Manual of Traditional Wood Carving

WITH 1,146 WORKING DRAWINGS AND
PHOTOGRAPHIC ILLUSTRATIONS

Edited by
Paul N. Hasluck

Dover Publications, Inc., New York

This Dover edition, first published in 1977, is
a republication of *Cassell's Wood Carving*, as
originally published by Cassell and Company
Limited, London, in 1911.

International Standard Book Number: 0-486-23489-4
Library of Congress Catalog Card Number: 76-58574

Manufactured in the United States of America
Dover Publications, Inc.
180 Varick Street
New York, N.Y. 10014

PUBLISHERS' NOTE

THIS book is offered as a volume of practical instruction, and of designs and examples, covering every phase of the art and craft of wood carving. Most of the matter it contains has been complied from contributions to "WORK," and consequently the whole of the instruction here given in the use of tools has challenged emendation from a wide circle of practical carvers. The majority of the two hundred and sixty-two reproductions of photographs, however, are here published for the first time. Of special interest and importance is the introduction of a series of illustrations, made from photographs, showing carvers' tools in actual use; the value of this series—especially to the beginner who may not have the opportunity of seeing an experienced carver at work—can hardly be over-estimated.

The designs shown by the very large number of line drawings are of a kind from which the carver can easily work; and he is at perfect liberty to reproduce in wood any or all of them exactly as shown, or to modify or alter them to suit his own taste or requirements. It is believed that the instructions are so exact, and the illustrations so lavish, that the earnest worker is not likely to meet with serious difficulties in making practical application of the information here supplied.

The bulk of the practical instruction comprised between pages 26 and 99 is from the pen of Mr. Herbert Turner, of Scarborough, an expert carver and designer. To him also are due the sections on "The History of Wood Carving," "Figure Carving," "Carving for Industrial Purposes," and "Classes in Wood Carving," as well as the text accompanying the half-tone illustrations of miserere or misericord seats. Mr. Turner has helped in other ways, notably by supplying critical and descriptive remarks upon many of the examples illustrated. The following carvers and designers have kindly given permission to reproduce examples of their work in these pages: Mr. J. Phillips, Altrincham; Mr. J. P. White, Pyghtle Works, Bedford; and Mr. W. S. Williamson, Taunton. Acknowledgments for permission to use certain photographs accompany the illustrations to which they refer.

CONTENTS

CONTENTS

WOOD CARVING

PRACTICAL INSTRUCTIONS AND DESIGNS

INTRODUCTION

WOOD CARVING calls for the exercise of manual skill and artistic feeling. Both of these are essential to the production of any good piece of carved work. Manual skill comes from the knowledge of the shapes and uses of tools and by putting this knowledge into actual practice. Artistic feeling is largely instinctive, but it can also be inculcated and developed. Thus almost anyone with strength and eyesight can learn to carve, and he will find in this one book sufficient instruction to lead him up to an advanced stage of the art. Reference may be made to the scheme of this book. The woods in general use among carvers will be described, and all the necessary tools and the methods of keeping them in order will be explained. Then will come practical instruction in the actual cutting of the wood, explanations being given of all processes in general use. Design in relation to carving, and the historical aspect of the subject, having been duly considered, a full range of designs for carving applied to all kinds of articles will be presented, with notes on their execution; and final chapters will treat of chip carving, the carving of foundry patterns, appliqué decoration, and other matters. It is hoped that the great value of the photographic illustrations showing the actual manipulations of the tools will be appreciated by the student, who may not have the opportunity of watching an experienced wood carver at work. In this preliminary chapter, some notes on a few

general matters—largely culled from papers read before the Royal Institute of British Architects by Messrs. Romaine-Walker, W. S. Frith, Aumonier, and J. E. Knox—may serve as an introduction to an art which has exercised a fascination for craftsmen from very early periods in the history of mankind.

Relation of Designer and Carver

The part of the wood carver is to act as the exponent of the designer's ideas. The designer should express on paper his fancy and the object he wishes to develop, giving every possible detail to enable the craftsman to interpret him successfully; but (says Mr. Romaine-Walker) he should leave the exponent of his thoughts certain liberty of action, else he will take from the executed work its soul, and leave it but a lifeless production. Under the influence of the Gothic architects, wood carving was the handmaid of architecture, and ministered to her unobtrusively. Witness the sumptuous choir stalls of Amiens as a type of the most ornate period; in these the most striking feature is the architecture; the outline and wonderful massing of light and shade created by a wealth of delicate moulding and intricate tracery; the rich interlacing lines and gracefully formed arches, relieved by cusps and crotchets, pinnacles and brattishing. In these the designer trusted for their beauty. The carver merely heightened the effect by enriching the construction with carved crotchets, finials, spandrils, and panels.

Wood as a Sculptor's Material

There is no doubt, indeed, that wood was the sculptor's first material. It has, however, for certain purposes, given way to other materials which have more completely met certain requirements. Wood (says Mr. W. S. Frith) has not the dignity of marble or bronze, or the evenness of texture and colour which enables these materials to convey refined delicacy of form and expression. In marble or bronze the material allows the form and expression to dominate, to seize and hold the attention quite unimpeded by questions of material; while in wood the grain and colour are always so marked that delicate expression is more or less diverted by them. On the other hand, the texture and warmth of wood are qualities so agreeable that it is pre-eminently the comfortable material, the one above all others suited for what may be called architectural furniture, that which fits the building as a structure sustaining weight and giving space, with that which makes for intimate physical comfort; and the office of wood carving in this connection is to provide objects of interest, to give variation of texture, and otherwise to contribute to the grace and beauty. The refined degrees of facial expression are unsuitable to production in wood, which is, however, essentially the material for the display of imagination and fancy. The expression of action is distinctly invited. Groups or ornaments with projections and perforations, which would be inappropriate to stone or marble, are quite fitting in wood; and its lightness, as far as that can be obtained without fragility, gives a charm which the silky and variegated texture heightens. The knowledge that the object is not friable, or chilling to the touch, conduces to the quiet enjoyment of the work.

In What Does the Beauty of Wood Carving Consist?

Mr. W. Aumonier has said that all the beauty of wood carving should be evolved from the material itself; being wood, it should retain the characteristics of wood, and not be made to represent marble, bronze, silver, or any other material. Wood is quite capable of taking care of itself properly if properly treated; and by the very individuality of its treatment it may attain a charm and beauty equal to that of almost any substance the hand of man can fashion into art. It must be cut by someone fully alive to the capabilities and susceptibilities of his material. If he is a good workman, he will combine freshness and grace: freshness, because the work grows under his own hand, untrammelled by any mechanical appliance; he will show the cuts and gouge-marks in it freely and fearlessly to the last; he will concentrate his mind on the firm sweep of the gouge over all; tenderly treat the thin and delicate parts which fade into the ground, and boldly undercut the projections, even to the extent of cutting right away in places to make the work stand out free; and he will give grace, because there is no form the artistic mind can conceive but may be obtained in wood, if honestly sought after. The work should always appear to be carved out of a solid block; it should aim at broad lights and sharp shadows; the high parts should be comparatively smooth, or, at least, little disturbed by modelling, to catch light; the depths should be rough and choppy, the better to hold shadow; the ground should be by no means absolutely flat or smooth, but deepened in parts where strong shadows are required to strengthen the effect; and the relief so managed as to incorporate the ground and the work together as much as possible. Invention and lightness, combined with breadth and strength into one harmonious whole, the work sparkling with gouge-cuts to give it texture, constitute the essence of wood carving.

How the Appearance of Carving is Affected

Distance affects the appearance of wood carving, and therefore the position carved work is to occupy should influence the design. Mr. Aumonier shows that not only the design, but the actual carving itself should be carefully considered, with a view to the position it is to take and the light it will receive. Thus, even if quite close to

Fig. 1.—Tazza, Carved in Solid Walnut, by a
Florentine Workman.

the eye, where, of course, its position warrants or demands a certain amount of finish, it must be remembered that real finish rather means perfection of form than smoothness of surface ; so that even there it should still show its cuts and its tool-marks fearlessly, and be deepened in parts to make it tell its proper tale in the combined scheme of decoration ; while if it is to be placed a great distance from the eye, it should be left as rough as ever it can be left. The only points that have to be regarded then are the outlines, varieties of planes, and depths ; and if these are properly considered, everything else will take care of itself, and then the whole work cannot be left too rough. Its very roughness and choppy cuts will give it a softness and quality, when in its place, that no amount of smoothing or high finish can possibly attain to. Any effort towards more than this, or finicky striving after accuracy of detail, on work once treated in a rough, masterly manner, according to its position, will more than likely result in failure. Tool - marks in wood carving should not be visible on figure work in general, says Mr. W. S. Frith, since the form is the essential, not the manner of producing it ; and this rule necessarily applies wherever exact form is desired. But, as has already been shown, the clear cut best displays the quality of the material, the mastery of the craftsman, and his delight in his work, and makes that in which the dexterous use of the tool can be traced one of the most charming phases of wood carving.

Wood Carvers' Drawings

Drawings for architectural carvings should be studied at the same distance from the eye as the finished work will be, and should be designed especially for the place and position the work is to occupy. They should aim at a broad and vigorous treatment of light and shade, paying but little regard to small details, which can be better worked out on the carving itself towards the finish, because many of the parts will become different in size from the drawing, owing to the varied planes and angles into which they naturally fall in treatment. If the work is going up any considerable height, care should be taken to keep the drawing open in arrangement, as the tendency is for the projecting parts to appear to fill up the voids or grounds in looking up at the work, giving it a crowded effect. If the design is embodied in a model, it is more than ever necessary to place it, not only at the right distance, but also at the right elevation from the ground. In fact, what is really valuable in the case of either drawing or model is that the design should be judged in as nearly as possible its actual position, with all its surroundings just as they exist.

The Use of Models

The wood carver must, of course, take every opportunity of examining first-class examples of the art, but the models particularly alluded to below are those made of clay or plastic material for the guidance of the carver. As to whether or not such models are necessary, argument has raged fiercely. Mr. Romaine-Walker says a word for them, but his remarks apply to a carved model in wood, not to a model in clay or plaster. He holds that the preliminary model is of vital importance with the larger surfaces to be carved, such as panels, friezes, and the like, in order that there may be found most effective relief to give to the carving when placed in juxtaposition with its environment. Six inches square of the most salient feature, in pine, is ample ; unless, indeed, the wood to be used is not a familiar one, and then it is safer to make it the material of the experiment. The making of a preliminary model does not increase the total expense ; often it conduces to economy, provided that the models are but amplifications of the drawings, be they in charcoal, sepia, or pencil, and only made so far as is necessary to show the particular weight, cut, finish, and character it is wished to adopt. Again, it is always well to offer up these models to the actual position they will hold in the finished work, and, when possible, under the same conditions of light. Many surprises will be in store for the designer who adopts this plan. In a certain building is an effective band of guilloche enrichment. The right and left of the band have been

Fig. 2.—Mirror Frame, Carved by Panciera Besarel of Venice.

Fig. 2.—Carved Capital, etc., from Hindoo Temple.

carved running in opposite directions, meeting correctly in the centre. The result is that from whichever side it is viewed, one-half appears to be carved and the other half to be plain. This would have been obviated had the method above suggested been adopted. On the other hand, Mr. W. Aumonier condemns models, and says that the money spent in preparing them might be better spent on the actual carving. His strictures apply principally to clay models

retain the skill of making an accurate copy of the dead plaster he sees before him. Remember, too, that at the best he can only make a translation of a model in wood, because some effects which are easily obtained in clay by a skilful modeller belong to that art alone, and not to wood carving. But give the carver a rough charcoal drawing to work from, in which is shown in a broad and direct manner the relative heights of the different planes, the general effect of

Fig. 4.—Carved Course and Corbels over Capital from Hindoo Temple (see Fig. 3).

and plaster casts. Unless the worker is sufficiently skilled, and is allowed the necessary freedom to chop boldly at a block without any particularly preconceived design—in which way some very fine work may be produced—it is best to work from drawings—rough, full-size charcoal cartoons, which give the effect wanted by their light and shade. Mr. Aumonier regards clay or plaster models as being worse than useless. Once, he says, put a full-size model into a carver's hand to copy, and he easily sinks to the level of a mere copying machine, losing the power of concentrating his mind on his work as an art, only to

light and shade sought for, and he has to exercise all his ingenuity from the first to the last to interpret it. He has to keep his wits about him all the time, and has an opportunity to use his imagination and fancy with a certain amount of freedom in details, by following out and developing accidental forms and cuts which keep arising and suggesting themselves in the progress of the work. Of course, in working from a drawing, care must be taken, in the first place, to decide which are to be the highest points in the design, and then to work away from them until the whole work is brought into a pleasing effect of light and shade.

Suitability of Carving to its Environment

The necessity of carving being in harmony with its surroundings is emphasised powering than the same applied to a small room. Wood carving for a small room is from its nearness more liable to hard usage and damage than that in a large room. The carving, therefore, should be

Fig. 5.—Carved Wood Lattice, copied from Stone Lattice in Old Mosque.

by Mr. Romaine-Walker. The designer should be largely guided by the size and proportion of that part of the building for which the carving is destined, the height it is to occupy, and the consequent risk it will run. Nothing looks nobler than a large, well-proportioned room treated with carving in high relief ; nothing looks more over-subdued in relief, and the subject matter treated so that it can be grasped when viewed from a short distance. There is such a room (taken from a house at Exeter) at the South Kensington Museum. The lower panels are simply but very characteristically moulded. The upper, which take the width of two of the lower, are carved in excellent style, and yet the total projection the carver has allowed himself is one-eighth of an inch. Another room, of Jacobean workmanship, is in simple strapwork, very free in setting-out and execution—not the art England has ever known, in spite of all the severe strictures he has received at the hands of architects. His creations show an extraordinary knowledge of light and shade, of texture and quality. Note

Fig. 6.—Carved Wood Lattice, copied from Stone Lattice in Old Mosque.

a straight line nor a true circle; and yet what a charm it has! To those who wish the maximum of effect for the minimum of cost, a careful examination of these specimens is suggested. Carving in high relief is suited to a large room. In this connection, the name of Grinling Gibbons will occur to many. He, undoubtedly, was the greatest exponent of with what care he interspersed his sharp crisp foliage and flowers with soft and smooth fruit and waving ribbons; how he gave the impression of great lightness and delicacy, yet ever retained the maximum of strength. But it has been urged against him that his work is meretricious, because it was not carved out of the solid, but was "appliqué." But this fault, if fault it be, was not confined to Gibbons, but will be found in much earlier examples. When dealing with these great projections, if the carving is done in the solid, the grain of the wood will often run counter to the design, and a blow, or possibly a natural crack, will in time cause a portion to fall off. On the other hand, when the work is built up in appliqué style, the grain may be made to come as required; and Mr. Romaine-Walker believes the carving done thus to that this style of carving should never be polished; indeed, when it is good, it is impossible. In the early Victorian era it was attempted, but in so doing it was necessary to retain a uniformity of smoothness and a coarseness of detail to take the polish and stand the rubbing.

Fragile Carvings

It is a serious mistake in architectural work, says Mr. Harry Hems, to carve wood

Fig. 7.—Amorini, Symbolical of "The Arts." Designed and Carved by the late Luigi Frullini, of Florence.

be much more durable. When this mode is adopted, it is always well to have the ground board sufficiently thick to allow of the deepest part of the carving, and the tendrils, and those portions of the ribbons in low relief, being cut out of it. Of course, the difference in expense is very considerable. Nothing in an English treatment can look more impressive and dignified than a large room, some twenty feet or more in height, carried out in what may be called the Wren style, with columns, pilasters, and large panels, surrounded by bold and vigorously carved mouldings, the whole relieved with Gibbons's carving. It is needless to say too fragile, or indeed fragile at all. There is no real skill, in point of fact, in too much undercutting. In figure work, too, uplifted and extended hands or arms, and especially pointing fingers, are a weakness and a snare. Much anxious labour is spent in their creation, yet in a few years, it may be only weeks or days, those projecting parts, obtruding from niche or newel, will surely be knocked off by some careless duster. Of course, the broken places may be mended, stuck together with glue; but is there anything more humiliating to an ambitious craftsman than to see a statuette, the product of days or weeks, thus mutilated?

Yet the actual fault is not altogether that of the careless one who does the irretrievable damage. Surely a much larger amount of blame must belong to the craftsman.

Wood Carvings to be Polished

Wood carvings that are to be polished (and this applies to the majority of furniture) should be so treated that all the parts and every face can be rubbed without fear of damage. When it becomes necessary to lay polish on with a brush, it may be taken for certain that the carving is inappropriate. Polishing should be .done with a mixture of beeswax and turpentine ; and after this has been repeated several times, it should be rubbed down with a hard brush. This polish is very durable, and does not mark. The modern French polish, though quicker and cheaper, is not suitable. In the art of carving to receive polish, the English masters, the brothers Adam, Chippendale, Sheraton, Hepplewhite, and others, were very successful, for in the greater part of their work they expressed themselves in such a manner that the carving could not only receive real polish, and bear and improve by constant rubbing, but it had the double advantage of being as pleasing to the touch as to the sight. It is a golden rule for the carver, that on furniture, and particularly on chairs, his work must be soft to the touch, and devoid of all sharp projections which would catch and tear lace or other fine materials with which it is sure to come in contact.

Wood Carvings to be Gilt

For wood carvings that are to be gilt, Mr. Romaine-Walker says that special consideration and treatment are necessary owing to the strong and reflected light. A little more emphasis is required in the shadows, and the lights should be left smooth or strongly defined, only cutting them up where they begin to reach the shade, but always bearing in mind that even the deepest part must be carefully considered, as much reflected light is sure to reach it. The ground, too, where to all appearances flat, plays an important part in the ultimate effect, and should· never be really level, but have an undulating wave in it, the better to catch the various rays of light and give variety of tone. Carving that is to be gilt is usually treated with a fine coating of whitening and thin glue, and this is absolutely necessary where burnishing is to be employed. This is repeated over and over again—in really good work as many as ten

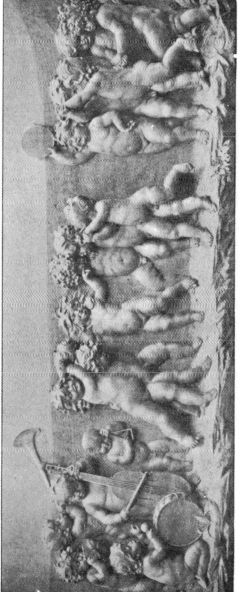

Fig. 8.—"Dance of the Hours," Designed and Carved by the late Luigi Frullini, of Florence.

Fig. 9.—Carved Table, Sixteenth Century.

Fig. 10.—Carved Panelling from House at Exeter.

times—being rubbed down between each application with pumice-stone and glass-paper, the parts to be burnished receiving a thicker layer. This process naturally takes off much of the crispness and life, and it may be desirable at this stage to return it to the carver to sharpen and revivify. Red gold-size is considered to have an advantage over the ordinary gold-size, more particularly when the work is liable to be handled. Should a little of the gold be

far surpassed them in their delicacy of treatment. Nothing can exceed the marvellous beauty and finish of their work, which rose under Louis XIV., and declined under Louis XVI.

Illustrations in this Chapter

The illustrations included in this chapter depict carvings of great beauty, and will serve as models to be emulated by all who make in these pages their first acquaintance

Fig. 11.—Reredos in Roman Catholic Church, Wimbledon. Designed by John Hungerford Pollen. Carved by the Students in Training of the School of Art Wood Carving.

rubbed, the effect is often enhanced; while with white gold-size the result is exactly the opposite. For gilt work, it is imperative that the carver shall adopt one or other of the two extremes, either very high or very low relief, after the manner of repoussé metal-work. The Venetians and the Florentines were the most successful masters in this former branch of the art, having grasped the value of large masses boldly undercut, and plenty of voids and open spaces to give depth. While these two contended for supremacy of breadth and vigour, the French, without doubt,

with the art and craft of carving wood. These illustrations have been selected as representing some of the best productions of Italian, French, English and East Indian carvers.

Tazza.—A tazza is a saucer-shaped vessel supported by a foot, and Fig. 1 shows a very fine example carved from a solid piece of walnut by a workman employed by Signor Pecchi, of Florence, Italy. It was shown at an exhibition in the Royal Albert Hall, London, held in 1880, and it presents a good example of the grace and ease with which the talented Italian carvers introduce the human figure into ornament. The three sea-horses support a decorated Renaissance column, in turn supporting a shell forming a cup. The erect head of the winged mermaid forms a sort of handle, and her locks fall into the shell.

Mirror Frame.—Fig. 2 illustrates a mirror frame carved by Panciera Besarel,

The capitals of the pillars are of the bracketed kind found in the hill temples in the neighbourhood of Simla. The ornament with which they are incrusted is so minute and in such low relief as to present very much the effect of embroidery or brocade. This is not uncommon in Hindoo carving, even in stone, which has sometimes all the

Fig. 12.—Carved Rood, with the Virgin and St. John. French Work in Peyre Collection.

of Venice. The frame, as can be seen by a glance at the illustration, is in the form of a wreath which is composed of the figures of nude children carved with a grace and vigour which are indeed wonderful considering the character of the material.

East Indian Carvings.—A beautiful example of carved work shown at the Colonial Exhibition in 1886 is represented by Fig. 3.

character of raised needlework studded with pearls and precious stones. In fact, if it were gilded and painted, the effect would be very much that of gorgeous trappings, horse - cloths and elephant - cloths, belonging to an Indian potentate. The ornamental course with corbels (of which a detail is given in Fig. 4) has many evidences of its Hindoo origin. Other exhibits at the Colonial Exhibition, 1886, mentioned at the beginning of this paragraph, are illustrated by Figs. 5 and 6. These carvings are executed in Rangoon teak, and are copies of stone lattices in old tices in wood, because the stone architecture of the Hindoo temples is itself founded upon the forms of wooden construction. The student of design will note the great value of the massive stems in the lattices.

Fig. 13.—Oak Door with "Labours of Hercules" in Lunette.   French Work, Sixteenth Century.

mosques. The specially Indian characteristic about their design is that the graceful lines seem always to grow, although the foliated ornament is always more Oriental than natural—that is to say, it is more strictly ornamental than related to any known form of foliage. There is nothing inconsistent in the execution of these lat-

Groups of Children.—The work of Luigi Frullini, of Florence, is among the most remarkable in modern carving. He worked without design, sketch, or preliminary model, and he specially succeeded in the figures of children (see Figs. 7 and 8). In the examples illustrated, every curve in the plump limbs reveals the acute student, a true artist and a clever craftsman. Frullini's exhibition in Paris of " The Dance of the Hours " (Fig. 8)—" babies that might have come from Donatello's chisel "— brought him the Legion of Honour ; and

Fig. 14.—Carved Door Panel. French Work, Fifteenth Century.

in England, also, he won medals and other honours.

English Examples.—A sixteenth-century table (shown by Fig. 9) is supported on a central row of arches, and has spreading feet, thus representing roughly a shape that survives in the " Pembroke " table. The original of Fig. 9 is to be seen at South Kensington. Panelling from a house at

Exeter (the actual piece now being at South Kensington) is illustrated by Fig. 10. The mouldings of small panelling of this kind are in very fine lines. The uprights seem to have been worked on the bench and then cut to the required length, while the top line and the weathering below on the base of the panel seem to have been worked with hand tools after the making up of the whole series. The lower weathering is a mere bevelling, whose only purpose is to avoid the accumulation of dust.

Reredos.—A carved pine reredos at the Wimbledon Roman Catholic Church is illustrated by Fig. 11. This was designed by Mr. John Hungerford Pollen, and carved by the students in training of the School of Art Wood Carving, London, under the superintendence of Mr. W. H. Grimwood, the instructor. The pine is silvered over and lacquered to a rich warm colour. The outside stiles are painted blue, and a blue band runs round the base and the cornice. The paintings are copies (by Miss Helen Blackburn) of the Borgognone in the National Gallery.

French Examples.—Some beautiful examples of French carving—all taken from the collection of M. Emile Peyre at South Kensington—are shown by Figs. 12 to 14. The first illustration shows a carved rood or crucifix, from a rood screen, together with the figures of the Virgin and St. John. Fig. 13 shows an oak door with a lunette above, in which are depicted " The Labours of Hercules." Beneath the lunette is a delicate scroll-work frieze. This work was executed during the reign of Francis I., who was King of France from 1515 to 1547. Fig. 14 shows a carved panel from a fifteenth-century oak door, and represents an amusing subject of a youth who has apparently been stealing plates and hiding them in his clothes. The owner has caught him, and is about to give him a thrashing.

WOODS USED FOR CARVING

ALTHOUGH obviously there are scores of varieties of wood that can be, and have been, carved, it will be found that ordinary wood carving does not employ more than about twenty different kinds. These twenty are favourites because their structure is such that the carver's tools leave a clean, sharp cut, or because their grain is so straight as to enable the wood to be worked with the least amount of trouble and risk of splitting. Of the greatest importance in all woods used for carving is thorough seasoning; where time and convenience allow, it is desirable for the carver himself to stock the wood for a year or two, so that when using it he can be sure that it is thoroughly dry. This chapter gives a few notes on the woods which are in common use by the carver. The woods in most general use are oak, Italian and American walnut, lime, holly, pearwood, chestnut, and mahogany, and these are described in this order below, after which notes on a few of the less-used woods are given.

Oak

Oak, the oldest of woods known to be used for wood carving, is *Quercus robur* L. (natural order Cupuliferæ), and is the chief hardwood of Europe. Many varieties of oak are grown in North America, India, Japan, and Australia. It grows to a height of 60 ft. to 100 ft. and has a diameter of 1 ft. to 22 ft.; a straight oak stem often measures from 30 ft. to 40 ft. high and from 2 ft. to 4 ft. in diameter. When seasoned, the specific gravity of oak is ·780 or ·597, and when freshly cut 1·280. Its weight per cub. ft. is 62—43 lb. Fig. 15 is a micro-

photograph (multiplied 30 diameters) showing the formation of oak wood. Oak is hard, firm and compact, glossy and smooth, with a variable surface. It is a good wood for the use of experienced carvers, but on account of its hardness is not so suitable for the beginner. As already mentioned, oak has great lasting qualities. Most of the carvings of the Middle Ages in the churches and abbeys were wrought from the true British oak. In colour, oak is a light fawn when freshly cut, but on exposure it turns to a handsome brown. The sapwood is very liable to insect attack, but the heartwood under any conditions is very durable. Oak can be obtained in logs from 25 ft. to 50 ft. long by 12 in. to 24 in. square.

Bog-oak

Bog-oak is often used for carving, and in Ireland the carving of this wood is one of the peasant industries, the work produced being small but of good quality. Bog-oak is so called from the fact that it is found embedded in the decaying vegetable matter of the bogs, and the oak itself has often entered on the first stage of putrefaction The wood is hard, close-grained, and brittle, but it is also capable of a very high polish. When ready for sale, it closely resembles ebony. It is a very dark-coloured wood, being almost black. Bog-oak is liable to violent splitting and "checking" after being excavated, and therefore should the carver himself dig it, he should remember not to remove it from the peat water until a store place is ready for its reception. Chip off the sapwood all round down to the heartwood, following the course of the bends.

17

Saw off all broken ends, and cut away all rotten places ; then stand it for a few days under cover, and allow it to drain. If the design of the proposed furniture is partly curved, take advantage of the natural bends of the wood, and so economise material.

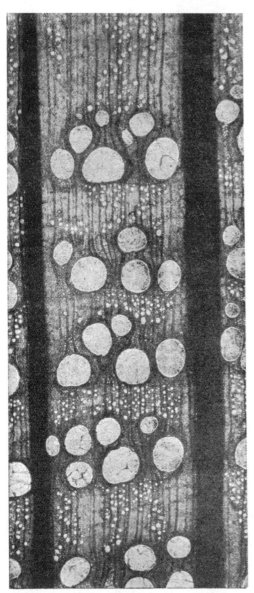

Fig. 15.—Micro-photograph of Oak Wood (Multiplication, 30 diameters).

Mark off the lengths of straight material in the same way. Then cut up the logs into the shortest lengths possible, allowing for waste, of course. Plank the stuff at the sawyer's, and rack it, preferably in an upright bar rack which is tight enough to prevent much warping. Cut the panels, seating, etc., out of the large logs, and use those of smaller dimensions for the square stuff. As bog-oak generally takes three or four years to season, and becomes much harder (and more brittle) as it dries, it is desirable to work it out before it gets thoroughly seasoned. In conversion little attention is paid to the silver grain of the wood. Being black, it does not show much. When, however, the medullary rays are rather pronounced, "pairs" should be matched as far as possible.

Walnut

Walnut comes from *Juglans regia* L. (natural order *Juglandaceæ*), now growing in Europe, but originally a native of Northern China and Persia. It grows to a height of 30 ft. to 50 ft., with a diameter of 2 ft. to 3 ft. When green, walnut weighs 58·5 lb. per cub. ft., and when dry 46·5 lb. A micro-photograph (multiplied 30 diameters) is presented by Fig. 16. It is a moderately heavy, hard, close-grained wood, and very durable if kept dry. It is dark brown in colour, and is beautifully marked. It is susceptible of a high polish. English-grown walnut is pale, coarse, and perishable, that from the Black Sea being more valuable (logs of this kind as imported measure from 6 ft. to 9 ft. long, and from 10 in. to 18 in. square). Walnut from Italy (Italian walnut) is the best of the walnuts; this is obtainable in planks measuring from 4 in. to 9 in. thick, 10 in. to 16 in. wide, and 5 ft. to 12 ft. long. Italian walnut is a rich and beautifully marked wood, very suitable for carving. Close-grained and hard, it amply repays the extra labour of working it.

American Walnut

American walnut (*Juglans nigra* L.), or black walnut, is grown chiefly in Eastern and North America, and grows to a height of 60 ft. to 150 ft., with a diameter of 3 ft.

to 8 ft. Its specific gravity is ·611 and its weight per cub. ft. is 38·1 lb. It is hard, tough, and rather coarse-grained. It cleans up to a smooth surface, and takes polish well. It is a capital wood for carving, and it is not liable to split. It is considered less liable to insect attack, more uniform in colour, and darker and more durable than European walnut. In colour American walnut is a violet or chocolate brown, blackening with age. Logs from 10 ft. to 20 ft. long and from 15 in.

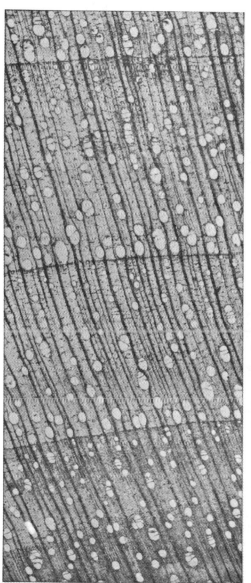

Fig. 16.—Micro-photograph of Walnut Wood (Multiplication, 30 diameters).

Fig. 17.—Micro-photograph of Lime or Linden Wood (Multiplication, 10 diameters).

to 30 in. square are imported. Planks of American walnut can be obtained 1¾ in. to 2 in. thick, and boards from ⅝ in. to 2 in. thick.

Lime or Linden

Lime (corrupted from " line ") is known also as linden, and appears to be produced

Fig. 18.—Micro-photograph of Holly Wood (Multiplication, 10 diameters).

by three varieties of trees in the order *Tiliaceœ*—*Tilia parvifolia* Ehrh., *T. platy-phyllos* Scop., and *T. argentæ* Desf., these being spread over Europe, the last-named, however, being found only in the south-east. It grows to a height of from 20 ft. to 90 ft., its diameter being from 1 ft. to 4 ft. Its specific gravity is ·794 to ·522. Fig. 17 shows a micro-photograph (multiplied 10 diameters). It is extensively used by beginners in carving on account of its cheapness and easy cutting qualities. Soft and pliable to the tool, it splinters less than any other wood. Owing to its colour being white to yellowish-white, it generally requires either staining or gilding. Grinling Gibbons executed much of his beautiful carving in this wood.

American Lime

American lime is known in America as basswood. The wood known in Great Britain as basswood is the product of *Liriodendron tulipifera* L., and is described under the title of basswood later in this section. American lime is the wood of the *Tilia americana* L. (natural order *Tiliaceœ*), and is also known by the names American linden, or lime or bee-tree. It is grown in the Eastern United States and Canada, reaching a height of from 80 ft. to 100 ft. and a diameter of 3 ft. to 4 ft. Its specific gravity is ·452, and its weight per cub. ft. 28·2 lb. Light, close-grained, soft, and tough, it can be easily worked, and is of remarkably even texture. It shrinks considerably in drying, but is durable.

Holly

Holly comes from the tree *Ilex aquifolium* L. (natural order *Ilicineœ*), and grows chiefly in Central Europe and West Asia. It grows to a height of 10 ft. to 40 ft. or even 80 ft., with a diameter of 1 ft. to 4 ft. or 5 ft., and it weighs 47·5 lb. per cub. ft. It is fine-grained, hard, and heavy, subject to considerable shrinkage and warping. A micro-photograph (multiplied 10 diameters) is shown by Fig. 18. It is a nice wood for cutting, but being so light in colour, generally requires staining. In colour it is white to greenish-white, and it approaches ivory in colour and texture more than does any other wood.

Pearwood

Pearwood comes from *Pyrus communis* L. (natural order *Rosaceæ*). It grows chiefly in Europe and Western Asia, and is also cultivated in other countries. The height of the tree is from 20 ft. to 50 ft., and the diameter from 1 ft. to 2 ft. Fig. 19 shows a micro-photograph of pearwood, the multiplication being 30 diameters. It is a close-grained, moderately hard, and heavy, tough, and firm wood, being very difficult to split. For carving, pearwood works well, cutting easily in any direction. If kept dry it is very durable. In colour it is a light pinkish brown, darker towards the centre.

Chestnut

Chestnut is the wood of the *Castanea vulgaris* Lamk. (natural order *Cupuliferæ*), a large tree which grows to an enormous girth. It is a native of the continent of Europe, and a closely related variety, americana, is grown in the Eastern United States. Its specific gravity is about ·450, and it weighs 28 lb. to 41 lb. per cub. ft. It is a moderately hard wood, but is much softer than oak, which it resembles in colour, toughness, and solidity ; it is light and coarse-grained, and is very liable to split with nailing. A micro-photograph (multiplied 30 diameters) is presented by Fig. 20. The sapwood of chestnut is white to a yellowish-white or light brown, and the heartwood darker brown, but distinguished from that of oak by the absence of broad pith rays.

Mahogany

Mahogany is a wood concerning which there is much misunderstanding. Spanish, Honduras, and the bay mahogany are all three produced by the true mahogany tree, *Swietenia mahagoni* L. The distinguishing names were originally given in reference to the localities from which the wood was principally shipped. Thus, Spanish mahogany came from Cuba, and some other West Indian Islands and ports belonging to Spain ; Honduras mahogany came from the province of Honduras in Central America —chiefly from the neighbourhood of the mouth of the Rio Hondo ; while baywood or bay mahogany was obtained from various places around the coast of the bay of Honduras. The mahogany procured from these three districts varied considerably in colour, in hardness, and in figure—the Spanish wood being much the best, and the baywood the poorest. Now, of course, mahogany wood is obtained from many other

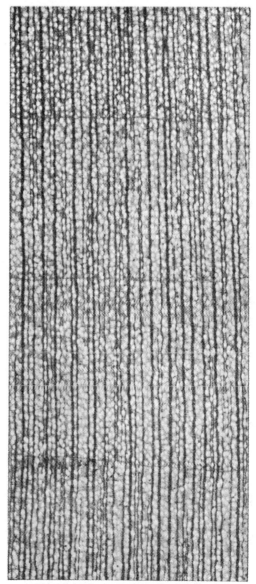

Fig. 19.—Micro-photograph of Pearwood (Multiplication, 30 diameters).

districts and ports in Central America, as, for example, Tabasco, Minatitlan, Tecolutla, Panama, Costa Rica, and St. Domingo ; but to the average woodworker in England only the three grades mentioned still exist, namely, Spanish, Honduras, and baywood, chiefly because each of these three names has come to represent an arbitrary standard of quality, colour, and figure, regardless of the origin. Beyond saying that the baywood is the soft, light, straight-grained, and pinkish (nearly white) material, and that the Spanish is the dark, ruddy-brown, often cross-grained, and curly wood, no

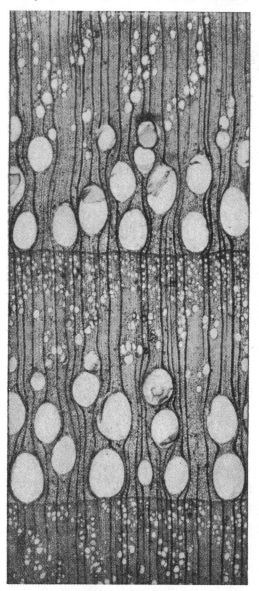

Fig. 20.—Micro-photograph of Chestnut Wood (Multiplication, 30 diameters).

Fig. 21.—Micro-photograph of Pine or Fir Wood (Multiplication, 30 diameters).

definite rule can be given ; observation will soon disclose the ordinary limits of each term. Some regard the chalky deposit in the pores of dark-coloured mahogany as conclusive evidence that the wood is of Spanish origin, but the occurrence of this substance is by no means an infallible test. Mahogany has the advantage of being durable, taking a fine polish, and improving in colour with age. Baywood is soft and easily worked. It may be obtained in widths up to 2 ft. 6 in., but the price per foot is much higher for wide than for narrow boards. Spanish mahogany is harder than the other varieties, and is often beautifully figured ; considerable skill is required in cleaning it up. Mahogany unites with glue better than any other wood.

Spanish Mahogany.—Spanish mahogany is obtainable in logs from 18 ft. to 35 ft. long and from 11 in. to 24 in. square. The specific gravity varies from ·720 to ·817, the weight per cubic foot being 53 lb.

St. Domingo Mahogany.—St. Domingo mahogany resembles the above, but the logs do not exceed 10 ft. long by 13 in. square, except occasionally. It is a wood of a horn-like substance, being extremely hard. More suitable for carving is Nassau mahogany, which is the favourite mahogany for turning ; this rarely exceeds 5 ft. in length. Honduras mahogany is obtainable in 25-ft. to 40-ft. logs from 1 ft. to 2 ft. square. This wood is liable to be brittle when thoroughly dry.

Pine or Fir

Pine (Northern Pine), known also in commerce as fir, red deal, yellow deal, etc., is produced by the Scotch fir (*Pinus sylvestris* L.). It is grown in Europe and Northern Asia, and the character and quality of the wood vary very much with climatic conditions. The height of the pine tree is from 80 ft. to 100 ft., and the diameter 2 ft. to 4 ft. Its specific gravity is ·774—·478, and weight per cub. ft. is 34 lb. to 47 lb. Fig. 21 shows a micro-photograph (multiplied 30 diameters). Yellow pine is a good cheap wood for carving ; being soft, it requires careful working, as it splits easily. In colour it varies from pale to deep reddish yellow. If thoroughly seasoned it is durable.

American Whitewood or Basswood

Basswood is the wood of the *Liriodendron tulipifera* L. (natural order *Magnoliaceæ*) ; it is also known as tulip-tree wood, saddle-tree, poplar, yellow-wood, whitewood, Virginian poplar, canary-wood, canoe-wood, American poplar, yellow poplar, and American whitewood. It is grown in Eastern North America, the tree reaching a height of 100 ft. to 150 ft., with a diameter of 3 ft. to 10 ft. Its specific gravity is ·423, and it weighs 26·36 lb. per cub. ft. It is

Fig. 22.—Micro-photograph of Sycamore Wood (Multiplication, 10 diameters).

soft, close, and straight-grained, compact but not very strong or durable. It is easily worked, and of a remarkably uniform texture; it shrinks and warps somewhat in seasoning. In colour basswood is yellowish green or greenish white. It is readily obtainable

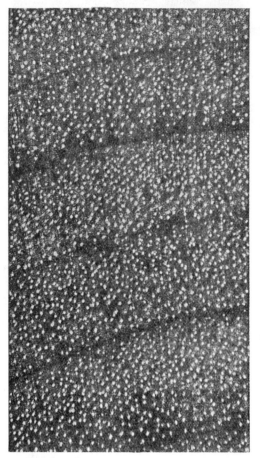

Fig. 23.—Micro-photograph of Boxwood
(Multiplication, 30 diameters).

in all ordinary lengths, and in widths of from 2 ft. to 3 ft.

Sycamore

Sycamore comes from *Acer pseudoplatanus* L. (natural order *Acerineæ*). It is grown largely in Great Britain, Central Europe, and Western Asia. In height it grows from 40 ft. to 60 ft., and in diameter

from 1 ft. to 3 ft. When newly cut it weighs 64 lb. per cub. ft. ; when dry 48 lb. to 36 lb. Distinct pith rays with a beautiful satiny lustre distinguish sycamore wood from limewood (see the micro-photograp Fig. 22, multiplied 10 diameters). It is of uniform texture and fine-grained, tough and rather difficult to cut ; it contains gritty matter, which blunts tools. In colour it is white, and is therefore used for the manufacture of domestic articles.

Satinwood

Satinwood comes from *Chloroxylon swietenia* DC. (natural order *Meliaceæ*), which is grown chiefly in Central and Southern India and Ceylon, another variety being grown in Australia. It grows to a height of 30 ft. to 60 ft., and has a diameter of 12 in. to 15 in. Its weight is 64·3 lb. to 55 lb. per cub. ft. It is close-grained, heavy, and hard, and is susceptible of an excellent polish. It is somewhat apt to split, and darkens if not varnished. It is not much used by carvers, as the figure in the wood is apt to mar the effect of the carving. In colour, satinwood is a light orange. Logs are obtainable 9 ft. long.

Sandalwood

Sandalwood, the wood of the *Santalum album* L. (natural order *Santalaceæ*), is grown chiefly in the south of India, attaining a height of 30 ft., 8 ft. to the lowest branch, and a diameter up to 2 ft. It is hard, close-grained, and fragrant, and is sold in billets weighing from 50 lb. to 90 lb. It is chiefly used in carving for fine delicate work, and is of a yellowish-brown colour.

Jarrah

Jarrah, sometimes known as mahogany or bastard mahogany, is from *Eucalyptus marginata* Sm. (natural order *Myrtaceæ*), and is grown in South-western Australia. It attains a height of from 100 ft. to 150 ft. and a diameter sometimes of 10 ft. Its specific gravity varies from ·837—1·120, and its weight is 54 lb. to 76 lb. per cub. ft. This tree grows very straight, yielding timber 20 ft. to 40 ft. long and 1 ft. to 2 ft. square, occasionally unsound in the centre. It is close-grained, hard, and very heavy ;

it works smoothly and takes a good polish. For carving, it is slightly coarse in the grain, but cuts fairly well. When sound, jarrah is extremely durable, resisting the action of water, earth ship-worms, etc. In colour it resembles mahogany, being of a beautiful dark-red. Jarrah is obtainable in logs up to 97 ft. long and 20 in. square.

Boxwood

Boxwood is the wood of the *Buxus semper-virens* L. (natural order *Euphorbiaceæ*), and is grown in Northern and Western Asia, North Africa, and Central and Southern Europe. It grows to a height of from 8 ft. to 30 ft., but with small diameter. The specific gravity is ·950 to ·980. In weight it is 80·5 lb. to 68·75 lb. per cub. ft. It is a very hard and firm wood to carve, close-grained, and very durable when thoroughly seasoned. A micro-photograph (multiplied 30 diameters) is presented by Fig. 23. Boxwood is best suited to figure carving and small, fine, delicate work. It is capable of a very high finish. In colour it is light yellow with a slight silky lustre. It is sold in billets from 3 ft. to 8 ft. long, and 3 in. to 12 in. in diameter.

Ebony

Ebony is hard, dense, heavy, and gene-rally black, and is the product of trees be longing to the order known as *Ebenaceæ*, native to Southern India and Ceylon. Its weight per cub. ft. is 70 lb. or more, and its specific gravity 1·187. It is a very fine-grained wood, and will take a high polish. It contains grit, which blunts the tools.

Cedar

Cedar comes from the tree *Cedrus libani* Loud. (natural order *Coniferæ*), and was introduced into England after the middle of the seventeenth century. It is a true native of the mountain ranges of south-west Asia, notably Lebanon, Taurus, etc. It grows to a height of 50 ft. to 80 ft., and has a diameter of 3 ft. to 4 ft. or more. It

is a straight and open-grained wood, easily worked, rather brittle, and liable to extensive cup shakes and heart shakes. Fig. 24 shows a micro-photograph (multiplied 30 diameters).

Fig. 24.—Micro-photograph of Cedar Wood (Multiplication, 30 diameters).

Cedar has a pleasant odour. The wood known as "cedar" in the English timber trade is chiefly West Indian cedar (*Cedrela odorata*), shipped from Cuba, Trinidad, Honduras, and other islands. The specific gravity of cedar is ·372 to ·664, its weight being 31 lb. to 47 lb. per cub. ft.

TOOLS AND APPLIANCES USED IN CARVING

THIS chapter and the following one will treat wood-carving tools from a practical point of view, and will describe the types (c) spoon-bit tools, and (d) tools of special shape. Types a, b, and c are shown by Figs. 25 to 28, and type d by Figs. 29 and 30.

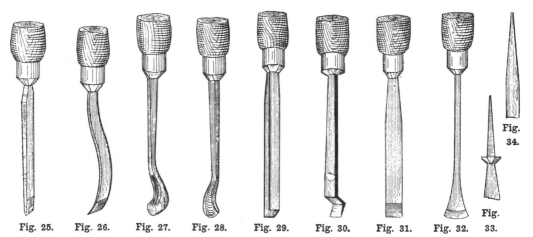

Fig. 25. Fig. 26. Fig. 27. Fig. 28. Fig. 29. Fig. 30. Fig. 31. Fig. 32. Fig. 33. Fig. 34.

Fig. 25.—First Type Carving Tool. Fig. 26.—Second Type Carving Tool. Figs. 27 and 28.—Third Type Carving Tools. Figs. 29 and 30.—Fourth Type Carving Tools. Fig. 31.—Ordinary Chisel. Fig. 32.—Spade Chisel. Figs. 33 and 34.—Shouldered and Unshouldered Carving Tools.

and shapes of tools, the proper manner of sharpening them and of keeping them in the best condition, the most suitable types of mallets, cramps, slips, and the other necessary accessories. Wood-carving tools are varied in shape, both in length and in section, but they can be classified into various types.

Tools of the First Type

Type a consists of those tools which are, viewed from the edge, quite straight. They are, of course, of various sections, and are used for all ordinary work. Indeed, it is only necessary to supplement this type when

Fig. 35.—Cutting Edges and Sections of Carving Tools.

The classification here adopted is as follows : The tools are divided into four types, referable to the shape of their stems, namely (a) straight tools, (b) curved or bent tools,

doing special work, such as under-cutting, pierced work, carving that is in high relief, or work which requires to be deeply sunk from the surface. These tools can be obtained either of the ordinary shape as regards their width, as in Fig. 31, or as spade tools (Fig. 32). They also can be had shouldered (Fig. 33) or unshouldered (Fig. 34).

Tools of the Second Type

Type *b* consists of tools so shaped (see Fig. 26) as to enable them to follow easily along internal or concave curves. It is obvious that a tool quite straight in its length would always have the line of force entering the wood in too direct a manner ; and if the tool made any progress at all, it would move in a series of jumps,

Fig. 36.—Sizes and Sweeps of Straight and Bent Carving Tools.

which would leave a rough and uneven surface. But by bending the tool, the line of force is also bent in such a manner that it leaves the tool free to move along the surface in a manner that allows the edge to cut evenly.

Fig. 37.—Sizes and Sweeps of Straight and Bent V Parting Tools.

Tools of the Third Type

The above description also applies generally to tools of type *c* (Figs. 27 and 28), which, however, are so shaped that they can cut curves of greater depth and less radius, thus working in much less space.

Tools of the Fourth Type

Type *d* (Figs. 29 and 30) are tools which are of quite a special nature, and can be used only for a specific purpose. All these types can be had either shouldered or unshouldered, and type *a* can be had as spade tools, in addition to the ordinary shape (see Fig. 32).

Fig. 38.—Straight Chisel, London Pattern.

Fig. 39.—Skew Chisel, London Pattern.

Fig. 40.—Straight Gouge, London Pattern.

Fig. 41.—Veiner, London Pattern.

Fig. 42.—Curved Gouge, London Pattern.

Fig. 43.—Spoon-bit Chisel (Right Corner), London Pattern.

Fig. 44.—Spoon-bit Chisel (Left Corner), London Pattern.

Fig. 45.—Spoon-bit Gouge (Front Bent), London Pattern.

It is recommended that only shouldered tools should be bought. They are stronger and far more serviceable than the others (see Figs. 33 and 34). An objection to unshouldered tools is that the tang drives into common to the first three types of tools (Figs. 25 to 28), so that it is possible to have a great number of different tools. The choice of tools suitable to general work, or to any particular form of it, is a matter

Fig. 46.—Spoon-bit Gouge (Back Bent), London Pattern.

Fig. 47.—Straight **V** Parting Tool, London Pattern.

Fig. 48.—Curved **V** Parting Tool, London Pattern.

Fig. 49.—Spoon-bit **V** Parting Tool, London Pattern.

Fig. 50.—Macaroni Tool, London Pattern.

Fig. 51.—Dog-leg Chisel, London Pattern.

the handle without any check, and almost invariably splits it.

Sections of Tools

The various sections of carving tools are shown in Fig. 35 (to which reference will be made later), the full range of sections being shown by Figs. 36 and 37. The tools are made in sizes varying from $\frac{1}{32}$ in. to $1\frac{1}{2}$ in. and 2 in. All these curves are

needing much judgment and care, and this will be dealt with later.

Sets of Tools

The tools shown by Figs. 38 to 51 comprise a set of London pattern (shouldered) carving tools, as made by William Marples and Sons, Ltd., Sheffield. Under each figure is an inscription giving the particular name of the tool, and Figs. 52 to 57 show a

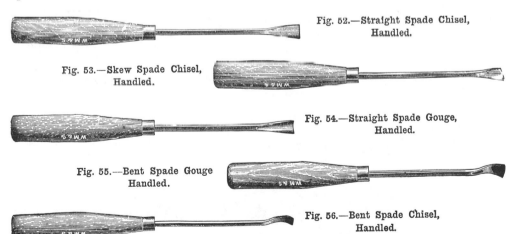

Fig. 52.—Straight Spade Chisel, Handled.

Fig. 53.—Skew Spade Chisel, Handled.

Fig. 54.—Straight Spade Gouge, Handled.

Fig. 55.—Bent Spade Gouge Handled.

Fig. 56.—Bent Spade Chisel, Handled.

Fig. 57.—Spade **V** Parting Tool, Handled.

set of spade tools with round beechwood handles. Figs. 58 to 66 show a set of fancy rosewood handled tools. Sets of tools in cases can be obtained, examples being illustrated by Figs. 67 and 68.

Tool Handles

Tool handles vary in size, in shape, and in the kind of wood from which they are made. They are known and regulated by the size of the ferrule, and vary from $\frac{3}{8}$ in. outside diameter of the ferrule to $\frac{5}{8}$ in.

for tools up to $\frac{3}{4}$ in. in width; and for larger tools, in proportion to the thickness of the tang. Two shapes have already been shown, and Figs. 69 to 71 show further shapes. That shown by Fig. 71 fits the hand better than most other shapes. The woods most generally used for tool handles are box, rosewood, beech, hornbeam, and mahogany. Of these, box and beech are the most lasting. All handles should be ferruled, and the handle itself should be about $\frac{3}{8}$ in. thicker than the ferrule. The

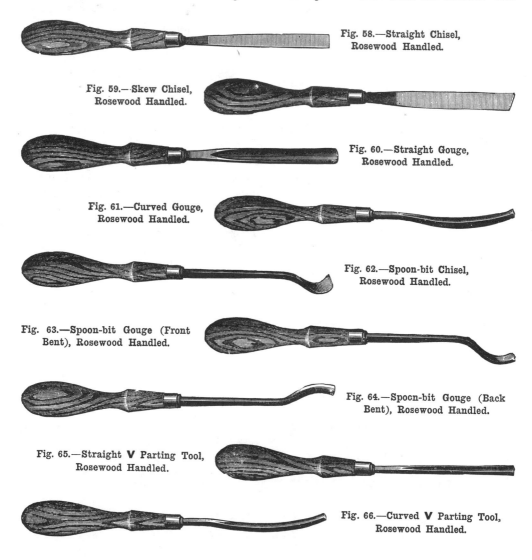

Fig. 58.—Straight Chisel, Rosewood Handled.

Fig. 59.—Skew Chisel, Rosewood Handled.

Fig. 60.—Straight Gouge, Rosewood Handled.

Fig. 61.—Curved Gouge, Rosewood Handled.

Fig. 62.—Spoon-bit Chisel, Rosewood Handled.

Fig. 63.—Spoon-bit Gouge (Front Bent), Rosewood Handled.

Fig. 64.—Spoon-bit Gouge (Back Bent), Rosewood Handled.

Fig. 65.—Straight **V** Parting Tool, Rosewood Handled.

Fig. 66.—Curved **V** Parting Tool, Rosewood Handled.

length of a handle should be 4½ in. or 5 in. If longer, they are, except for the very large tools, clumsy and awkward to use. If shorter, there is much loss of power in using

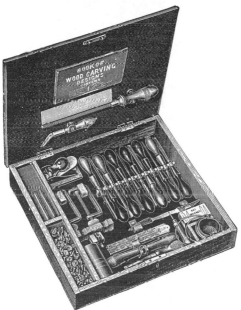

Fig. 67.—Wood Carver's Complete Outfit in Case.

them. A good plan in selecting handles for a set of tools is to have them in various woods, and marked distinctively with respect to the position and number of the rings that are often turned on them. If all are of the same wood, they can be stained in different colours whilst still in the lathe; the object being to enable the worker to distinguish the tools easily when they lie grouped together.

Fixing Handles on Tools

It is important to have the handle fixed to the blade in a proper manner. The tools are generally bought with the handle fixed. But even then it is advisable to know when the tool is handled in a business-like manner. To begin with, in most cases the blade should be in perfect alignment with the handle. Especially is this the case with the setting-in tools. It is not so much a necessity with **V**-tools and fluters, because the force transmitted through these tools

does not, as a rule, proceed in a perfectly straight line, but moves in the direction of a curve. A tool whose blade is so fixed in the handle that it forms a concave curve

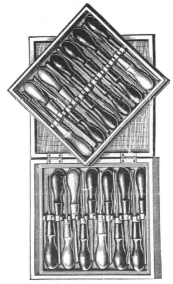

Fig. 68.—Set of Lady's Carving Tools in Case.

on its face side is often of greater advantage in getting round a concave curve than one in which the blade is in perfect alignment with the handle. But in all tools to which force has to be applied by

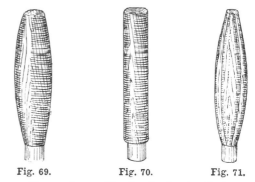

Fig. 69.   Fig. 70.   Fig. 71.

Figs. 69 to 71.—Handles for Carving Tools.

other means than mere hand pressure, the blade must be fixed quite straight. To retain all the force given by the mallet, it is necessary that it should be directed by the shortest possible route, which is a straight line. If the blade is in the least degree out of this straight line, then some of the force is lost just where the bend occurs.

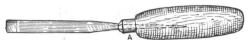

Fig. 72.—Chisel with Blade not in Straight Line with Handle.

In Fig. 72, which shows a tool badly handled, the force is lost at A. Not only is force lost, but a probability occurs of the tool getting broken because of the jarring that is caused. To handle a tool, fix the handle in a bench vice, and bore a hole with a nose bit less than half the size of the diameter of the tang of the tool. Then with a taper bit proceed to widen the hole at the top, taking care not to make it so wide that the tang does not get a good grip from the handle. A good plan is to make the tang itself act as the taper bit, in the following manner : The blade is firmly fixed in an iron vice, the tang projecting upwards. Then taking the handle (which has already been bored with the nose bit) firmly in one hand, push it on the tang, and begin to twist it round. This action helps to make the hole wide at the top, and in direct proportion to the diameter of the tang. Then draw it off, shake out the chips, and with the

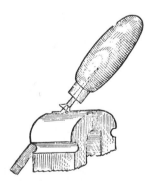

Fig. 73.—Holding Tool in Vice whilst Fitting Handle.

mallet knock it a little farther on. Twist it round again, remove and shake out chips, and again knock it on the tang. Proceed

gradually in this manner until the shoulder of the tool is within $\frac{1}{4}$ in. of the ferrule, when it may be driven down quite

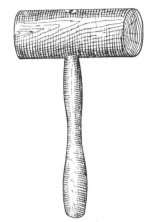

Fig. 74.—Cylindrical-headed Mallet.

tight. Although this method may appear to be slow, the hole made by it is perfectly adjusted to the size and taper of the tang. Fig. 73 shows how the operation is performed.

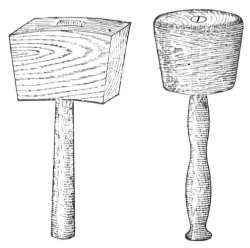

Fig. 75.—" Square "-headed Mallet. Fig. 76.—Round-headed Mallet.

Mallets

Mallets are indispensable, and are made principally from the wood of the apple tree, plum tree, beech, and elm. They vary in shape, three of the varieties being shown by Figs. 74 to 76. That shown at Fig. 76 is the best, for the reason that it always presents the same face to the tool handle. The usual diameters for ordinary work are 3 in., 3½ in., and 4 in. They can be had either polished or unpolished. Polishing merely makes them more present- able when new and after use. One draw- back, which is not so noticeable with the other types of mallets, but which can scarcely be avoided, is that as the blows become in time fairly evenly distributed over the whole surface, those which are parallel to the grain wear the mallet more quickly, because on those sides it becomes more easily bruised. The only thing to minimise this is always to endeavour to use the end grain, which is a somewhat difficult thing to do. In handling a mallet, let the handle come right through to the head, and fix it with a wedge at right angles to the grain of the head. Do not cut the wedge off close to the head, but let it, for a time, project beyond about ¼ in. As the wood dries and seasons, the handle is apt to work slack, and it is when this occurs that the usefulness of having the wedge longer is appreciated. It can be driven in until all is tight again.

Use of the Mallet.—Although a mallet is not so necessary a tool to a wood carver as it is to a carver in stone, to whom it is absolutely essential, its use cannot be too systematically cultivated, says Mr. Harry Hems, who recommends that all roughing out should be done with it ; and bosses, cor- nices, and other work intended to be fixed at a height from the eye, should invariably be finished with the mallet. When the carver is engaged on these classes of work the mallet should never leave his hand ; for the cut left by the chisel with the mallet behind it is always the most effective when looked up at from the ground. Further, by the free and continuous use of the mallet the work is got over in half the time it would otherwise take. Particularly in architec- tural carving, the great end to be attained is general good effect. If it is to be suc- cessful, the lights and shadows, the out- lines, and general grouping must be happy

and telling when seen from the real point of sight—that is, the floor. Half-a-dozen strokes judiciously administered may make a really effective patera ; whereas half a day's minute work upon a bench may produce something which, when placed in position upon the wall-plate at the springing of a roof, will not only be disappointing, but practically invisible. It is a general practice of wood carvers to use the half- closed palm of the hand as a sort of mallet, and for light work this is a good custom. Mr. Hems notes that most experienced wood carvers have a large hoof in the middle of the palm as a result thereof, and, un- fortunately, cannot open their right hands quite straight. In course of time the habit causes the fingers to become rigidly bent inwards, although the flexor tendons and joints are unaffected. Subcutaneous divi- sion of the contracted bands sets the fingers free, but a relapse is nearly sure to occur. An eminent surgeon states that there are quite half-a-dozen different operations in vogue for this deformity, but he does not know one that is really successful—that is to say, which results in a permanent cure.

Cramps

The principal cramps used are illustrated by Figs. 77 to 79. All work has to be held fast in some manner, and opinions differ as to which is the best way. All that is necessary is that the work should be held quite firmly, and without damage to it. Fig. 77 shows what is known as a G-cramp, presumably because of its rough resemblance to that letter. These are made in sizes varying from 2 in. to 1 ft., the size referring to the width between the jaws. These are the strongest cramps used, especially when of the best make. An objection to their use is that the part that corresponds to the top of the G stands above the level of the top jaw, and is much in the way of the free use of the hands during actual work. The form of cramp shown at Fig. 78 is as free from this objection as it is possible to be ; and, although not so strong as the G- cramp, yet its strength is quite sufficient for the purpose. This is, in the writer's opinion, the best form of cramp to use. It can be obtained in sizes from 3 in. to 8 in., and may be had bright, japanned, or polished. The last-named is the best, as it does not mark the wood, the jaws of the other kinds being somewhat rough ; but of course this can be overcome by using a small strip of leather or paper. The cramp shown

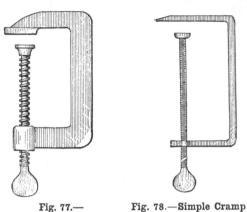

Fig. 77.— G-cramp.

Fig. 78.—Simple Cramp of Good Design.

at Fig. 79 is known as " the carver's screw," and is used as follows : Holes corresponding in size to the thickness of the screw are bored through the bench top. The wing nut is then taken off the screw, and the latter's gimlet point screwed well into the back of the panel. Then the whole screw is threaded through one of the holes, and the wing nut screwed on under the bench top until the panel is drawn down tight to the bench. This keeps the work quite firm, and, moreover, possesses the advantage of leaving the whole of it quite clear, so that neither the hands nor tools are impeded in any way. Objection may be taken to the holes made in the back of the work by the screw. To overcome this, a block of deal is often glued on, and the screw driven into this. Then, when carved, the deal block is damped and separated from the work. In purchasing a pair of cramps, remember to take into account the thickness of the table or bench top, and allow at least 2 in. more. Sometimes it is necessary to have specially large cramps.

Special Methods of Holding Work

The carver has sometimes to work on articles of such a shape or size that they cannot be securely fixed by the ordinary methods of cramping and screwing. Objects of a larger size than can be accommodated by the ordinary cramps, such as a glove-box, are often a source of difficulty. All articles of this type should, if possible, be carved in pieces, and fixed together after the carving is finished. But when the article has been made up first, then difficulties arise respecting the carving of the ends, at least ; and often the box is too thick to be gripped by the cramps so that the top and sides may be carved. Of course, the carver's screw cannot be used, because it would disfigure the bottom and perhaps split it. For all work of this type the best way is to make a case in deal, in which the box may be jammed tight, so that the sides and top may be carved (see Fig. 80). The case consists of a bottom, long enough to have projecting ends to allow of their being cramped to the table ; and two ends and two sides nearly the same depth as the box. The case is made so that the box jams tightly in ; thus the top can be carved. To carve the sides, turn the box over, and, if there is any difference between the width and the depth of the box, have a piece of wood of

Fig. 79.—Carver's Screw.

the thickness of the difference to jam in. For carving the ends, a different arrangement is necessary, as is shown by Figs. 81 and 82. To carve the ends, unscrew the sides and ends of the case, and screw one of the sides A (Fig. 81) to the bottom B as shown. Then cramp the box to the bottom, and cramp the projecting side to the table, as shown in Fig. 82. Another convenient way is to utilise a drawer. The drawer is opened, the box placed on its end in a corner of the drawer, which is then shut tightly against the

Fig. 80. Case to Hold Box for Carving.

edge of the table top. Two pieces of wood are prepared, one to jam the box tightly up to the inside of the drawer front from the back, and the other to jam it tightly up to one of the drawer sides, from the other side. A circular piece of work, such as a turned pillar, can be held as shown in Fig. 83. This apparatus consists of a bottom piece with two ends. The ends are 1 in. thick, and have holes bored to accommodate the pins that are turned on the ends of the pillar. If the pillar has no pins turned on it (as in the case of a table leg), then a screw can be put through. To keep the pillar from turning round, the holes can be keyed as in the case of some marking gauges. This

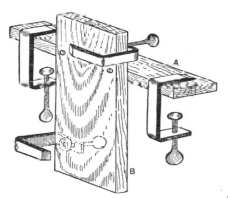

Fig. 81.—Cramps arranged to receive Box to be Carved.

allows the pillar to be turned round as desired, and fixed securely in any required position. Work that is known as " carving in the round " often presents some diffi-

culty in fixing. One side can easily be done, but it is when the other side comes to be carved that difficulty arises. Work of this kind should be fastened to a board

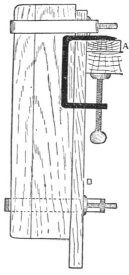

Fig. 82.—Box in Cramps ready for Carving.

by means of screws. If it is, for example, a lion lying down, then it may be screwed to a board, and the board itself screwed or cramped to a bench. If it is a piece of work to occupy eventually a vertical position, then screw it face on to the board, and screw or cramp the board to an upright pillar or door-post. Work the back, and then reverse the block, bringing the face to the front. Panels and similar work may be held in position by means of blocks such as are shown at A and B (Fig. 84).

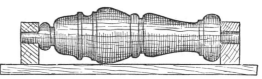

Fig. 83.—Holding Turned Pillar for Carving.

These may be of any size for small or large work. Fig. 85 shows a form of wood block that may be used with advantage. It should be made of ash, and the distance between the points A and B should be little less than the thickness of the block being

Fig. 84.—Cleats or Blocks for Holding Work on Bench.

carved, so that the bridge of the ash block may bind tightly on it.

Punches

These tools (Fig. 86) frequently have designs worked on their faces, and are used to give a more or less uniform appearance to the groundwork. Usual designs are shown by Fig. 87. Also, roses, acorns, hearts, crosses, anchors, etc., are obtainable (see Fig. 88). Good and economical punches can be made by heating out the ends of ordinary nails and then filing them into points. The punch should be used as little as possible.

Punching

Punching is a method of treating the ground after the carving is finished. The best manner of treating it is to leave it quite plain ; but this necessitates a perfect treatment. " Perfect treatment " means not so much a quite smooth surface, but a clean cut surface. It is not advisable to get a surface that would appear to have been worked by means of a plane ; but it is highly essential that it should be cut clean and bright, and that all the tool marks should be smooth and shiny. No " ragging " or tearing should be shown. Punching is resorted to when the ground is rough and

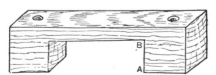

Fig. 85.—Block for Holding Down Work on Bench.

uneven, in order to hide the bad work. This may sometimes be excused as a matter of expediency when the worker is incapable

of doing better work. But the real reason for the use of the punch should rest on a sounder basis than that of expediency. Punching a ground should be resorted to only when a real artistic necessity exists for its use. In any case, in punching the ground in wood carving, it is a great mistake to cover it regularly. To be a little sparing with the punch lightens the labour and heightens the effect. Well-finished carving very rarely requires the punch to show it up. It is only at times that the punching of the ground of a flat panel, that is intended to stand close to the eye, is a help to work. Generally, it simply means common work ; because, of course, punching, which anyone can do, takes much less time than careful cleaning up with a chisel. A big star punch may be used effectively sometimes, as on the ground of carved barge-board panels.

Supplementary Tools

There are some tools which do not belong

Fig. 86.—Wood Carver's Punch.

exclusively to the wood carver's craft, being common to the woodworkers' trades, but which are often used by the carver, generally in the higher branches of the craft. These will be briefly described, and their uses pointed out. These tools and implements are : Brace and bits ; compass, bow, keyhole and fret saws ; spokeshaves ; files ; rasps ; rifflers ; routers ; scrapers ; and glasspaper. These tools are shown in Fig. 89.

Brace and Bits

The brace shown in Fig. 89 is that of the American ratchet kind. It is exceedingly useful, as, besides working in the ordinary way, it can be worked either left or right hand in an enclosed space where the hand cannot get its full swing round. The bits used by the carver are chiefly the shell and the centre bits. The use to which the brace and bits are put is chiefly in pierced carving, and in carving in the round ; and also in doing work with irregularly shaped edges. Their particular application will be dealt with when treating of these forms of carving.

Saws

The compass saw is in appearance something like a hand saw. It is shorter, vary-

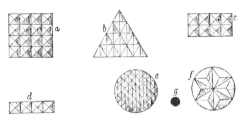

Fig. 87.—Usual Designs made by Punches.

ing from 12 in. to 18 in., and much narrower in the blade, to enable it to be twisted round, in order to saw curves of not less than about 6-in. radius. There is on the market a compass saw that has three blades, which can be fitted into the same handle. This obviously increases the value of such a tool, as the blades, being of various lengths

and widths, can be used for a greater variety of work. The bow saw is not more than ¼ in. wide, and is held stretched in a frame. The blade can be tightened or loosened by twisting the string stretched across the top. This form of saw can be used for curves of very small radius, and is especially useful for work which has an irregular outline. It is the best saw (worked by hand)

Fig. 88.—Other Designs made by Punches.

to use for curves which are on the outside of the work. It can also be used for the inside curves of pierced carving; but to do this the saw has to be taken out and threaded, and then fastened and tightened. This, in a saw of this kind, is somewhat tedious; moreover, the frame is often in the way, especially in big work. The fret saw is used in pierced work, and if the

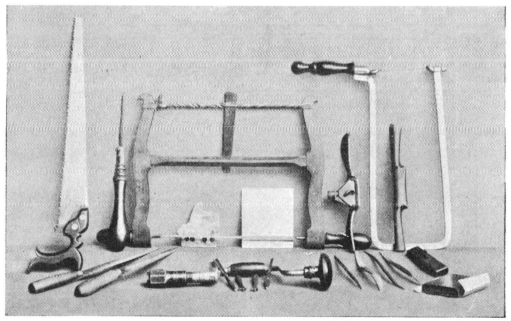

Fig. 89.—Set of Carver's Supplementary Tools.

wood is not more than 1 in. thick it makes a cleaner job, and it is possible to cut closer to the work, especially in corners, than w th any other saw. The keyhole saw has a tapering blade not more than $\frac{1}{2}$ in. wide, about 12 in. or 15 in. long, fitted into a handle known as the pad. This handle is

means of a wedge or screw. The amount of projection on the blade depends on the depth of ground that is desired. The blade may be a broken carving tool, and the widths used may vary from $\frac{1}{8}$ in. to $\frac{1}{2}$ in. Handles can be fitted at each end of the body if considered necessary. The form

Fig. 90.—Riffler.

pierced in its length, so that the blade can be passed right through, and so be shortened or lengthened as may be necessary. This saw is often used in pierced work, because it can be worked without any necessity for its being loosened and threaded. It does not make such a clean finish as the fret and bow saws, but is nevertheless a useful, strong, and reliable type of saw.

Spokeshaves

These may be used for cleaning edges, rounding corners, and other similar work, especially where the curved edge is a long one. The blade, having the frame as a guide, takes off the chips more uniformly than the carving tool, and ensures a more shapely and more uniform outline.

Files, Rasps, and Rifflers

These are used to work down rough edges and uneven surfaces, as a preliminary step to the use of glasspaper, when a perfectly smooth surface is necessary for polishing, such as in the case of worked mouldings. The rifflers (Figs. 89 and 90), of which many shapes can be obtained, are used in undercut and pierced work, where it sometimes occurs that the carving tools cannot quite successfully reach some of the undercut parts in cleaning up ; this the rifflers do quite well.

Routers

Routers are useful in clearing the ground quickly and uniformly, providing the setting in has been well done. A router is a piece of wood at least 4 in. long, 2 in. wide, and $\frac{1}{2}$ in. thick, through which a steel blade is placed, fixed perpendicularly by

of router shown in Fig. 89 is very serviceable for all ordinary work, but for larger pieces a much stronger form should be used. This is shown in Fig. 91. Plough bits can be used with this type of body, and much greater weight and purchase can be applied to the wood.

Scrapers and Glasspaper and Other Accessories

Scrapers and glasspaper are used when the work has to be quite smooth, but they are seldom necessary, and they are not employed in the very best work. The plane, hand and tenon saws, drawknife, etc., are sometimes used, but not often enough to specify them as being tools that come

Fig. 91.—Carver's Router.

quite within the carver's set. It will, however, be seen that it is an advantage for the carver to be able to draw on the resources of a cabinetmaker's shop.

Choice of Tools

A carver cannot be expected to own a set of tools that would cover all carving operations, including carving of the most advanced kind. His object, then, is to obtain a really good set of tools to begin work with, without going to too great an outlay. The following suggested set of

baize or canvas (Fig. 92). As progress is made, and work of a higher nature is undertaken, thus causing a demand for a more extended outfit, the worker will be in a position to decide for himself exactly

List of Hand Tools Essential to Wood Carving

No. on Sheffield
Tool List.

No. 1.—Straight Chisel (Fig. 38) $\frac{1}{2}$ in. wide, chiefly used for setting in.
No. 3.—Straight Gouge (Fig. 40) $\frac{1}{16}$ in., $\frac{1}{8}$ in., and $\frac{1}{4}$ in. wide, for grounding small spaces.
No. 3.— ,, ,, (Fig. 40) $\frac{3}{8}$ in. wide.
No. 4. ,, ,, (Fig. 40) $\frac{3}{8}$ in. wide, for setting in, grounding, and modelling.
No. 5.— ,, ,, (Fig. 40) $\frac{3}{16}$ in. and $\frac{5}{16}$ in. wide, for setting in and grounding.
No. 5.— ,, ,, (Fig. 40) $\frac{1}{8}$ in. wide, for setting in, grounding, and modelling.
No. 7.— ,, ,, (Fig. 40) $\frac{3}{8}$ in. wide, for grounding and modelling.
No. 8.— ,, ,, (Fig. 40) $\frac{1}{8}$ in. and $\frac{1}{4}$ in. wide, for modelling.
No. 8.— ,, ,, (Fig. 40) $\frac{3}{4}$ in. wide, for grounding and modelling.
No. 11.— ,, ,, (Fig. 40) $\frac{3}{16}$ in. wide, for modelling.
No. 21.—Spoon-bit Chisel, Square (Fig. 62), $\frac{1}{8}$ in., $\frac{3}{16}$ in., and $\frac{3}{8}$ in. wide for grounding.
No. 28.—Spoon-bit Gouge or Front-bent Gouge (Fig. 45), $\frac{1}{4}$ in. and $\frac{1}{2}$ in. wide, for modelling.
No. 30.—Straight V Parting Tool (Fig. 17), $\frac{5}{16}$ in. wide, for outlining and modelling.
Mallet, pair of 4-in. cramps, three punches for the groundwork, two oil slips, oil-can, and strap.

tools constitutes a representative collection that will enable a carver to execute all flat work, and as much pierced and solid work as he will be likely to have to do in the first few years in his trade. There are twenty tools, known in the Sheffield Tool List by the numbers attached to them in the accompanying list. The size also is given, as

what tools he will require, and these can be added as the necessity arises. Routers, files, glasspaper, scrapers, and similar implements should be avoided as much as possible. The set above enumerated will be sufficient for executing all flat work, and a great amount of the undercut and solid work, and other similar elaborate carving.

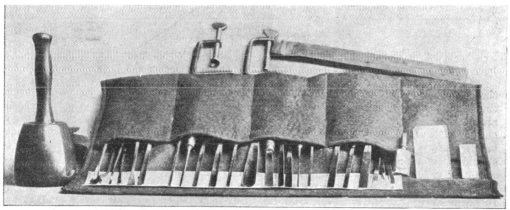

Fig. 92.—Set of Hand Tools Essential to Wood Carving.

well as the principal uses. The number of the tool is generally stamped on the blade, and the size can be ascertained by measuring the width. This set can be kept in a case of

Remember that a multiplication of tools is not to be desired. One tool should be put to as many uses as possible. This principle of economising, if applied in reason, saves the tools, and increases the ability of the carver.

Care of Tools

Needless to say, the greatest possible care should be taken of the tools—especially steel ones. Sometimes, when left in a damp place, steel tools rust. To prevent this, the tools should be occasionally rubbed with an oily rag. Rub the whole tool, handle included. The oil, besides cleaning the handle, also helps to harden it. By constant use, the handles begin to fray at the top, especially

Tool Cases

The life of the carving tools can be much prolonged, and the trouble of sharpening them lessened, if proper care is taken of them. This applies not only when the tools are in use, but also when they are not being used. Suitable cases or boxes should be provided, and arranged so that the tool required can be taken out at once. A case made of green baize, felt, or brown canvas, and divided into pockets, will be suitable for holding the tools, cramps, slips,

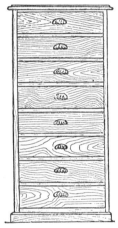

Fig. 93.—Pedestal of Tool Drawers.

Figs. 94 to 96.—Plan and Two Sections
of Tool Drawer in Pedestal.

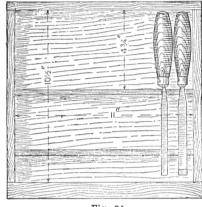

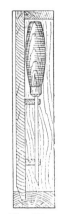

Fig. 94.   Fig. 95.

Fig. 96.

those tools which are most used for setting in. In time, if this fraying is not attended to, the fibre ends turn over, and, acting as tiny wedges, begin to split the handle. To guard against this, the handles should be continually trimmed with glass-paper or a flat tool. The cramps should also be given a drop of oil occasionally; this will ease the friction and prevent the wearing and cutting of the thread. The oilstone slips are brittle and liable to break easily. They will be safe in a drawer; but if they have to be carried about to classes, it is a good plan to wrap them in a large piece of corrugated paper; or a small tin box is useful for the purpose.

etc. It rolls up, and can be packed away in a drawer. Fig. 93 shows a small pedestal of drawers to hold about ninety tools. It consists of a carcase fitted with eight drawers, each being capable of holding about a dozen tools. The drawers can be used as trays for use on the bench; and it is suggested that the two lower drawers be stocked with a general set for constant use, and the upper drawers with tools that are only occasionally used, or *vice versâ*. The tools are arranged with the cutting edge to the front, so that the tool required is easily seen (see Figs. 94 to 96). The arrangement of the laths keeps the tools from knocking against each other, a necessary precaution, and the use of the lath close to the shoulders of the tools is to prevent the tool edges knocking up against the drawer front, and so damaging them. Fig. 97 shows a case designed for carrying about two dozen carving tools and mallet. Fig. 98 is a longitudinal section, Fig. 99 a horizontal section, and Fig. 100 a cross section. The outside dimensions of the box are 15 in. by 12 in. by 5 in. For making this case, oak, mahogany, or any similar wood would be suitable. The broad sides and divisions are $\frac{3}{8}$ in. thick, and the narrow sides $\frac{5}{8}$ in. The rim to the lid is dovetailed together at the angles, as shown in Fig. 97. The pieces forming the

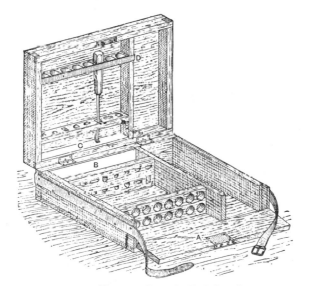

Fig. 97.—Carver's Tool Box Open.

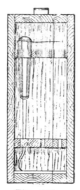

Fig. 100.

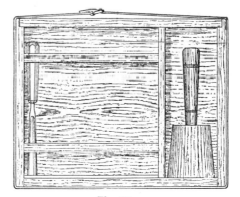

Fig. 98.

Figs. 98 to 100.—Longitudinal, Horizontal, and Cross Sections of Carver's Tool Box.

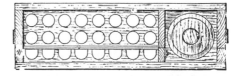

Fig. 99.

three sides of the box are dovetailed together where the lid hinges, whereas the
other ends are rebated for the flap A. This
is hinged so that it can be dropped down,

Fig. 101.—Carver's Bench.

and thus allow the tools to be readily withdrawn, as indicated by Fig. 97. To hold
the tools in the lid portion, a strap is tacked
fast at the left-hand end, and the other
end is passed over a brass pin at D. To
protect the edges of the tools whilst being
carried about, pieces of cork lino are inserted, as at B and C (Fig. 97). Holes are
bored in the upper divisions for the handles
of the tools, while the lower divisions are
bored to receive the blades. The lock

Benches

To obtain good results in wood carving,
a satisfactory bench is essential. The two
principal conditions are size and rigidity.
In size the height is important. All workers
should stand to carve; this should be accepted as a firm and unalterable principle,
only to be modified in case of physical
infirmity. Even then, if possible, the
worker should be so seated as to be able
to get the toes on the ground, with the
bench at standing height. Thus the bench
should be from 3 ft. to 3 ft. 3 in. high. A
good guide is to measure the height up to
the elbows, with the forearm raised horizontally. The top should not be less than
3 ft. long by 1 ft. 8 in. wide, which is sufficient for one person. But it is an advantage to have the bench longer and wider, in
order to get sufficient bearing for the legs
to make the bench stand quite firm. The
bench must be able to resist the firm thrusts
and sudden jerks constantly being given
during the progress of the work. Therefore, the bench should be built of heavy
material, and should be of the best construction and workmanship. Deal is quite
suitable, but the legs should be at least 3 in.

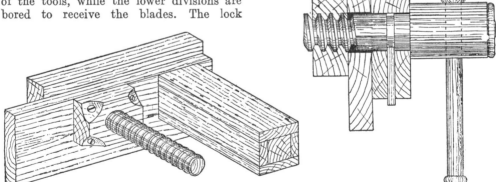

Fig. 102.—Inside View of Bench Screw.　　　　Fig. 103.—Section through Bench Screw.

should be fixed on the flap and the staple on
the lid. The lid should be hung with brass
hinges. For carrying, a strap should be
passed right round the box.

by 3 in., and better still $4\frac{1}{2}$ in. by 3 in.; the
rails should be about $4\frac{1}{2}$ in. by $2\frac{1}{2}$ in. To
make the bench rigid and immovable, it
should be braced with diagonals; or it can

be fitted with rails and shelves, or with drawers. Fig. 101 shows a suitable bench for one person. The shelf below is useful for holding work not actually in hand, boxes of tools, etc., and the drawer under

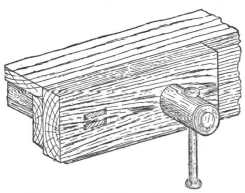

Fig. 104.—General View of Bench Screw.

the top holds tools and other apparatus. The top projects at least 3 in., to give room for the cramps in fixing the work. If a carver's screw is used, the drawer should be placed lower down, or omitted, otherwise there will not be space enough to work the wing-nut. In very advanced work, a bench screw is indispensable. For a bench of the kind here shown, the screw can be fitted at the end. An ordinary wooden screw (Figs. 102 to 104) is useful, but one of the "instantaneous grip"

be made to serve as a substitute. To increase the height, a false top, as shown in Fig. 106, can be adopted. Two strong boards, between which are two or three cross pieces of substantial section, are arranged as shown, and they can easily be cramped to the table top when required. This arrangement gives the projecting top

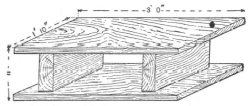

Fig. 106.—False Top to Convert Table to Bench.

which is so desirable. Another way, where economy of space is an object, is to utilise a chest of drawers about four drawers high, fitting it with a strong top that projects the necessary 3 in. One very important matter that should not be neglected is that the bench top, or table top, should be quite level, and, owing to wood being apt to warp, the tops should be constantly inspected and tested.

Carver's Portable Bench and Vice

A description will here be given of a construction which has been designed especially for the use of carvers. The bench shown

Fig. 105.—Instantaneous Grip Vice.

screws (Fig. 105) is better. If a tail vice is fitted to the bench, so much the better.

Substitutes for Benches

When it is not possible to have a separate bench, a good strong kitchen table may

in plan and elevation at Figs. 107 and 108 is 3 ft. long by 2 ft. 4 in. wide, and has been designed to fix on a strong table 3 ft. by 1 ft. 9 in. It is not necessary, however, to make the bench as long as the table, but it must not be any longer. If the table is more than 1 ft. 9 in. wide, the width of the bench must be increased accordingly. Fig. 109 is a section on the line x x (Fig. 107), and of a pair of wedges c and D (Fig. 107); the wedge D is operated by a lever, and presses the work against the stop E, which is fixed

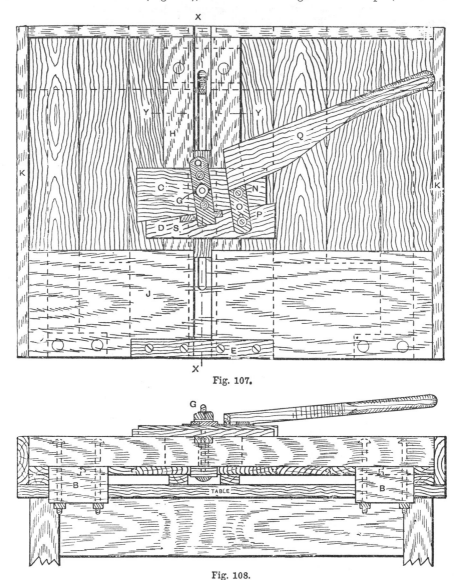

Fig. 107.

Fig. 108.

Figs. 107 and 108.—Plan and Front Elevation of Portable Bench and Vice.

shows how the bench is clamped against the edges of the table-top by means of the screw A and blocks B (see also Fig. 108). The bench is fitted with a vice, consisting simply flush with the edge of the front board. The vice may be secured at any desired distance, up to 1 ft. 6 in., from the top, to suit the work in hand, by means of a

$\frac{1}{2}$-in. bolt and nut G, passing through a slot in a cross piece H (see also Fig. 109). The work is secured by drawing forward the lever handle Q, and released by pushing it back. White deal should be used for the general construction of the bench. Note that the front board J (Fig. 107) is 3 ft. long by 9 in. wide by $2\frac{1}{2}$ in. thick; this front carries the cross piece H, which is fixed at

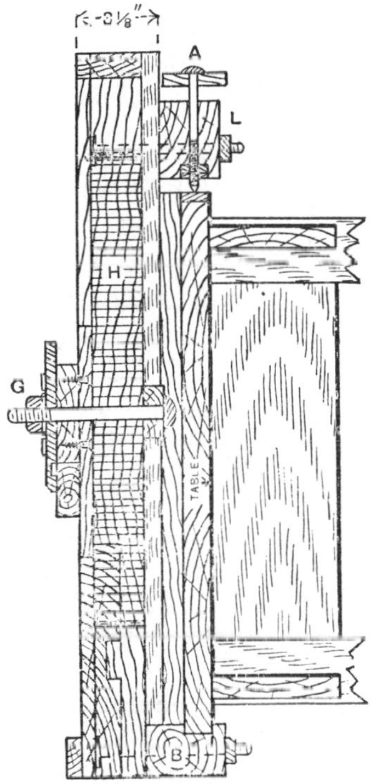

Fig. 109.—Section of Portable Bench and Vice (on Line X X, Fig. 107).

right angles $11\frac{1}{2}$ in. from the left-hand end. The cross piece H is 2 ft. $3\frac{1}{8}$ in. long by $6\frac{1}{2}$ in. wide by $2\frac{1}{2}$ in. thick, and is grooved and slotted in the middle as shown in the cross section, Fig. 110. The groove at the top, $1\frac{1}{2}$ in. wide by $\frac{1}{2}$ in. deep, is carried the whole length of the piece, and the ends of the slot, which is $\frac{5}{8}$ in. wide, are 3 in. from the back end and 9 in. from the front end. The cross piece is fitted to the front board with a glued cogged joint, as shown in Fig. 109. When the glue has set, the groove is carried across the front board, and the slot prolonged to within $5\frac{1}{2}$ in. of the edge; the cross piece should then be screwed to give greater firmness. The two blocks B (Figs. 108 and 109), 5 in. long

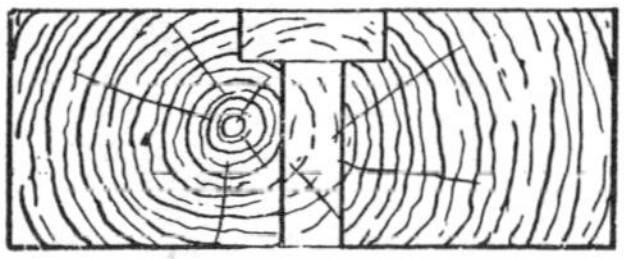

Fig. 110.—Enlarged Section of Bench's Cross Piece (on Line Y Y, Fig. 107).

by 3 in. deep by 2 in. wide, and grooved $\frac{1}{4}$ in. deep to fit over the front edge of the table-top, are fixed to the under side of the front board with two $\frac{3}{8}$-in. bolts and nuts. The wo end rails K (Fig. 107), 2 ft. 4 in. long by 4 in. deep by $\frac{7}{8}$ in. thick, are nailed to the ends of the front board and back rail. The back rail is 2 ft. $10\frac{1}{4}$ in. long by $2\frac{1}{2}$ in. deep by $\frac{7}{8}$ in. thick, and is nailed to the end of the cross piece H. The bottom is made up of seven $\frac{5}{8}$-in. boards, grooved and tongued; the two end boards are 2 ft. 4 in. long by $4\frac{5}{16}$ in. wide, and are nailed to the under side of the front board and back rail, and to fillets, $1\frac{3}{4}$ in. wide by $\frac{7}{8}$ in. deep, nailed and glued flush with the bottom of the side rails. Pieces $2\frac{3}{4}$ in. by 2 in. must be cut out of the front ends to allow the blocks B to bed direct on the front board. The two bottom boards which come under the cross piece are 5 in. wide, and are fixed with their edges $2\frac{1}{4}$ in. apart, to form a groove to guide the washer of the holding-down bolt G of the vice. The three other boards are only 1 ft. 0 in. long, as indicated by the dotted lines in Fig. 107. Bearers, 1 ft. 9 in. long by $1\frac{3}{4}$ in. wide by $\frac{7}{8}$ in. deep, are nailed under the cross piece and front board, as shown in Fig. 108. The block L (Fig. 109) carrying the clamping screw

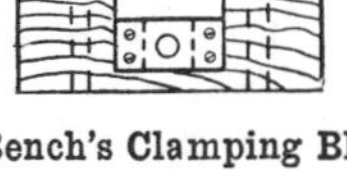

Fig. 111.—Bench's Clamping Block Screw.

is shown separately at Fig. 111; this is $6\frac{1}{2}$ in. long by 3 in. wide by $2\frac{1}{2}$ in. deep. A notch $2\frac{1}{4}$ in. long by $\frac{7}{8}$ in. deep is cut on the top to allow the washer of the bolt G to pass

through. The hole for the clamping screw
—which is an ordinary $\frac{3}{8}$-in. bolt and nut,
with a wood handle fixed under the head—
is bored $1\frac{3}{8}$ in. from the top ; the nut is let
in on the front and secured with a thin
iron plate. The screw is pointed, and fits

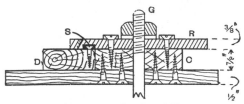

Fig 112.—Section of Vice.

into a countersunk hole in a $\frac{3}{16}$-in. iron plate
let in flush with the edge of the table-top,
which is taken as being 1 in. thick. The
oak stop E (Fig. 107) is 1 ft. long by $1\frac{1}{2}$ in.
wide by $\frac{5}{8}$ in. thick, and should be fixed
with glue and stout screws. The vice is
shown in cross section at Fig. 112. The fixed
piece C (see also Fig. 107) is a beech or oak
wedge 11 in. long, $4\frac{1}{2}$ in. wide at the thick
end and 3 in. at the thin end, and $\frac{7}{8}$ in.
thick. A guide piece 9 in. long, and made
a sliding fit for the groove in the cross piece,
is screwed to the under side to keep it
parallel with the stop. Square a line from
the top edge in the middle, and gauge down
$1\frac{7}{8}$ in. for the hole for the $\frac{1}{2}$-in. holding-
down bolt G ; measure from the small end
on the sloped edge $2\frac{1}{16}$ in., square a line
across, and gauge $1\frac{1}{4}$ in. from the edge ;
the intersection of these lines is the position
for the No. 14 by 1-in. wood screw N (Fig.
107) forming the pivot for the iron lever O.
The movable wedge D is 11 in. long, 3 in.
wide at the thick end, and $1\frac{1}{2}$ in. at the thin
end. Measure from the thick end on the
sloped edge $2\frac{13}{16}$ in., square across, and
gauge $1\frac{1}{4}$ in. ; this gives the position for
another screw P, which works through a slot
near the end of O. Figs. 113 and 114 are respectively a longitudinal section and a plan
of a turned-iron pivot that may be used in
place of the screws N and P (Fig. 107). These
pivots are riveted on an iron plate 3 in.
long by $1\frac{1}{4}$ in. wide by $\frac{3}{16}$ in. thick, and
are then put through the lever O and secured
by riveting the ends over washers, being
fixed to the wedges with four No. 10 by

1-in. screws. The pivots make a stronger
job than the screws, although the latter, if
made a tight fit, answer the purpose. The
lever O is made of strip-iron, $7\frac{3}{4}$ in. long
by $1\frac{1}{2}$ in. wide by $\frac{3}{16}$ in. thick. Scribe
a line up the middle, and mark with a
centre punch $1\frac{3}{16}$ in. and $1\frac{1}{2}$ in. from the
front end ; drill two $\frac{5}{16}$-in. holes, and file
away the metal between to form a slot
about $\frac{11}{16}$ in. long. Drill another $\frac{5}{16}$-in.
hole $3\frac{1}{2}$ in. from the same end for the fulcrum pivot N. The wood handle Q (Fig. 107)
is made of 1-in. oak, 1 ft. 8 in. long by $3\frac{3}{8}$ in.
wide at the butt end and $1\frac{1}{2}$ in. at the other.
Gauge $1\frac{1}{2}$ in. across the butt end on the
under side, and $\frac{1}{8}$ in. up on the end, and plane
down to the lines ; this will raise the other
end clear of the bench. The handle is fixed
to the lever O with five No. 10 by $\frac{7}{8}$-in.
screws ; the ends of both the handle and
lever are cut to an angle of 1 in 4. When
the work is fixed in the vice, the ends of
the two wedges should be even, or nearly
so, and the slot in the lever should be just
long enough to allow the movable block
to be withdrawn $1\frac{1}{2}$ in. The fittings for
holding the wedges together are shown at
R and S in Fig. 112. They may be made of
iron or brass. S is $3\frac{1}{2}$ in. long by $\frac{1}{2}$ in.

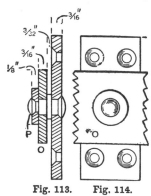

Fig. 113.   Fig. 114.

**Figs. 113 and 114.—Section and Plan of Pivot and
Plate of Portable Bench and Vice.**

wide by $\frac{3}{16}$ in. thick, and is screwed flush
with the edge of D, $2\frac{7}{8}$ in. from the small end ;
it slides in a groove in R, which is $5\frac{3}{4}$ in. long
by $1\frac{1}{2}$ in. wide by $\frac{3}{8}$ in. thick. R is fixed
to C with two screws with washers under
their heads as shown ; the holes for these

screws and the bolt G should be elongated to allow for adjustment. Figs. 107, 108, 109, and 111 are one-eighth full size ; Figs. 110 and 112, one quarter full size ; and Figs. 113 and 114, one half full size.

Lighting of the Carver's Workshop

A few words respecting the arrangement of light will be useful. To get the best work, the lighting must be suitably planned. The best arrangement is to have two sources of light at right angles to each other, one directly facing the worker and the other on his right. With this arrangement, the light will strike, or can be made to strike, across all the ridges, and produce a proper amount of shadow. For the shadows which lie in the direction of the front light, this front light should be shut off, and the side light used alone, and *vice versâ*. It is difficult to do good work when the light is so arranged that it does not throw any shadows. All lights should be low, with as little top light as possible. Thus, if the windows are high, cut off some of the top light with a blind. The same general remarks apply to artificial light. A centre chandelier is not desirable, because it throws the light down on the face of the work in such a manner that no shadows appear. If gas is the illuminant, have a folding bracket of three arms, so that it can be moved as required. If the light cannot be otherwise arranged, candles can be utilised. Electric light is suitable, because it is possible to place the lamps as convenient, and a lamp that can be raised and lowered is perhaps the best arrangement of artificial light that can be secured. The electric light offers the important advantage over most other illuminants that it is not so productive of heat. With a paraffin lamp this latter difficulty may be serious. In such cases the best arrangement is to have the benches on the wall, and have the lamps, with reflectors behind, placed about 1 ft. above the bench.

SHARPENING CARVING TOOLS

THIS chapter will deal with the slips, strop, oil, and other materials for sharpening the tools, and the methods of keeping

Fig. 115.—Gouge before Grinding.

the tools in a condition that will enable them to work in a proper manner.

Cutting Edges of Tools

When the tool blades arrive from the manufacturer, their ends or cutting edges are quite thick; the curved and **V**-tools, too, are quite long in the point. As a rule, the quicker the curve of the tool, the longer is the point. This is shown in Fig. 115, which represents a tool of No. 11 curve (see o, Fig. 35, p. 26). The tool blades require grinding down to a fine edge, and this edge should lie in a plane at an angle not exceeding a right angle to the direction of the blade. This is shown in Fig. 116. If a carving tool is long in the point, this part begins to cut the wood first, before the rest of the edge of the tool has begun to cut the surface of the wood. Consequently the chip which comes out is pushed rather than cut out, the result being rough surfaces to the cut, and torn edges. Thus the tools should always be made so that they cut the surface first. That part of the tool which lies below the surface should follow, not precede, the upper part of the tool.

Grindstone

The first thing required is a grindstone (see Fig. 117); one of about 3 ft. in diameter,

and about 6 in. or 7 in. wide is very useful. If this size is too expensive, some very serviceable stones mounted in iron troughs, down to 10 in. in diameter, can be obtained. A stone that is in constant use should always run in water; thus, a wood or iron trough is necessary. A stone that is somewhat hard is better than a soft one, but it should not be extremely hard. Grindstones are not always of the same consistency throughout; they often have soft patches that quickly get worn away. In this case the stone requires constant attention to keep the surface square and true, and the circumference regular.

Grinding Tools

In grinding the tools, first grind the edge quite square, as indicated in Fig. 117, which shows a grindstone with the water trough. The dotted lines on the tool show the extent and shape to which it should be ground down. This makes the edge quite thick. It is then ground on the grindstone to as fine an edge as possible, without entirely destroying it. It is important to know the correct angle at which to hold the tool whilst grinding its edge. It is sometimes thought that a carving tool necessarily requires a very long "grind," as in Fig. 118. But, although for light modelling this is more or less so, for general work this is a mistake, because a tool so

Fig. 116.—Properly Ground Gouge.

ground, if used for setting in, is liable to have its edge suddenly snapped off. And, as it is impracticable to keep a separate

48

set of tools for each of the several processes of carving, tools must be ground to serve all purposes. A short grind, as shown in Fig. 119, is best. In grinding curved tools, they must be rocked from side to side in order to get an evenly ground surface and edge. The very quick curves, such as those shown at *m*, *n*, and *o*, in Fig. 35 (see p. 26), are rather difficult to manage, and require great care in grinding the extreme points. Much practice is necessary to make the grinding a success, and good results cannot be expected at the first few attempts. Plenty of water should be used, and when the grindstone is very hard

Fig. 117.—Grinding Tool on Grindstone.

some sand will assist in getting it to bite. In frosty weather, and especially when the stone is exposed in the open air, use warm water; cold water would freeze. Always have the surface of the grindstone quite straight, or, at any rate, convex rather than concave. The stone should always be revolved away from the tool, as shown by the arrow in Fig. 117. To turn it the other way wears away the tool edges too quickly. To ensure an even and accurate edge, the steel requires wearing away somewhat slowly. The straight tools require grinding from both sides, to throw the cutting edge towards the centre of the thickness of the tool, as shown in Fig. 120. In Figs. 118 and 119, at the end of the grind A, is an angle formed by the meeting of the ground surface with the back of the tool. This should

be left as shown, and not rounded off as is often done. This ridge really is a very important part of the tool, and increases its effectiveness. It acts as a fulcrum, on which the cutting edge can be levered up at all times, and this prevents it running

Fig. 118.—Long Ground Tool.

down into the wood and splitting up large pieces, as might otherwise be the case.

Oilstones

After grinding, the tools require finally setting on an oilstone. There are many stones on the market, some of the best known being Turkey, Charnley Forest, Washita, and Arkansas. These can be obtained in slabs, and in smaller pieces called slips. The average size for a slab

Fig. 119.—Short Ground Tool.

is 8 in. by 2½ in. by 1½ in. The slips, the average size of which is 4½ in. by 2 in., have the edges rounded to suit the many curves of the tools. For general home use, it is advisable to have a slab of the above size. Turkey stone, when good, is the best, but the quality greatly varies, even in the same stone. A Washita stone is perhaps the best for general use. It should be mounted in a case, the bottom half of which is shown in Fig. 121. About half a dozen slips, both Washita (Fig. 122) and Arkansas (Fig. 123), should be obtained for doing the

Fig. 120.—Tool Ground on Two Sides

inside of the curved and **V**-tools. Arkansas stone, ground or cut to a fine edge, can be used for **V**-tools and veiners. Washita stone is too coarse to be taken to a finer edge than $\frac{3}{16}$ in. For use at classes, or to carry about in a case, two slips will serve all purposes. The oil used for the stones should be a mixture of neatsfoot oil and paraffin, about 1 part paraffin to 4 parts neatsfoot. This is the best oil, but sweet oil, ordinary greasing oil, and olive oil, are also suitable; but always avoid linseed oil.

Fig. 121.—Oilstone in Case, Lid removed.

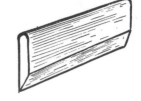

Fig. 123.—Arkansas Slip.

Strop

A strop is necessary; a soft leather strap, into which a mixture of tallow and emery flour has been well rubbed, is suitable.

How Carvers' Tools Differ from Joiners' Tools

The method of sharpening carving tools differs from that for joiners' and cabinetmakers' tools. The cutting edge of the latter is in the plane of the tool's face, as in Fig. 124, but the cutting edge of carving tools is situated nearer the centre of the tool's thickness, as in Fig. 125. This rule applies to all the carving tools, with the possible exception of a few for special use, and the greatest attention should be

Fig. 122.—Washita Slip.

paid to the method of sharpening in order to make sure of attaining this result. There are very definite reasons for adopting this form. In the first place, the angle at the cutting edge is greater in a carving tool

than in a cabinetmaker's tool, and therefore the carving chips come off shorter and more brokenly. This militates against the splitting tendency of the tools, especially when cutting cross grain or against the grain. In the second place, the ridge formed by the intersection of the ground surface with the oilstoned surface acts as a fulcrum on which to lever the tool, as already mentioned, and this ridge being on both sides of the tool gives it a double advantage in this respect. The amount of leverage so obtained is small, but it is sufficient to prevent the beginning of a split or tear in the wood.

Setting Flat Tools

The flat tools will be dealt with first,—those whose sections are shown at a in Fig. 35 (see p. 26). Pour a little of the neatsfoot oil on the stone, just sufficient to enable one tool to be sharpened; more can be added for each succeeding tool. Then, grasping the tool handle firmly in the right hand, and steadying it with the tips of the fingers of the left hand, push the tool backwards and forwards, nearly the full length of the stone. First one side of the tool, and then the other, should be pressed on the stone, until the two new

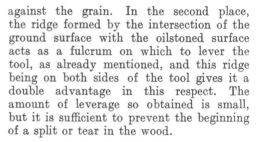

Fig. 124.—Edge of Cabinetmaker's Chisel.

Fig. 125.—Edge of Carver's Chisel.

surfaces so formed intersect in a sharp-cutting edge. The angle at which the tool should be held depends on the angle the ground surface presents to the stone. The former should be just slightly greater than the latter. Fig. 126 shows approximately what this angle should be, and also shows how the angle increases for each subsequent sharpening. This means that the tool handle has, at each subsequent sharpening, to be held a little higher than at the last operation, and consequently the edge gradually becomes too thick to cut at the proper angle ; the tool then requires regrinding. In pushing the tool from end to end of the oilstone, the general and natural tendency is to lower the handle when pushing forwards, and to raise it when pulling back ; this is known as " rolling." The result is that an edge somewhat like that shown at Fig. 127 is obtained. This

of the tool. This is done during the grinding process, and the subsequent treatment is as already described.

Setting Gouges

The gouges (c to l, Fig. 35) can be ground from the outside only ; but, with the aid of the oil-slips, the cutting edge can be pushed a little towards the centre of the tool's thickness. The gouges should be held to the oilstone in the same way as the straight tools ; but, being curved more or less on their cutting edge, they require to be rocked from side to side at the same time as they are pushed backwards and forwards. This must be done uniformly, so that all parts

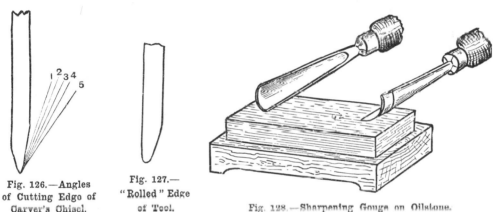

Fig. 126.—Angles of Cutting Edge of Carver's Chisel.

Fig. 127.— "Rolled" Edge of Tool.

Fig. 128.—Sharpening Gouge on Oilstone.

makes the actual cutting edge too thick for effective carving. To avoid this, carry the hand forwards and backwards at one uniform level ; this keeps the angle uniform, and the sharpened surface quite flat. When a sharp cutting edge has been formed, it is often the case that the two surfaces have not quite intersected one another, and that, consequently, what is known as a wire-edge, or a feather-edge, is left. This can be removed by rubbing the edge of the tool quickly on the prepared surface of the strop, leaving the cutting edge quite sharp and keen.

Setting Skew Tools

The skew tool (b, Fig. 35) differs from the flat tool in having its cutting edge inclined at a greater or lesser angle to the direction

of the edge receive an equal amount of wear. Some carvers prefer to hold the tool at right angles to the stone, and rock the tool in that manner (see Fig. 128). The former way is recommended as being preferable, especially with very quick gouges, because of the great difficulty of turning the gouges quickly enough to get a uniform wearing away of all parts of the cutting edge. The slips should now be applied to the inside of the gouges, so as to obtain the cutting edge nearer to the centre of the thickness of the tool. To do this, the particular slip which most nearly fits the curve of the tool must be held to the edge, and inclined at an angle corresponding to the angle at which the straight tools are held to the oilstone. This is shown in Fig. 129. The slip is rubbed backwards and forwards, and from side to side of the tool, to get a uniform sharpening of the edge. All the gouges are sharpened in this manner.

Setting V-Tools and Small Veiners

The V-tools and very small veiners (the latter being really the small sizes of k and l, Fig. 35) are sharpened in the same manner, the sharp edge of the Arkansas slip instead of its rounded edge being used for the in-

Fig. 129.—Finishing Gouge with Oilstone Slip.

side. An Arkansas slip, which is more expensive than the other kinds of slips, is used for these tools, because most other stones cannot be cut down to an edge fine enough to fit them.

Shape of Tool Edges

The edges of all tools except skew tools should be quite straight and square with the direction of the blade. An edge that is slightly convex is better than one that is concave ; the latter should never be allowed. Figs. 130, 131, and 132 in the next column show the three types of edge ; the first is correct, and the others are wrong.

Stropping Tools

Gouges and V-tools should be stropped ; but, obviously, a straight strop will not do for the insides. Therefore, what may

Fig. 130.—Straight Edge of Gouge (Correct).

Fig. 131.—Concave Edge of Tool (Incorrect).

be called strop slips will be required. These can be made of wood slips, similarly to the oil slips, with the edges covered with strips of thin prepared strop fixed with glue. To use a strop slip, hold it in the left hand, and, with the right hand, draw the tool downwards about half a dozen times. This will take off the wire edge, and will leave the edge of the tool sharp and keen. The strop should always be handy for immediate and constant use. When the tools have been used a little while they become slightly dull, and a few strokes on the strop will make the

Fig. 132.—Convex Edge of Tool (Incorrect).

edges keen again. When sharpening the tools, have a piece of soft pine at hand on which to try them. If they cut without tearing, they can be relied on to cut any harder wood.

DESIGNING FOR WOOD CARVING

THE wood carver, to ensure anything like success, must be well acquainted with the principles of design. He may be skilled in the actual work of wood cutting, but, unless he understands the art of design, his powers are severely limited. He need not be a first-class designer, but he should be able to produce designs that are at least passable. To do this, a more than ordinary knowledge of design is necessary. This chapter will describe the steps to take to begin the study of design, and will give an outline of the subject generally, with its application to wood carving in particular. In wood carving the variety of objects forming the designs is so great that it seems a somewhat hopeless task, at the first, to sort these objects into divisions or classes. Thus, in the chapters on practical work which will follow this, tulips, roses, dragons, the acanthus leaf, the lily, vases, geometrical figures, and the maple leaf have been used for the designs. The objects thus used are generally termed the elements of ornament.

Elements of Ornament

These can be classified as follows : (1) Dots, lines, and geometrical figures, as in chip carving ; (2) natural forms, such as the rose and tulip ; (3) artificial foliage, as the conventional acanthus leaf ; (4) artificial objects—for example, musical instruments and weapons ; (5) grotesque forms, such as the mask and the griffin ; (6) the human figure. These elements are arranged to form designs according to certain principles, some of the chief of which are here given : (1) Even distribution ; (2) order ; (3) fitness ; (4) symmetry ; (5) contrast ; (6) variety ; (7) repetition ; (8) alternation ;

(9) balance ; (10) proportion ; (11) radiation ; (12) harmony ; (13) unity. The elements of ornament are selected and arranged in accordance with various combinations of these principles.

Even Distribution

Even distribution is perhaps the most important principle of all, much judgment and taste being required in arranging it. To obtain really judicious distribution, cultivated judgment and refined artistic feeling and perception are required. Whatever the space at disposal, the design should be spread over it, so as to emphasise it and produce the best possible effect. Even distribution does not merely mean that all the space should be completely filled ; it rather means that a perfect balance should exist between the extent of the design and the extent of the ground. Thus, the design presented by Fig. 164 (p. 73) for incised carving is not a well-filled design, but the balance is preserved between the extent of the design and that of the grounds.

Order

It is possible to have a design that, while evenly distributed, does not produce a good effect, unless it is arranged with regard to order. The elements of ornament, whatever they may be, should be arranged on a definitely organised plan. This implies that, first of all, a skeleton of the design should be conceived, and the elements built up on it, thus getting the whole design to appear in an orderly manner. More will be said respecting this when dealing with the method of building up a design.

Fitness

Fitness means that the elements chosen should bear some relationship to the object to be ornamented, and that the style of ornament and its treatment should be such as will harmonise with the object itself. Thus, for example, a sideboard whose outlines and general plan are conceived in the Renaissance style should not be ornamented with Gothic carving ; the different spirits that produced these two great styles are entirely opposed to each other, both in their aims and in their effects. The question of how much ornament to employ is one that comes under this head. Then, again, the choice of the situation for the placing of ornament is one that is decided by the application of this principle. To place carving, for example, on table tops, chair seats, and other horizontal surfaces intended for use, is an offence against fitness ; also, the character of the carving to be employed in various positions is one that fitness should decide. For instance, the back of a chair may be carved ; but as, like the seat, though not to the same degree, utility is its chief purpose, the carving should not be in high relief, but in a flat style, such as Scandinavian chip carving ; or Elizabethan strap-work is even more suitable. It should be understood that fitness is always a very important factor in deciding the character of a carving design.

Symmetry

Symmetry consists in having corresponding parts to balance each other. It does not necessarily mean that each side or part should correspond exactly in every particular. If they correspond so that a perfect balance is maintained, it is sufficient ; but as soon as the parts are so arranged that the balance is destroyed, then this principle of symmetry is transgressed. Thus, in Fig. 135 (p. 56) a perfect symmetry is observed, because each side corresponds in every respect. But the principle of symmetry could still have been observed if some of the details had varied. For example, the flowers on each side could have been different, provided the idea of mass was preserved in the same relative

quantity. It follows, then, that so long as the main curves and outlines of the design duly correspond, the principle of symmetry is not violated. The details may vary up to the point when such variation tends to destroy a perfect balance of parts, but not beyond. Symmetry also applies to the treatment of the design. This may now be noted, although it belongs more properly to the actual handiwork of the craft. A design that is in itself symmetrical may be made to look quite lopsided and ill-balanced because of a variation of treatment in the two, or more, corresponding parts. But, as with the construction of the design, this symmetrical treatment need not be carried to the extent of making each particular corresponding part absolutely similar, or it may appear too rigid and unbreakable in its character. A little variation is of much advantage to the ultimate effect.

Contrast and Variety

These, being so closely connected with and dependent on each other, may be classed together. Without variety there could not possibly be contrast, and without contrast there could be no character. There would be effect, certainly, but this would be of a monotonous kind that would be better absent. There should be contrast both in respect of the elements used and in respect of their arrangement. This contrast should also extend to the treatment. Contrast means the judicious arranging of the elements of ornament with regard to their relative size, shape, and character. Thus, again referring to the design for incised carving given in a later chapter (see p. 73), the tulips vary in size, position, and shape. The same applies to the leaves, and the variety thus introduced gives point and character to a design that, using only one plant form, could easily fall into the category of monotonous and characterless designs. In order to produce good effects it is not necessary to have violent contrasts. A variation in the twist of a leaf, the thickness of a stalk, the placing of a flower, the curve of an outline, may be quite sufficient. Needless to say, the treatment of a design has to be well thought out, and should be a principal consideration in its planning. This again emphasises the necessity for a carver being a designer, because he knows the effects that can be obtained with the carving tools, and can thus arrange his design so that it shall be suitable for executing in wood, and avoid having to attempt the grotesque exercises with the carving tool that some ill-considered designs render necessary.

Repetition and Alternation

These, again, may be considered together. Repetition may be credited with a large percentage of good effects. Symmetry may be termed the sum of a series of repetitions, because it is by the more or less exact repetition of elements that the symmetrical effect is produced. Repetition, perhaps, renders the best service of which it is capable when it is used in designs that contain the simplest and least significant elements, which consist of lines, dots, and geometrical figures. Chip-carving designs are good examples of the use of this principle. The rule for repetition is that the more unmeaning an element, the more it will bear repetition ; and the nearer to the human figure, the less may this principle be applied. Thus chip designs consist almost entirely of lines, and these alone are about as unmeaning as anything can possibly be. But, by means of repetition, they can be made capable of very charming effects. Alternation is the alternate repetition of two or more elements, such as may be observed in many borders. Bands of ornament, such as occur on mouldings and narrow borders, rely, in their planning, on these principles very largely. Thus, the effect of the very familiar egg-and-tongue moulding depends entirely on the alternate repetition of the bold and obtuse form of the egg, with the more acute lines of the tongue. Alternation is bound up with contrast ; the object of using the former is to produce the latter. This dependence of one principle on another is a matter that should be noticed somewhat particularly. All the principles are merely parts of a whole, and cannot exist independently, however much they may appear to be separated by classification, which, after all, is a mere matter of convenience.

They are brought into existence as the effect of combination, and the success of a design depends largely on the skill with which these interacting effects are brought into relationship. It is impossible to set definite limits to the action of any of these principles.

Balance and Proportion

These also can be treated together, because of their dependence on each other. Without a proper proportion there could be no balance. Balance is connected with symmetry, contrast, and variety, although a design need not necessarily be symmetrical to be well balanced. Balance really means the rhythmic and more or less regular succession or placing of the elements of which the design consists. Balance has to do with the placing of the masses. A design may be easily spoiled by bad judgment in arranging these. In a symmetrical design the proper balance is not difficult to get ; but a design that is not symmetrically arranged requires much thought, care, and trained judgment.

Radiation

Radiation concerns the arrangement of curves in a design, and the way in which they spring from a common source. It binds a design together, even the remote parts of a large design feeling its influence. The easy flow of the lines in a well-radiated design is illustrated in the style of the Renaissance. Here radiation is employed to a large extent. Faults in radiation are perhaps more easily detected than faults of any other kind. Therefore it is imperative that this principle should have careful consideration in the planning of design.

Harmony and Unity

Harmony is dependent on unity more than on the other principles ; but it is really the effects produced by a good combination of all the principles. Harmony decides how far each principle should be used so as to avoid distracting effects. It in fact exercises a discriminating supervision in the use of all the elements. Harmony necessarily implies unity ; but unity also means that, besides the harmonious selection of the elements, their general arrangement shall be of such a nature that the design is complete without any further addition. Also, that any subtraction from it would seriously injure its effect.

shape. It is quite impossible, and it is equally undesirable, to take natural forms and attempt to portray them in wood, or, indeed, in any material, just as they occur

Fig. 133.—Daffodil with Leaves (Natural Style).

Fig. 134.—Three Forms of Conventionalised Daffodil Motif.

Conventionalisation

In examining wood carvings it will be found that they do not portray natural forms just as th y appear in nature, not even those wonderful works of Grinling Gibbons and his school. The reasons for this alteration of shape and character are

in their living form. The second reason is that the material that is being worked imposes limitations that forbid the exact representation of the natural form. The original disposition of the features of the object to be imitated may be supremely beautiful in natural surroundings; but when the object is no longer helped by its

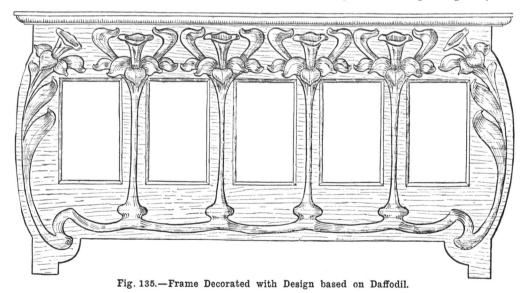

Fig. 135.—Frame Decorated with Design based on Daffodil.

twofold. The first is that in all wood carving the design has to conform to a definite shape, whilst natural forms are not limited to any arbitrary boundary of line and

natural environment, its lines must be modified in accordance with the altered circumstances. They must be arranged on a more or less regular, rhythmic, and orderly plan. This alteration of arrangement is termed conventionalisation. Fig. 133 shows a daffodil with leaves as it occurs in nature. Fig. 134 shows various conventionalisations of the flower and leaves that are suitable for expression in wood, and Fig. 135 shows this motif used for the purpose of ornamenting a photograph frame. The method of conventionalising a natural form is to fix on some characteristic feature possessed by the form, and arrange it in a decorative manner that is suitable to the object decorated. Thus, in the daffodil, the leaves are capable of being made into a variety of shapes and forms that have an extremely

the natural forms can be modified with considerable freedom of treatment, and less objection can be taken to such alteration in the treatment than in the general planning. But even in the treatment, modes that are so artificial as to kill natural strength and vigour must be carefully avoided.

How to Build Designs

The elements out of which ornament is built up, and the principles which govern the building-up processes having been dealt with, it will be shown how these principles are to be applied to the elements

Fig. 136.

Fig. 137.

Figs. 136 and 137.—Frieze Illustrating the Planning of Design by Mass.

decorative value ; and a face view of the flower with its six petals and deep cup can be made into many conventional shapes, without quite disguising its identity. It is a matter of opinion how far it is legitimate to take this principle of conventionalism in respect of natural forms. Some advocate taking it to any length, even to the extent of entirely losing the identity of the original form. However, it is thought that sufficient should be left to enable the original type to be identified. Truthfulness, too, should have some consideration. Thus, the number of petals should correspond to the number possessed by the original form, however much their shape and arrangement are altered ; and the relative strength and width of the leaves should be maintained so that the distinctive character of the daffodil, as a natural form, can be secured and made permanent. In the actual carving,

for the production of good ornament. In the first place, choose the particular elements out of which it is intended to form the design. This choice is conditioned by (1) the character of the object to be decorated ; (2) the space available for the carving ; (3) the material of which the object is made. Thus chip carving would be quite unsuitable for a large modern sideboard ; and if only narrow spaces, such as mouldings or narrow friezes, were to be ornamented, the introduction of a large-membered element, such as a sunflower, would be an offence against fitness. Similarly, an object in boxwood would need a very different kind of design from an object made in English oak. The elements will now be arranged, which is done from either or both of two points of view, that of mass and that of line. By the first method, that of mass, begin the design by planning

the prominent masses of ornament, afterwards inserting connecting lines as subordinate secondary members. To design from
the line point of view, the leading lines
should be planned first, and the masses
placed afterwards. The first method is
eminently suitable for work that has to be
placed, when completed, at a considerable
distance from the eye, and therefore has
to be in high relief. The second method
is more suitable to work in low relief that

For high relief, elements that are big enough
to be noticeable without an undue increase in size should be chosen, which in
this case is the tulip. Fig. 136 gives a
suggested arrangement of the masses. These
may be developed afterwards either into
the flowers or into masses of leaves and
stalks. Then the stalks and other subordinate members (subordinate to the purposes of ornament) are put into position,
and the design completed, as shown in

Fig. 138.

Fig. 139.

Figs. 138 and 139.—Panel Illustrating the Planning of Design by Line.

is subject to closer inspection, and in which
the beauty of a line arrangement is more
perceptible than would be possible at any
considerable distance. Generally, however,
designs are considered from both points
of view, and not from one point exclusively.
In beginning to make a design in high
relief, a frieze will be taken as an example.
This will need a considerable use of the
principles of repetition and alternation,
because of its length. First divide its
length into smaller spaces, squares, and
oblongs arranged alternately, as shown by
the fine lines in Fig. 136. The second step
is taken by choosing the character of the
ornament, and by arranging the masses.

Fig. 137. Figs 138 and 139 show the stages
in the building of a design based on the
consideration of line. First, the space is
divided into smaller spaces, if necessary;
sometimes this need not be done, because
the lines can be arranged over the space as
a whole. In beginning, an oblong panel
is divided by a vertical centre line, from
which the ornament is planned. Lines,
known as leading lines, are carefully arranged throughout the space, as shown
in Fig. 138, for the subsequent design to be
built on. The next stage is to place the
masses, and it should here be borne in
mind that, as the line arrangement is to
predominate, these masses must be so

arranged as to be subordinate in characte , and therefore not of an aggressive nature. Fig. 139 shows the finished design. The procedure, therefore, in building a design is as follows : (1) Choose the elements and arrange the character of the ultimate design ; (2) plan the space available according to its requirements, whether it is to be in high relief or in low relief—if the former,

Fig. 140.—Planning of Design by Temporary Geometrical Division of Field of Ornament.

plan its masses first; and if the latter, its leading lines first ; (3) then build up the design by filling the spaces between the masses, or by filling the skeleton consisting of the leading lines.

Geometrical Aids to Planning.

Much assistance may be given in planning by the application of geometrical principles in dividing the field of ornament into smaller and more convenient spaces. This assistance has already been noted in the frieze shown

in Figs. 136 and 137. This spacing by means of geometry may be of two kinds, temporary spacing and permanent spacing. In the first case, the divisions made are, after being filled with the ornament, done away with, and no trace of them remains, save that which may be traced in the general arrangement of the full design. Fig. 140 shows an example of such temporary spacing. In the right half of the design the original spacing lines are left in to show how the design has been planned. In the left half is shown the completed design. By permanent geometrical spacing is meant an arrangement by which some part, or the

Fig. 141.—Planning of Design by Permanent Geometrical Division of Field of Ornament.

whole, of the original lines is left in to form essential and permanent parts of the completed design. This is shown in Fig. 141, where some of the lines ultimately form part of the design in the shape of strapwork. Elizabethan strapwork affords admirable illustrations of the application of this principle of geometrical division in which the dividing lines are represented ultimately by bands of strapwork, the spaces between being filled with conventional flowers, leaves, and grotesques.

TRACING AND OUTLINING IN PRACTICAL CARVING

A KNOWLEDGE of the tools and other implements, and of the method of building up the design, having been obtained, the actual work of wood carving can now be proceeded with.

each in turn, and obtaining the mastery of each, a sound knowledge of those successive mechanical processes necessary to master the technical difficulties is gained.

Fig. 142.—Fixing Design for Tracing on the Wood.

It is proposed to divide the subject into the following stages : (1) Tracing, or otherwise putting on, the design ; (2) outlining or wasting away ; (3) setting in ; 4) grounding ; (5) modelling. By dealing with

Such a technical knowledge, however perfect it might be, does not constitute as that is necessary. Wood carving should be considered as possessing two sides, the mechanical and the artistic, and the latter is by far the greater. The would-be carver should train his artistic intelligence by attending art classes, especially for lessons in design, and in the application and the history of ornament. He should also study the works of the best artists of all ages in the way of sculpture and ornament, and in these and other ways help to develop the powers of conception.

manner, but as a rule most wood carvers have to depend on tracing and transferring with carbon paper to get the designs on the wood. The following are the stages in getting the design traced: (a) Have the design on tracing paper; (b) always work from centre lines; and (c) pin the design along one edge, slip the carbon paper under, fix along the other edges where necessary,

Fig. 143.—Left, **V**-tool Trench Work; Right, Wasting Away with Gouge.

Tracing the Design

Whatever work is engaged on, the limits of the design and its principal disposition must be known. In certain forms of work, such as carving in the round, some wood carvers have so perfect a development of the sense of form that they can dispense altogether with any pencil indication of the design; but, generally, some such indication is necessary. Some are able to sketch this indication or design on the work in a direct

and trace. If the design is drawn on tracing paper, it can be easily fixed in the centre and quite square. By working from centre lines, the design is always central and square. Whatever the character of the design, always draw lines through the centres of the length and width of the design, and make similar centre lines on the wood. By making these lines coincide, accuracy is assured in the process of fixing the design. Take care that the carbon paper is used black side to the wood. There are various kinds of carbon paper, but that which is black on one side only is the best because it is cleanest. In pinning the design, the pins should be placed inside the margin, otherwise they will mark the margin permanently. Fig. 142 shows the design fixed on, and one side traced. In this case the design was pinned

cutting a **V**-trench about $\frac{1}{8}$ in. away from the outlines, and then setting in; and (3) by wasting away the wood with quick gouges up to about $\frac{1}{8}$ in. of the outlines, and then setting in. The first method is often employed, but is unsuitable because by this method thin stalks, and other thin parts of the design, nearly always

Fig. 144.—Left, Setting in; Right, Grounding.

down the centre line first, the carbon paper then slipped under, and then pinned on the margin. An ordinary pencil is generally used for tracing, but a style (say, of ivory) is the best. A pencil often spoils the outline of the design for future use.

Outlining or Wasting Away

When the design is successfully placed, the first thing to do is to cut away the wood to form the ground. There are three ways in which this can be done : (1) By setting in along the outline first ; (2) by

get broken and dislodged, owing to the lateral pressure due to the rapid driving in of the tool. The second method consists of cutting, with a **V**-tool, a trench about $\frac{1}{8}$ in. away from the outline of the design. This is shown in the left half of the panel in Fig. 143. This **V**-tool work is done in all the corners and channels of the design, and especially so across the thin parts of the design. Then the setting in is done on the outline (see Fig. 144). The third method is somewhat similar to the **V**-tool method, except that the whole of the ground gets wasted away instead of merely a trench being formed. This is done with various quick gouges, the sizes of which will vary with the width of the space to be cut out, as shown in the right-hand half of Fig. 143. It is then set in, as shown in Fig. 144. Either of the two latter methods should be employed in preference to the first method, for the reason that when a tool is driven into a piece of wood, it exerts a lateral pressure in both directions because of its thickness. This must be so, as the first blow does not cause any cutting away of the wood. The proportion of lateral pressure in each direction

slides completely along, bodily. This is the cause of the splitting and loosening of the thinner elements of the design, especially those lying across the grain, which is a feature of the first method. By either of the two latter methods, the evil effects of this lateral pressure are nullified, as the V-tool trench, and the wasting away of the ground with a gouge, make the lines of least resistance invariably lie in the direction of the groundwork. And, as this is bound to come out, any splitting that occurs in this direction can be ignored. Fig. 143 shows clearly what is meant. In the left half of Fig. 143, A shows part of a stalk set

Fig. 145.— Holding Carving Tool on Work.

varies inversely to the amount of resistance. Force moves along the lines of least resistance, and therefore it is obvious that if the tool is driven in about $\frac{1}{2}$ in. away from the edge of the board, the greatest pressure would be exerted in the direction of the edge, because of the greater bulk of resistance lying in the other direction. This transmission of lateral pressure cannot occur without some result ; as a matter of fact, a slight sliding of the grain takes place at the level of the greatest depth of the cut. This sliding of the grain varies inversely as the resistance, and, obviously, the nearer the edge of the wood the greater the volume of force that streams through in the shorter direction, until the varying resistances become so disproportionate that the wood along the shortest direction

in by the first method. The first blow (that on the right) was quite successfully done, but when the second cut was made, the line of least resistance lay across the stalk and, being quite narrow, it slid away towards the first cut, to the depth of the cut. This can easily be seen in the illustration. At B, two trenches are made, one on each side. The result of this is to make the line of least resistance lie away from the stalk, and consequently the stalk escaped any transmission of lateral pressure and remained intact. In grounding, both V-cuts, and the wasting away, should be made at a uniform depth. The proper way of holding the carving tool is shown in Figs. 145 and 146. The handle of the tool is held firmly in the right hand, and the blade is also held firmly in the left hand. It is sometimes advised, that only the fingers of the left hand should be laid on the blade of the tool, and used for guidance only. But the more firmly a tool is held by both hands, the greater safeguard there is against inaccurate cutting and the slipping of the tool over the edges. The progress a tool makes depends on the balance of pressure that exists between

The direction and the shape of the stroke, viewed from the side, is shown in Fig. 147. It is in reality a segmental curve. Fig. 146 shows the under side of the hands when holding the tool as in Fig. 145. Referring to the left hand, the three points of grip are, the thumb, the two middle fingers, and the fleshy edge of the hand. By suddenly bringing heavy pressure to bear by

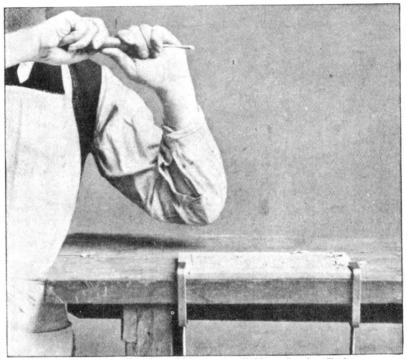

Fig. 146.—Position of Fingers in Holding Carving Tool.

the forward (right-hand) thrust and the backward (left-hand) thrust. The smaller the balance of pressure, the less risk there is of false cuts and slips. The left hand, near the wrist, should always rest on the wood—that is, wherever possible. This forms a pivot round which the tool can revolve, and limits the length of the cut, and helps to prevent it cutting too far. Short strokes to the cut are the best. The longest lines should be cut with a succession of short strokes. An even continuity both of depth and direction can be insured better by this means than by any other.

the thumb and two middle fingers on their respective sides of the tool, a perfect "brake" is obtained to its further progress, and the possibility of slipping is diminished. In wasting away, make the cuts across the grain, wherever possible; the wood cuts more uniformly thus. In Fig. 143 this has been done, the only exceptions being the narrow spaces that lie in the same direction as the grain.

Wasting Away with Machine.

An engineer approaching wood carving from the point of view of his profession deviced the machine shown by Fig. 148, for wasting away the wood, his contention being that the first stage of wood carving is preparatory and mechanical only, and calls for an artisan rather than an artist. This stage terminates when the design has the appearance of having been fret-sawn out of one planed board, the thickness of its relief, and stuck to another planed board which forms the ground. His appliance is a means of executing the first, or preparatory, stage not only more quickly, but also more perfectly, he claims, than is possible in the usual way to a person of only ordinary skill. The appliance is a sensitive drilling machine (Fig. 148), which can be put on the lathe bed and driven from the cone pulley. It stands on a hardwood bed-plate, having a fillet to fit between the lathe bearers,

Fig. 147.—Diagram showing Side View of Short-stroke Cutting.

and can be lifted on or off the lathe in an instant, not requiring fixing. To fasten permanently on the iron drilling table, a much larger hardwood table is strongly recommended. After squaring up a board to the outside dimensions of the panel that is to be carved, he rips off with a circular saw a rebate all round by two cuts along each edge. The depth of this rebate is just the amount of the proposed relief (or a shaving less to allow for cleaning up), and its width is such as to leave the raised portion the size of the sight opening of the panel. Next he transfers the design to the wood, and takes the wood to the drilling machine, in which a slotting bit as shown in Fig. 149 (not a pointed drill) is set so that it can just barely reach the face of the rebate when the panel is on the drilling table. He uses a $\frac{3}{8}$-in. bit in the first instance, and bores a series of holes about $\frac{1}{32}$ in. from each other, and the same distance clear of the outline of the design. The flat bottom of each hole is, of course, at the level of the " ground." Each hole only

takes about a second to drill, and in this way he completely honeycombs all the wood that has to be reduced to ground level. When this is done he changes the $\frac{3}{8}$-in. bit for a $\frac{1}{8}$-in. bit, bores to the same

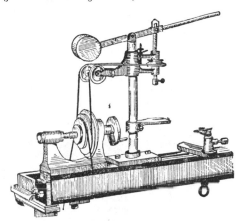

Fig. 148.—Drilling Machine suggested for Wasting Away.

depth, and completes the honeycombing in those parts where there was not room for a $\frac{3}{8}$-in. hole. Then with the panel on the bench, and with a flat gouge and mallet, he roughly lowers the ground, which is not only so weakened by the honeycombing that its removal is rapid and easy, but is covered all over with marks at the right depth, so that there is no need for slow, careful work to avoid going too deep. He does not try to obliterate the drill marks, but merely levels to them very roughly. The process is a very quick one. Then he stabs out the design, not very carefully, but well on the outside of the outline, as the final outlining will be done later. This is comparatively quick and easy, as it is only the trimming of an

Fig. 149.—Bit used in Wasting-away Machine.

edge, not setting down in the solid. Then from the drilling machine he removes the counterbalance of its lever, so that the drill is now held down, instead of up, by the weight of the parts. The work is then pulled about with both hands under the revolving drill, which acts as a very rapid and efficient router, and leaves a "beautifully flat ground of absolutely uniform depth all over." Then the final trimming of the outline is done, nearly entirely with the chisel. For this purpose he finds that the best tool is a keenly set bevel-edge paring chisel. To use a gouge is to be often changing the tool. Besides, he states, gouges are ground to a bevel on the convex side, and so are highly unsuitable tools for vertical stabbing of concave outlines. Even concave curves of sharp radius he stabs out with the chisel, and the subsequent trimming they require, if any, is slight. Bevel-edge chisels down to $\frac{1}{16}$ in. wide are obtainable, and a substantial portion of the work, if the curves are quick, will be done with chisels $\frac{1}{8}$ in. to $\frac{1}{4}$ in. wide. The walls of the design should now stand truly vertical. It is usual to lean the handle of the tool a little over the design in outlining, which makes the walls slope a little outwards. But it should be remembered, he states, that this is a minor evil, and is only recommended to guard against the major evil of the walls sloping inwards, that is, undercutting them. The ideal condition is absolute perpendicularity, so that, whatever depth it is cut, the outline will be as true as it was marked on the surface. The drilling method of getting out the ground is of great assistance here, as the sides of the drilled holes—very close to the final outline—are truly vertical. His drilling machine drills up to 7 in. from its standard, so it will reach all over panels that are not more than 14 in. wide. A little practice is required before the slotting bit can be safely used, as it tends to run along the surface of the work if the latter is not rigidly held till it has got an entry. This is soon got over. Another point is that the bit, which of course should be kept sharp, must be gripped very firmly in the chuck; otherwise it will creep down and cut below the surface intended, especially when routing. In criticism of this machine method of wasting away, it may be admitted that, as the engineer claims, the first part of the work is more or less mechanical, and may legitimately be done

with labour-saving mechanical appliances; but the advisability of finishing with these tools is questionable, even though they do make an absolutely level surface. In fact, this particular result is one that it is better to avoid. Such a groundwork may be exact and trim, but it is fearfully mechanical. The value of any wood carving is to a large extent in its virile, nervous cutting; because it is that which gives it life, and therefore character; and it is obvious that a mechanical process is the best possible method to adopt to kill completely any strivings after life and character. If it were the regular thing to punch the ground, then of course the mechanical treatment is legitimate and, indeed, is recommended, because of the time saved. But it should be taken for granted instead, that wherever the tool can get, there it should make its evidence seen; and there it should play its part in giving life and vigour and character to the work, even if it is only the ground that is in question. This is why punching should be avoided; it is itself purely mechanical, and can never be productive of a highly ideal or artistic effect. It therefore follows that whilst mechanical means may be employed to waste large tracts of groundwork (corners and other similar places), at least the finishing process should always be done by hand, to give life and character to the work — to the ground as well as to the modelled design. Further, the punching, being itself a mechanical process, should only be used when the work is of such a poor quality that the mark of the punch is preferable to the work of the tool. It is a vitiated taste which assumes that a punched ground has any intrinsic value. A carved ground, provided it is well cut, is infinitely preferable. The use of the paring chisel in connection with the above method is good; being thin at the edges, the chisel goes easily into acute angles. Its general use for concave curves is not advised, however. A gouge makes a better curve, and any difficulty with regard to its grinding angle can easily be got over by sloping the tool slightly outwards, so that the grinding face is perpendicular.

SETTING IN, GROUNDING AND MODELLING

Setting In

WHEN the outlining, or wasting away, of the ground space is completed, the design is " set in " as a means of finally and completely separating it from the ground space (see left half of Fig. 144, p. 62). It con-

handle ; this enables an effective pressure to be applied at once to the tool, when required. In Fig. 151 another method of holding the tool is shown. The blade, in this case, is held with the forefinger and the thumb of the left hand, close to the cutting edge. By this means the hand is always

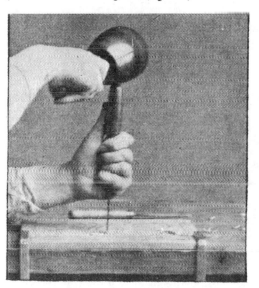

Fig. 150.—Setting In : Holding Tool Midway, with Thumb on Handle.

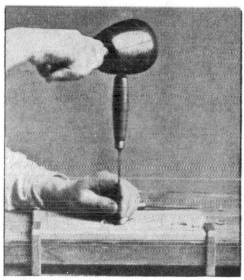

Fig. 151.—Setting In : Holding Tool close to Cutting Edge.

sists of holding suitable tools perpendicularly on the outline of the design, and then, either by hand or mallet pressure, forcing them into the wood, until the outline of the design is represented by a continuous line of tool cuts, taken to a uniform depth (see Figs. 150 and 151). In Fig. 150 the left hand is shown grasping the tool firmly about midway down its entire length. Notice the position of the thumb on the

resting on the wood ; this assists in quickly recovering the tool from the previous blow of the mallet, and enables it to be placed ready for the next blow, in the quickest possible time. With the tool held as in Fig. 150, a particularly quick eye and steady hand are necessary to place it instantly where required, so that no pause or break ensues in the successive blows of the mallet.

Precautions in Setting In

The principal precautions are as follows : (1) Hold the tool slightly away from the perpendicular, with the handle leaning slightly over the design. (2) Set in deep enough. (3) Set in to a uniform depth. (4) Make all the cuts meet one another. (5) Set in across the grain first, whenever possible. (6) Set in only on the outline. Reference to Fig. 150 will show what is meant by the first precaution. The object of this is to ensure the strength of all the elements of the design. If the handle is allowed to lean over the groundwork, the thin member is ensured. These false cuts should be made a little distance away from the lines, gradually working backwards towards the design, making each succeeding cut closer to the preceding cut than it is to the farther side of the thin member, and thus always securing that the line of least resistance lies away from the design.

Uniform Depth in Setting In

Respecting the second and third precautions mentioned above, all cuts should be uniform in depth, and of a depth that is sufficient for the purpose of taking out

Fig. 152.—Method of Using Router.

cutting edge naturally is driven under the outline of the design, and makes the member narrower the deeper the tool goes ; also it weakens the edge of the design, and causes breakage and splitting. This is a serious matter, especially with narrow members such as stalks. The amount of divergence from the perpendicular should not be greater than that perceptible in Fig. 150; otherwise it creates another difficulty— that of making the design wider, in proportion to the depth the tool is driven.

Setting In Stalks and Thin Members

In setting in a stalk or other thin member it is sometimes advisable to make false cuts, even when the ground has been wasted away, or outlined. Thus the safety of the the ground neatly. Many beginners fail at this point, because of a lack of vigour, and the result is that the groundwork cannot be cut evenly and neatly. The edges of the design therefore become chipped and untidy. Too much force should not be used, as this will tend to split the wood. Reliance should be placed on light, smart taps of the mallet, rather than on heavy and " dead " blows. A light blow accomplishes its work of driving in the tool by a minimum of force ; because the tool is withdrawn before the whole force contained in the blow has time to spread through the wood adjacent to the cut. But a blow of the " dead " variety works havoc with the grain of the wood, as all the force contained in it is allowed to spread beyond the cut; and when thin stalks are being set in, much damage results.

Overlapping Cuts in Setting In

To make all the cuts meet one another means that each cut should overlap slightly the previous one to produce a continuous outline. This also enables the ground space to be cleared with ease, and without danger to the outline of the design. Much judgment has to be exercised in selecting the tools for setting in, so that they fit the curve of the outline, and thus follow the design exactly. If the design contains

Other Points in Setting In

To set in only on the outline means that only as much of the design as the groundwork touches should be cut in at this time. The cutting in of these parts which lie within the boundaries of the outline is included in the modelling process. The flatter tools, say up to curve No. 5 in the tool lists, are principally used in setting up. If a curve requires a bigger tool than No. 5, use flatter tools of narrower width, and make a great number of strokes. The reason why this should be done is that

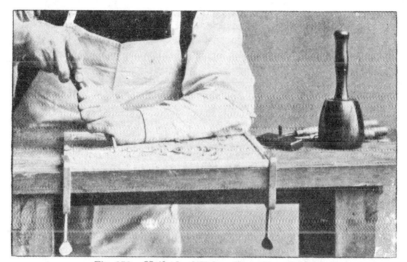

Fig. 153.—Method of Using Grounding Tool.

curves which are not represented by any tool in the worker's set, act as follows: if the curve of the design is concave, use a tool whose curve is slightly more concave, rather than one whose curve is flatter; and if the curve is convex, use a tool which is flatter than the curve.

Setting In Across the Grain First

Cuts lying across the grain should be made first, wherever possible; whilst those lying with the grain should follow in the order of setting in. The reason is that the wood has a greater tendency to split with the grain than across the grain, but the wood cannot split further than the cross cuts if these have already been made.

a tool of quick curve is much more apt to be subject to the lateral pressure exerted by the wood, because of the greater circumference of its curve, than a tool of flatter curve. Consequently it gets broken much more easily, even with careful use. Care should be taken to equalise the power used in setting in. Small enclosed spaces require less force than spaces which are of larger area. Setting in with the grain, too, requires less force than when setting in across the grain.

Grounding

When setting in is finished, the work of taking out the superfluous wood in this ground space is proceeded with. To do this, take a tool of about No. 5 curve and from $\frac{3}{16}$ in. to $\frac{1}{2}$ in. wide, and cut the wood away around the outline. Then with the same tool roughly level the whole

Figs. 154 and 155.—Diagrams showing Advantage of Bent Grounding Tool.

area. Further to level the ground, take tools of No. 3 curve, and from $\frac{1}{16}$ in. to $\frac{3}{8}$ in. wide, to suit the varying spaces, and bring the ground to a uniform level. Do not use a tool that is quite flat (straight tools), because its corners invariably scratch the ground. A tool of No. 3 curve is just curved enough to lift the corners off the ground, and yet is flat enough to produce a ground of the necessary smoothness. It is not necessary to get the ground so smooth as to suggest that it has been done with a plane. Tool marks may show, but all the cuts should be smooth, clean, and shiny. If the ground has been outlined

pear somewhat as shown in the right half of Fig. 143 (p. 61). Then follows the flattening and smoothing of the ground as already described. When all this has been done, the ground should appear as in the right half of Fig. 144 (p. 62). To assist in removing the superfluous wood in the ground space, the router is often used. Fig. 152 shows it in use. This tool gets the masses out quickly, and to a uniform depth. It does not do this by cutting the wood, but by tearing or scraping it. For this reason it is not recommended for the most artistic work, unless the traces of its work are destroyed by going over the ground with the flat cutting tools. It should be accepted as a sound principle that all wood that has to be taken away should be cut out, and not scraped, levered, torn, or split away. In using the router, the bulk of the wood should be cut away first with a quick gouge. Keep the body of the router firmly on the wood, and use sufficient pressure to prevent it jumping. Fig. 153 shows the grounding tool in use. This tool is well adapted for clearing small

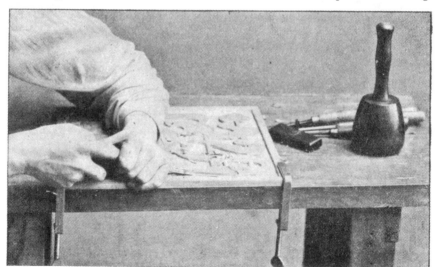

Fig. 156.—Trimming Rough Edges with V-tool.

only, the mass of wood in the centre of the ground spaces should be cut away by means of a quicker gouge, say a $\frac{3}{8}$-in., No. 7 or 8 curve. This would make the ground appear as shown in the right half of Fig. 143 (p. 61).

spaces which could not be done with a tool having a perfectly straight blade. By means of the bend in the blade, the cutting edge can be taken almost all the way across the space ; whilst a straight-bladed tool could only begin near the centre of the space (see examples given in Figs. 154 and 155). It is a somewhat difficult tool to use. The handle should be held much higher than in the case of the ordinary carving tool. Compare Fig. 153 with Fig. 145 (p. 63). The hand holding the tool should always be carried at the same height. The common

require trimming must be done with the ordinary tools, by means of setting in. The design is now quite ready for modelling.

Modelling

It is in this stage that the artistic attainments of the wood carver show themselves, and the success attending one's efforts in modelling are dependent far more on the

Fig. 157.—Left, Setting In : Right, Modelling.

tendency is to dip the hand as it goes forward ; consequently the tool's edge ceases to grip the wood. The V-tool is useful at this stage, by applying it to those edges of the design that are slightly faulty in their definition and direction. By holding it to one side, so that that side of it which is nearest the edge of the design is nearly perpendicular, the faulty outline can easily be reduced to its proper proportions and definition. Fig. 156 shows the V-tool in use, correcting a curve in the lower part of the design. The V-tool can also be used for longer curves. Quicker curves that

development of these than on any perfection of technique. There are two sides to modelling : the life side and the form side. The latter is a matter of the training and cultivation of manual dexterity. The former is a matter of conception first, and afterwards one of the training and the cultivation of the higher faculties. Therefore few remarks can be made that will be helpful in more than a very general way ; and what remarks are made are intended to apply to modelling in general, and not necessarily to the particular panel here illustrated. Fig. 157 shows the panel finished, and a portion of tne ground punched. Variety and contrast are the life of the carving, and constitute the larger share of importance in modelling, in producing the greatest effect. To this end, the whole surface should vary in height, both in the length and the width of a member. Alternate elevation and depression of surface is absolutely indispensable. And yet all this must not be done in a purely mechanical manner ; so much depends on the development of one's individual judgment and artistic sense. To obtain the best contrast, and therefore the best effect, certain parts of the carving have to be selected as being essential masses ; these are, generally speaking, flowers, fruits, animals,

course of the stalks, and gives greater emphasis to the line arrangement of the design. If the ground is taken to a comparatively great depth, use this depth to its greatest possible value. That is, make the leaves twist down in some part, at least, to the ground, making the greatest use of whatever relief there is. Respecting the finish of the groundwork, it is the greater ideal to try to get it so neatly done as to do without any punching, especially when working in the more valuable hardwoods. Sometimes punching is necessary from an artistic point of view, but only if this is so should punching be resorted to. The aim should be, in every case, to do such tool work as will render this quite unnecessary.

Fig. 158.—
Ordinary Margin.

Fig. 159.—Margin, Edge
Bevelled Back

Fig. 160.—Margin Hollowed
with Gouge.

Fig. 161.—Margin Sunk Below
Level of Carving.

Fig. 162.—Development from
Fig. 161 : Margin Removed.

Fig. 163.—Margin, Ground
Gouged in.

and the human form. These essential parts have to be given the greatest prominence, and thus they are left the full height. Other parts, such as leaves and stalks, are quite as essential, viewed as line ornament, but they can be subordinated in height, to give the greater contrast and prominence to the masses. In this particular example this has been done. The flowers are given prominence as the masses, together with the more important leaves, whilst the stalks and all the leaves are treated as line ornament. The leaves, which otherwise would have been plain to the point of baldness, are made effective by twisting them and folding their edges over, and thus causing that play and contrast of light and shade which is essential to the true effect. In modelling stalks it is better not to make them of a half-round section, but to make them slightly hollow, as in this example, or with a decided ridge along the centre. The latter treatment enables the eye to readily follow more the

Margins

There are many ways of treating the edges of carved work, some of them being illustrated in Figs. 158 to 163. Fig. 158 shows the ordinary margin, Fig. 159 the edge bevelled back, and Fig. 160 the margin hollowed with a gouge. Fig. 161 shows a margin which is sunk below the level of the carving, and Fig. 162 gives a further development of this, in which the margin is entirely removed. This treatment enables the carving to stand off the ground in a very bold and striking manner. Fig. 163 shows the ground simply gouged in, thus making it rise in an unbroken curve to the surface of the wood. In plan, there is no necessity for keeping the margins with straight lines ; thus they may be of varying curves, and the corners may be arranged otherwise than with sharp angles. Margins should conform to the artistic requirements of the work, and should not be introduced merely for the purpose of variety.

INCISED CARVING

INCISED CARVING is often suitable for space in which relief carving would be impossible or improper. Such examples occur in table tops, trays, stool tops, the tops

square, the work should be securely cramped to the bench. Then take the **V**-tool, and holding it firmly in the right hand, with the butt of the handle in the palm, and the

Fig. 164.—Design suitable for Incised Carving.

of revolving bookcases, chair seats, and similar surfaces, these generally occupying horizontal positions. Incised carving consists of carving a design without any groundwork. There is very little if any setting in, the designs being generally arranged to avoid this, by contriving that the outlines shall be as far as possible of a continuous curve, that can be cut with the **V**-tool. Therefore the only setting in required is

fingers of the left hand holding and steadying the blade, proceed to make a cut of uniform depth, with the point of the tool, exactly on the outline of the design. The tool should be held perfectly upright as shown in Fig. 165, which compare with Fig. 166, where the **V** tool is shown held in an inclined position. The depth of this cut will be regulated by the character of the design, the nature of the work, the position

Fig. 165.   Fig. 166.

Figs. 165 and 166.—Correct and Incorrect Positions of Tool for Incised Carving.

when very short lines cannot be avoided. Fig. 164 gives a design which can be taken as a typical example of incised carving. When the design is traced quite true and

it will ultimately occupy, and the use to which it will be put. Generally, the depth should not be more than $\frac{3}{16}$ in. All the long stretches of outline will be done with the V-tool. The shorter lines and the lines that are much curved, as at A (Fig. 164), will need setting in. In doing this, make the cut as nearly like a V-cut as possible by means of an inclined cut on each

Modelling

The next process is to model the work, and this is done just as if a groundwork had been prepared. The outside edges

Fig. 167.—Section of Wide Part of Leaves (see Fig. 164).

Fig. 168.—Section of Stalk (see Fig. 164).

Fig. 169.—Section of Tulip (see Fig. 164).

side. Care has to be exercised to keep the V-tool exactly on the line all the way, so as to make good curves. To do this, take short cuts with the tool; do not attempt a long outline with one continuous stroke. Make a point of getting good angles; do not let the V-tool slip too far, but keep it just a trifle short of the junction, so that it can be easily trimmed without danger of jumping over. The work will now present

are rounded off, the leaves are separated with the V-tool, and, with the surfaces of the flowers, are gouged. Certain parts are rounded, and the petals are sunk, just as if the work was in ordinary relief. Greater care, however, has to be taken than in ordinary relief carving, in order that the tools do not slip and cut the wood outside the outlines. This is the greatest source of danger, and too much care cannot be

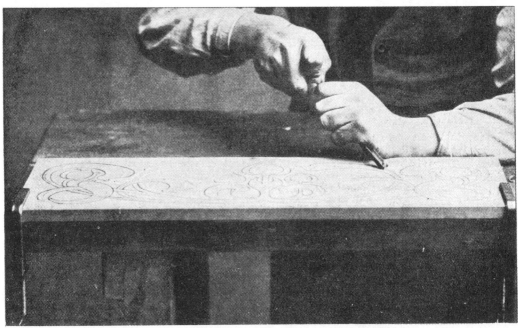

Fig 170.—Method of Using Tool for Incised Carving.

an appearance similar to that obtained in the exercise described in the previous chapter, but with the exception that in the present instance no ground has been taken out.

exercised in avoiding it. Figs. 167, 168, and 169 give sections of the various parts of the carving; these and the shaded design (Fig. 164) will give an idea as to how the modelling is done. Glasspaper should not be used, but all the work should be clean from the tool. Sometimes that which in ordinary carving would be the groundwork is punched, although this is not recommended. Occasionally, also, oblique cuts crossing each other are made with the V-tool; this produces an effect which is sometimes very useful.

Designs for Incised Carving

Some judgment is necessary in choosing designs for incised work. As the V-tool is largely used, designs with long sweeping curves and outlines should be favoured, so that nearly the whole design can be cut with the tool mentioned. The style of treatment adopted in the modelling is, of

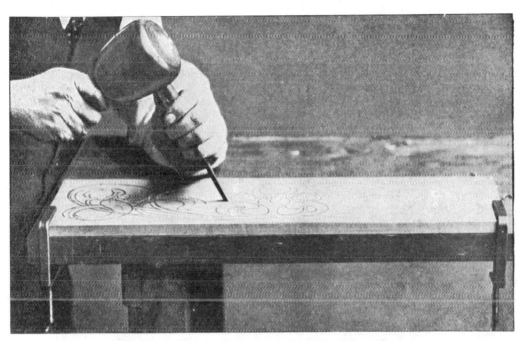

Fig. 171.—Setting In (Taking Second Cut) in Incised Carving.

Further Hints

Fig. 170 shows how the V-tool is used in cutting the outlines of a design in incised carving. Fig. 171 shows how the setting in of small lines and quick curves is accomplished. The inside cut is first made with the handle of the tool inclined over the design to correspond with the angle of inclination of the side of the V-tool. Then the chip is cut out by making the outer cut necessary to complete the V-shaped incision. In doing this part of the work it is necessary to have the edges of the tools perfectly square, or the tool cuts will not meet, and a ragged outline will be the result.

course, limited to objects of a somewhat flat form; but some variation can be made to get the contrast required for good effect, by sinking the incisions of the outlines of the flowers, for example, a little deeper, so that a more rounded section, and therefore an apparently greater relief, may be obtained. The deep cuts in the leaves may also be taken deeper than the depth of the incised outline, so that a greater strength of character may be given to the design, with stronger contrast of light and shade. But, of course, these deeper cuts must be made within the limits of the outline of each member, and must not touch the outline.

Fig. 174.—Incised Carving on Box Lid or Panel.

Fig. 175.—Repeating Border in Incised Carving.

Fig. 172.—Incised Carving on Marriage Coffer or Chest.

Fig. 173.—Incised Border on German Gothic Cabinet.

Adaptability of the V-tool

Where the overlapping of the stalks and leaves occurs, it might appear to be necessary to take the incised outline deeper than usual, in order to get the various levels required ; but this is not so. It will be noticed in Fig. 164 that those parts which lie under other parts are not elaborately or deeply modelled, and therefore there is but a slight difference between the depths of the two parts. In addition to outlining, the V-tool can be used for modelling, for rounding over the edges of the leaves and flowers, and for parting the petals of the flowers ; and if the ground is to be treated with the crossed and incised cuts before mentioned, it can be used for these also. Thus the importance of thoroughly mastering the use of this tool cannot be too strongly emphasised.

Some Examples of Incised Carvings

That the mediæval craftsmen understood how to decorate their productions by simple means and with the use of but few tools and appliances will be evident to all who look carefully at the many examples of their work to be seen in the museums. Fig. 172 is taken from a portion of a marriage coffer or chest, one of many similar specimens to be seen in the Italian Court of the South Kensington Museum ; the whole front has been covered with a very spirited design of animals and foliage, simply incised on the cypress wood of which the chest is made, to a depth of about $\frac{1}{16}$ in., and the details and groundwork are filled in with coloured mastics, in this case the colours employed being green and red. The decoration serves its purpose admirably, and although nearly five hundred years have elapsed since it left the hands of the Venetian decorator, the design is almost as plainly to be seen as ever, and it serves fully to illustrate the principle so clearly advocated by Pugin —the Gothic revivalist—that " all ornament should consist of enrichment of the essential construction," a precept which has been sadly ignored in much modern work. Another example (Fig. 173) is taken from a German Gothic cabinet in the same museum, but of about a century later,

Fig. 176.—Sunflower Panel in Incised Carving.

and forms part of the cornice and base moulding. This piece, although not so rich in design, is nevertheless equally suitable for its purpose; and although the workmanship of this example is by no means of a very high order, yet it holds its place among its more ambitious rivals. Many similar pieces of work to these two specimens are to be found both throughout England and on the Continent, and serve to show the amount of popularity this class of decoration enjoyed. There are many who, while possessing the ability to construct many articles of household woodwork, are yet deterred from decorating their productions because of the difficulties of learning to carve, and of acquiring the knowledge of modelling necessary for doing really good carving in relief. To these and others the examples here given may serve as an incentive, helping them to direct their efforts towards a class of work from which the results will be more speedily accomplished; and after but little practice they will be enabled to produce decoration which, if not of the highest order, shall yet be based on sound and artistic principles. After some facility in the use of the tool has been gained, a simple running pattern, such as the German pattern in Fig. 173, may be attempted, after which any of the other designs given may be successfully executed. The design in Fig. 174 would be suitable for a box lid or panel for a cabinet, and the running pattern in Fig. 175, being arranged to repeat itself, could be used in a variety of ways as a border, frieze, cornice, or dado rail. The conventional sunflower pattern (Fig. 176) has been designed for the decoration of a door panel, but it could be adapted for many other purposes. The leaves and stalks, and the seed centres and petals of the flowers, should be very carefully outlined with the veiner to a depth of about $\frac{1}{16}$ in.; the ground could be either left quite plain, or, what would be preferable, worked across in a similar manner to the other examples shown. The addition of colour to any of these designs may be a great improvement in the eyes of some workers, and a very good effect may be gained if the groundwork only is painted in with any oil colour, a dark rich blue being, perhaps, as good as any; but if a very rich effect is desired, the sunflower design would be improved by painting the ground in cream colour, made by mixing a little raw sienna with white; the leaves and stalks in warm green, of raw sienna and a very little Prussian blue; and the petals in Venetian red, with the centre seeds gilded.

PIERCED CARVING

PIERCED CARVING has been known for centuries as a most effective form of ornamentation. In mediæval churches it figures in the shape of rood screens. Pierced carving is less difficult than is commonly supposed, and very beautiful effects may be obtained with comparatively little labour.

Bow saw or fret saw; brace and three shell bits, say $\frac{3}{8}$ in., $\frac{1}{4}$ in., $\frac{1}{8}$ in.; wood file; and about three rifflers of various shapes. The wood being prepared, and the design traced on, fix the panel firmly in the bench screw, with about half the panel showing (see Fig. 178). Then bore holes of various sizes

Fig. 177.—Design suitable for Pierced Carving.

Panel in Pierced Carving

The exercise given in Fig. 177 is suitable for a panel. The design is of modern style or character, and is based on the tulip. The panel is 1 ft. 6 in. long by 8 in. wide, and it should be $\frac{3}{4}$ in. thick. Being a modern design, the flowers and leaves should be treated in the freely conventional way that is characteristic of the style. In addition to the ordinary carving tools, the following will be necessary:

in the angles of the design, so that the fret saw can be inserted (see left-hand end of Fig. 179). If a fret saw is to be used, then the smaller bit ($\frac{1}{8}$ in.) will be sufficient; but if a keyhole saw is to be employed, the larger bits will be necessary. Then saw out the wood between the outlines of the design, keeping close to the lines, but not obliterating them. It is important that the saw be kept perfectly perpendicular, or square to the face of the wood, in all ways; otherwise the work will suffer either in appearance or in strength, or in both, because of the lines becoming displaced when the wood is cut into. If a keyhole saw is used, it should be a fine-toothed

Fig. 178.—Panel Fixed in Bench Screw.

enables the leaves to be well twisted and sunk, and nicely varied. The tools should be well sharpened, so that as little pressure as possible shall bear on the weaker

Fig. 182.—Cross Section of
Leaf (see Fig. 177).

Fig. 180.—Cross Section of
Tulip (see Fig. 177).

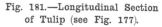

Fig. 181.—Longitudinal Section
of Tulip (see Fig. 177).

Fig. 181.

one, to avoid rough work at the back. A treadle fret saw is of great use in sawing out the wood. When this has been done, lay the panel, face upwards, on a flat board, and with a flat carving tool, or a joiner's paring chisel, clean up the outlines. Then fasten down the panel tightly, and

parts of the work; these weaker parts, such as the stalks that are lying across the grain, should be carefully treated. In carving the leaves, vary them in height from stalk to tip, and from side to side. Fig. 180 gives a section of the flowers across their width, and Fig. 181 a section through their

Fig. 179.—Various Stages in Execution of Pierced Carving.

proceed as in ordinary flat carving—that is, the wood being in this instance fairly thick, sink the underlying leaves and stalks to a good depth. The thickness of the wood

length. Fig. 182 shows the appearance of the surface of the leaves in cross section. To finish the panel, the back edges of the leaves and flowers should be trimmed by

Fig. 183.

Fig. 184.

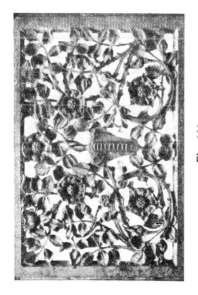

Fig. 185.

Fig. 186.

Figs. 183 to 186.—Panels in Chancel Screen at St. John's Church, Windermere.

taking off a small chamfer, as shown in the cross sections of the tulips and the leaves.

Using Files and Rifflers

The wood file and rifflers already mentioned are needed in pierced work, to correct any rough or badly sawn outlines. When the ordinary carving tools have taken off as much superfluous wood as they possibly can, these files and rifflers are used to finish. A quick movement

every direction. It often occurs that what is shapely and proportionate, and of good curve, viewed from one point, is often uneven and discontinuous viewed from other points ; and the depth of pierced carving increases the liability to this fault. Therefore, in sinking the stalks, take care to sink them evenly and gradually, and with due regard to their connection with the roots and flowers. The tips of the leaves should touch the stalks, and the tips of the

Fig. 187.—Panel in Chancel Screen at St. John's Church, Windermere.

backwards and forwards is what is required, so that not too much of the downward pressure is distributed into the wood ; if this latter occurs, it is apt to force off a back edge, or tear the wood out, with disastrous results. Work these tools as far as possible with an oblique stroke ; that is, not quite straight through, but with the tip of the file pointing either upwards or downwards. It should always be remembered that these tools are to be used only when their employment is essential.

Securing Strength and Grace

In carving the stalks and leaves, look at them from all possible points of view, to see whether their surface curves are good in

flowers the margin. Do not saw clean through, or the ultimate strength of the panel will be endangered. The object of pierced carving is to introduce into the work a degree of light and airy grace that could not possibly be attained to in any other way ; but the above-mentioned precaution must be taken, otherwise the work fails as a work of art.

Five Panels in Pierced Carving

Five panels of extremely good execution are illustrated by Figs. 183 to 187 (pp. 81 and 82). These form part of the chancel screen at St. John's Church, Windermere, and are examples of pierced carving of a refined and delicate character.

UNDERCUTTING

When it is desired to give prominence to carving in order to produce full contrast of light and shade, and thus to secure a bold and striking effect, undercutting is resorted to. This consists in cutting away to a greater or a less extent the wood that lies under the surface and within the limits of the design. The result is that the shadows thrown where the undercutting is are darker and much more distinct than when the " walls " of the design are cut quite perpendicularly ; and the depth of the shadow varies proportionately to the depth of the undercutting and of the relief. With undercutting some very remarkable effects are obtained, as may be seen, for instance, on examination of the carved woodwork of the fourteenth and fifteenth centuries, especially the screens of some of the churches of Norfolk and of the western counties. The remarkable work of that master of the craft, Grinling Gibbons, owes much of its great effect to the employment of discreet undercutting.

Value of Undercutting

At this stage it will be well to consider the reasons for the use of undercutting, and how far it may be adopted. There is a prevalent idea that undercutting marks a very high level in wood carving, and that if a piece of work is undercut it must therefore be good. So long as the life side and the form side of wood carving (see p. 71) are confused, this will always be the case. But if the two are considered separately, and the great difference that lies between them is realised, it will be seen that it does not follow that undercut work is necessarily of the highest value. From the point of view of form—that is, of the actual cutting and shaping of the wood into the form required to express the worker's ideas—undercutting occupies a high place. As a matter of technique, the difficulties attending its execution undoubtedly place a great value on it, and require an educated ability to deal successfully with it. But from the life point of view—that is, of the idea or ideas which give rise to the necessity of form or shape with which to express the idea—the matter assumes a different aspect. The result of a consideration of the matter from this point of view leads to the conclusion that the use of this kind of work is governed by conditions of necessity. That is to say, undercut work is only of value where it is necessary to fulfil a certain definite and particular part in a general scheme. Another reason against its general use is, that by undercutting, the strength of the wood is considerably weakened, because of the cutting of the grain or fibre ; and as true carved ornament should always be subservient to the strength of the wood work and to the rules of proper construction, an excessive or undue use of undercut work, however striking and effective it may appear to the uninitiated, should be avoided.

Grades of Undercutting

There are various grades of undercutting, which may be classed as follows : Simple undercutting, elaborate undercutting, combined pierced and undercut work, and undercutting on mouldings. These grades will be separately considered.

Simple Undercutting

This can be applied to carving of very

low relief. This must be emphasised, because many think that the term " undercut " should be, or is, applied only to that class of work that is sunk in such great relief

Designs for Simple Undercutting

Fig. 188 is a design to which this kind of undercut work may reasonably and effec-

Fig. 188.—Design suitable for Slight Undercutting.

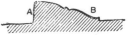

Fig. 190.—Section of Leaves without Undercutting.

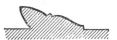

Fig. 191.—Section of Leaves Showing Amount of Undercut.

that portions of the design can be completely detached from the ground. Any carving, the walls of which incline under the pattern, as drawn on the surface, is undercut work. What may be designated as simple undercutting is that class of work which is in no part detached from the ground, but is simply cut under to intensify the depth of the shadow, and so cause a

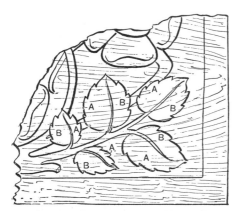

Fig. 189.—Part of Fig. 188 Enlarged.

greater contrast between it and the high lights ; or where it is done merely to take away the bald and wooden effect of a thick edge to a leaf, for example.

tively be applied. The depth to which it may be taken need not be more than $\frac{3}{8}$ in. at the greatest, the size of the whole board being about 1 ft. 6 in. by 10 in. With this depth (and bearing in mind the remarks given on p. 72 on making full use of the depth of relief), a good variation of the surface can be obtained, and this means that certain parts of the leaves and flowers will be almost at full height from the ground. This occurs on the portion of the panel enlarged in Fig. 189. Here the leaves are raised at A and depressed at B, the sections of them being somewhat as shown by Fig. 190. The result is that at A, the high part of the leaves, a high perpendicular wall occurs, and this, viewed from the side, is uninteresting and objectionable. If, however, the wall is cut away as in Fig. 191, by undermining the surface edge, the wall is quite lost in the deep shadow that results, or is made nearly invisible by being made to coincide with the line of vision. The result justifies the use of undercut work of this kind, and, providing the actual edge of the leaf is left thick enough to bear the strain of brushing or cleaning, this method of not only minimising harsh places, but turning them into strongly effective members, can be safely used. The actual method of working is to set in and clear the ground as usual, but not to undercut when setting in. Then model the design, getting as much variety and contrast of surface as

Fig. 192.—Beginning to Undercut.

possible. When this is done, the effect can be increased by judicious undercutting of the edges. Fig. 192 shows the edge of a leaf being undercut, and Fig. 193 the use of a grounding tool in clearing away the super-

not to use too much force—which in a panel like the one illustrated need not be applied with a mallet—or the ground will be cut up too much. Work of this kind is better left unpunched.

Fig. 193. Using Grounding Tool to Clear the Chips.

Elaborate Undercutting

This is especially favoured by the student, because of the wonderful effect supposed to be obtained by it; and the question

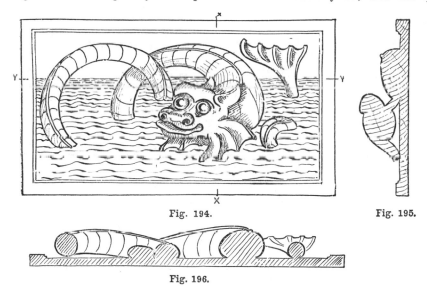

Fig. 194.

Fig. 195.

Fig. 196.

Figs. 194 to 196.—Design, with Sections on X X and Y Y suitable for Complete Undercutting.

fluous wood. In undercutting a curved edge, use a tool the curve of which is flatter than the edge itself. Beware of splitting the wood; always cut it, and be careful

appears to resolve itself into how much of the design can be separated from the ground, rather than how much support can be given to the design by as complete an association with the block of wood as possible. Fig. 194 is a design suitable for elaborate undercutting. It is that of a creature of the sea-serpent type, and a complete detachment of the creature from the ground is here reasonable enough. It may be supposed that a sea-serpent

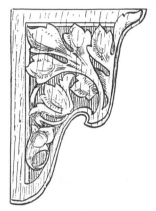

Fig. 197.—Side Elevation of Bracket with Pierced and Undercut Carving.

would have at least its head projecting from the sea; and that the convolutions of its body would suggest that in parts they should be quite detached from the ground. But it should be particularly noted that the limits of the strength (or weakness) of the wood should not be exceeded. Not so much of the body should be completely clear of the ground as would tend unduly to weaken that part and render it liable to be knocked off. This is where the real mistakes in undercutting are made; for instance, a design is chosen that is not at all suitable for undercutting, and it is treated in such a manner that, although the technique may be good, the carving is quite a failure on the grounds of art and commonsense. Fig. 195 is a section of the board through x x (Fig. 194), and Fig. 196 a section through y y (Fig. 194), showing in each case the amount of undercut that has been given. In completely detaching the serpent's body from the ground, the tools in an ordinary set will do the greater amount of cutting necessary to complete this design. The quick

spoon-bit gouges are very useful in cutting away the wood under the serpent's body, to clear it from the ground, and an addition might be made to the set of a spoon-bit **V**-tool about $\frac{1}{4}$ in. or $\frac{5}{16}$ in. in width. This tool will help to clear the corners and angles cleanly and neatly. Great care must be exercised in getting quite clean and level the ground under the parts of the body that are completely raised from the ground.

Pierced and Undercut Work

There are two ways of producing the appearance of a network of tracery that is yet in nearly all its parts raised quite away from the ground. First it may be cut out of the solid block by very elaborate and difficult undercutting. To do this, the ground spaces are cut down to a great depth, as usual, and then the undercutting is commenced. In this case, in addition to the set of tools, a few spoon-bit gouges, both quick and flat, will be required. In every respect the work will be carried out as already indicated. The second way in which this kind of work can be done is by piercing and carving on both front and back of a piece of wood, which is then glued to the face of another piece, so giving the effect of work in very high undercut relief. A good effect is sometimes obtained by carving two pieces in this manner and fixing them together. Brackets to shelves

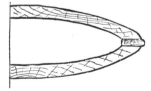

Fig. 198.—Cross Section of Bracket (see Fig. 197).

may be treated in this way, and a rich effect is the result. Fig. 197 shows a side elevation and Fig. 198 a cross section of such a bracket. This method, as compared with the other, saves a great amount of labour, and is certainly safer, as there is less danger of breaking the design. It is sometimes objected to as being to some extent artificial and misleading, giving the appearance of very complicated and elaborate undercut carving.

Undercutting on Mouldings

The shape of a moulding can often be adapted to emphasise the prominent features of an undercut design, and any design that is to be applied to a moulding should be so built as not to injure the contour. This as the third type does. Nevertheless, very fine effects can be obtained by adopting the simpler form of undercutting, namely, that of cutting back the walls of the design to secure a deeper shadow. When the background is cut to quite a dissimilar section there are opportunities for a very deep and detached form of undercutting. Examples of this can be seen in some of the Devonshire rood screens of the

  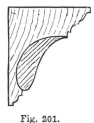 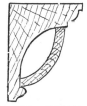

Fig. 199.   Fig. 200.   Fig. 201.

Figs. 199 to 201.—Sections of Carved Mouldings with (a) Background of Similar Shape, (b) Background of Similar Shape but Varying in Depth, and (c) Background of Different Section.

Fig. 202.—Section of Carved, Pierced and Undercut Moulding, with Carving on Separate Portion.

means that enough of the design should be arranged to be of full height, so as to ensure the possibility of the eye being easily carried over the sunk and undercut parts, without a perceptible break or jar, and thus ensure the continuity of the original moulded surface. Concerning the contour of the ground, this can be either : (a) The same section as the surface, as at Fig. 199 ; (b) a similar section to the surface, but somewhat deeper in parts, as at Fig. 200 ; (c) an entirely dissimilar section, as at Fig. 201. Sections of the first and second types do not allow of so much undercutting fifteenth century. Sometimes these mouldings were made as shown in the section (Fig. 202). The detached part was pierced and carved, and then fixed to the cove moulding, thus giving the representation of very deeply undercut work. In designing for all pierced work which has to be undercut, the greatest attention should be paid to the planning of the details, so that all the elements have sufficient support ; and this advice applies to all undercut work. It must be taken as an invariable rule that strength should never be sacrificed to any attempt to gain effect.

GOTHIC CARVING

AT the present time most of the eccle-siastical woodwork that is executed is either purely Gothic in style, or is very largely influenced by Gothic. Such work requires special treatment—a peculiar manipulation of the tools being rendered necessary by the distinctive and exceptional characteristics of the Gothic style, which place it in a class apart. Gothic wood carving follows in its style and character the features of the architecture of the same period. The wood carvers, however, were, apparently, more conservative in their methods than the masons, with the result that the wood carving of a later period commonly retains many of the character-istics of the architectural period immediately preceding it. The Gothic style of archi-tecture is divided into three principal periods, the Early English, extending from about 1190 to 1275 A.D.; the Decorated, from about 1275 to 1375; and the Perpen-dicular, from 1375 to 1536. The latter period is sometimes, and perhaps quite rightly, divided into two parts, the Per-pendicular proper and the Tudor period. There is little carved woodwork of the Early English period left now; the best pre-served and most complete example being perhaps the misericorde seats in Exeter Cathedral. More carving of the Decorated period is left, but there is little in proportion to what was executed. In the Perpendicular period, however, a great proportion of what was done is still retained; and in its earlier part it resembles work of the Decorated period. The characteristic features of this period are: (1) A use of natural forms as elements of design, such as oak leaves and acorns, maple leaf, the vine leaf and grapes, ivy, and similar forms. (2) A very natural treatment of these forms, which is yet conventional enough to fulfil the re-quirements of decorative art. The char-acteristic feature of this treatment is the unusual nature of the relief of the elements making up the design. A reference to Figs. 203, 204, 205, and 206 will make this clear. These figures show a Gothic boss, with various sections giving the depth and character of the relief. These bosses were used principally in wooden roofs at the intersections of the beams. It will be noticed that the contour of each leaf of the boss follows that of a double ogee curve (see Fig. 207). This is distinctive of carved work of the Decorated and Early Perpen-dicular periods. The effect produced by the alternation of the parts in high relief with those cut down to a great depth is extremely rich and tasteful, and the work-manship required to give the fullest effect to such carving as this is of such a high stan-dard that the majority of Decorated carvings are of a high quality. The size of this block is 12 in. by 12 in. by 3 in., and the sections (Figs. 205 and 206) show that full advantage is taken of the thickness. The peculiarity of the cutting of the depth lies in the fact that it is confined to such a short distance. Thus, from the diagonal sec-tion (Fig. 206) it will be seen that a depth of $1\frac{3}{4}$ in. has to be obtained in a space not more than $\frac{3}{4}$ in. in length. This necessi-tates the use of a tool known as the spoon-bit tool (Fig. 45, p. 28), and half a dozen tools of this kind should be obtained; the particular sizes obtained will depend, of course, on the character of the work on which they are intended to be employed.

Practical Gothic Carving

To begin work of this kind, the best thing to do after the design has been traced on is to fix some essential point, or points, that are of such a depth that they cannot be cut out by subsequent work. The eight points marked in Fig. 208 by circles are deeper than any other parts, and form the essential points in the skeleton of the design. These holes may be cut down by means of a quick gouge, about $\frac{1}{4}$ in. or $\frac{3}{8}$ in., No. 8. Fig. 209 shows a quick and ready way of doing this. The tool handle is held perpendicularly between the palms of the hands, and twirled rapidly backwards and forwards, with a downward pressure; a clean, well-defined hole is the result. The next step is to mark the divisions of the component parts of the design—in this case the leaves or petals—and to cut down the outlines of the design. Then proceed to cut away the superfluous wood, to get the various parts of the boss to their proper proportions all round, so far as the general contour of the surface is concerned. The dotted line at A (Fig. 206) shows the position of this. Then the particular contour can be cut, as at the dotted line B (Fig. 206). It is here where the greatest care is required, and the greatest amount of judgment and artistic sensibility can be shown, as well as the greatest perfection in the actual cutting of the wood. The deep channels can be cut out, in their initial stages, with the ordinary gouges of suitable curve; the quicker tools will cut them the most effectively. Then when these tools will no longer cut the quick and sudden curves, the spoon-bit gouges can be used. To use these tools, considerable practice is necessary to make them cut cleanly and easily. The pressure applied with the left hand has to be even and continuous throughout the whole sweep of the stroke. Also, the pressure applied by both hands is in a different direction from that applied to an ordinary straight tool. In the latter, the direction taken by the pressure is more or less coincident with the length of the tool, and is, at most, contained within the limits of the thickness

of the handle of the tool. With a spoon-bit tool, the line of pressure is best represented by a curved line, whose shape is determined by the direction of the ground surface of the back of the tool in relation to the butt end of the handle (see Figs. 210 and 211). In Fig. 210 the dotted lines represent some of the curves that are possible when

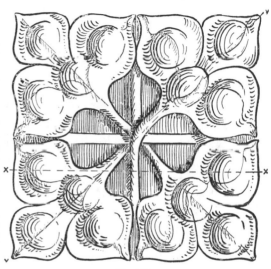

Fig. 203.

Fig. 204.

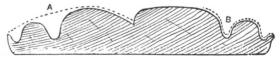

Fig. 205.

Fig. 206.

Figs. 203 to 206.—Gothic Boss, Plan, Side View, and Sections on Lines X X and Y Y.

an ordinary straight tool is used, and it will be seen that the pressure to be applied through the hands will be transmitted within the limits of these curves. In Fig. 211 is given a diagram showing a tool that is not subject to the limitations of the straight tool when a very deep channel has

Fig. 207.—Double Ogee Curve : Contour of Leaves of Boss.

to be cut. With this tool, the curves possible vary within the limits of the curves A D and B D. In cutting a curve of the short radius of A D the tool handle will move along the concentric arc B C, whilst at the same time it is moved forwards in order to cut the wood. The same applies to all curves of large radius in varying degrees. Thus the curve shown by the line B D represents roughly a mean value of the direction of the pressures to be applied to a tool of this kind, in making its different cuts. Thus the pressure is applied not more or less directly through the length

of the handle, but in a direction through its thickness. The application of the pressure in this direction tends to make the

Fig. 208.—Diagram showing Beginning of Carving the Boss.

cutting edge of the tool fly away from the work. This is only prevented by the pressure of the left hand as already mentioned.

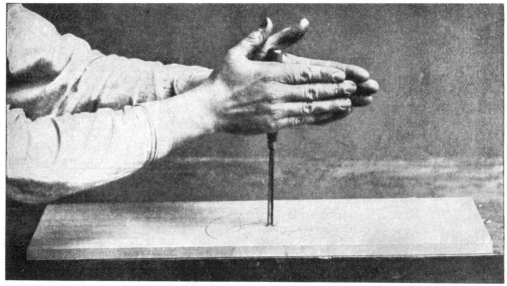

Fig. 209.—Twirling Carving Tool to make Deep Hole.

Boss Leaves, etc.

The edges of the boss are slightly under-cut to make them stand out clear and dis-

of the leaves are each traversed by a ridge, which is formed by a junction of two parallel gouge cuts, as shown in Fig. 212, which is a cross section. The dotted line in Fig. 212

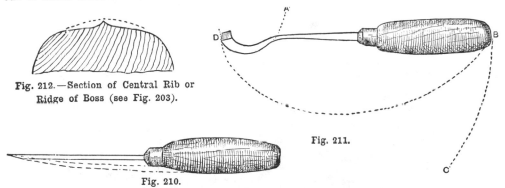

Fig. 212.—Section of Central Rib or Ridge of Boss (see Fig. 203).

Fig. 211.

Fig. 210.

Figs. 210 and 211.—Diagrams showing Capabilities of Different Tools.

tinct. Otherwise, they would appear, from some points of view, somewhat distorted when in position, if from that position the line of the back edge projected in front of the line of the front edge. The lobes

shows the original surface. In any place where the edges of leaves, or parts of them, overlap other parts, they should be undercut for the same reason as for the outside edges.

Fig. 213.—First Position of Spoon-bit Gouge in Carving Boss.

Using Spoon-bit Gouges

In using the spoon-bit gouges, allowance must be made for the unusually large the tool in the position shown by Fig. 213. Fig. 214 shows the finish of the same cut, and it will be seen that the butt of the handle has to make a large sweep to secure

Fig. 214.—Second Position of Spoon-bit Gouge in Carving Boss.

sweep of the handle, and to get a sufficiently good start—that is, a start that will ensure the tool getting a good hold on the wood to enable it to be taken steadily and uniformly, and yet quickly, round the curve. It is well to begin with such a slight cutting distance of the edge of the tool. It is this that causes so much difficulty in getting the tool to bite evenly all the way. Much practice is necessary to secure clean cutting; and the work should not be glasspapered or scraped.

CARVING IN THE ROUND

CARVING in the round is a term applied to the carving of a figure, or a group of figures, of the human form, of the animal form, or the form grotesque ; plant forms are also carved in the round. The roods, the figures of the saints, and the Jesse trees that adorned the rood screens of pre-Reformation times, the fifteenth and sixteenth century pulpits in Holland and Belgium, and some of the work of Grinling Gibbons, notably that magnificent group, " The Stoning of St. Stephen," which is in the South Kensington

Fig. 215.—Front View of Eagle : an Exercise for Carving in the Round.

(Victoria and Albert) Museum, are some examples of carving in the round that readily occur to the mind.

What is Carving in the Round?

This form of carving is that in which the objects to be carved are completely

Fig. 216.—Side View of Eagle.

detached from the rest of the block, or where the whole of the block is used for the production of the figure. In doing this work, an appreciation of form and proportion and conception of mass are so largely necessary as to make this quite a special form of carving. Large examples of this work, such as "The Stoning of St. Stephen," already mentioned, require build-

ing up, and this adds to the difficulty, because in many cases the separate parts are fitted together after they have been carved, the pieces where the joints occur being carved and finished after the building up.

Built-up Work

The wood should be dry and clean, and the workmanship of the very best. Any fault in these particulars will make open joints that will disfigure the finished work. When the work is large enough to need thus

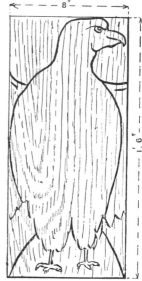

Fig. 217.—Cutting Out Timber for Body of Eagle.

building up, the parts should be fastened together by means of wood dowels. Much solid work of this kind can be done out of an entire block; but it is always well not to use large pieces, because of the much greater strain caused by the shrinkage of the wood. With any large piece of work it is better to build it up of smaller pieces, for at least three reasons. The first is, that this minimises the effect of the large amount of shrinkage attending the use of big pieces of timber. The second reason is, that the outlying parts, and those which lie across the grain, and cannot well derive any support from the main body, can be built up with the grain of the wood running in a direction that gives the most strength. The third reason is that it is more economical of material to build up in this way than to employ one solid block.

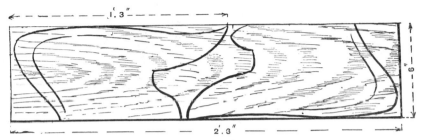

Fig. 218.—Cutting Out Timber for Wings of Eagle.

Carving of an Eagle

As an example, the carving of an eagle, shown in Figs. 215 and 216, will be considered. Eagles are much used in ecclesiastical carving, the eagle being the representative symbol of St. John. In this piece of work there are three separate portions, the body and the two wings. The three reasons already given apply very aptly to the method chosen. This is well illustrated in considering the sizes of timber required for (a) cutting the whole from a solid block, and (b) building it up in three pieces. For the first method, a block 1 ft. 7 in. long by 1 ft. 9 in. wide by 5 in. thick is required. For the second method, the wood necessary is, one piece for the body, 1 ft. 7 in. by 8 in. by 3 in., two pieces for the wings, each 1 ft. 3 in. by 6 in. by 2 in. In the latter method the body is tilted forward slightly to save material, and the wings are dowelled to the body. Figs. 217 and 218 show in front view the method of cutting the body and wings out of the board, Figs. 219 and 220 being the side views of the same operation. The wings are cut out of 6-in. by 2-in. stuff, and the body out of 8-in. by 3-in. stuff. The wings can, for further economy, be cut out of one board 2 ft. 3 in. long, as shown in Fig. 218. The wings may now be bored and dowelled ready for gluing up afterwards. It is best in this case to carve them first, and then fix them. The pieces should be sawn out with the bow saw. One

great difficulty that will be experienced at this stage will be the holding of these pieces quite firmly, and yet leaving a clear surface. The carver's screw illustrated by Fig. 79 (p. 34) will be found of great use for this purpose. The screw can be fixed into any part of the back that has to be cut out, so that its marks are not afterwards visible. If a carver's screw is not available, a somewhat similar result may be obtained by screwing a $\frac{1}{2}$-in. board to the

Fig. 219.—Side View of Timber Cut Out for Eagle.　　Fig. 220.—Side View of Timber Cut Out for Wings of Eagle.

back of the wings, and cramping it down to the bench in the usual way, leaving the ends a little longer for fixing the cramps. The first thing to do is to cut the wings and body to a roughly proportionate shape. A large gouge, No. 7 curve, about 1 in. or 1¼ in. wide, is very useful for this purpose. Fig. 221 shows the first stage in this operation.

effect. At the same time, an undue straining after conventionalism is not to be commended. Thus the feathers will not show every constituent part of each, and

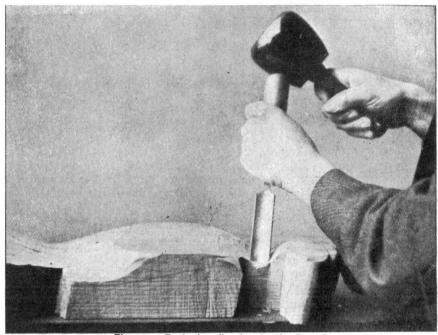

Fig. 221.—Beginning Carving in the Round.

It will be noticed that the wood for the body is cut somewhat on the bevel, owing to its being tilted to economise both material and labour. The same bevel should be maintained throughout. When the front has been done, the pieces are turned over, and the backs treated in the same way. An instantaneous-grip vice (Fig. 105, p. 43) is an excellent apparatus for holding the pieces at this stage. First the parts are all shaped roughly, and afterwards they are taken to a definite and final shape. Fig. 222 is a cross section of the wing. The edges of the wings should be taken fairly sharp, to avoid an appearance of woodenness. The feathers of the wings and body may now be carved. It is well to bear in mind that these objects are intended for decorative purposes, and that therefore it is a mistake to try to get a very naturalistic

will not be cut as an exact copy of nature. The decorative lines of the feathers, however, should not be forced out of all natural

Fig. 222.—Cross Section of Eagle's Wing.

shape. The surface of each feather should be slightly convex; the accumulated effect of them all is to give a full, rounded,

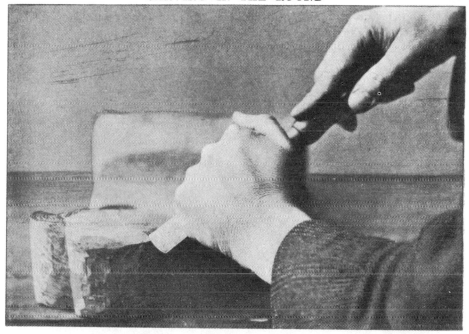

Fig. 223.

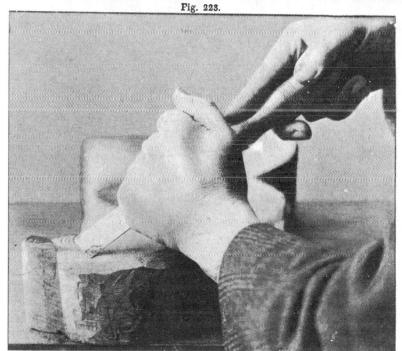

Fig. 224.

Figs. 223 and 224.—First and Second Positions of Tool for Cutting End Grain in Carving Eagle.

and substantial appearance to the whole wing. Keep the top edges of the wings fairly sharp, and do all that is possible to avoid a has been carved as far as possible, the portions can be fitted together with dowels, and the parts near the joints can then be levelled

Fig. 225.—Owl, Carved by T. H. Kendall.

clumsy appearance. The backs of the wings are carefully rounded, and then the feathers carved. The feathers should be cut in slight relief, so as to obviate as far as possible resting places for dust. When each part off. In carving in the round, there is a great amount of cutting on the end grain. In oak, this is very hard to manage. The best way to cut this end grain is to incline the edge of the tool to the direction of the cut, and carve with a slicing motion. (Compare Figs. 223 and 224.) All end grain can be most conveniently cut by this method, which can also be applied to cross grain. Many places occur where the carver has to cut against the grain, but the cuts can always be managed without mishap, provided this particular manner of using the tool can be employed. In trimming the body and wings, the spokeshave is of value in shaping them, after they have been roughly carved. For a piece of work of this kind, files, rifflers, and glasspaper are not necessary, although they are used in some forms of carving in the round, but it is best to do without them if possible. The most essential thing in carving of this kind is to get the masses proportionately grouped, so that the parts balance each other in proportion. After this, the carving consists in drawing on the surface with the carving tools instead of pencils. Any elaboration can be effected on the prepared surface, such as hair, feathers, scales, leaves, or whatever is considered appropriate and desirable; but the surface must first be properly prepared. Care must be taken that any surface work that is done does not cut too far and too often into the block, and so disturb the continuity of the surface

Owl Carved in Limewood

Fig. 225 illustrates an excellent example of carving in the round. It is the work of T. H. Kendall, and was exhibited in 1880 at the Royal Albert Hall.

FINISHING CARVINGS

Unsuitability of High Polish

CARVING may be finished off in various ways, but much discretion should be exercised in determining on the mode of finishing employed. Much depends on the wood, of course, but there are general rules that apply to all woods. The first is that wood carving should never be highly polished. Carving should always be finished clean from the tool, and consequently the tool marks always show to some extent. The application of polish tends to emphasise the marks of the tool, and therefore the more highly polished a surface is, the more do the tool marks stand out. It is an essential condition of highly polished work that the surface should be so perfectly smooth that no marks or ridges of any kind should be present to mar the ultimate effect, which should be like a mirror, capable of reflecting a good image. Therefore, to qualify carved work for french polishing, it should be, as other surfaces are, prepared by means of the scraper and glasspaper of varying grades, so that a perfectly smooth surface results, quite free from any ridges or marks that would militate against the final surface obtained by the process of polishing. This would, of course, completely destroy the individuality of the work, and would make it quite valueless as a work of art; and the carver who wishes to avoid this result will refrain from the use of french polish—or, at any rate, will not aim at producing a very high polish. It may be remarked that in the middle of the nineteenth century, from about 1830 to 1860, much furniture was carved with such patterns as could easily be scraped and glasspapered to take a high polish, but the result was never artistic.

Process of French Polishing Carvings

In polishing two carved panels in a sideboard, if they are of mahogany or walnut the colour may be enriched by brushing over with red oil, which consists of 2 oz. of alkanet steeped in $\frac{1}{2}$ pt. of raw linseed oil. The panels should then be allowed to stand for at least twelve hours. Grain fillers are not used, but roughness may be removed and the pores partly sealed up by well rubbing the surface with a wad of fine soft shavings, pressing firmly till a slight lustre appears. The same appliances and materials are required as for french polishing flat surfaces, but, owing to the irregular surface, the wads must be kept very soft. The wad is a piece of wadding enclosed in a soft, fluffless rag, the whole forming a pointed rubber, which is held as in Fig. 226. When the surface has been brushed quite clean, apply polish wherever possible, then rub in a little thin varnish, using a camel-hair brush ; dab it well into the inner or undercut portions, and allow it to get thoroughly hard. Afterwards rub down with very fine glasspaper all parts that can be reached. Apply another coat of varnish, which will flow better if it has been slightly warmed. When this is quite dry, work over all prominent parts with a small rubber having a rag covering, using the polish rather thin—say about half polish and half spirits. Rub till the whole of the surface becomes bright, and use less polish as the brightness increases, till a surface is gained similar to that obtained by spiriting off. But, as already mentioned, the french polishing of carving is not advised.

Wax Polishing Carvings

The treatment of carving by means of raw linseed oil, beeswax, and some kinds of furniture polish, is to be recommended as being the best treatment that can be applied. Oak may be oiled with raw linseed oil, left to dry, and then treated with beeswax, well rubbed in—the plain parts with a cloth, and the carved portions with a stiff brush. The wax should be shredded, or cut finely with a knife, and dropped into a jar

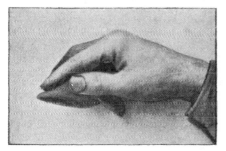

Fig. 226.—Method of Holding Rubber when French Polishing.

of turpentine; use enough wax to form a mixture the consistency of butter. It should be heated in an oven or other warm place until all the wax is dissolved, and then for use it simply requires heating until it is soft enough to apply by rubbing. In applying it, see that it does not lodge in corners and stiffen, but rub it about well. The applications should be thin but many. For wax polishing carved work, benzine wax is preferred by many workers to turpentine wax because the former has less tendency to clog the fine lines and notches. To prepare benzine wax, put small pieces of white wax into a vessel, cover the wax with benzine, and closely stopper the vessel and allow to stand for a day in a cool place. Care is needed in these operations, as benzine is highly inflammable. A thick paste will form; remove a little of this with a knife or spatula, dilute it with benzine in a flat dish to about the consistency of milk, and apply

this to the carved work by means of a moderately soft bristle paint brush. After allowing it to stand for a few minutes, brush out all the cavities with a good bristle brush, when a faint lustre will appear. To give a red tinge to the wax, add a little of an infusion of alkanet in benzine; for blue, add a solution of Prussian blue in benzine; and for a mahogany colour, use Cassel brown. After use, clean the brushes, etc., with a hot soda solution.

Treatment of Oak

Oak is sometimes fumed and then waxed. Fuming is done by exposing the oak to the fumes given off by liquid ammonia. These fumes darken the oak in proportion to the strength of the ammonia and the length of time the oak is exposed. An airtight cupboard or chamber of some kind is necessary, so that the fumes do not escape, and so that they may thus exert their fullest effect. A saucerful of ammonia is quite sufficient for a chamber containing 50 cub. ft., unless a very deep shade is required, when the amount could be doubled by the addition of another saucer. An important point to be noticed is that the ammonia should be in flat vessels, so that a wide surface is left for the giving off of the fumes. The oak may then be oiled, which darkens it still further; or it may be waxed without any preliminary oiling. The addition of turpentine to the oil tends to make it dry quickly, but no more than 1 part turps to 3 parts oil should be used.

Treatment of American Walnut

American walnut may be treated in the same way—that is, it may be oiled first with raw linseed oil, which makes it a rich dark brown colour, and it can then be waxed. The best way, however, is to use only the oil, and to depend on frequent applications subsequently to give a good finish. A fine colour and surface are eventually produced by this combination of oil and plenty of rubbing.

Treatment of Various Woods

Satin walnut may be oiled and waxed, or oiled only; the same with kauri pine and pearwood; or all these woods may be waxed without a previous oiling. White woods, such as sycamore, may be waxed only, or they may be stained various colours, and then oiled and waxed. If it is thought advisable to french polish any work, polish only the edges and those parts which can be made perfectly smooth. But keep the carving either the natural colour of the wood, or oil it, and polish it with wax; or polish by rubbing it continually with an oily brush. For fuming, oak should be chosen clear of sap, as the sap always shows white; it is only the heartwood that takes the fumes of the ammonia. Austrian wainscot takes the fumes the best, and is the best wood for carving, being clean, straight, and fine grained. American white oak takes the fumes fairly well, but red oak does not, and should not be used if it is intended to fume the work. English oak fumes nicely, but is rather hard for carving purposes. It may be taken as a rule that fine varieties of wood should not be stained. Walnut, pear, oak, plum, and mahogany retain their natural colour, and are waxed only and subsequently brushed, by which means they attain a somewhat darker tone and antique appearance. A handsome dark-brown shade on walnut is obtained by first coating the wood with linseed oil in which alkanet root has been infused, and polishing after twenty-four hours. A simple method of staining carvings is to coat with a dilute solution of potassium chromate and then with a dilute solution of potassium permanganate. By varying the strength of the solutions and the number of applications, all woods, from the hardest to the softest, can be stained effectively. It is wise to try the stains on a piece of board first; after staining with the potassium permanganate, wash out the brush in water, or the salt will destroy the bristles. An antique shade on oak carvings is obtained by staining with umber which has been boiled in water with a little potash. Wood stained in this manner is not polished, but it receives a covering of limpid varnish.

Worm=eaten Carvings

Old oak furniture and carvings, beside being dirty, are often encrusted, and the carvings and mouldings clogged with many coats of beeswax; they may have been varnished or even painted, or they may be worm-eaten. This paragraph will give some instructions on how they should then be treated. In case there are any insects in the joints and crannies, take a feather and thoroughly dress all doubtful places with a mixture of paraffin and benzoline. Any greasy marks left by the paraffin will be removed afterwards. But there may be insect life in the wood itself, and that of a kind less easily disposed of—the grub. Of wood-boring grubs there are more kinds than one, but that which is chiefly to be dreaded is the larva of a small brown beetle, about $\frac{1}{12}$ in. in length, which takes wing in its mature state in the month of July. It may then be seen on ceilings, walls, etc., near worm-eaten woodwork, and as a means of preventing further mischief it should be destroyed. It is easily killed, for it is a sluggish insect, and makes little attempt to escape. The baby beetle, a tiny white grub, affects beech and pear more than other woods. It is slow to attack woods of the fir kind; indeed, some of the conifers seem to possess an immunity. In oak these pests quickly riddle the sap or outer part, but do not readily penetrate the heart. It is generally after exposure to damp that heart of oak becomes subject to their attacks. The grub buries itself so deeply in the wood that it is not easily reached. There are many recipes for destroying it, of which the following are a few approved ones : (1) Corrosive sublimate, 1 oz. to 1 pt. of warm water. This is a deadly poison, to be handled with care. (2) Vitriol dissolved in warm water. This also is poisonous. (3) Oil of cassia. (4) Camphor dissolved in paraffin. (5) Decoction of bitter apple. (6) Fumigation by sulphur, the wood to be treated being shut in an air-tight box. (7) Benzoline, which is very penetrative and effective. Each recipe should be repeated after a few days, and the grub holes stopped with a mixture of 3 parts of beeswax to 1 of resin.

Cleaning Old Carvings

For removing dirt from old carvings, nothing is better than scrubbing the article with warm water in which soda has been dissolved. This also removes any beeswax which has been put on. But if hard varnishes have to be removed, scrub with the following mixture: American potash, soft soap, washing soda, and rock ammonia, ½ lb. of each, dissolved in 1 gal. of hot water, and with a few drops of nitric acid added. At the beginning of the nineteenth century it was the fashion to paint oak panelling, etc., so that some old oak has several coats of paint on it. This can be removed by covering the painted wood, to the thickness of about 1 in., with a mixture of a strong solution of American potash thickened with sawdust, and leaving it for about twelve hours. The paint will then be so softened that it can be washed off with a sponge and cold water. If the paint is thicker in some places and does not come off, repeat the process. Old varnish, etc., may also be removed in the same way. When the wood is dry, its rich dark colour can be restored by well rubbing with boiled oil.

Repolishing Carvings

In repolishing, varnish should be applied only when the oak is much worm-eaten, or when age or exposure has rendered it unusually tender. Generally, beeswax and turps, with a little resin melted to a jelly, is the proper and best polish, and this should be used sparingly, the wood being thoroughly rubbed.

CLAY MODELLING FOR WOOD CARVERS

Desirability of Models

THE opinion of expert wood carvers is divided as to the desirability — from an artistic point of view—of building up a preliminary model in clay. This matter is briefly discussed in the Introduction to this work (see p. 4). But notwithstanding this, the average carver does better with a preliminary model than without. Craftsmen of the rank of the Florentine carver—the late Luigi Frullini—who gave embodiment to ideas straight away in the wood without preliminary sketch or model, are extremely few in number. Luigi Frullini was a genius, but even he left in his studio "numberless figures in graceful poses, one lacking an arm, another a bit of floating drapery." "He often found that the block from which he worked was not of sufficient size to contain the work of his imagination." It may be taken as a rule applying to all ordinary wood carving, that a charcoal or similar drawing, shaded, is necessary. Further, a model will invariably be extremely useful. Drawing and model will allow of the work being set out the better, and will enable the carver to avoid starting to carve a piece of wood that is not large enough for the purpose intended. The wood used in carving is an expensive item, and for this one reason alone the average carver will prefer first to work out his ideas in the plastic clay, in which, of course, the design can be freely altered without the slightest waste of material. The more frequently the clay is used, the better does it serve the modeller's purpose. The greatest advantage, however, of the preliminary clay model is that it shows approximately how the executed design will appear, and important modifications—easily made in the clay — may at once suggest themselves; but in the case of a finished carving any serious alteration is, of course, out of the question.

Scheme of this Chapter

The practical processes involved in the modelling of clay cannot be summed up in a few sentences; and if the reader, who is assumed to be quite ignorant of even the elements of the modelling art, is to be benefited at all, a lengthy chapter must be devoted to the subject. This course, it will be observed, is here followed. This present chapter is a comprehensive survey of the whole art of clay modelling, and is taken from "Clay Modelling and Plaster Casting," a handbook prepared under the direction of the Editor of this present work. It may therefore contain information on some phases with which the wood carver may not desire to become minutely acquainted. But it nevertheless presents a course of practice which should be followed by all who wish to get a knowledge of the art of modelling clay; and the student who has worked through this course will be the better for the acquired skill in the manipulation of the clay, and will be perfectly prepared to build up original designs which can afterwards be expressed in the wood.

Modellers' Tools and Appliances

Modelling Stool.—A modelling stool is very handy. A useful stool is one with a top 15 in. square; it should be stoutly made, for models are heavy. It should be 3 ft. 3 in. high, and the legs should spread slightly, to give greater firmness. The top should have a turntable so that all parts of the work may be readily brought under the eye, and into different lights. Fig. 227 is a diagram of a turntable; the top, it will be seen, is double. In the middle of the lower part is a round hole, through which passes a pin or peg A fixed in the

allows a relief model to be readily turned to get new lights, but also enables the clay model to be laid on its back for wrapping in wet cloths. Modelling stools are sometimes made with a screw like music stools, which allows them to be adjusted to different heights. Theoretically, this arrange-

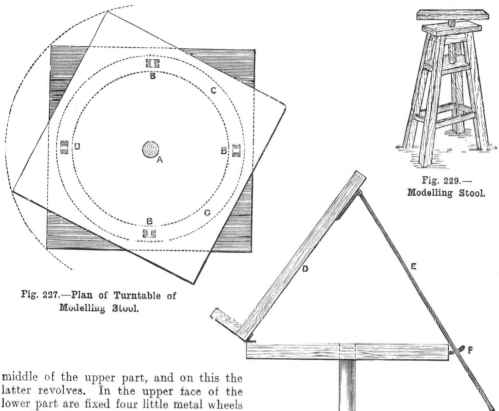

Fig. 227.—Plan of Turntable of Modelling Stool.

Fig. 229.— Modelling Stool.

Fig. 228.—Side Elevation of Adjustable Top of Modelling Stool.

middle of the upper part, and on this the latter revolves. In the upper face of the lower part are fixed four little metal wheels or rollers B, and on the lower face of the upper part is an iron ring C, which runs on these rollers. This allows the top to be turned easily, even when a heavy weight may be upon it. A useful form of top which may be made to fit on the same stool is shown by Fig. 228, and will come in handy for reliefs, models, etc. The board D is hinged to the upper half of the stool-top, and may be adjusted to any desired angle by means of the iron tongue E, which is pierced with a series of holes and hasps over the pin F. The tongue is attached by a hinge to the board D. This arrangement not only

ment is convenient, but it does not always work well in practice. Such stools are apt to be shaky, but firmness in the stand is essential to satisfactory modelling. If the model is too low, it is always possible, without a screw, to pack under it; and if too high, the modeller, who commonly works in a standing posture, can generally find something to stand on. The modeller may sometimes sit whilst working on small reliefs, or whilst finishing details; but he has to stand up to do work on anything of size and importance, especially whilst roughing out, and whilst determining general forms and throwing in action and expression. The moisture which is being continually used causes another objection to

Fig. 230.—Modeller's Proportional Compasses.

the screw, which, if of wood, gets swelled, and, if of iron, rusted, and in either case becomes unworkable. A stool of a simple and serviceable pattern is illustrated in Fig. 229. A wooden pin is fixed to the top, and on this pin the top revolves. The legs are spread, to give stability to the stool, and a number of rails tie the legs together.

Callipers, Compasses, etc.—The modeller's most useful measuring tools are callipers and compasses. Ordinary callipers are in constant employment, and the proportional callipers shown by Fig. 230 are used when a model is to be made either smaller or larger than the original.

Modelling Tools.—For roughing-out on a fairly large scale, the modelling tool shown by Fig. 231 will be found useful; it is 9 in. long. That shown by Fig. 232 is about $5\frac{1}{2}$ in. by $2\frac{1}{4}$ in. by $\frac{1}{3}$ in. at its thickest part. Both these tools are somewhat deeply notched, for it is found that a toothed edge will work far better in the clay than a plain one, whilst on the unfinished model it leaves a surface more pleasing to the eye and better fitted to retain the water sprinkled over the clay to keep it damp. Large modelling tools such as are shown in Figs. 231 and 232 may well be made of some wood —elder, for instance—that is more easily obtainable in large pieces than box. Among large roughing-out tools, a straightedge is indispensable for preparing clay grounds on which to model reliefs, etc.; a strip of plum-tree does admirably for this. For ordinary work the straightedge may be 15 in. long by $2\frac{1}{2}$ in. wide and $\frac{1}{4}$ in. thick. This tool must, of course, be planed true on the bench, the tooth notches, about $\frac{1}{2}$ in. apart,

being afterwards put in with a file. After roughing-out the model, the finer work is attempted. For this purpose, the modeller's first and best instrument is one provided by nature, the thumb; and next to it come those tools which most resemble the thumb in shape. Of tools of this class, that shown by Figs. 233 and 234 may be taken as a type. These are sometimes called "spoon-shaped tools." They are about $6\frac{1}{2}$ in. long. They ought to be less pointed than an ordinary spoon, and should more nearly resemble the thumb in the breadth of their ends. The form admits of some variety from that shown—the points may be made slightly more blunt, thus approaching the thumb shape, or more sharp, thus approaching the spoon shape. For moderately small work a tool not more than $\frac{1}{8}$ in. across at its narrowest blade is valuable; and at times one even smaller, having a blade $\frac{1}{12}$ in. in width, is very handy, but will be better if made from bone. Figs. 235 and 236 show a useful tool in somewhat the same class but more globular in its ends; this also is $6\frac{1}{2}$ in. long. Another similar tool is illustrated by Figs. 237 and 238. A most handy little tool (Figs. 239 and 240) is allied both to those already mentioned and to the scrapers. Its length is $5\frac{1}{4}$ in. In some kinds of work, as in modelling hair loosely arranged on a bust, both ends will alike be found valuable. It will be observed that in the examples of tools given there is no part sharp or angular; and, as a rule, in a wooden tool there should be no sharp or angular parts. Breadth and softness

Fig. 231.—Modeller's Roughing-out Tool.

are the qualities required in clay modelling, and in consequence the tools must present only soft and easy curves. The tool illustrated by Figs. 241 and 242, with its sharp claws, is an exception to this rule; but this

Fig. 232.—Modeller's Roughing-out Tool.

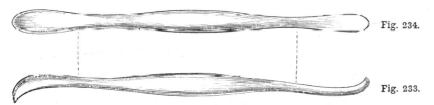

Fig. 234.

Fig. 233.

Figs. 233 and 234.—Thumb- or Spoon-shape Tool for Modelling.

Fig. 236

Fig. 235.

Figs. 235 and 236.—Thumb-shape Tool with Globular Ends.

Fig. 238.

Fig. 237.

Figs. 237 and 238.—Tool for Fine Modelling.

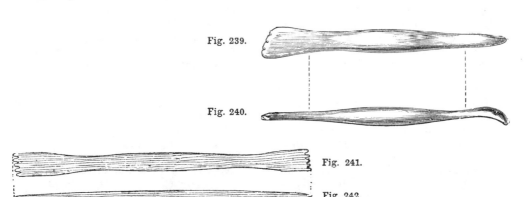

Fig. 239.

Fig. 240.

Fig. 241.

Fig. 242.

Figs. 239 to 242.—Modeller's Hair Tools.

tool is intended for giving roughly the effect of crisp hair, of fur, or of wool, etc., in which a certain abruptness is necessary, though the harshness may have to be partly softened down later on. This tool is 6 in. long. Of small scraping tools serviceable examples are shown by Figs. 243 to 248. In scrapers a toothed edge is preferred generally, but not always ; each of these has therefore one end plain. These tools also are 6 in. long. A scraper with two toothed edges is shown by Figs. 249 and 250. Fig. 251, though edged like a scraper, is an admirable tool for general use on busts, etc., in their earlier stages. It is a flat tool, 6 in. long by $1\frac{1}{2}$ in. at its widest, while its greatest thickness at the middle is $\frac{1}{4}$ in. A modeller who has once used this tool would not care to be without it.

Making Modelling Tools.—The material for tools is some kind of wood, hard, smooth-grained, commonly box. The modeller can buy tools at shops at about 6d. each ; but those sold are rarely of good forms, and often are useless. Instead of buying these, the worker is advised to make his own from the illustrations here given. He is advised to content himself at the beginning with three or four tools, and he will soon find out what others he requires, and what forms best suit him (for different modellers fancy different tools), and he can make such as he requires. Boxwood is costly as commonly sold in towns by the pound, and the intending toolmaker is advised to find, if possible, some turner, whose stock generally includes sticks of box of sufficient size. In cutting a length for a modelling tool, knots should be avoided ; and after the piece has been sawn out, all the tools required to finish it are a sharp chisel and a half-round wood file, the latter being the more useful of the two. After the wood has been roughly shaped with the chisel, it is finished with the file, for with this there is little danger of tearing the grain in the wrong direction. Finally, all roughness is removed with glasspaper, first of medium and afterwards of very fine grade ; for perfect smoothness is most essential in a modelling tool. Small tools are made of bone or ivory. Old toothbrush handles form a very suitable material. For fine work a bone tool resembling Figs. 233 and 234 (which are shown half full size), but only two-thirds as long and one-third as thick, would be found most useful. Bone tools are desirable for minute work in clay and for working in wax and on plaster. They are not more difficult to make than wooden tools, but the work requires more patience, because little of it can be done with the chisel, and filing makes slow progress. There is nearly always a difficulty in buying factory-made tools which work quite satisfactorily, so the ability to make one's own tools is not to be regarded merely as a way of saving money.

Wire Tools.—One or more wire tools (Figs. 252 and 253) are desirable. They are made of brass wire fitted to a handle, and in its working part the wire is somewhat flattened and notched with a file on one side so as to form teeth. These tools are not so easily made as the others, and most persons prefer to buy them, though some modellers make them for themselves. The bent wire is secured in the ferrule as shown. Wire tools are useful in the earlier stages for scooping or scraping away superfluous clay ; and in finishing, many accidental irregularities may be removed by drawing one lightly but firmly over the surface. The tooth marks left can be softened away afterwards.

Surfacing Clay.—A method of getting a good surface on clay is to wrap over the thumb a scrap of the ribbed material of which most cotton stockings are made, the ribs lying crosswise ; then damp it, and work it firmly over the clay. The ribs cut in, and reduce the inequalities ; the marks left by them are removed by dabbing with a damp sponge. For very large surfaces, such as the drapery of life-sized figures, a broad, flat brush (Figs. 254 and 255) having very stiff bristles is often used to procure a true surface. This does its work by cutting more deeply into the clay than does the cloth. An artist's brush called a " hog tool," with the bristles cut down to $\frac{1}{2}$ in., is useful in levelling small parts ; in delicate work a camel-hair brush is good for softening down delicate details. In artistic modelling, breadth and softness are the qualities to be striven for ; to this

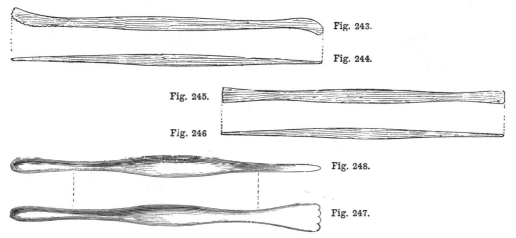

Fig. 243.

Fig. 244.

Fig. 245.

Fig. 246

Fig. 248.

Fig. 247.

Figs. 243 to 248.—Scraping Tools used in Modelling.

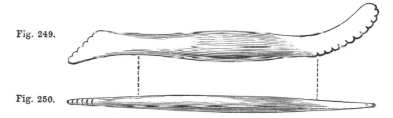

Fig. 249.

Fig. 250.

Figs. 249 and 250.—Modeller's Scraping Tool with Two Toothed Edges.

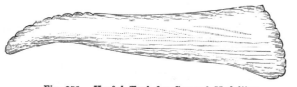

Fig. 251.—Useful Tool for General Modelling.

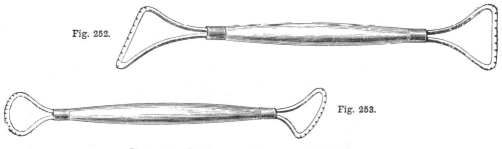

Fig. 252.

Fig. 253.

Figs 252 and 253.—Wire Tools used in Modelling.

end modelling tools are all more or less rounded instead of being left angular.

Modellers' Clay

The best clay for modelling is generally considered to be Devonshire pipeclay. It is highly plastic, yielding readily to the touch ; its cool grey colour is pleasant to the eye ; it is cleanly ; and in most places it is to be procured readily and cheaply. However, any tolerably pure clay will serve the modeller's purpose, and some workers prefer clay which, owing to the presence of iron, has a warm brown tone. This is merely a matter of taste. As dug from the pit, clay is never fit for use. It needs to be tempered and prepared. When the modeller buys his clay in the rough, the ordinary treatment is to lay it on a strong table or bench, and thoroughly beat it with an iron bar, picking out all stones and other foreign matters that are revealed in the process. Some persons sift a little fine sand into the clay during beating to make it work more freely, and this is an improvement if the modelling is to be on a large scale. Newly dug clay is generally deficient in tenacity, but weathering, or exposure to the weather, will toughen the clay. The clay, when dug, is laid in heaps and occasionally turned over. The water and oxygen of the atmosphere and the influence of frost disintegrate, wash, and purify clay, thus greatly improving its quality. Clay is also toughened by being well worked or kneaded. For modelling there is nothing so good as old clay—that is, clay that has been repeatedly used. Consequently, when a mould has been made from a clay model, the clay is thrown back into the bin, becoming tougher and more ductile by this continual usage. For use, the clay should be so soft as to be easily moulded into any shape and spread out smoothly by the thumb, but it should not be so soft as to be sticky. If clay is too soft, exposure to the air will soon dry and harden it sufficiently ; if any lump should be a trifle too hard, two or three holes may be made in it with the finger and filled with water, and a wet cloth wrapped round it. This will soften it in a few hours ; but if clay should be

much too hard, the better plan is to break it up in small pieces, soak it for a time in water, and then beat it up again as at first. In no other way can it be brought to that regular consistency of softness which is essential to proper modelling.

Clay Bin

Some arrangement is necessary for keeping the clay moist. If the modeller uses a large quantity of clay, he should have a bin made of stout boards, lined with zinc soldered together at the corners, and having a tightly fitting lid. For work on a smaller scale, a glazed earthenware pan with a lid answers the purpose admirably. A red clay pan known as a " bread pan," capable of holding enough clay for a bust, is sold at earthenware shops for about two shillings. Provided the lid fits well, a very little water in the bottom of the bin or pan will keep the clay in proper working order for months.

Working Up Dry Clay

Clay that has been allowed to become perfectly dry can be soaked again with water, but it will then crumble down to a kind of mud, which will seem for the time to have lost its cohesive properties. It will need drying to some extent, and after that it will need quite as much beating and tempering as at first. It is, therefore, better not to allow clay to get quite dry, if it can be kept moist by any means.

Re=using Clay from Plaster Moulds

It has already been pointed out that clay is not only none the worse, but decidedly the better, for having been used. The tempering it receives in use makes it work more smoothly and freely than new clay. When dug from a mould—in the process of making a plaster cast of the clay model—however, it will not be fit for immediate use, because it will be too hard. The best way of treating it is at once to break it up into pieces of about the size of walnuts and put water to it. After due time for soaking, it will need beating up again, but it will want less tempering and work better than if t had been allowed to get quite dry. In the process of casting, lumps and chips of plaster are sure to have found their way into it; these should be carefully picked out.

Keeping the Clay Model Wet

With regard to the management of the clay forming the actual model, the necessity for keeping it wet has already been spoken of; though, at the first building up, the clay model needs rather drying than damping, and has to be left uncovered for some hours in order that it may set. But in the later stages wet cloths have to be kept over it, except during the time that the modeller is at work; and should this be for long periods, a moistening now and then will be desirable. For throwing water over a model, some sculptors use a syringe having a rose pierced with minute holes. A toilet syringe or scent sprayer would give a finer spray. For busts and small works the sprinkling can often best be done with the mouth. The plan is to fill the mouth with water, and blow it out through a small opening at the middle of the lips; the knack of doing this is easily acquired. The clay work before being left should be wrapped in wet cloths. In the earlier stages it matters little what these cloths may be, or how they are put on; but as the work proceeds, tolerably fine calico is put nearest to the clay, and thick, coarse wraps outside. As more delicate work is put in, and the surface receives greater finish, the model must not be touched by any cloth whatever. The ordinary plan is to stick wooden skewers into those parts where there is no delicate modelling to be injured. These skewers keep the cloth away from the clay: spots are always to be found where the skewers will do no harm; and the holes made by them are easily stopped before casting. A better and safer plan than the use of skewers is to surround the model with a regular frame of woodwork or wire made to fit over the model. Wood is better for such a frame than metal; for when exposed, as it must be, to constant damp, iron wire rusts and iron-moulds the cloths, and copper gets green and poisonous. For busts and the like, a large frame covered with oil-cloth to put over the inner wrappings is an excellent thing; and, thus protected, the model may be kept in good working order for months, and even for years. Another way in which models in relief may be kept damp is by working them on a background of plaster; but this is only applicable to medallions and other small articles which are raised but little from the background. The plaster is soaked in water, and the highly porous nature of the material enables it to take up a great deal of this, and the clay will suck in enough to keep it sufficiently moist for a reasonable time without wet wraps. A minor point in connection with the keeping of claywork models is that of avoiding fungoid growths. To this end it is well that wherever wooden

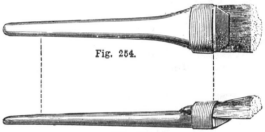

Fig. 254.

Fig. 255.

Figs. 254 and 255.—Brush for Levelling Modelled Drapery.

supports are used in the clay they should be of pine or deal. These resinous woods do not encourage the growth of fungus as do elm and most other woods.

Starting Clay Modelling

Some simple piece of ornament often serves for the first lessons in modelling, but the best teachers usually start with the human figure. In mere ornament, comparatively little can be done without tools, whereas it is important that the beginner should learn to model as much as possible with his thumbs, and it will be in some portion of the human figure that he will find those large forms and broad surfaces which will give freest scope for their use. Early practice, therefore, should be chiefly from the figure, even though the student may aim ultimately to become a modeller of ornament. Casts are best for the learner to copy from. They are rigid, and therefore do not change and perplex the modeller as does the living subject. Also the lights and shadows on them are clear and decided, which is a great point, for it must be remembered that it is wholly through the shadows cast by it that the modeller is able to recognise and reproduce form.

Modelling Part of Colossal Statue

Sculptured figures that are of a size only slightly larger than life-size are termed " heroic " ; but if they greatly exceed life-size, they are termed " colossal." The beginner should start by attempting some portion of a colossal statue. A cast of the hand, or foot, or mask (that is, merely the face) of such a statue should be got and copied in clay as closely as possible, callipers and compasses being used to get all dimensions correct. Place the cast as near as is convenient, and on a level with the top of the modelling stool ; then proceed to build up the model in clay. For a foundation, place a piece of board or slate on the stool. Taking a lump of the prepared clay about the size of a couple of fingers, slightly roll it between the hands to form a rude cylinder, and lay it where the middle of the model is to be. With the thumb press it down closely to the board beneath, which should have been previously damped. Then take another roll of clay, and lay it beside the first, and by drawing the thumb along it so work it down as to make it adhere closely to that already laid. Do this firmly and quickly with a single motion of the thumb. The clay forming a model should be made into one compact mass, without air spaces left within it, as these would probably cause future trouble, the air being gradually pressed out and the clay sinking in, thus causing depressions on the surface. Continue to add rolls of clay, and work them down till the model is built up to a suitable bulk. Do this almost entirely with the hands, only using a large roughing-out tool occasionally. The tool shown by Fig. 232 (p. 107) will be found of most service. When clay is thus first put together it is highly plastic, and yields readily to every touch ; it may easily be bent, moved, or altered, and in a

model like the present of no great size it is therefore desirable to complete the roughing-out in the first day's work. It is not easy to make considerable alterations when the clay has stiffened and set, though the firmer state is necessary for the putting in of details and for finish. In roughing-out the model there is a temptation to make the masses unnecessarily large, and to cut them to shape with tools. As far as possible this should be avoided. It is among the advantages of the modeller's art that he can freely add to, take from, or alter any part at pleasure, but the proper method is to build up and not to cut away, and this is the means of attaining a good style of modelling. When roughing-out, with a view to the additions to be made when finishing, keep everything somewhat smaller, and especially somewhat narrower, than the cast, and make angles and planes instead of curves and rounded surfaces serve to represent the forms of the cast, leaving these to be softened into curvatures later. In modelling, as in drawing, the most masterly roughing-out is always angular. In a few hours a small mass of clay will be sufficiently stiff for the more minute work. Now the clay has to be laid on in much smaller pieces ; as the work proceeds, with the thumb and finger roll these into little pellets, so as thoroughly to temper the clay, and make it work quite smoothly. Proceeding in this way, gradually reproduce upon the model every form seen in the plaster cast. Occasionally alter the position of both cast and model, so as to see them under different lights ; for if it is seen in one light only it is easy to be deceived as to a delicate form. It is better to work by turns all over the model, and to keep every part fairly equally advanced, than to work on any one part and advance it to the neglect of the rest ; it is thus only that the modeller can see whether his work generally is progressing properly. In the anxiety to see the effect, there is a temptation to build up particular parts too hastily, without blending and working down the clay properly. In modelling flesh it is quite possible to give a good finished surface in the broader parts with the thumb alone, but in the smaller parts, for which the thumb is too large, it will be necessary to use tools for shaping and smoothing. The broad flesh surfaces will be difficult to produce as the first work approaches its finish. Instead of being even and regular, they will have hills and hollows where smoothness ought to be. This will result from a want of firmness in modelling with the thumb, a fault which can only be corrected by practice. A passable surface can be produced by mechanical means, but it is better for the beginner to practise and so get good firm surfaces with his thumb, for thus only can the more delicate curvatures be expressed with due tenderness, and thus only will he be able to attain what is called " feeling " in his modelling. When the work is well advanced, look over it again and again with care, and probably many parts will be found capable of improvement. High finish may not be of great importance in a first effort, but it should be remembered that every part ought to be well finished in the clay, and nothing left to be done in the plaster.

Round and Relief Models

Modelled work is either in the round or in relief. The round is not attached to a background, and includes busts, etc. ; whilst whatever is attached to a background, however slightly, is included under the head of relief. Reliefs are of three kinds—low relief (sometimes called basrelief), in which the work has no undercutting and lies flat upon the background ; middle relief, in which the work is somewhat more raised, and in which there is some amount of under-cutting ; and high relief, in which the figures, etc., often stand out so boldly from the background as to be almost detached from it. Works in the round demand most skill and care, because they ought to appear satisfactory from whatever point of view they may be looked at ; whereas a work in relief is supposed to be looked at from one point of view only —namely, from the front. The merely mechanical difficulties of modelling a figure in the round are also much greater than those of modelling a work in relief. Hence those who are learning modelling usually do much more work in relief than in the round.

Modelling in Relief

A study in relief will now be discussed. The bust of that well-known statue the Apollo Belvedere (Fig. 256) affords good practice, as the modelling in it is large and grand, and has much beauty and expression to make it interesting. Though it is in the round, a study in relief can be made from it ; the one about to be described will be a profile view, of the size of the original, but in somewhat low relief. The head is about 12 in. high and 10 in. across, so that, allowing for that portion of the bust which it will be desirable to show, the

Fig. 256.—Apollo Belvedere Statue.

background must not be less than 24 in. by 18 in. The best background is a slab of clay supported on a board or slate. Slate is heavy, but it does not warp ; the clay model is less easily secured to it, and may be liable to slip off should it get too dry. Therefore, a modelling board is more commonly used ; it will need cross-clamps or ledgers to keep it from warping, and a projection along the bottom in front, to support the clay. Fig. 257 shows a modelling board in section. Such a board stands better if the screws which fasten on the ledgers are driven through slots rather than round holes, so as to allow freedom for swelling and shrinking of the wood. This board may be used on a modelling stool like Fig. 228 (p. 105), or on an ordinary easel of moderate strength. A slab of clay about an inch thick will be necessary. Damp the board to cause the clay to stick, and in making the slab take care not to leave air holes, or by-and-by the surface will become uneven; a similar result will also be caused if the clay used is not well tempered and is softer in some parts than others. When sufficient clay has been laid on, smooth it with a modeller's straight-edge. One about 12 in. long by 2 in. broad,

Fig. 257.—Modelling Board for Relief.

made of boxwood, and toothed in the same manner as the roughing-out tools, is useful for this and similar purposes. A slab to be pleasant to work upon should always have a toothed face. The slab is left uncovered for some twenty-four hours, that it may set; then it will need again working over with the straightedge, and making quite level and true. The outline of the relief can now be drawn in with the rounded end of the tool shown by Figs. 239 and 240

(p. 107). Upon the clay slab draw as with a stick of charcoal on paper, any false stroke being obliterated by finger or tool, taking care to make the outline correct in all essentials, as this will save much future labour. It should be determined how far the relief is to project. Then within the outline lay on clay in larger or smaller pieces, according to the bulk required in any particular part, and work it down with the thumbs. In this case the projection might be about 2 in., and, in building up, take care to keep the highest parts somewhat lower than this, for they are sure to grow higher as the work proceeds. All forms are to be represented much flatter than they are in the cast, and some attention will be necessary to give to each its proper relative amount of projection. An unpractised eye is often deceived on this point, and it will be found necessary to look frequently at the cast at right angles to the surface, and to use a plummet. In roughing-out, remember to sketch mainly in straight lines and angles. The different slightly rounded surfaces will be represented by planes, and much attention will be given to making all these planes at such inclinations as are relatively correct. By looking well to these matters in the early stages, much future labour, and many after alterations and corrections which involve the destruction of elaborate work, may be avoided. Keep everything large and broad, and at present make no attempt to represent details which detract from breadth—such, for instance, as eyelids; but judiciously indicate the main features in their correct positions, and so obtain a general resemblance to the cast. It is this sketching out of a model which chiefly demands the worker's energies, his powers of perception, his judgment, and his dexterous handling of the plastic material. The finishing may be taken far more leisurely.

The Lighting.—The lighting of the cast and model is important. The light should fall upon both of them from the same direction. Some studios have sky-lights, and under the light so thrown forms are strongly brought out, but the work thus lighted does not look so well when taken, as it generally must be, into a less forcing light.

Perhaps the best light is one which falls obliquely from above at an angle of about 45°, and the most approved arrangement for studios is to have a high window above the level of the head and open towards the north. The north aspect is desirable as admitting no sunshine. A strong artificial light is even better than daylight for modelling from the cast, since it throws more decided shadows.

Advantages of Clay Background.—As the relief advances, the advantages of the clay background over one of plaster or bare slate will be made apparent. Reliefs of moderate size like the present are best laid flat when work is over and they have to be damped for the night, and most of the skewers which support the wet cloths can be stuck into the slab rather than into the work; besides, by adding considerably to the bulk of clay, it allows the figure to be kept in a state of more regular moisture than would otherwise be possible. Other advantages are purely artistic, though these are less apparent in a tolerably bold relief like the present than in one of greater delicacy. One of these is the more tender outline of which this ground admits. A hard continuous outline has a crude effect in low relief, and a clay background allows it to be softened and almost blended with the slab in parts, which could not be done were the ground of another and a hard material. Again, much labour may be saved at times, when the ground is of clay, by sinking it a little so as to bring in some receding form. Moreover, in very delicate work the parts are less likely to be brought into proper harmony when the eye is disturbed by difference of colour in figures and background. Other conditions regulate the modelling of mere ornament in low relief. It is perhaps necessary in the majority of cases that this should be upon a curved ground; and to keep such a ground true through the operations of modelling may be a difficult matter if it is in a material so yielding as clay. Often therefore in ornamental work it is better to model the ground roughly in clay, to cast it in plaster, and in that material to bring it to its proper form and level. In the case of a curved surface, this is more readily done in the firmer material

than in the clay. For ornament the outline will rarely be too firm or decided. The adhesion between clay and plaster is not strong, and the former is likely to peel from the latter if the work is not kept regularly damped.

Final Hints on Relief Modelling.—The broad flesh surfaces which the Apollo figure offers will give admirable practice for finishing with the thumb, though, of course, the outline and more intricate parts of the features will need tools. The hair will be all tool-work. In working from nature, hair is a difficult thing to treat; but here, as in the antique generally, it is conventional and simple. A little drapery is thrown across the bust; and in finishing this, a flat wire tool, such as is shown by Fig. 252 (p. 109), will be found most serviceable. For further practice in relief, whole antique figures or groups of figures, modelled to perhaps a third of their original size, are usual subjects. Of these, simple figures in high relief are the most easy, and groups in quite low relief demand the most skill. In choosing a view of any statue or group for this purpose, some judgment is needed; it should be one in which the lines compose gracefully; and if they can be to a great extent in one plane, so much the better. It is not well to have a leg or arm projecting straight out towards the spectator; it is difficult to foreshorten such limbs, and they always look awkward. After all care taken in sketching, it will sometimes be found, as a work of this kind progresses, that an arm, a leg, or a head is not just in the right place. It is far easier to correct such an error in modelling than in drawing. All that has to be done is to cut the part from the background with a wire or string, and move it to its proper position. Or the part may have been modelled in a relief relatively too high or too low; if the latter, it is easy to detach it from the ground with the wire, and by putting clay under it to raise it to its proper height; if the former, a slice can be cut from under it, and the relief thus lowered as required.

Modelling Ornament

Mouldings.—In modelling ornament, the first stages may consist in attempting some simple moulding as shown at Figs. 258 and 259. All that is required by way of an outfit is a board, some modelling clay, and two or three boxwood tools. In the

parts at right angles to the board as shown at Fig. 260. The next thing to do is to fill up the angle thus formed by adding clay till it has assumed the appearance

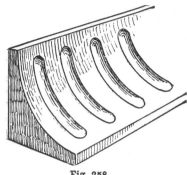

Fig. 258.

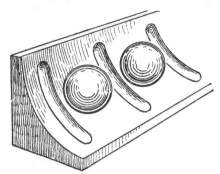

Fig. 259.

Figs. 258 and 259.—Modelled Ornamental Mouldings.

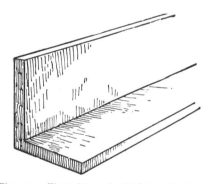

Fig. 260.—First Stage in Making Moulding.

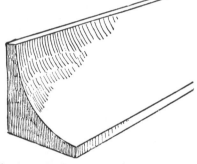

Fig. 261.—Angle of Moulding filled in with Clay.

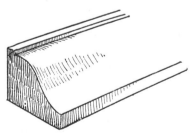

Fig. 262.—Modelled Plain Moulding.

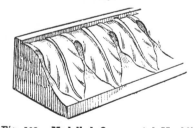

Fig. 263.—Modelled Ornamental Moulding.

earlier of the examples given here, on tools of any sort besides thumb and finger need be used. The moulding (Fig. 258) may be begun by laying out on the board a bat or slab of clay to a depth of, say, 2 in. Cut this bat in two and set up one of the

of Fig. 261. Do this very carefully, and try to avoid having to carve or cut any clay; for the great rule in modelling is to build up as much as possible, and carve or cut away as little as possible. If, on the moulding now formed, equal distances of, say, 1 in. be marked off and the finger pressed along these marks, a design like Fig. 258 will be made. This may be further elaborated by making little balls and adding these as shown at Fig. 259. Indeed, there are many mouldings that may be taken as early exercises in modelling. Take a moulding like Fig. 262, and ornament it with a leaf similar to that shown at Fig. 263. Of course, in actual work no

be used, but in the present examples the idea has been to give exercises as a training in using the fingers only. If the ornament is modelled on the bare board, it will be necessary first of all to wet the board in order that the clay may stick to it. It is much better, however, to lay out a bed of clay an inch or so in depth, and, if smoothed and levelled, this is much better to work, or because the modelled ornament will remain

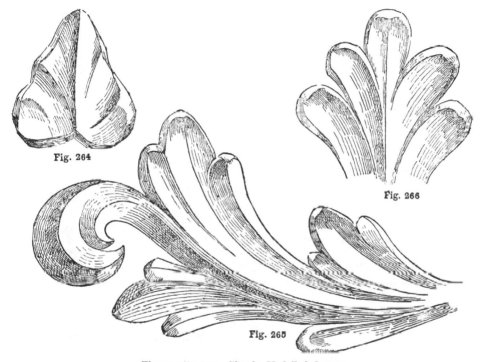

Fig. 264

Fig. 266

Fig. 265

Figs. 264 to 266.—Simple Modelled Leaves.

attempt would be made to model each leaf, since all are alike. What is done is, after having modelled the first leaf, to make a mould by simply pouring a little plaster-of-Paris over it. Into this mould clay is pressed and an impression taken of the leaf, which is then stuck on the moulding. This is repeated till as many have been added as are required.

Leaves.—An attempt will be made to explain the method of handling the clay in making leaves like Figs. 264 to 266. In more intricate work, tools of some sort must

longer moist and pliable, and is much less apt to dry and crack. In modelling a leaf like Fig. 265, make a start by rolling between the hands a piece of clay, and lay this out in the direction the leaf is lying, as at Fig. 267. This really constitutes the centre rib of the leaf, all details being added and made to flow into this line. If a pinch of clay is next taken and rolled between the finger and thumb, with a little pressure it will be made to adhere to the finger as shown at Fig. 268. This little piece of clay is then placed in position on the ornament; and if the hand is then drawn with a sweep along the direction of the main stem, as shown at Fig. 269, the tip of this part of the leaf will be formed. Do the same with the other parts, drawing the hand along in the direction of the curve of the ornament (Fig. 270). This is again illustrated at Fig. 271, where the hollow part of the leaf is simply made by the pressure of the thumb. The different stages shown at Figs. 267, 269, and 270 are given to show that the general method is to work from the centre outwards. It will be found advisable to have a wet sponge at hand to moisten the fingers so that they may be drawn smoothly along the curves of the design. Do not attempt to polish the work or make it too smooth; this serves no good purpose, besides being unnecessary and liable to destroy the finer markings.

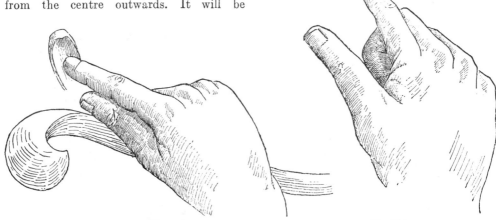

Fig. 269.   Fig. 268

Figs. 268 and 269.—Method of Modelling Tip of Leaf.

Fig. 267.—First Stage in Modelling Leaf.

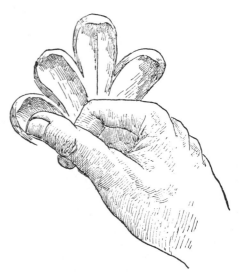

Fig. 270.—Part of Modelled Leaf.

Fig. 271.—Method of Modelling Leaf.

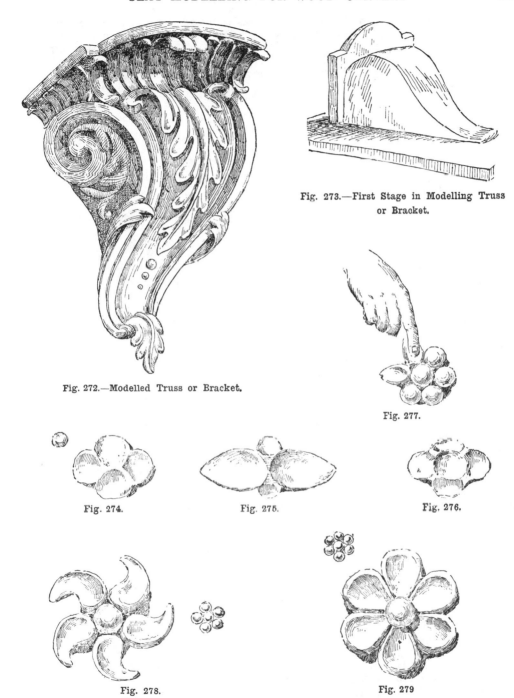

Fig. 273.—First Stage in Modelling Truss or Bracket.

Fig. 272.—Modelled Truss or Bracket.

Fig. 277.

Fig. 274.

Fig. 275.

Fig. 276.

Fig. 278.

Fig. 279

Figs. 274 to 279.—Modelling Exercises with Balls.

Truss or Bracket.—Up to this stage in the modelling of ornament, only details have been attempted; the next thing might be to try a complete design, and the illustration (Fig. 272) of a truss or bracket may serve as a fairly good exercise

These are made by laying on a roll of clay, squaring and finishing as may seem most convenient. This will give the principal contour of the bracket. The front is the next part done. The shape of this is such that it may be modelled entirely without

Fig. 280.—Modelled Wing.   Fig. 281.—Early Stage in Modelling Wing.

without necessitating any special knowledge of ornament, as would be the case in designing a pilaster. It would be better, however, before anything original were attempted, that some experience had been gained in copying from casts of ornament, as this will give practice in noting the variety of relief and light and shade, the principal elements which go to make up a successful design in modelling. As to the truss, a rough mass of clay must first be laid out, giving an approximate idea of the eventual shape. This is shown at Fig. 273, and on this groundwork the ornament has to be modelled. It is better to allow this basis to become fairly firm and stiff before beginning the design. The slab on the top is best made by making a sheet of plaster-of-Paris of the required thickness, and sawing this to the desired shape. The plaster is easier and quicker to shape than

the aid of tools, as the forms of the grooves may be made by simply pressing with the finger in the manner shown at Fig. 269. Next add the details underneath the top. These also may be made by using the fingers only, though it may be found necessary to use a flat tool here and there to trim them up. The large leaf at the top and the small one at the bottom are now done. Both these leaves are somewhat similar in character to Fig. 265, and may be modelled in the same way. No further difficulty should be experienced in finishing the bracket; any details too small to finish with fingers alone must be done by using suitable tools.

Elementary Ornament. — The exercises about to be given are elementary, and partake to a great extent of the nature of drill forms. The clay must be in such condition that it can be handled plea-

Fig. 282.—Modelled Bird.

wood, and the reason why this part is not modelled in clay is simply that, as it is of a rigid and severe outline, there would not be the same likelihood of getting it accurate as when made in the manner indicated. The spirals on each side may be done first.

santly and freely. If too soft, it will stick to the fingers; if too stiff, its plasticity is partly gone, and it will more readily dry and harden with handling, the bench soon becoming covered with little crumbs of clay. To work the examples, roll a pinch

Fig. 283.—Example of Modelled Rococo Ornament.

Fig. 288.—Modelled Ornamental Scroll.

Fig. 285.

Fig. 284.

Figs. 284 and 285.—Two Examples of Modelled Rococo Ornament.

Fig. 289.—Modelled Ornament worked with Tools.

Fig. 287.—Method of Modelling Scroll.

Fig. 286.—Modelled Scroll.

of clay between the fingers and thumb, making it as spherical as possible. Form groups of two or more, endeavouring to get them as nearly of the same size as possible. Figs. 274 to 279 show various numbers of balls placed side by side, and also how, simply by pressing with the finger, the balls may be made to assume different shapes. For the wing (Fig. 280), make a roll of clay 3 in. or 4 in. long and lay it out on a board. Flatten one side, as in Fig. 281, by drawing the finger along it. Do the same with the other long feathers, and add the shorter ones afterwards. Form the general shape of the wing first, and notice that the tips of the feathers are much lower in relief than the quill end; therefore begin by roughly suggesting this relief (Fig. 281). Next a bird, without much detail (Fig. 282), may be attempted. Examples of rococo ornament are given by Figs. 283 to 285. The chief characteristics of this style are lack of balance, either as a whole or a part; but however doubtful rococo may be as a style of ornament, it certainly yields admirable exercises leading towards freedom in plastic art. In working, the general shape of the figure may be roughly sketched in, the details being the outcome of the vagary of the modeller. The exercises in ornament treated so far may be almost entirely executed by thumb and fingers, but those shown by Figs. 286 to 290 necessitate the use of tools. The particular tool to be used will depend on the shape of the work. Thus, for the scrolls shown at F.gs. 286 and 287, after making a roll of clay and pulling it into shape on the board with the fingers, a flat tool will be all that is required to finish the work. A cartouche, or scrolled shield, is given at Fig. 290; the general shape and relief of the ornament must first be set out, and the rest of the work almost entirely done by tools. This design should be worked on a thick bat of clay spread over the board. The sunk parts may then be raked out with a wire tool.

Modelling the Human Figure from the Antique

When copying a bust or other work in the round, it is well that both cast and model should be on turntables, that all sides of them may be readily brought under the eye, and that both shall be on the same level. The bust frame (see p. 125) is damped, and the clay built up around it. It must not be thought that in putting together a comparatively large mass it does not matter whether the clay is well tempered or otherwise, or whether the building up is or is not done methodically. All clay shrinks as it becomes drier, and in badly tempered clay the soft parts shrink more than the hard, and produce a lumpy and irregular surface. Roughing-out a bust, though only from the antique, is highly interesting work. The modeller needs to discern clearly the characteristic points of his original, so as to get resemblance by the disposal of his great masses only. This he ought to be able to do quickly; and all the leading features may be expressed by a few effective touches. The thumbs pressed deeply into what will afterwards be the inner corners of the eyes, and then drawn outwards, marking the line of the eyebrows, will at once give a human look to the upper part of the face. Make a deep, somewhat crescent-shaped indentation at the opening of the ear, and an oblique line drawn with the thumb-nail, to mark its hinder limit. A few sharp incisions of the tool indicate hair where it falls upon the flesh. The position of the mouth, and something of its expression, are given by a slight depression at each of its angles, and drawing the thumb downwards from them. In this stage, an ingenious modeller can throw a vast amount of resemblance into his copy with marvellously little labour; and it is well that the learner should practise the means of doing this. It at once gives interest to his work, and facilitates after-labour. Although in some respects it is more difficult to copy in the round than in relief, the worker has this advantage— he can now take measurements in all directions. This should be done freely, but in an intelligent manner—that is, the dimensions of each form should first be judged by the eye, and afterwards tested by the callipers. The eye is thus trained to accuracy, and will after a time become so exact that scarcely any measurements will be needed. It is well to acquire this habit before working from the life, for a frequent application of the callipers is not pleasing to sitters for portraits. In working up the forms of the more intricate features—such as the eye and mouth— the main part of the work will have to be done with tools; but in life-sized work the eyeball is best formed by the thumb. The upper eyelid cannot be completed without the tool, and it plays so important a part in the expression o the face that form should be given to it at a comparatively early stage. The lower eyelid is rarely put in till later. This, in an unfinished state, takes off from breadth of effect in a painful

with a fine moist sponge blends all together and makes a good surface. For small work a scrap of sponge tied to a bit of stick is useful for parts which cannot be reached with the fingers. The mechanical plan of producing a presentable surface on flesh, etc., has already been mentioned. The

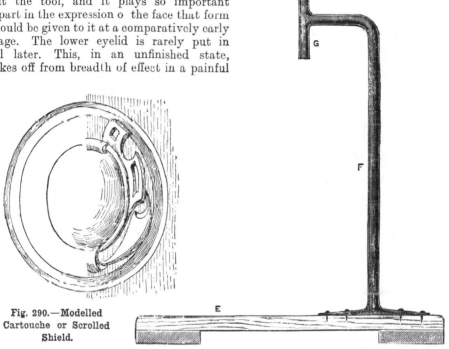

Fig. 290.—Modelled Cartouche or Scrolled Shield.

Fig. 291.—Support for Modelled Statuette.

manner, and, to keep it from being offensive, needs a great deal of softening down. It may be well to see how this is done. In large forms, where the thumbs can work freely, softness seems to come naturally; but in less accessible parts the harsh marks left by tools have to be removed in order to give finish. Working across any line —say, as this of the eyelid—with a fine tool and a light touch, will do much. Sometimes a painter's hog-tool, with the bristles cut rather short, is used, it being first dipped into water. In delicate matters, a sable brush, also cut short, may be used instead of, or after, the hog-tool; and a final dabbing

modeller wraps a piece of cotton stocking material tightly and smoothly over his thumb, with the ribs running across it, and, having damped it, works it firmly but lightly over his surface. The ribs to a slight degree cut into the clay and reduce it to smoothness, and this, with an after-dabbing with the sponge, produces a good finish. Those who are learning modelling rarely copy a whole life-sized statue in the dimensions of the original. The great quantity of clay required, and the cost and difficulty of providing sufficient support, deter them from doing so. For the purposes of study, it is held sufficient to copy some of the antique statues on a smaller scale—that is, to reproduce them as statuettes. In Fig. 291 is shown a section of a frame for the support of a standing figure about 2 ft. high. To any unusual attitude the frame must, of course, be specially adapted. The figure stands on the board E, and strongly screwed to this, near one end, is the upright bar of iron F; this is bent near its upper end, that it may enter the figure at the small of the back. At its termination is the shank G, which will occupy the centre of the lower part of the body. When this frame is prepared for use, three pieces of gas-piping will be bound with copper wire to this shank. Two of these will descend to the board below, and will be arranged to run down the middles of the legs; their upper ends, after being carried straight upwards to the height of the shoulders, will branch off, to support the arms; and the third pipe will run up to the centre of the head, and will be tightly bound to the arm-pipes for so far as it keeps company with them; and to its top some cross-bits of wood will be wired, for the better support of the clay forming the head. The clay will hold more firmly to the pipes generally if wires are wound spirally round them. For figures of moderate size, lead or "compo" gas-piping admirably serves the purpose of skeletons; for whilst strong enough to bear the weight of the clay, it admits of being freely bent in any direction. It is not easy to give the proper pose and action to a figure in the round, or to make it balance so as to give the idea of standing securely. The plummet will be freely used, and the pieces of gas-piping will have to be bent and re-bent many times. If figures of this kind have to be kept long in the clay it is desirable to have an oilcloth-covered frame to fit over and keep them moist. Nothing more than what has been said already need be observed with regard to copying from the antique. Such copying, though pleasant and interesting work, is, of course, but a means to an end. Those who do it are generally only seeking to fit themselves for dealing with portraits, or for expressing the inventions of their own imaginations in ideal sculpture.

Modelling from the Life

In modelling from the life, two things are apt to bother the beginner—the forms before him are constantly changing, more or less, and colour (which was absent in the cast) is apt to mislead him as to the real nature of form. It is therefore well that he should not come to this work till eye and hand have been somewhat practised. Modelling from a living person is far harder and more exhaustive work than mere copying from a cast. Living flesh and bone cannot retain the same pose for an unlimited period as a lump of plaster does; and the modeller, knowing this, has to put forth all his energies to make the best use of his time. With the strain put upon brain and eye and nerve, he tires before long. The sitter, too, grows weary, and falls into attitudes or assumes an expression which it is not desirable to copy. Hence it is generally allowed that, whether for the purposes of portrait or for mere study, the length of a sitting ought not to be more than about two hours. Half a dozen such sittings will commonly suffice for a medallion portrait, and frequently for a bust. By this, it is not intended to be implied that such a portrait should be modelled in twelve hours—far from it, for much must be done between sittings, in completing what has then only been roughly sketched. Photographs may also be made use of in off-times; and after the sittings are over, much finishing will be required to fit the model for casting in plaster.

Medallions Modelled from the Life.—With the general public, perhaps, the most popular form of portrait sculpture is the medallion. It is a favourite with modellers —it does not offer technical difficulties. it can be modelled in an ordinary room. and it can be easily and safely cast. A medallion looks best on a flat circular ground, with the head in profile and some where about 4 in. high, and with a projection of perhaps some $\frac{3}{4}$ in. For such a head, with so much of the bust as it is necessary to show, a background of some 14 in. in diameter suffices. Medallions in which the head is mor than 5 in. high, but less than life-size, are rarely satisfactory. Life-sized medallions in middle relief are better suited for large galleries and monumental purposes than for ordinary rooms, in which they are apt to look clumsy; whilst in very low relief, and especially on concave grounds, they are best adapted for decorative purposes, and are far more difficult to manage than when in the style recommended. Most modellers find that they can model a profile with greatest facility when it looks to the spectator's left, but it is not well to fall into the mannerism of working from one side of the face only. Practice should be made from both sides—a pair of medallions should look towards each other. For reasons already discussed, a clay ground is to be preferred if the medallion is to be of the kind and size indicated. It is well to form a square slab on the modelling-board of greater breadth than the proposed diameter. The modeller will not then be obliged to waste time in bringing the head scrupulously to the centre. Striking a circle round the head, and leaving a proper space on every side, can be far more easily arranged in the process of casting. A small medallion like the present is best modelled on an easel, which will permit of its being readily raised and lowered. The sitter should be placed for the light to fall somewhat from above and somewhat from behind him; this will best bring out the features. The model should be placed in much the same light, with the back of the head towards the window; but as the work goes on, the easel will need turning occasionally to different lights so as to correct errors. A delicate and conscientious finish is very necessary. In a female head, especially, all harsh and crude modelling is to be avoided; slightly lower relief than in the male subject is also desirable; and what has been said on softness of outline in low reliefs ought particularly to be borne in mind. The male head calls for more vigorous and decided work. The exact flow of the curved line in which a medallion portrait usually terminates a little below the neck is very much a matter of fancy, though some hold that by the management of its curves may be indicated whether the sitter is stout or thin.

Modelling Life-size Portrait Bust

A more serious undertaking than any yet described is the modelling of a life-size portrait bust, and one for which such simple arrangements as the above will scarcely serve. It will take somewhere about half a hundredweight of clay, and will need a strong frame. Figs. 292 and 293 show elevation and section of a good and simple frame for the purpose. The flat bottom board A, say 15 in. by 11 in., is braced together by two ledgers to prevent warping. B is an upright of sufficient height to reach to about the centre of the head; a tenon at the bottom of this upright passes through a mortice in the middle of A, where a wedge C, removable at pleasure, tightens and secures it. Through a second mortice near the top of the upright passes the short and tapered cross-arm D, also removable. On this arm will chiefly rest the weight of the head. The cross-arm and upright are made easy of removal from their places, to facilitate taking the clay from the mould in the process of casting. Wood has an advantage over iron, as forming the support of a bust, in this respect—that if through alterations in the model in course of the work any part of the frame should become exposed, that part may be easily cut away. Lead piping is very often used for the upright, wood being better for modelling a bust from the antique in which the position of the head is absolutely settled beforehand. Many modellers prefer a frame with only a short upright of iron or wood which does not reach to the neck, and to which is tied such a strength of gas-piping as will bear the weight of the head. The object of this is to allow of the head being turned and its position readjusted, if desired, up to a comparatively late stage of the work. The "pose," to use the technical term, of the head is always a matter of great importance in a bust. The way of carrying the head—whether erect, stooped, or inclined to either side—is often highly characteristic of the individual, and must be reproduced if the bust is to be a striking likeness. The flexible support gives special facilities for doing this. The modeller ought, however, to be able to satisfy himself on this point during his first sitting, whilst his clay can still be moved freely on the wooden upright. Fig. 294 shows a general form of bust frame. This consists of a wooden upright with a cross-bar fixed to a board, and it will be found a convenience if this upright is so arranged as to be easily detached. This may be managed by some such method as that

difficulty in getting the soft clay to remain in position. It is therefore advisable to build up the core of the figure with as stiff clay as possible, as being less liable to sink or settle. The base or plinth of the bust is not usually modelled unless some particular or fantastic design is required. This part of the work, whether square or round, is made separately of plaster-of-Paris, and separately moulded and cast. As objects

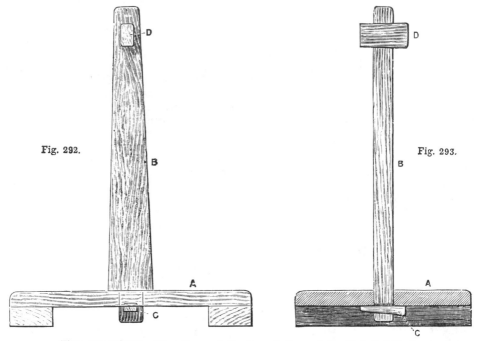

Figs. 292 and 293.—Elevation and Section of Support for Modelled Bust.

shown in Fig. 294. This upright should not rise much, if at all, above the level of the neck, as it would then render the head immovable and prevent any change of the pose. In order that any alteration may be effected, a piece of lead piping is used as shown in Fig. 294. The lead is strong and flexible, and may readily be bent in any direction. Fig. 294 shows the armature required for a bust; the wire, with two small pieces of wood attached—called a " butterfly "—is sometimes added as a support for the chin. Even with the aid of the wooden upright and lead pipe, it may be found that, at first, there is some

in the " round," like a bust, have to be viewed from every point, both back and front, a modelling stand on which the model may be turned about is a great convenience. When a bust has to be modelled in an ordinary room, the best position for the modelling stool is facing a tolerably lofty window, the lower half of which has been darkened by shutters or a thick blind. The sitter is placed in a chair beside the stool, with his head on a level with that of the model; the head also of the modeller, as he stands at his work, should be on the same level. The turntable, moving freely round, allows all parts of the work to be brought readily beneath the eye and hands of the operator; and in the later stages, when mere finish is being put in, the modeller, if so inclined, sits to his work: but not in the earlier ones, and never when the sitter is present. Whilst he is busied with those manipulations on which the vigour, likeness, and expression of his portrait depend, all his faculties of eye and hand must be exerted to the uttermost; he needs to be frequently stepping backwards and forwards to judge the effect of what is done, or to observe the forms which he sees in his sitter from new points of view, and for these things a standing attitude is indispensable. It is usual to build up a bust roughly two or three days before the first sitting, making it resemble more a barber's block than anything human. It ought, however, to be carefully and regularly put together; air holes should not be left in it, and there should be no hard lumps in the clay. The cross-arm of the frame will be embedded in the middle of the mass representing the head; the chest portion, standing on a broad base, does not need a cross-arm to support it. Before the first sitting takes place, it is well that the modeller should, if possible, settle in his own mind what the pose of the head shall be. Only in very formal works is it usual to make the face look directly to the front; such an attitude is stiff and inartistic, and the effect is more pleasing if the head is turned a little to the right or left. Most persons have some mannerism, more or less marked, in the way in which they carry their heads; and this characteristic, if it can be caught, adds not a little to the likeness. The clay for the first few days is sufficiently soft to allow of the head being turned between the two hands into any desired position, even on the rigid wooden frame. In the first sitting the general proportions ought to be well massed in, and, however much the modeller may have trained his eye, it is prudent to take two or three of the main measurements with the callipers. He will thus have some certain standard by which to judge minor matters. It is not pleasant if, after several sittings and much labour, he finds that he has made some serious error as to size—too much

width in the head from ear to ear, or too much length from back to face, for instance. Still, there are means of correcting such errors without sacrificing any great amount of work. A clean cut may be made into the head with a wire, and a slice taken out, or in like manner clay may be put in to increase width, etc. Working from the life is a severe strain on the powers of the modeller, whilst, in a different way, the sitter also finds his part wearisome. As has been said, a sitting rarely lasts longer than two hours. Yet, after the sitter has gone, the modeller will find much that he can do, working in a more leisurely

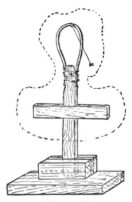

Fig. 294.—General Form of Frame for Modelled Bust.

manner; for those forms which during the sitting have only been roughly put in, can now be completed and smoothed down.

Roughing-In.—At the first sitting the modeller makes it his business broadly to rough-in the main forms without details, and, in doing this, much of the individual character of the head may be secured with little labour. The chief points are indicated by bold touches, and may be briefly recapitulated: The thumbs, pressed deeply into the inner corners of the eyes and drawn outwards along the line of the eyebrows, will impart a human look to the lump of clay. A pressure, sloping obliquely to each side, determines the length of the nose, and a couple of slight indentations mark the corners of the mouth.

The opening of the ear is shown by a deep and somewhat crescent-shaped depression, and the hinder limit of that organ is expressed by an oblique line drawn with the thumbnail. A few deep touches with the end of a tool suffice for the present to give the character of the hair.

Taking Measurements.—In order to ensure correctness of proportion, a few of the most important dimensions should be measured with the callipers—such as the length, breadth, and depth of the head, the width of the shoulders, etc. In the after sittings, when the forms which at first were merely

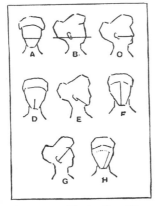

Fig. 295.—Diagrams illustrating Measurement of Sitter's Head for Modelling Purposes.

sketched are elaborated and filled with detail, it may be well to take some minor measurements with the compasses; but, so far as is possible, the eye should be accustomed to judge distances accurately without such help, for frequent measurements are always annoying to the sitter. A suggestion as to how to set about measuring the head is given in Fig. 295 : A, from ear to ear ; B, horizontal line to find level of nose ; C, from each ear to point of nose ; D, from nose to chin ; E, from chin to ear ; F, from chin to root of hair ; G, from ear to root of hair ; H, from chin to eyebrows. Each measurement, as soon as taken, should be marked on the clay model, without any attempt at introducing detail. By employing some such method as this a certain degree of mechanical accuracy

is guaranteed, both in the position of the features and the shape of the head.

Obtaining " Likeness."—All minutiæ or characteristics of a face must be regarded as work to be done after the general form has been massed in. When this is done, the features may be more defined in detail, and any peculiarity noted. In all modelling from the life, a hand looking-glass will be found of great use. The reflection shows up faults which escaped notice when the sitter was looked at in the ordinary way. The power of rapid sketching will be found of especial value when roughing-in a portrait bust. It goes far towards securing a vigorous, as well as a faithful, likeness ; worth consideration also is the greater satisfaction which it enables one to give to the sitter by getting some sort of resemblance early, for sitters are apt to take some disgust at the uncouth and often ridiculous appearance of a bust in its first stages. As noted on p. 124, photographs help in carrying out work that has to be done between sittings. During sittings the modeller has to content himself with roughly getting in what he sees, and most of the smoothing and polishing he leaves till off-times. After the last sitting, also, a great deal of finishing will have to be done before the bust is fit for casting.

Treatment of Hair.—It should be borne in mind that no special parts should be finished to the neglect of others, but that the whole work should be carried forward in its varying degree of completeness. The treatment of the hair is more or less of a conventional nature, and an examination of heads from the antique will show several methods of how this is done. In painting, the different colours of skin and hair are clearly defined, whereas in sculpture of wood or stone, where no colour is used, this effect is arrived at by variety of texture or mass. In modelling, the hair has to be done with tools, and its texture is expressed by curved lines drawn with a tolerably sharp point, more flowing and continuous for smooth, and more abrupt and broken for curly hair. Unless just at the parting line, or on those parts of a female head where it is brushed smooth, hair needs no softening down, but best shows its character by being left crisp from the tool. The little ragged fragments of clay which stick along the edges of the tool marks aid the effect, and should be left untouched. Something even of colour may be indicated in modelling if by bold touches the shadows are kept deep and strong in reproducing dark, and softer markings are used to bespeak light, hair. If the locks are long, wavy, or massive, especially in the male sitter, they should be dealt with whilst the clay is still so plastic as to admit of free and bold handling. If smooth or closely cropped, the hair is better worked upon when the clay is harder. A source of annoyance is, that on the heads of most sitters the arrangement of the hair varies from day to day, so that the work put in at one sitting may at the next be found to be altogether wrong. It is therefore generally best merely to indicate its character in the earlier stages, and to devote a whole sitting to it later on.

Eyes.—The effect of the eyes in the bust is obtained by making a hole to represent the pupil, its depth varying according to the depth of shadow or suggestiveness of colour desired.

Draping a Bust.—The best way of draping a bust is a point which admits of much discussion. The likeness is increased by giving the ordinary dress, but modern costume is generally considered inartistic. Variety and artistic effect can be produced without absurdity by making use of an academic or official robe, if the sitter is entitled to wear one, by a cloak, by a dressing-gown, etc. Sometimes the difficulty is overcome by a mere piece of loose drapery thrown round the figure, this admitting of artistic, if not of specially consistent results. And sometimes an excellent effect is produced, particularly with a male subject, when the bust is of the stiff and formal terminal type, by leaving so much as is given of the chest wholly nude. Sitting for a portrait is an occupation of which people soon grow weary. Few care to give more sittings than are absolutely necessary. The modeller therefore studies to do all that can then be done in the absence of his sitter. If the person's actual dress is to receive artistic treatment, a photograph

of the sitter will serve for this purpose as well as the sitter himself. If a piece of fancy drapery is to be used, a plaid is thrown round a plaster cast or a lay figure, and copied at leisure. Drapery for such a purpose, however, needs to be arranged in good and effective folds, and must not be taken at random. A lay figure, it may be observed, is a life-size doll with movable joints. If academic or other loose robes are employed as drapery on a bust, they are best disposed for modelling from upon such a figure. Drapery on a large scale, though laid in with the thumbs, needs to be shaped and worked up with flat toothed tools, and afterwards roughly levelled with the brush shown half size by Figs. 254 and 255 (p. 111). The bristles cut well into the clay, and make the folds level and uniform; and an amount of finish can afterwards be given by dabbing with the sponge. But only in parts should the drapery have a smooth surface, and it is considered artistic to leave the marks of tool and brush in many places.

Casting Clay Model in Plaster

It may be desirable occasionally to give the model a permanent form by taking a plaster cast of it, an operation which, as usually conducted, involves the destruction of the clay model. Other processes are available, but it is most often convenient to adopt the one above alluded to, this being known as casting by the waste-moulding process. Only the best superfine plaster-of-Paris, especially sold for this purpose, is used. Taking a handful of plaster, sprinkle it into a basin two-thirds full of water. Do this carefully with the hand, so as to detect and lay aside any lumps, etc. The plaster falling on the surface of the water becomes gradually soaked, and sinks, and the sprinkling is continued until, instead of sinking, the plaster begins to stand in a heap above the level of the water. This shows that no more plaster is needed. This is the proper way of mixing plaster; the gradual saturation from below expels the air quietly, without causing bubbles; also, by this method the moulder is able to see when exactly the proper proportion of plaster has been added to the water. The mixture is now beaten up with a spoon. A silver spoon is the least likely to cause discoloration. In beating plaster, put the bowl of the spoon to the bottom of the basin, and by moving it rapidly with a circular motion, and without bringing it to the

Fig. 296.—Edge of Plaster Mould with "Keyholes."

surface, make the mixture thoroughly "boil up." Avoid bringing the spoon-bowl to the surface lest it should carry down air with it and cause bubbles; for air-bubbles must be most carefully avoided. When the plaster is well mixed, skim off and throw aside any bubbles or scum that may have arisen, and the plaster—which is of about the consistency of cream—is ready for use. Assuming that the model is in the round, the mould is best made in two or more pieces. Where the line of separation between these pieces may best come must depend on the pose of the figure, but generally the mould will be formed in front and back halves. Make a parting along the line of separation with slips of zinc an inch wide, by sticking their edges into the clay of the model. Say that the back half of the mould is first made. Throw the mixed plaster over the model, as far as the zinc parting wall, with the hand or a spoon till a thickness of $\frac{1}{4}$ in. is reached. It is well to tinge the water with which the plaster for this inner mould is mixed with some colouring matter—say ink. Wait five minutes for the plaster to set, then brush it over with a mixture of clay and water as thick as pea soup. This is to cause this inner mould to separate from the outer one when required. Then mix plaster for the outer mould with clean water, and throw it over the inner mould to a depth of $\frac{3}{4}$ in., embedding in it pieces of bent thin iron rod to strengthen it. The back portion of the mould being thus finished, remove, when it has set, the slips of zinc, and in the edges of

the mould thus left exposed, bore at intervals conical holes. These "keyholes" are shown in Fig. 296. These, with the corresponding projections which will be formed in the front part of the mould, will serve as keys to ensure the accurate fitting together of the two parts. Brush clay water over the exposed edges, and make the second half of the mould in the same manner as the first. When the whole has set, the two halves can be divided by inserting a chisel at the line of separation. The clay water will prevent the parts from adhering too firmly together. As the chink between the two begins to open, a little water poured in, and gentle working of the parts to and fro, will help the separation. Remove the clay from the model, and well wash out the mould with soap and water. Lash the pieces of mould tightly together (see Fig. 297), and pour in the plaster to form the cast. Move the mould about so as to let it flow equally over every part. Strengthen with copper wire where required. When the cast is set, chip off the mould with a blunt chisel and mallet. The outer mould can be removed by a few strokes; the inner (tinted) mould must be broken off with more care; its colour will cause it to be easily distinguished

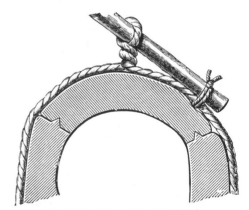

Fig. 297.—Tying Plaster Mould.

from the white cast. Parts of the figure which project much, such as the hands in some positions, it is often desirable to cut off, cast separately, and stick on again. If the model is in relief, a mould made in a single piece will generally suffice.

HISTORY OF WOOD CARVING: STYLES OF CARVED ORNAMENT

CARVING in wood is undoubtedly of very great antiquity. To realise this, upon the theory that the life history of the individual represents the life history of mankind generally, one has only to see how readily boys take to whittling pieces of wood, sometimes making a well-finished article, such as a boat, or sometimes, apparently, cutting the wood for the pure joy of feeling the knife go slashing through it. It is well known, too, that savage races have their war clubs and other weapons, besides their domestic utensils, paddles, and other wooden implements, decorated with carving. No one knows when man first rose to that level of developed ability which made him capable of executing a distinct design, even though of the vaguest kind. Certain it is that the very first piece of wood carving, historically considered, is of the very highest degree of excellence. It is that of a human figure, and is known as the "Sheikh-el-Beled," a name given to it because the Arabs who found it noticed that it bore a very close resemblance to the Sheikh of the village where it was found, who was ruling at that particular time. This statuette is done in sycamore, as was much of Egyptian work, and stands on a base of similar material; it is 3 ft. 8½ in. high. It is not remarkable for its detail; but it is most undoubtedly a strong, well-proportioned, and clever piece of work, showing a masterly handling of the human figure such as can only have proceeded from the brain, and through the hands, of a master of craft. Between the earliest vague attempts to express the feeble workings of the spirit of wood carving on the part of early man, and this clever and strong representation of the human figure, there lies a gulf covering many centuries—centuries not only in point of time, but in point of development and progress too.

Ancient Chip Carving

Turning to the ornament of some of these early peoples—that is, early only in their period of development—we find that their wood carving is practically that of the kind we know as chip carving. That is, it is of the kind the pattern of which is preserved as ridges, formed by the chipping away of the wood on either side in the shape of, generally, geometrical patterns. Relief carving, on the other hand, is formed by taking away the wood on both sides of the design, and leaving it raised an appreciable distance from the ground. The carved ornament of Oceania is of this type principally, varying, it is true, in different parts of the wide expanse of islands, but varying only between simple incised carving—that is, rude designs simply cut, or scratched in outline in the wood—through chip carving, to simple flat relief. Early as is this form of carving, it is yet comparatively well developed; because these craftsmen had a definite idea as to what they wished to represent, and they most certainly had developed more or less ability to put their ideas into concrete form. It may safely be taken for granted that the earliest form of carving would be in the form of incised or chip work, but of a much lower and cruder order than that of Oceania.

Ancient Egyptian Work

To take, now, the subject in chronological order, a beginning is made with a period showing a very high standard, that of Egyp-

Fig. 298.—Carved Doorway in Church of Aal, Hallingdal, Norway. Date, about 1200 A.D. (Scale : $\frac{1}{2}$ in. = 1 ft., approx. See p. 148.)

tian ornament of quite 6,000 years ago. In addition to what has already been said about the Sheikh-el-Beled statuette, it is interesting to note that it is, with the exception of the

Fig. 299.—Chevron, Norman Moulding.

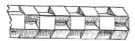

Fig. 300.—Billet, Norman Moulding.

Fig. 301.—Sunk Star, Norman Moulding.

right arm, carved out of one solid block of sycamore; the arm is mortised and tenoned in, and the eyes are formed of inlaid bits of shell and crystal. There are also, belonging to this date, or thereabouts, some panels from the tomb of Hosi, about 4 ft. high, with figures of men, and hieroglyphs, carved in low relief in the quaint style peculiar to Egyptian bas-reliefs. The Egyptians, at this time, appear to have employed wood carving to a considerable extent as ornament; it is found applied to furniture, boxes, and toilet implements.

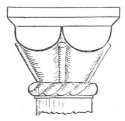

Fig. 302.—Beak Head, Norman Moulding.

Fig. 303.—Norman Capital.

plements. These were carved in what may be termed surface relief, the elements used being animals or plants, and the lotus and papyrus being largely used. Almost all, if

not quite all, their carvings in wood and stone were eventually coloured. Each craftsman's outfit included his bag of paints; and, mixing them himself, he laid them on in

Fig. 304.—
Three-lobed Foliage,
Early English.

Fig. 305.—
Spiral Plan, Early
English.

flat washes of red, green, blue, and yellow. It is to the earlier dynasties that the best carvings belong. There was undoubtedly a decline of ornament, and during the later dynasties little wood carving was done, unless the wooden coffins are considered to be specimens of the craft. It must be remembered that in Egypt wood was not plentiful, and the best Egyptian carving was done in stone, chiefly granite and basalt. In the British Museum can be seen two statues of kings carved in sycamore that are typical of the mode of treatment (date, about 1350 B.C.). One is a statue of an unknown king and the other of Seti I. (known also as Sethos), both of the nineteenth dynasty. They are strong and vigorous representations, suggestive of power and decision; the limbs are well proportioned, although they are smooth, and do not show the muscles clearly. The principal elements used by Egyptian craftsmen are: The lotus, papyrus, and palm; the winged globe; winged beetle or scarabeus; the egg and serpent; the rosette; the human figure, and the various animals necessary to

Fig. 306.—Dog-tooth Moulding, Early English.

the representation of the chase; fishing, and the various industrial arts and national pursuits, which were commonly used as frieze decorations.

Chaldea and Assyria

Chaldea and Assyria, which come next in chronological order, and whose art resembles

Fig. 307.—Maple Leaf, Decorated Period.

to some extent that of Egypt, afford very little that is of interest or value in connection with wood carving. Lower Mesopotamia is a flat, marshy country, abounding in reeds, which grow sometimes to 14 ft. high, but it is devoid of both timber and stone. Sir Austen Layard and Mr. George

Fig. 308.—Ogee Plan, Decorated Period.

Smith have shown that the furniture was ornamented with the heads of bulls, lions, and rams ; but this furniture was made largely of metal, gold and silver and bronze entering largely into its construction. It was inlaid with ivory, and sometimes with coloured glass ; the feet were carved to re-

Fig. 309.—Ball Flower, Decorated Period.

present the feet of lions and the hoofs of bulls. However, many of the patterns that have become familiar in the ornament of nearly all periods from that time to this

—especially in the Greek and the Roman, and later in the Renaissance of the fifteenth century—appear to have originated, or at least were very largely used, in Assyrian

Fig. 310.—Tudor Flower, Perpendicular Period.

art. Some of these are the palmette, the guilloche pattern, lilies, and the fir cone.

Greek Carvings

Greek art covers a period of from 800 B.C. to 140 B.C. During this period there are many references to wood carving, chiefly given by Pausanias, a Greek topographical writer, who lived about 150 A.D. His principal work, still extant, is " A Description of Greece," and in it he describes apparently everything he saw during his extensive travels. He shows that the art of carving in wood was of some considerable importance. At the present time, few examples survive, and, indeed, the only places where ancient wood carvings are now to be found are in Egyptian tombs. It must be remembered that wood is much less enduring than stone Wood suffers not only from fire, warfare and other violent destructive agencies, but soon perishes of natural decay. The earliest example of any wood carving in this period is 655-625 B.C., and refers to the famous chest of Cypselus of Corinth, which is said to have been made of cedar, carved and decorated with figures and bas-reliefs, some in ivory,

Fig. 311.—
Four-leaved Flower,
Perpendicular Period.

Fig. 312.—
Tudor Rose,
Perpendicular Period.

some in gold or ivory part gilt, and inlaid on all four sides and the top. Illustrations from bas-reliefs of this time show chairs whose four legs are carved to represent the

Fig 313.—Gothic Style Frame, showing Alternative Designs.
By F. L. Schauermann

legs and feet of lions, and the back
legs, which are carried up to form a
back, terminate at the top with a
carved representation of the anthemion.   This representation of the legs
and feet, in addition to the heads,
of lions, leopards, and sphinxes, is
common enough to form a distinctive
feature of Greek furniture, and it, too,
forms another link in the connecting
chain of art tradition that exists
between Greece and Assyria and
Egypt.   From the descriptions given
by Pausanias, it appears that the
earlier examples of wood carving were
the wooden images of the gods, many
examples of which were preserved
down to historic times.   One of these
ancient statues is that of Apollo,
dedicated in 428 B.C., in the Campus
Martius at Rome.   This, like the
chest of Cypselus, was done in cedar
wood.   Another statue, that of Zeus
Larissæus, at Argos, was remarkable
because it had three eyes.   Pausanias
also mentions a statue in wood of
Hermes, on the shrine (a figure in
wood) of Athena Polias, on the acropolis
at Athens, and also a colossal statue of
Apollo, carved in cedar, at Thebes,
which was attributed to Canachus, a
wood carver who held a high position
as an exponent of his craft.   In
Olympia, too, were statues in cedar
by Theocles, one of them representing Atlas bearing the universe.   One
peculiar feature of many of the large
wooden sculptures was that they were
covered with gilt or gold plates.   As a
necessary consequence, the carvers
had principally to consider the general
proportions and pose of the figures
and the arrangement of the masses,
rather than any elaboration of detail
in the shape of muscles, bones, etc.
In addition to this, wood was combined in many instances with marble.
Pheidias is credited with carving a
colossal statue of Athena, or Minerva,
at Plataea, the head hands, and feet
of which were of marble of Pentelicus,
the body being of wood and
gilded, or covered with gold plates.

Fig. 314.—Carved Panel in Gothic Style.   By F. L. Schauermann.

Fig. 315.—Church Door at Valthiofstad, Iceland.   Date, Middle Ages.
(Scale: 1 in. = 1 ft., approx.   See p. 156.)

The Greeks appear to have had a fair choice of woods for their work. Cedar was the wood used for many of the statues already mentioned.

Roman Wood Carving

Pliny speaks of a statue of Jupiter made of cypress, which was erected in Rome in the year 97 B.C. The gates of the Ephesian temple were also said to have been made the Romans (100 B.C. to 337 A.D.); but there is enough to show that it occupied a position of some importance. Roman ornament is really the continuation of the Greek and Etruscan styles; and as Grecian art finds its sources to a considerable extent in that of Assyria, it is not surprising to find that the arms and legs of chairs and couches are carved to represent the limbs of animals, thus closely following the examples succes-

Fig. 316.—Oak Boss, carved, with Arms of Hanningfield. Date, about 1400.
(Scale: 3½ in. = 1 ft. approx. See p. 156.)

of cypress, and they were credited with having lasted for 400 years. Pliny also mentions that the gates of the Temple of Apollo, at Utica, which were made of cedar, were in daily use in his time, and had been for 1,500 years. Ebony is also mentioned as being used for statuary—not, it may be thought, a very happy or suitable medium for the purpose. A great statue of Hercules carved in beech is also mentioned; and oak, box, olive, and pear wood were used for carved work. Little is mentioned in historical works respecting wood carving under sively set by Egypt, Assyria, and Greece. This idea was apparently carried out in the building of their war vessels and galleys. These were built of chestnut, cypress, pine, elm, oak, and fir; and in some of the bas-reliefs that still remain, the prows are shown ornamented with the heads of animals and similar elements. Thus one is shown with a boar's head carved on it; another has an entire crocodile; whilst one is shown with a swan's head and neck. One ship shown has a cable moulding carved the whole length of the ship, whilst the handles of the oars are carved at the place where they project through the sides of the vessel. Roman furniture was also decorated by carvings in bas-reliefs of subjects taken from Greek mythology. Some of the woods used in the making of Roman furniture were cedar, pine, elm, olive, ash, ilex, beech, and maple ; and these, with the exception of the elm, and the possible exception of the ash, are quite suitable for the purposes of carving. The elements of ornament that occur the

mented with the acanthus, whilst the body is covered with a highly raised and very elaborate design of scroll foliage of varied composition, consisting, as it does, of oak leaves, corn, ivy leaves, and berries, poppy leaves and seed vessels springing from one branch.

Fifth Century A.D.

The Roman Empire, so long the mistress of the world, had been slowly, and now was

Fig. 317.—Oak Boss, carved, with Arms of Badewe. Date, about 1100.
(Scale : $3\frac{1}{2}$ in. $= 1$ ft. See p. 156.)

oftenest in Greek and Roman ornament are the anthemion, which is derived from the conventional bud and lotus of Egypt, Assyria, and India ; the scroll ; the rosette, again a survival of the traditional Assyrian rosette ; the acanthus ; and with the Romans especially, birds and cupids and reptiles, and the griffin. A chariot in the museum of the Vatican is a remarkable example of a varied mixed ornament. The yoke ends in heads of birds, the bosses of the wheels in lions' heads, and the pole in the head of a ram. The spokes are orna-

rapidly, tottering to its fall. The Goths, Sarmatians, and other warlike and semi-civilised tribes, were feeling the strange stirrings within them of the lust for war and conquest ; and they were setting forth on their 150 years of savage warfare, to overrun practically the whole of Europe. The Saxons, in the fifth century, overran England, and, later, the Scandinavians, in their viking ships, came sweeping down the western seaboard, including in their wide embrace the British Isles as well as the western countries of Europe. From the

Urals came down the fierce tribes of the Huns and the Magyars, to help in the general dismemberment of the great Roman Empire, and, later, the Arabs and the Moors were pursuing a victorious career through Spain and France. What wonder, then, that during these turbulent and violent times the arts and crafts should be overshadowed, and their progress retarded, and that, in some cases, they should be completely submerged ?

the countries in which Christianity was the state religion became highly symbolic.

Byzantine Carvings

The main doors of S. Sabina on the Aventine Hill have carved panels, the carving taking the shape of sculptured figures whose costume decides the date to be in the fifth century. The doors are arranged in a number of small panels, on each of which is carved

Fig. 318.—Oak Boss, carved, with Arms of Robert Braybroke. Date, about 1400.
(Scale: $3\frac{1}{2}$ in. = 1 ft. See p. 156.)

Further than this, too, during this violent period, so full of warfare and destruction, many art treasures were destroyed; and, as wood is a thing that perishes much more easily than stone, the consequence is that there are but few examples of the work of this and earlier periods.

The Influence of Constantine

Christianity was, during the reign of Constantine the Great, made the state religion, and this circumstance had a great influence upon art generally. The art of Rome and Greece was almost purely æsthetic; that of

(450 A.D.) a scene from the Old and New Testaments, the details being of a debased classical type. Whilst the western Roman Empire was slowly dying, the eastern portion was being built upon a sound enough foundation to enable it to endure for over 1,000 years, and to give to the world a very remarkable type of art and architecture. Constantine removed his capital from Rome to Byzantium, afterwards called Constantinople, in 324 A.D. This, together with the uncertainty of life in the Western Empire, caused a migration of wealth and genius eastwards. The proximity of Constantinople

to Greece and Persia naturally paved the way for the assimilation of Grecian and Persian ideals ; these were assimilated, together with those of Rome, and, being subordinated to the influences and needs of the new religion, gave rise to an art and architecture of great vigour and significance, whose symbolism was in marked contrast to the great styles which it had principally drawn upon for its materials. Thus the conventional type of the Greek acanthus was combined with various symbols of Christianity such as the cross-circle, vine, and the dove. One feature of the actual working of Byzantine carvings was that the whole field was covered with the design, the extent of groundwork being very small. There are now, unfortunately, but few examples of

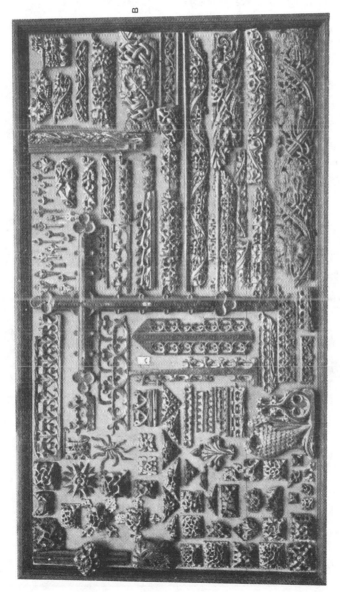

Fig. 319.—Fifteenth-century Carved Bosses, Mouldings, etc.

Byzantine wood carving, and none of the earlier periods; wood carving does not appear to have received the attention that stone ornament and glass mosaics and ivory carving did. The ivory carvings of the Byzantines are, however, exceedingly fine specimens of the carver's craft. The subjects of these are principally taken from the Bible, and it is reasonable to suppose that whatever wood carving was done would have its *motifs* drawn from the same source. In the British Museum there are two ivory boxes belonging to the sixth century, which show (1) Daniel in the lions' den and (2) the martyrdom of St. Menas. The actual workmanship is somewhat crude; but the conception, the symbolism, and the imagery are very marked, and bear witness to the great change in the aims and the ideals of the ornament of the times, from a purely æsthetic, like that of the Greeks and the Romans, to this highly symbolic ornament of the Byzantines. As time went on, various influences arose that had, eventually, a far-reaching effect upon the development of the arts of carving and sculpture, and upon the spreading of these arts to countries outside the borders of the Byzantine empire. One of these events was the prohibition by the emperor, Leo III., in 726 A.D., of image worship. This caused internal wars and disorders in the Byzantine empire itself, and had the effect of driving away from the capital, and from the empire eventually, all craftsmen and artists whose special work it was to produce these images. Many migrated to Italy, and as Venice was a rising star at the time, many settled there, and began that development and culture of

Fig. 320.—Cresting from Church at Littleham (see A, Fig. 319).

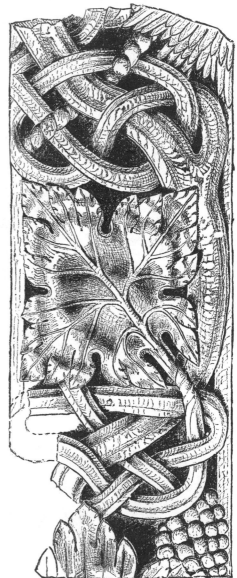

Fig. 321.—Pierced Band from Rood Loft of Stoke Gabriel Church (see B, Fig. 319).

wood carving which two or three hundred years later culminated in some of the finest work being done in Venice that has ever been done in wood during historical times. Of the period about to be considered, there are so many existing examples or records of wood carving, that one can more definitely and accurately judge of its work

and of its value. And, further, a consideration of the wood carving of the periods about to be touched upon has greater interest, because in so many cases there can be traced the influences that have been at work in the production of English styles. First of these the Celtic and the Scandinavian periods must be noticed.

Celtic Carving, 150–1400 A.D.

This covers a period of from the second century to the fifteenth, the principal characteristics being a most complicated and remarkable interlaced *motif*. In the earlier part of this period these interlaced forms were without life of any kind. From the eighth to the fourteenth centuries, interlaced bird and animal forms were used—probably the result of Byzantine influence. The serpent, or dragon, which is such a prominent feature of Scandinavian carvings, was introduced by the Norsemen and the Danes during their voyages of conquest in the seventh, eighth, and ninth centuries, and obtained so strong a hold as to find a place in the ornament of this style until its final decline in the fifteenth century. Students will be familiar with the dragon in designs of this period.

Fig. 322.—Carved Band, supposed to be French Work.

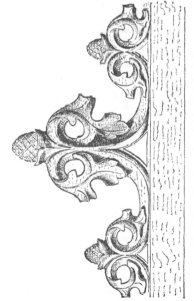

Fig. 323.—Cresting (probably Belgian) in Mr. G. A. Roger's Collection.

Scandinavian Carving, 550–1450 A.D.

Wood carving was a most prominent feature of Scandinavia quite from the earliest viking times, as might be expected of a country so richly endowed with the material necessary to the craft. Wood carving was applied during this period to objects both great and small. Churches and houses were built of wood, and their carved portals are amongst the most remarkable wood carvings done during historical times. In the old churches of Borgund and Hitterdal much of the seventh and eighth century wood carving may still be seen. Much of this early carving

plant forms appeared, and wooden sculpture, of a somewhat rude kind, became included to represent the legends of the gods. In treatment, generally, the bodies of the dragons were carved flat, the sole projections being the heads, which were often raised in good relief from the rest of the work. In the Christiania Museum are the portals of the Church of Hyllestad, Sætersdal, belonging to the twelfth century, the subject being the representation of the legend of Fafni, which legend forms the basis of the dracontine nature of Scandinavian wood carving. The same subject is again portrayed in a more developed form in the portals of Hedals

Fig. 324.—Two Carved Bosses. Date, Fifteenth Century.

is plainly influenced by the art of the Byzantine empire, showing the tremendous extent of its "sphere of influence." Much of the early Russian carved woodwork may legitimately be included under the heading "Scandinavian," because in the year 911 Ruric the Jute led an excursion into Russia, and became the head of a dynasty that reigned for 600 years ; and much of the work done during the Ruric dynasty shows undoubted traces of Scandinavian origin. Besides its application to churches and houses, the craft of wood carving found expression through the medium of wooden tankards, jugs, caskets, and chests, and other domestic objects. The wood carving itself consisted up to the twelfth entirely of animal forms twisted and interlaced in the manner peculiar to Scandinavian art (see Fig. 298). After the twelfth century,

Church, Balders, of the date of 1400 A.D. In these portals, which are entirely covered with the dragons, and their folds and interlacements, a good contrast is obtained by making the dragons themselves very prominent, and by filling up the spaces with small convolutions of narrower width, that act as subordinate members to the larger elements, and give a contrast that is remarkable, considering, too, that the elements used in the building of the design are nearly all drawn from one class. Scandinavian wood carving is most admirably suited to the material, in respect of both the patterns and their treatment. They are flat ; they are close enough to cover the surface with little groundwork ; and they have no projection beyond the heads of the dragons here and there, which, being thick, or, rather, of considerable extent compared with the bodies, have enough support given to them to make their projection quite legitimate.

Early British Carving

Having got to this point, it will be as well to confine attention mainly to the development of wood carving in Britain, reference being made to the wood carvings of other countries only when it is necessary to show how far these have influenced the develop·

Fig. 325.—French Panel, Carved with Open Gothic Tracery. Late Fifteenth Century.
(Scale : about $7\frac{1}{8}$ in. = 1 ft. See p. 159.)

ment of English wood carving. The capabilities of the ancient Britons in the craft are not known ; but as Britain itself was an outlying province of the Roman empire, Roman art in Britain was certainly not remarkable for any great development. Much the same can be said relative to the wood carving of the Saxons, who came to Britain in 449 A.D. The Saxons were a section of that active, restless Germanic people who were causing so much disturbance in Europe in their efforts to break up the existing empires of the time. The influence of Roman art was still being felt; and, naturally, the decorative art of the Saxons is very much influenced by that of Rome, and constitutes a great part of the road through which this particular phase of the Romanesque passed, finally to appear as Norman ornament and architecture. Wood was the principal material used in the construction of buildings and the making of furniture, during this period ; and, although there are very few existing examples of Saxon wood carving, and although information about it is meagre, yet it can reasonably be assumed that the Saxons did a great amount of it. On some of the illuminated manuscripts of the time, ships are represented having carved prows very much after the manner of the Roman galleys, the prows taking the form of dragon heads and other grotesque creatures. Chairs, too, are said to have been carved with the heads and feet of animals, in this respect following the example of the Egyptians, Assyrians, Greeks, and Romans. As time went on, this Roman influence was modified, but by no means subordinated, by the art of the Danes and Scandinavians, another Germanic tribe, who, in turn, invaded Britain, burning, destroying, and ravaging wherever they went. Their peculiar " dragon " carving has already been noticed ; and it became incorporated with the ornament of the time, as is evidenced by the scraps of ornamental remains still preserved in many churches of ancient foundation—especially in the northeast of England. There is in the British Museum a carving in whalebone, done on the cover of a casket of the eighth century, which shows the varying influences at work during a time of transition. It represents an

attack upon a house, which is being defended by its owner. In the house itself is represented a round-headed arch resting on columns having both caps and bases ; round the arch, which is of two orders, are borders of zigzag or chevron pattern, which were to become, eventually, such a prominent feature of Norman ornament 250 years later. The columns, or pilasters, are ornamented with a guilloche design. In various corners, which otherwise would be vacant spaces, are carved small interlacing patterns of Celtic origin.

1100 to 1174 A.D.

Generally speaking, the state of the country was so unsettled that little progress could be made in the industrial arts. But towards the end of the tenth century, French influence was making itself felt, and resulted in many additions and improvements to both houses and furniture. There were carved oak chests, oak armoires enriched with carving, carved chairs, and carved bedsteads. These would be carved in the Norman style, a particularly strong and vigorous offshoot of Romanesque architecture. There is but little direct evidence in the shape of actual specimens of Norman woodwork, and especially carved woodwork. Perhaps the first wood carver whose name is preserved is William of Sens, who restored the choir of Canterbury Cathedral after the great fire. He is described as a " workman most skilful both in wood and stone."

Norman Style

The style immediately preceding the Gothic is known as the Norman style, which was in use from about 1040 to 1189. This style is classical in spirit, being an attempt to revive the Roman architecture. Its principal ornamental features are : Its characteristic mouldings, which were, especially from 1120 to 1189, very much enriched, the enrichments employed being known as the zigzag or chevron, the round and square billet, the hatched, the pyramid, the lozenge, the sunk star, the cable, the double cone, the beak head, and the embattled ; the capitals, which were carved sometimes in rude imitation of Corinthian and Ionic capitals, sometimes with rude sculpture, and very

Fig. 326.—Openwork Carving on Buffet Door. Date, about 1500.
(Scale : 5¼ in. = 1 ft. See p. 159.)

Fig. 327.—French Panel, Carved with Gothic Tracery
and Shield of Arms. Date, Early Sixteenth Century.   (Scale : 1⅔ in. = 1 ft.   See p. 161.)

often in scalloped design ; the shafts, or
columns, supporting the arches were often
ornamented with a zigzag pattern. The
doorways are a very characteristic feature
of the Norman schemes of ornament, being
in the latter half of the Norman period
very richly ornamented. One feature may
be noticed as showing foreign influence, and
also as showing the source of that vigorous
spirit that gave the Norman architecture
distinction and strength as compared with
contemporary forms of the Romanesque :
this is the employment of chip-carving
patterns, such as the sunk star and
other designs, which are found on the abaci
and the capitals of some churches, and
undoubtedly show a northern influence.
Dragons, too, which are decidedly Scandinavian in character, often form part of
the ornamental schemes of the Normans.
Figs. 299 to 303 (p. 133) give details of
Norman ornament.

Norwegian Doorway

A remarkable example of carved work,
dating from about 1200 A.D., is shown in the
museum of the University of Christiania. It
is a doorway (see Fig. 298) standing about
12 ft. 6 in. high, and 6 ft. wide, and was
originally in the church of Aal, in Hallingdal,
Norway. The illustration is from a plaster
cast exhibited in the South Kensington
Museum.

Gothic Period, including the Early English

The Gothic style is the finest and most prolific in wood carving that England has known.
It extends from the close of the Norman in
1189 to the beginning of the Renaissance in
the early years of the sixteenth century. The
Early English does not offer many actual examples, but the few that are still fortunately left are quite sufficient to show the
kind of work done, and the great advance
made, by the wood carvers of that time.
In the cathedrals of Exeter and Salisbury are
two remarkably fine series of misericorde seats
carved in oak. Those at Exeter were done
during the time of Bishop Bruere (1224-
1244), and are carved with rare spirit. (Illustrations of them appear later in this book.
They are remarkable, too, for the varied

character of the subjects employed. These comprise foliage; the three-lobed foliage characteristic of the Early English period; figures from real life, such as lions, fishes, an elephant, various combats between beasts and men, etc., and grotesques. It is interest- ing to note that the elephant is carved with hind legs like a dog or horse, whereas it should have knees, similar to those of a man. The seats in Salisbury are remarkable for having the dog-tooth ornament, another characteristic Early English feature, carved on

Fig. 328.—German Panel, representing Christ bearing the Cross. Date, Early Sixteenth Century. (Scale: about **4** in. = **1** ft. See p. 161.)

them, this being the earliest known example of this form of ornament. In Ufford Church, Northamptonshire, were some stall ends of the thirteenth century, carved to represent the passions—hate, anger, jealousy, etc. This illustrates what was the keynote of Gothic ornament, namely, symbolism. Nearly all ornament was used, not for its artistic possibilities, but for what the elements of which it consisted represent. In the fourteenth century much fine woodwork was done, of which the principal remains are in the churches and cathedrals. The Early English work of the thirteenth century had been heavy and somewhat coarse in detail, even though the stonework done during this period was light and graceful. But invariably carving in wood was fifty years to one

Fig. 329.—Elizabethan Strapwork.

hundred years behind carving in stone; thus the fourteenth-century work, although much of it was good, did not reach by any means the state of excellence attained by stone carving during the same period, one reason being that the forms used were more suited to expression in stone than in wood. Stall ends, screens, misericorde seats were commonly carved, the elements of ornament used being generally a little later than those used in stone carving. Besides foliage carving, large recumbent effigies were carved in wood. One of the best known is that of Robert, Duke of Normandy, in Gloucester Cathedral. This was done during the twelfth century. In the south choir aisle of Abergavenny Church is the figure of a young knight, George de Cantelupe, who died in 1273. It is a remarkable thing that these wooden effigies were covered with gesso or fine stucco, on which various ornaments

were modelled or stamped in relief, and then were richly decorated in go'd and colour; this appears to have been the case on the Continent as well. The Coronation Chair, made in 1296-1300, was covered at one time with a coating of plaster, gilded over; and stall ends and screens were painted and

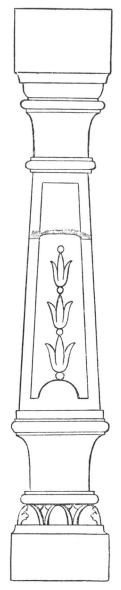

Fig. 330.—Elizabethan Pilaster.

gilded, such as a perclose screen at St. Margaret's, King's Lynn, belonging to the middle of the fourteenth century, which was originally painted blue and gold. The Bishop's Throne in Exeter Cathedral, built during the episcopate of Bishop Stapeldon, 1308 to 1326 A.D., is a very magnificent piece of woodwork, having a profusion of carved crockets and pinnacles ; and it has the reputation of being the finest episcopal seat in the world. The vine, oak-leaf and acorns, thistle, maple, and ivy were commonly used

Fig. 331.—Carving Design in Cinque-Cento Style (Italian, Sixteenth Century).
By F. L. Schauermann.

during the fourteenth century, besides the trefoils, quatrefoils, cinquefoils, and tracery work. Foliage was remarkable for its treatment, which was of a peculiarly " bossy " nature (*see* the section " Gothic Carving," pp. 88 to 92).

Fifteenth-century Carving

During the thirteenth and fourteenth centuries wood carving in England became general ; but it was during the fifteenth century that it reached its culminating point. Thousands of the magnificent rood screens,

Fig. 332.—Design in Italian Renaissance Style.

with their roods and figures of St. John and the Virgin, their galleys, their wonderful tracery work, their panels painted with figures of the saints, were built during this prolific period. Pulpits, stall ends, choir stalls, with their misericorde seats ; the fine hammer-beam and other wooden roofs of the eastern counties ; the font covers, lecterns, and other furniture of the churches, are numerous enough and remarkable enough to require volumes for their adequate description. The mode of detail treatment varies in different parts of England ; thus, for instance, whilst poppy-heads are numerous enough in the Midlands and the eastern counties, only five examples occur in Devonshire. One important feature of fifteenth-century wood carving is the very

fine way in which the work suits the material, and the manner of its arrangement with regard to the suitability of the object to its ultimate use. " Linen panelling " was much used during this period. This is an attempt to represent folded linen in a very conventional manner as an ornament in wood. The crockets of this time were carved with greater spirit and vigour and strength than in the preceding century. The Tudor flower and the four-leaved flower are characteristic of this, the Perpendicular, style. The vine, maple, and ivy were still much used. The misericorde seats of this and the preceding century are remarkable, not only for bold, powerful, and suitable treatment, but also for the peculiar, and, in many cases, utterly ridiculous, character of their subjects. In Beverley Minster there are about sixty-eight of these seats, and in only two is the ornament based on scriptural subjects ; the remaining sixty-six are of a purely secular, not to say absurd, nature : rats hanging a cat ; wolves dressed in friars' garments, preaching ; a woman shoeing a goose ; man riding a pig ; pig playing a harp ; these are some of the subjects of this remarkable series. And this style of seat is the rule throughout the country. At the same time, however absurd in subject, these carvings are, in most cases, the work of master minds and hands, the conception being powerful and to the point ; while the manner in which they are executed is exceedingly clever and thoroughly suited to the material and the purpose for which they are intended. The furniture of the Gothic period followed the same style as the ecclesiastical work ; and, consequently, the same kind of carving is found on the chairs, bedsteads, and other furniture. A chair in St. Mary's Hall, Coventry, is a most remarkable example of the application of Gothic carving patterns to furniture. It has a back surmounted by pinnacles carved into the shape of animals, from which the arms curve downwards, terminating, one conceived in the true Gothic spirit, as a peculiarly grotesque figure of a man, the other in an animal ; the sides, as was a common feature of Gothic chairs, are solid, and carved in tracery work ; the back is treated in the same manner, and the same is the case with the front of the chair. Bosses were a feature of Gothic work, and were carved sometimes with grotesques, sometimes with delicate foliage, sometimes angels, and so forth. The chancel screens were generally finished at the top with brattishing, or carved open fretwork above the cornice. English wood carving during the Gothic period was, like the Gothic architecture, a thing of strong and vigorous growth; and although foreign influence was brought to bear upon it—as, for example, German and Flemish influence in the eastern counties, and French influence in the south-western, notably Devon and

Fig. 333.—Italian Renaissance Carving Design.
By F. I. Schauermann.

Cornwall—yet these various influences were absorbed and assimilated, and were not allowed to dominate the work of the Gothic wood carvers.

Gothic Considered as a Style

The Gothic was not a development of the Norman, but was quite a new growth, characterised by quite different manifestations of ornamental detail, and showing in every way the influence of a quite different spirit. It is most generally divided into three principal parts : The Early English, 1189-1275 ; the Decorated, 1275-1375 ; and the Perpendicular, 1375-1536. The Early English is remarkable for the complete change in style

Fig 334.—German Renaissance Carving Design.   By F. L. Schauermann.

as compared with the Norman. Its principal ornamental characteristics are: The beautiful suites of mouldings; its graceful three-lobed foliage, arranged conventionally and on a spiral plan; and the dog-tooth ornament. Figs. 304 to 306 (p. 133) give various Early English details. The Decorated Period is often spoken of as being in two parts: the geometrical and the curvilinear. It is distinguished by its foliage, which is of a very natural kind, the elements being the oak-leaf and acorn, the maple leaf, vine, ivy, and similar natural forms. They are arranged on the plan of a double ogee, and the surface

Fig. 335.—Flemish Renaissance Carving Design, after Holbein.
By F. L. Schauermann.

treatment, especially in the middle stages, conforms to this line. The Percy shrine in Beverley Minster is one of the finest examples of the carving of this style in England. One feature of the early Gothic styles is the use of so much grotesque ornament. Especially is this so in the case of the misericorde seats in the choirs, which, while often most absurd in subject, were carved with great power

Fig. 336.—Design in French Renaissance Style.

and ability. The development of window tracery that took place in this style has given rise to the arbitrary division that has been made. The geometrical, as its name implies, is that style in which the tracery is constructed on a geometrical plan. In the curvilinear, the tracery is arranged in a much freer manner, the lines consisting of free-hand curves. The ball-flower ornament is characteristic of this period, especially in the Midlands and the West. Figs. 307 to 309 (p. 134) give various decorated details. The

Perpendicular is often divided into two portions, known as Perpendicular and Tudor. The Perpendicular is distinguished for its panel treatment both in wood and stone. The windows are very large, and have the mullions carried up to the window heads, with transoms dividing the length of the windows, these transoms often being embattled. The ornament generally is of a much flatter nature, the mouldings being flatter, too, and more insignificant. Most of the magnificent rood screens date from the fifteenth century, and should be closely studied by the wood carver. The period is remarkable for the development of fan-vault tracery, the principal examples of which are to be seen in Henry VII.'s Chapel at Westminster; St. George's Chapel, Windsor; and King's College Chapel, Cambridge. As the style merged into the Tudor, the window heads became flatter, until they became what are known as four-centered arches. Then the influence of the Renaissance became powerful, and the Gothic gradually faded. The four-leaved flower, the Tudor flower, the Tudor rose, are the principal ornamental details which were employed. Shields and the portcullis are characteristic of the later portion of the Perpendicular. Figs. 310 to 312 (p. 134) give various Perpendicular details.

Illustrations of Carvings in Gothic Style

Two designs by F. L. Schauermann for carvings in the Gothic style are presented by Figs. 313 and 314 (pp. 135 and 136). The first is for a portrait frame, and gives alternative designs of acorn and vine, and the second is for a panel.

Icelandic Carving

Fig. 315 (p. 137) shows a carved door in the church of Valthiofstad, Iceland, the actual photograph having been taken from a plaster cast in the South Kensington Museum. This is an example of the work of the Middle Ages. The door is 6 ft. 10 in. high and 3 ft. 3 in. wide.

Three Carved Bosses

Belonging to the late fourteenth or early fifteenth century are the three bosses shown by Figs. 316 to 318 (pp. 138 to 140),

Fig. 337.—Door Panel, Carved in Spanish Renaissance Style.
(Scale : 3 in. = 1 ft.   See p. 167.)

these having ornamented the north aisle roof of Braintree Church, Essex, and at the time the photograph was taken being owned by the Rev. J. W. Kenworthy, M.A. The bosses bear the arms of Hanningfield (?) (Fig. 316), Badewe (Fig. 317), and Robert Braybroke, Bishop of London from 1382 to 1404 (Fig. 318). These bosses present

Fig. 338.—Pediment Design in Renaissance Style.

some points of interest to the wood carver. Their treatment has been considered in relation to the ultimate position they had to occupy. There is no delicate finish, and no careful tooling; but there is a strength and vigour, obtained by intelligent "roughing out" with a mallet and tools, which was indeed essential to the position each boss eventually had to fill. Twenty feet above one's head is no place to perceive delicate and minute effects. A broad, strong play of high lights and strong shadows is required, and the bosses show these effects in a marked degree. It should be noted that the cuts produced by means of the mallet and the tools are more effective than those smoother cuts resulting from continuous hand pressure; therefore, for high-relief work the mallet should always be used. The use of shields and coats of arms was developed during the fourteenth century and culminated in the fifteenth. The grapes in the boss shown by Fig. 316 are not to be commended as an example of the ideal treatment, however; they may be somewhat effective, but they are too crude and mechanical to be really good. The ease with which they can be done possibly influenced the choice of this method; and it affords an indication of the growing spirit that later in the fifteenth century was responsible for much inferior carving, whose evident intention had been to produce maximum effect with a minimum effort, thus tending to the sacrifice of honest and sound work.

More Fifteenth=century Bosses and Mouldings

Some fragments of oak carvings collected by Mr. Harry Hems, of Exeter (see Fig. 319, p. 141), include typical fifteenth-century bosses and mouldings. Fig. 319 was an illustration to a paper on Devonshire screens read by Mr. Hems before the Society of Architects in 1896, and two of the examples (A and B) are shown enlarged by Figs. 320 and 321, other work of much the same kind being illustrated by Figs. 322 to 324. Fig. 320 (A, Fig. 319) shows cresting from Littleham, Devonshire, where it was the crowning feature of a rood loft. Fig. 321 (B, Fig. 319) shows a pierced band from the rood loft of Stoke Gabriel Church, and is an instance of simple design and treatment having produced a highly successful result; this band has been lauded as an example of Gothic genius for apt decoration. Fig. 322 shows a carved band assumed to be of French origin; but it is of a too ornate character, and is too closely massed to be appreciated from a distance. Fig. 323 shows a piece of cresting (probably Belgian) from Mr. G. A. Roger's collection, of value from an æsthetic point of view, it was employed by the Gothic craftsmen, and can be so employed to-day, because of its symbolic possibilities. Thus this panel is a beautiful example of a double trefoil interlaced, the trefoil representing the Trinity. French Gothic ran a different course from contemporary English work. In France, the Renaissance made its influence felt earlier because of the proximity of the country to Italy, and in this panel

Fig. 339.   Fig. 340.

Figs. 339 and 340.—Bracket Design in Renaissance Style.

and represents a clever treatment of foliage. Two bosses are shown by Fig. 324 (p. 144); in these the cutting is direct and simple, and not a line of the design is wasted. These bosses were not ornaments only; they each covered the joint of two ribs in the vault of a rood loft.

Panel with Open Gothic Tracery

An oak panel of the late fifteenth century and having open Gothic tracery is shown by Fig. 325 (p. 145). This panel well illustrates the value of pierced carving as applied to decorative purposes. Besides being its sway can be felt in the peculiar shape of the cusps which converge towards the centre of the panel. In carving pierced tracery the greatest care has to be taken in following absolutely the setting-out lines, especially where the intersections occur, and it follows that an intelligent carver will perfect himself in the art of drawing and designing.

Carving on Buffet Door: Date, 1500

A fragment of a buffet door in oak, carved partly in openwork, is shown by Fig. 326 (p. 147); this is English, and dates from about the year 1500. It is a remarkable mixture

Fig. 341.—English Oak Panelling. Date, 1600–1650.
(Scale : $1\frac{3}{16}$ in. = 1 ft. See pp. 167 and 169.)

of open work and incised carving. The incised work is of the simplest and easiest kind, approximating very closely to chip carving. There is little modelling, and practically no opportunity for artistic expression. The effect really depends upon accurate cutting. The serrations round the leaves, although suited to the tools used, yet have a somewhat cheap effect; it is another illustration of the way in which the craftsmen of this period were aiming at a great effect whilst expending but little time or trouble to obtain it. The open tracery has lost its cusping—another method of saving labour.

Illustrations of Early Sixteenth-century Work

A very beautiful oak panel carved in relief, with Gothic tracery surrounding a shield of arms, is shown by Fig. 327 (p. 148); this is French work, dating from early in the sixteenth century, and formed part of the collection of M. Emile Peyre, acquired for the South Kensington Museum. It is an exceedingly fine piece of carved tracery of the period known as François Premier, 1515-1547. The Renaissance had got a good hold upon the art affections of the cultured classes, although the Gothic spirit died hard; and one effect of the combined influence of the two styles can be seen in this example. The general effect is Gothic, but the details show evidence of the later spirit of the Renaissance. The circular band of quatrefoils enclosing the square diamond-wise is quite characteristic of the later Gothic, and is commonly met with in English churches, Great St. Mary's at Cambridge being a very typical example. The crockets on the ogee arch, too, are characteristic of Gothic ornament; and the long bevel, or chamfer, on the sill, and the way in which the upright muntins of the tracery run into this sill, are also Gothic. The general effect is essentially Gothic because of the tracery; but in examining details, the student will be struck by work which bears evidence of another influence. The crockets have the serrations of the leaves of a more rounded type than is common to Gothic crockets. Their surface treatment, although approximating to Gothic, is yet not so strong and vigorous, because

of its more rounded "bossiness," which gives a much softer finish than that rugged finish typical of the Gothic carving. The cusps in the tracery work are arranged to give a rounded and continuous effect, especially in the row of traceried arches on the second row or tier from the top. The interlaced circular arches of the lower tier are also a reminder of the new spirit then demanding recognition.

Early Sixteenth-century German Carving

An example of German work will now be referred to : Fig. 328 (p. 149) shows an oak panel carved with a curious representation of Christ bearing the cross. This also dates from early in the sixteenth century.

Cinque-cento Style

Cinque-cento was a division of the Renaissance style, now about to be described. It was developed by sculptors and painters from north and central Italy, the most famous of whom were Raphael, Michelangelo, Giulio Romano, Lambarde, Bramante, Bernardino Luini, Pinturicchio, Agostino Rusti, and Andrea Sansovino. A design, by F. L. Schauermann, in this style, is shown by Fig. 331. (Figs. 329 and 330 will be referred to later.)

The Renaissance

In the period about to be discussed, a new influence was stirring, an influence that was quite different in spirit from that of the Gothic; and this influence was brought to bear upon the native craftsmen to such a degree that the new style was enabled to gain a foothold that it has not yet lost. This new style was that of the Renaissance. It began in Italy, and rapidly spread to the surrounding countries, especially gaining a stronghold in Flanders, and influencing Flemish work to a most remarkable extent. Thence it came over to England; and the earlier years of Renaissance wood carving in England are influenced very largely by Flemish craftsmanship. It began to be felt in England during the reign of Henry VIII., and for a time, especially in the ornament of the period, a great struggle went on between the old style and the new. The im-

Fig. 342.—Carved Oak Door from Dutch Church Screen. Date. about 1700.
(Scale: about $1\frac{5}{16}$ in. = 1 ft. See p. 169.)

mediate consequence of this is that a style, or a class, of work ensued which combined details of the two styles, and produced in most cases a very quaint effect. A change of style nearly always begins with the ornamental details; and it was so in this case.

Renaissance mouldings and carving patterns were executed on Gothic framework; and being executed, too, by Gothic craftsmen, accustomed to the strength and broad treatment of the Gothic spirit, the result, even if at times humorous and strange, was yet

Fig. 343.—Mirror Frame, Carved in Limewood, attributed to Grinling Gibbons.
(Scale: about $\frac{7}{8}$ in. = 1 ft.   See p. 172.)

decidedly interesting. The new style or class of carving that resulted from this combination of styles is termed Elizabethan, and this later merges into what is known as Jacobean. One of the finest pieces of early Renaissance woodwork is the organ screen

Fig. 344.—Carved Drop in Limewood, Grinling Gibbons Style (Modern). Photo supplied by Mr. John P. White.

at King's College Chapel, at Cambridge, 1532 to 1536 A.D. The ornamental detail of this, like much of the work done during Henry VIII.'s reign, is decidedly French in character. After his death, and especially during Elizabeth's reign, it was moulded very much by Flemish influence. The fine screen and hammer-beam roof of Middle Temple Hall, dated 1574, is a good example of the combined influence of the two styles. Heraldry was taking, at this time, a prominent place in the life of the nation, and, as a result, it occupied a large part of the ornament of the time. The Tudor rose and the portcullis are characteristic of the Tudor period; and coats of arms and shields play a large part in the carved ornament of the time. The strapwork patterns, known as Elizabethan strapwork, are a great feature of the period. They are most admirably suited to the peculiarities of wood as a material, and some of the finest wood carving, considering it as a decorative feature of ornament, was done during the latter half of the sixteenth century. At the Red Lodge, Bristol, there is some magnificent carved panelling, dated 1590, and at Burton Agnes may be seen more fine panelling, not so richly conceived, but perhaps more suited to the material and the purpose for which it is required. At the latter place there is, too, a very fine carved block of oak, 8 ft. by 5 ft., representing the "Dance of Death," showing Death, represented as a skeleton, dancing upon sceptres, crowns, jewels, money, old men, young men, babies, and all the material paraphernalia of life. This is supposed to have been done by a Flemish wood carver. During the Gothic period, much the greater part of carved ornament was to be found in churches, but during the Elizabethan and Jacobean periods the reverse is the case, for the obvious reason that then the country, owing to the breaking up of the feudal system, was in a much more settled state; and castles being no longer absolutely necessary, opportunity was found for building large domestic buildings, and the great houses such as Montacute, Kirby Hall, Barlborough Hall, Knole, Haddon Hall, and others, had their origin between 1570 and 1625. The interiors were invariably panelled in oak, and, generally, were most elaborately

Fig. 345.—Design for Carved Panel in Louis XIV. Style
By F. L. Schauermann.

Fig. 346.—Part of Arabic Carved Ceiling, from Damascus.
Date, Eighteenth Century.   (See p. 173.)

carved. The suppression of the monasteries and the withdrawal of their large incomes told against a widespread activity in church building and decoration such as had marked the fifteenth century. These two facts, too, considerably helped the progress of the new spirit of ornament, and during the seventeenth century it made very great strides. It is, however, somewhat surprising that the Jacobean, which followed the Elizabethan style, should have yielded such poor results so far as wood carving is concerned. The wood carving of this short period is, generally speaking, poor and flat in conception, and coarse in execution. It would seem as if the attempt had been made to produce as much effect as possible with as little effort as could be made ; and a greater contrast than exists between the work of this period and that of the palmy days of the rich Perpendicular style could not well be imagined. As the century advanced, more elaborate work began to be attempted, until, in the times of Charles II. and of James II., we get wood carving that, while based on Renaissance models, is done in very high relief—and a relief, too, that is not at all suited to the necessities of the object and the material.

Some Renaissance Carvings

Fig. 332 shows an Italian Renaissance design. Three designs by F. L. Schauermann, shown by Figs. 333, 334, and 335 respectively, represent Italian, German, and Flemish Renaissance. Fig. 336 is typical of French, and Fig. 337 of Spanish Renaissance ; the latter is a door panel, the original of which, at the time of taking the photograph, was the property of Mr. George Salting. This panel undoubtedly shows Flemish influence. Flanders was a great centre of decorative art, and considerably influenced all the countries around her. Spain, during the time of the Renaissance, was at the height of her power, and had brought the Netherlands under her yoke ; consequently, many craftsmen found their way to Spain, either voluntarily or under compulsion, and therefore there is, in Spanish ornament (especially carved ornament, of which the Flemish were past masters), a considerable degree of Flemish feeling. The cartouches, well

known in England throughout the whole of the Elizabethan and well on into the Jacobean periods, came from the same source ; Fig. 337 should be compared with

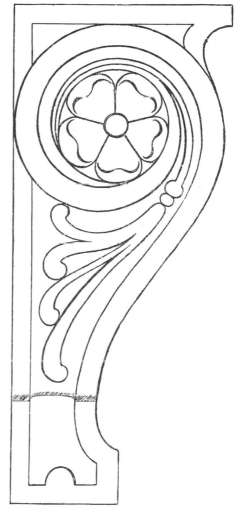

Fig. 347.—Bracket in Neo-Greek Style.
By F. L. Schauermann.

Fig. 341. A pediment and a bracket in Renaissance style (due to F. L. Schauermann) are illustrated by Figs. 338 to 340.

Seventeenth=century Panelling

A specimen in the Victoria and Albert Museum, South Kensington, is represented

Fig. 348.—Design for Carved Panel in Late Nineteenth-century Style.
By F. L. Schauermann.

by Fig. 341 (p. 160), which shows a piece of oak panelling. This is English work, and dates from the first half of the seventeenth century. The heavier treatment spoken of in connection with the next example (Fig. 342) is apparent in the oak panelling here shown. The conception of the whole, too, is more architectural, and shows well the model on which it is based—namely, the Greek temple. The pilasters represent the columns ; and there is the frieze which in the old Greek temples consisted of the ends of the cross beams, with the carved marble slabs between. The characteristic features of the late Elizabethan period, of which this is an excellent example, are the tapered pilasters, the carved cartouches, the moulded panelling, the split turned work fixed to the pillars, and the broken pediment in the centre ornament.

Carved Doors: Date, 1700

One of a pair of carved oak doors from a screen in a Dutch church is illustrated by Fig. 342 (p. 162). The door has brass fittings, and dates from about 1700. The carving on these screen doors shows very clearly the difference in ornament between the earlier and the latter parts of the sixteenth century, as compared with the pierced tracery shown in Fig. 325 (p. 145). In Fig. 342 there is pierced tracery, but it is characteristic of the full flood of the Renaissance. Gothic tracery is principally composed of geometrical figures ; but here there is a form of tracery based upon the scroll, all in freehand drawing. The arrangement of the spaces is remarkably well conceived ; they are not, for one thing, too big—a very common fault which designers who are not carvers often fall into. When designing for pierced work, always blacken the open spaces as shown in Fig. 342 ; this gives a much better idea as to their size ; when the spaces are left white, one is very apt to minimise their size, and the result is that the design when carved looks thin and unimpressive. This design gives a most admirable result because of the attention paid to this point. Dutch ornament was of a heavier and more substantial type than that of the southern countries—especially Italy and France. As the Renaissance movement went northward,

it came to countries whose peoples were slower in assimilating new thoughts and influences ; and the craft work of Germany and Flanders is especially marked by a strength that amounts often to heaviness, an example of which is seen in Fig. 342. Compare this with Italian or French carving of the sixteenth century, and the difference will at once be apparent. Much of the English work is influenced by Flemish or-

Fig. 349.—Panel, Designed by C. M. Rogers, and Carved by Edwin Fairchild at School of Art Wood Carving.

nament, and, in fact, much of it is actually the work of Flemish craftsmen ; and this explains why English work appears to be of a heavier nature than that of French contemporaries.

Development of the Renaissance Style

The Renaissance, this vigorous revival of classic architecture and ornament, began in Italy in the thirteenth and fourteenth centuries, and rapidly spread to Germany,

France, Spain, and the smaller countries adjoining, penetrating even as far north as Scandinavia, and then later to England. Although purely Italian in the first place,

Fig. 350.—Panel, Designed and Carved by
Charlotte Moore, at School of Art
Wood Carving.

it soon became altered in character by adaptation to the native abilities and requirements of the artist-craftsmen of the countries through which it was passing. Consequently there are, at least, these important divisions or manifestations of it :—Italian, German, French, Spanish, and English.

All these developments of the Renaissance reflect the national characteristics of the various people who adopted it. The Italian and the French Renaissance is characterised by lightness, airiness, and grace, the elements used consisting of a profusion of fruits and flowers, cupids, ribbons, dolphins, sea-horses centaurs, satyrs, and griffins, all arranged on a scrollwork basis, and in as light a manner as possible. Much the same can be said about the Spanish Renaissance, except that this development is more powerful, whilst at the same time more luxuriant. With the German and the English Renaissance, the development partook of a different nature. In both countries the Gothic had obtained an unusually strong hold, and it did not lose this hold without a keen struggle, and without strongly impressing and influencing the incoming style. Consequently, these forms of the Renaissance differ materially from the Italian and French and Spanish, in being stiffer, stronger, and more suggestive of power and stability ; and they show a deeper symbolism. In England, the first result produced by the Italian ornament was to form the Tudor style, which is a peculiar mixture of the Gothic and Renaissance, characteristic of English ornament. In it the depressed Perpendicular four-centered arch is used along with the round-headed Roman arch. Gothic mouldings are strangely altered in an attempt to make a compromise between them and the classic moulding. Designs of a Renaissance character are executed by Gothic craftsmen, and the whole spirit of their original conception is quite altered. Out of this grew the Elizabethan style, in a period prolific of beautiful carving, most admirably suited to the material in which it was worked. It is characterised by beautiful and appropriate strapwork ; square-worked newels and balusters and shafts ; tapered pilasters, being narrower at the bottom ; the use of caryatides ; the general use of the round-headed arch ; and the extended employment of panelling, plain and elaborate. Fig. 329 (p. 150) shows an Elizabethan strapwork panel. Towards the end of the seventeenth century, carved ornament became more and more elaborate, heavy, and unsuited to expression in wood, and some of the work of the Stuart period is quite remarkable for its ungainly and debased appearance. Following this came the glorious revival of wood carving by Grinling Gibbons, still under the influence of the Renaissance, and, in fact, being only a phase or development of this revival of classic ornament. Gibbons's work set the style for the next hundred years. Flowers and fruit, dead birds and animals, were treated in a quite natural manner, being heavily undercut, and were arranged in festoons and hanging bunches and strings. Ribbons, shells, dolphins, cupids, horns of plenty, and other Renaissance elements, were used side by side with the elements drawn from the natural world. But although the influence and the spirit were Renaissance, yet the interpretation was decidedly original, and has stamped this period as essentially an English development. During the eighteenth century the influence of the Renaissance became more pronounced still, and details and elements of Italian origin became more in evidence as the century advanced. In addition, there were influences at work resulting from the creation of national styles in France, Germany, and Flanders; a distinctive style arising in each case from the fusion of the Italian spirit with the native craft of the country concerned. One great result was the impetus given to furniture making, and it is during this period—say from 1680 to 1780—that those fine creations, known successively as William and Mary, Chippendale, Sheraton, Hepplewhite, Shearer, Ince, and Mayhew furniture, and others similar, were produced. In all these can the various influences at work be traced. The Dutch, as in William and Mary furniture; the French of the Louis XIV. and XV., as in much of Chippendale; the Louis XVI., as in Sheraton.

Renaissance after the Restoration

With the Restoration came a French queen and court and foreign influences of all kinds in all departments of life. The effect this had on architecture and wood carving was to give a great impetus to the Renaissance, which had already made great strides on the Continent. The great plague, followed by the fire, in 1666, gave those architects and craftsmen who were expert in the new style their day of opportunity; and the French and Dutch influence thus begun lasted throughout the succeeding century, and left an indelible impress upon the craftsmanship of the eighteenth century. A description of the Master's chair in the Hall of the Brewers' Company will show how thoroughly the art of the Renaissance had gripped English craftsmen; and a comparison of this chair with the Gothic fifteenth-century chair previously described is decidedly interesting. The chair has arms, each terminating in a grotesque head; the back has a shield placed on drapery carved from the solid, under which are two swags of fruit, flowers, and ribbons, and hanging from scrolls at the top corners are two drops of the same elements. The back is continued up in the centre, and terminates in a grotesque head with carved scrolls at each side. There is, too, a carved oak mantelpiece, which has a shield with a winged head, palms, and swags of fruit and flowers, while on the shield is an inscription giving the date 1670. Besides Grinling Gibbons, other noted wood carvers of this time were Samuel Watson, who did a great deal of the carving in Chatsworth; Drerot of Brussels; Launeans of Mechlin, who were all three pupils of Gibbons; Jonathan Maine and Philip Wood, who both worked in St. Paul's Cathedral; and Selden. Another great carver in both wood and stone was Nicholas Stone, an artist who was doing his chief work about 1620.

Grinling Gibbons

Grinling Gibbons was born in Rotterdam on April 4, 1648. He early came to England, where he established a style of carving which, though based on the Renaissance, and partaking of the feeling of this period, is yet a distinct phase, or style, marking it as being essentially English. In the Gothic periods, the elements used by the wood carvers were taken, in most cases, from nature, the ivy, vine, maple, blackberry, oak, being typical illustrations. During the Tudor and Elizabethan periods, strapwork, coats of arms, the Tudor rose, caryatides, shields and cartouches, figures of animals, grotesques, and the human figure, were the subjects most commonly adopted. The Jacobean period gave, besides strapwork, a crude conventionalisation of natural forms, sometimes reduced to geometrical outlines. This became more florid, until the late Stuart period showed elaborate scrollwork; and public buildings of this period invariably have, as a principal part of their decorative scheme, carved work of the Grinling Gibbons type. Birds, both living and dead, fruit and flowers arranged in festoons or swags,

Fig. 351.—Screen at Iwerne Minster, Carved by J. Phillips.

trophies, weapons, and musical instruments came gradually into the field. Gibbons raised wood carving again to an important place in architecture, as is witnessed by the great development that occurred during his lifetime, and the extent to which his work, or work after the school or style he established, was adopted. Churches, mansions, colleges, and ribbons, shells, dolphins, cupids, are all carved with the greatest spirit and with extraordinary ability.

A Grinling Gibbons Frame

The wonderful mirror frame shown by Fig. 343 (p. 163) is attributed to Grinling Gibbons, and there cannot be much doubt that the assumption is correct. This frame is executed in limewood, and is in the Victoria and Albert Museum, South Kensington, and will be dealt with at greater length in a later chapter devoted to frames. Enlarged views of it will also be given later. Fig. 344 illustrates a drop carved in limewood, after the style of Grinling Gibbons, presumably at the Pyghtle Works, Bedford, whose principal, Mr. John P. White, has

Fig. 352.—Lily Buds and Flowers: Detail of Screen at Iwerne Minster, Carved by J. Phillips.

kindly supplied the photograph from which the illustration has been made.

The Gibbons Style

The school or style of wood carving begun by Gibbons set the style for the whole of the eighteenth century, and throughout the Georgian period there was little carving except in this style. Additions and modifications were made from time to time, especially after the return of Sir William Chambers from his travels in China (1750), which

caused a decidedly Chinese character to be given to furniture; the influence of France from the time of Louis XVI. gave the art a French turn; and the finding and working of the remains of Pompeii and Herculaneum caused a corresponding modification in the carved as well as in the other ornament of the time. Carved friezes, capitals, pilasters, and mouldings were more favoured by the carvers than were panels, the latter generally being left quite plain. Furniture during this century was often elaborately carved, Chippendale using the craft to a large extent, very often to excess. From Gibbons's time to well into the nineteenth century, wood carving declined, and little or nothing of merit was done until one of the comparatively modern wood carvers, Thomas W. Wallis, who was born in 1821, began to raise its level.

A Louis Quatorze Design

A design by F. L. Schauermann, presented by Fig. 345 (p. 165), is typical of French carved ornament in the reign of Louis XIV. This king ascended the throne in 1643, and during most of the years between then and his death in 1715 gave every possible encouragement and impetus to the erection of buildings in the particular grand style which he affected.

An Arabic Ceiling

Fig. 346 illustrates the carved ceiling of a Damascus room. This is Arabic work, and is painted and gilt. It dates from the eighteenth century.

The Victorian Period

The carved ornamental detail of the furniture of the Early Victorian period was of the kind known as "Baroque," or debased "rococo." This came in with the Restoration of the Monarchy in France, from which country England had obtained its fashions since Gothic times. The use of this ornament appears to have been prompted more by a desire for display and show than for the real necessities of ornament. A certain school of architects, the greatest of whom was Augustus Welby Pugin, made an effort to revive Gothic architecture and ornament, but the effort met with great opposition;

and although the school had an influence subsequently upon architecture and the minor arts generally, yet for a long time a debased style, having the classical as its basis, held the field. The Great Exhibition of 1851 contained many undeniably clever and ingenious pieces of furniture in which the wood carving is extremely gorgeous. Indeed, it can be said that the ability to execute has always existed ; what has been wanting has been the power to originate and to conceive.

Modern Wood Carving

Recent ornament shows a decided reversion to natural forms, especially forms such as the tulip, daffodil, iris, rose, water-lily, apple, and such simple and well-known flowers and fruits. These, too, are treated in a natural manner, being conventionalised only so far as the limitations of the wood require such conventionality. A peculiarly sudden, yet boldly graceful, form of bend or twist is characteristic, too, of this modern tendency. Examples of this style are shown by Figs. 164 and 188 (pp. 73 and 84), and may be referred to as being somewhat typical of the modern development of carved ornament. One important point that obtains consideration is that the limitations of the wood as a medium of ornamental expression are very well considered and worked up to, but not exceeded. Thus, flat carving predominates, any work standing in high relief being confined to the large elements in any design. At the same time, the Gothic and Renaissance ornaments are still largely used, the former in church carving, and the latter in furniture. But there are evidences that the more vigorous and more reasonable forms of the new art have come to stay, and it is to be hoped they are forming the groundwork of a new style that will distinguish the ornament of the twentieth century from the dull, lifeless copy work that characterises a good proportion of the work of the nineteenth century.

Nineteenth-century Examples

An example of the neo-Greek style of carving (the design being by F. L. Schauermann) is shown by Fig. 347. This style is a modern French imitation of the work of the ancient Greeks, and it began in the reign of Louis Philippe. Its principles " enjoined a most careful studying of design based upon the materials of the structure, and of decoration strictly rational, and called for by the forms themselves." Absolutely different is the example of the " modern style " (see Fig. 348) offered by the same designer. This illustration cannot be regarded as representative. Two pieces of work executed at the School of Art Woodcarving, London, are illustrated by Figs. 349 and 350. The first panel was designed by C. M. Rogers and carved by Edwin Fairchild, and the second was designed and carved by Charlotte Moore. An example of the work of Mr. J. Phillips may conclude the illustrations to this chapter. Fig. 351 (p. 172) shows the screen at Iwerne Minster, for which Mr. C. E. Ponting was architect and Mr. Phillips carver. The upper part of this screen fits into a pointed arch, and is filled with tracery. Just below the springing of the arch a carved beam with cresting divides the open part from the solid door and flanking panels below. The posts of the door are carved with a similar pattern to the cross-beam—a pattern of roses—and these uprights are continued till they strike the arch, being crossed by small shields in two places where the perpendicular lines are broken by ingeniously designed bands of tracery. The lowest panels are filled with an ordinary linen-fold design, but the upper panels of the door are ornamented with an exceedingly graceful treatment of lily buds and flowers (see detail, Fig. 352) used as crockets and finials to a traceried head to the panel, while at the bottom a band of design of a similar character, but much smaller, runs across, enriching and emphasising the principal rail.

MISCELLANEOUS PANELS

Thɪs chapter includes a number of illustrations which are capable of being adapted by the wood carver to a great variety of applications. Most of the panels here shown have no special application, but that is not to say that any one of them is suitable for all purposes. The law of fitness, upon which emphasis has already been laid (see p. 51), must not be transgressed. Many of the designs may be used without the alteration of any part, but others will serve to provide the carver with instruction, ideas, and food for thought ultimately leading to his designing anew for himself.

Panels representing the Plum, the Blackberry, and the Wild Rose

The three designs shown by Figs. 353 to 355 are based on familiar forms, the larger panel (Fig. 353) showing the plum, and the smaller panels (Figs. 354 and 355) the common bramble or blackberry and the wild rose. (It should be noted that in order to get these illustrations into the restricted space available, the top and bottom margins have been sacrificed, thus somewhat detracting from the appearance of the designs.) Every carver should seize every opportunity of studying plant form, for all design may be said to be based on an intelligent study of plants. Draw any plant rather than none, but exercise the faculty of selection, and study particularly the plants that are "ornamentally suggestive"; for a form like the bramble is full of suggestion, almost all its features giving the craftsman opportunities. The leaf itself, made up of five small leaves growing from a common stalk, is most adaptable, and

can be rendered effectively in wood (see Fig. 354). Then the way the leaves articulate from the stem in what is termed a "whorl," or around the stem on the principle of a spiral, is a point to be noticed. The stem, again, with the spines, is an ornamental feature, and one that can be made much of. The panel introduces a flower and buds as well as fruit, in order to enforce practically the axiom that every suggestion should be made the most of by the craftsman; and as the flower is seen at the same time as the fruit, such a trait should be utilised and insisted upon. The fruit, again, with its numerous little beads or "drupes," is most effective in carving, as the surface, being broken up, catches the light, and casts numerous shadows, which give brilliancy and relief to work, and prevent any tendency to tameness. The skill in wood carving is seen in the way the surface is broken up, or "thrown about" as carvers say. In other words, it depends for its effect on some forms being prominent and receiving light, and others being kept back and producing shadows. The "throwing about" can less easily be studied in a sketch than in modelling in clay, for one is more occupied in disposing the various forms, filling out the space, and arranging "lines," than in studying it as a piece of carving. In Figs. 353 to 355, an attempt has been made to suggest by means of light and shade which parts should be prominent and which should be kept back, but in actually carrying out the design many modifications would doubtless present themselves. Many wood carvers model the design roughly in clay, and work from this rather than from the design on

Fig. 353.—Panel based on the Plum.   By Fred Miller.

Fig. 354.—Panel based on the Blackberry. By Fred Miller.

paper, and undoubtedly a more accurate estimate of the finished work can be thus obtained than by the most elaborate of pencilled drawings. To make the best use of plant form, it is necessary to draw the plant many times, until one is thoroughly imbued with its spirit and knows all its salient features by heart. For the designer must avoid thinking of any one particular specimen he has seen, but must endeavour to put into the design the characteristics of the plant, and not the adventitious and individual peculiarities of an individual specimen. And to get freedom as a designer one must be able to depend largely upon recollection rather than upon reference to fragments. The planning and disposition of the main lines of the design should, at all events, be studied apart from any individual specimens ; for if one has recourse to such data, the design is apt to be local and petty instead of general and dignified. In other words, the letter instead of the spirit will be found in work when the recollection is not largely depended upon. A designer has first of all to dispose his forms so that they occupy the space without crowding it, and the skeleton of the design should have balance, proportion, and grace. A most excellent drawing of a bramble may have been made, but only failure may come of any attempt to adapt a portion of it to occupying a particular space agreeably, or in such a way as shall give the beholder the feeling that the bramble filling out the panel was designed for that space, and that alone, and could not have been employed elsewhere. Then the capabilities of material and the possibilities of the craft have to be considered. Remember always that the carver does not, as a wax modeller does, imitate a piece of bramble in wood, but that he carves a design suggested by the bramble. A great deal must be generalised ; for evidently the carver cannot cut all the stamens in the centre of the flowers, or make the spines on the stem as sharp as they are in reality, or put every vein in the leaves. But the carver can hint that the stem is set with excrescences (thorns), and can suggest that the leaves are veined in one way and not another, and that the stamens are many. The result will be truer by the

generalising than it would be if the carver attempted to reproduce all he knew to be there, for then he would fail, owing to the impossibility of carrying out such a task. Reverting to Figs. 353 to 355, start with the main stems, and get these placed so that they form either agreeable curves or " nervous " angles with each other. At the same time put down the leading features, as the plums in Fig. 353, for the objects that are prominent must be thoughtfully arranged so that they do not (a) all come in one place and leave the rest of the space vacant, and (b) fall one under the other in perpendicular lines, but are spread about, so that lines drawn from one point to another make a series of triangles instead of squares. The position of stems and fruit having been roughly determined, the leaves must be carefully arranged. There must not be too many leaves—not nearly as many, in fact, as might be found on a piece of plum tree, for the design is to be kept simple. Then some leaves can fall over the fruit and stems, for the stems should here and there be broken up by leaves or fruit, to take away the look of stalkiness. It stands to reason that, as all forms have a relation to each other, the introduction of a leaf or fruit may cause the designer to modify slightly the disposition of some particular piece of stem, though adhering generally to the first suggestion. Thus a design is gradually built up, and not set down as a whole, complete in all its details from the outset.

" Nervous " Angles in a Design.— Reference to the stems making " nervous " angles with each other is made above. A design is said to be " nervous " when there is vigour, crispness, angularity in it— qualities, in short, the reverse of tameness. Instead of the edges of leaves being round or continuous, they should be in a series of angles (as in Fig. 356), and not rounded (as in Fig. 357). Natural forms will be found to be full of angles. The leaves break vigorously from the stems, and the stems again form most beautiful angles with each other. " Round " lines are always a sign of want of skill, and are sure to produce a feeling of insipidity and feebleness.

Carving the Panels.—In carrying out the three designs (Figs. 353 to 355) a draw-

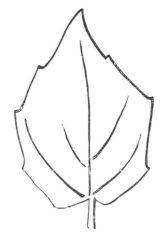

Fig. 356.—Desirable Angularity in
Leaf Form.

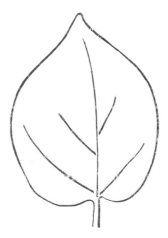

Fig. 357.—Undesirable Rounded Outline
in Leaf Form.

Fig. 355.—Panel based on the Wild Rose.
By Fred Miller.

Fig. 358.—Panel with Chrysanthemum as Motif.   By Fred Miller.

Fig. 359.—Panel with Poppy as Motif.   By Fred Miller.

ing should be made to the size of the proposed carving, fully the natural size. The enlargement should then be transferred to the wood as already explained. The depth to which the background is taken out depends upon the thickness of the wood; but beginners should not attempt very much relief. Try the designs not more than $\frac{1}{2}$ in. in depth; even $\frac{3}{8}$ in. would be sufficient. The " grounding out " is much more difficult the deeper it is taken into the wood, and at the outset the general difficulties are quite enough to overcome, without courting others. Do not be afraid to see the marks of the chisel in the work. Good wood carving looks as though the craftsman had executed his work by a series of well-directed bold cuts rather than a number of nerveless, timid ones.

Enlarging a Design

The simplest way of producing an enlarged design is as follows : Suppose that it is wished to produce a copy of Fig. 355 twice its scale (that is to say, the area covered will be four times the area of the original). Divide the original into $\frac{1}{2}$-in. squares by drawing lines across it and from top to bottom at intervals of $\frac{1}{2}$ in. Then rule a piece of paper in the same way with lines 1 in. apart. Having done this, copy the outline, square for square, on the paper thus prepared. A purely mechanical method is to use an instrument such as a pantograph.

Panel with Chrysanthemum as Motif

It is apparent that there is much in plant form that cannot adequately be rendered by carving in wood. Grinling Gibbons has shown how far in an imitative direction wood carving can be carried, in those wreaths and festoons of flowers and fruit he was so fond of working (see Fig. 343, p. 163). He compels admiration of such work because of his skill in almost hiding the insurmountable difficulties of his task ; but it is generally felt that this is not the direction in which wood carving should be carried, and very few wood carvers, either professional or amateur, have such a command over their tools as to carve a lily with the petals almost as thin as the real flowers. The Gothic school of wood carving is content with a much simpler character of work ; it does not attempt much in the way of imitation ; it has robustness, vigour, and an almost archaic simplicity. It suggests that it is better to succeed in a quiet, unaffected way than to fail by aiming too high ; as long as the carver keeps to well-known plant forms, attempting no great amount of relief, and just simplifying and fitting in the growth to the particular space to be filled, he can hardly help succeeding. In panels such as that presented by Fig. 358 for a hanging cabinet, the work is concentrated, and the carver can attempt a little more elaboration than if the work were on a large scale and extended over a large surface. In designing such a panel as is shown by Fig. 358, if the carver were working direct from nature, he should first of all make a study of some characteristic piece of chrysanthemum, and in choosing the specimens draw on his power of selection. He should not take a very complicated specimen, in which the growth is too full and prevents the skeleton, as it were, being seen. Do not choose a specimen that is eccentric through some malformation or individual peculiarity; for in carving the desire should be to give the first principles of plant form. Make a careful and life-size study in pencil, or sepia, or charcoal (colour tends to confusion, and may prevent perception of the general form and growth). Always make studies life size, for it is easy to reduce afterwards, whereas in working from one's own studies one is apt to get the work out of proportion if the study is not life size. Note all the peculiarities and characteristics of the plant : the way the leaves articulate from the stem, the curves and angles the stems themselves take, the contour of the leaves, the way the flower is set upon the stalk, and so on. Disregard minute points such as how many veins there are in a leaf (but observe the deviation the veins take, and any striking feature about them), or the number of serrations to the leaves (but notice the form of such serrations) ; these are matters that more concern the botanist. Strive for breadth, mass, line, for these characteristics wood carving can reproduce.

Fig. 360.—Panel with Vine as Motif.

Panel with Poppy as Motif

The poppy as a motif is utilised in the panel shown by Fig. 359. The remarks made in the previous paragraph apply in this case also. The drawing of a plant from nature makes one see for the first time what is in the plant that gives it its individuality. A man may have looked at a poppy a hundred times, and may think because

with some free implement—charcoal or a brush and colour. Think of the panel as a whole all the time the work is being blocked out, for, by so doing, the leaves will be made to fall agreeably from the stem, making pleasing angles and occupying the space without crowding it. It is impossible to get proportion or balance by dwelling upon some one feature, or, beginning at the top, by working downwards without

Fig. 361.—Panels showing Alternative Treatment of Vine Motif.

he can always recognise a poppy that he knows the plant. But let him attempt to make a sketch from memory, and his ignorance will then be the chief thing he is conscious of, so little does he remember what the growth of the poppy is. It might almost be said that an object is not seen correctly until the observer draws it. In working from studies, do not think of details at all; let these come of their own accord. Place down the chief forms, such as the principal leaves, and in these panels (Figs. 358 and 359) start naturally with the chief object, the flower. Work with freedom and

regard to what else is coming. Do not be too neat in designing. Brown paper and Chinese white and lampblack are the best materials to use. Put in the forms boldly, for with white and black the designer can soon get an effect on brown paper.

Panel Designs based on Vine Leaves and Foliage

Figs. 360 and 361 are illustrations of panels in which the vine has been used as the motif. Fig. 362 shows a rosette design in Byzantine style. Remarks already made apply in these cases. Bear in mind that the serrations on the edges of the leaves should be correctly drawn (see Fig. 363, which illustrates a leaf characteristic of the Byzantine period).

Circular Panel with Figure Design and Border

In drawing the ornament which fills the circular border of Fig. 364, the leading

of the principal forms are elliptical. The figure forming the principal feature of the centre panel in Fig. 364 must be carefully drawn, separately, and transferred to its position. The proportions must be religiously preserved in order to keep the grace and freedom of the pose. The lines of the figure have been carefully studied in relation to their harmony with the space

Fig. 362.—Rosette in Byzantine Style.

Fig. 363.—Serrated Leaf in Byzantine Style.

lines form practically the skeleton or framework, and must be defined at the outset; otherwise, the whole will prove a disjointed failure. The circular lines of the plaque itself will suggest the inclination and direction of these lines. Having determined these, and decided as to the manner in which the ground-lines are to be clothed, draw in the details firmly and deliberately. In the repetition of the forms, be careful that the lines flow sweetly into one another. Each line in itself is of vital importance to the whole; take it away, and its absence will be painfully evident. In analysing the forms it will be found that the curves

occupied. In treatment it must be strictly decorative. The drapery will require careful studying, lest, while preserving the lines of the figure, the designer falls into the trap of making the drapery too "pipey." Three different designs have been suggested for the border, but it is intended that one only should be used at a time.

Panels with Iris and Narcissus Motifs

The carved panels shown by Figs. 365 and 366 were designed by the late J. W. Gleeson-White for the folding doors of a small cabinet, but they can be adapted to

a variety of purposes, since an oblong upright panel is infinitely useful. The pattern is so arranged that for those who wish
to shirk the labour of carving out of the
saw the thin section for fret-cutting off
the solid block, so that, when replaced, the
grain of the wood should correspond exactly
in each instance. The idea of each panel

Fig. 364.—Circular Panel with Figure Design and Border.

solid, the design may be traced and cut
out with a fret saw, in wood about $\frac{1}{4}$ in.
thick, and then mounted on a block of the
same wood for carving. When practicable,
it would be best, in working this way, to
is a single group of the plant, with some
lesser flower nestling about its foot-stalks.
The stalks and the leaves of the principal
flowers are planned so that they appear to
grow up through the dividing bar of the

Fig. 365.—Panel with Yellow Iris as
Motif.

Fig. 366.—Panel with Poet's Narcissus as
Motif.

Fig. 369.—Ornamental Panel. By John Law.

Fig. 367.

Fig. 368.

Figs. 367 and 368.—Designs for Corners. By John Law

panels. In carving from nature, no production of the chisel can show the full subtlety of the actual object. Yet it must not be forgotten that in conventional carved work, a broad effect, whereby the more salient points of the flower are seized and treated by Figs. 367 to 374. The panel shown by Fig. 370 may be referred to particularly. This is a simple design, but a highly effective one providing the modelling is skilfully done. It is a case in which everything depends on the carver.

Fig. 370.—Panel based on Fruit and Foliage. By John Law.

boldly, is preferable to a painfully minute and laborious imitation of every detail. The yellow iris and the poet's narcissus are both adapted for this treatment (see Figs. 365 and 366), as the simple masses of their form can be expressed with comparatively little detail.

Some Effective Corners, Panels, and Borders

A Liverpool carver, John Law, designed the corners, panels, and borders illustrated

Jacobean Wall Panels

The designs presented by Figs. 376 to 381 are more especially intended for wall panelling, in dadoes or otherwise, but the carver will doubtless find other uses for which they will be acceptable. Figs. 376 to 378 are selected from good examples of the Jacobean period. Fig. 376 is perhaps most characteristic of the reign of James I., to which it belongs. It has the features which are associated with the ornament of this period—the flat strapwork, and the scroll-edged cartouche. These are points which conclusively fix its style and date. It will not, however, be found a particularly easy panel to carve. In thick board, where the forms could be treated boldly, it would be

for in some one or other of its varieties it is found frequently recurring in work belonging not only to the time of James, but to most other times in the seventeenth century. Indeed, among panel patterns old oak, none is so frequent as this diamond

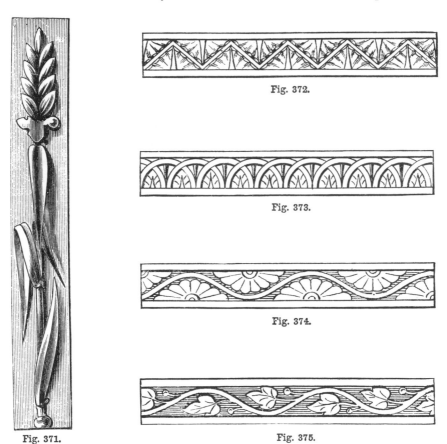

Fig. 372.

Fig. 373.

Fig. 374.

Fig. 371.   Fig. 375.

Figs. 371 to 375.—Narrow Panel, Borders, and Edges.   By John Law.

sufficiently simple, but in the thin substance of a panel, which necessitates a very low relief, clever management is needed to render it effective. The ends of the strapwork which approach the scrolls have, of course, to be somewhat lowered, whilst the central parts, in and around the rosette, are left at the original level. The sprays which occupy the corners are formed by incised lines merely. The diamond pattern (Fig. 377) is less distinctively Jacobean,

This is no doubt owing to the fact that whilst it is effective it is a thing easily and quickly carved. Two deeply incised parallel lines mark out the diamond, whilst the band formed between them is sunk into a rounded hollow with a large gouge, some enrichment being afterwards given to it as shown. The fleur-de-lis ornament at the angles has an incised line running round the outside edge of each petal; the rest is merely cut out with a couple of strokes of the gouge. Fig. 378 is drawn from an example somewhat more recent in date, though probably not later than 1660. It will be noticed that, apart from the central rosette, it has no relief carving, the rest being incised work. Though not bold in

Modern Wall Panels

In the modern design (Fig. 379) it will be seen that the manner of the old work has been followed. The ornamental band is formed in the same manner as the band

Fig. 376.—Jacobean Scrolled Cartouche.

Fig. 377.—Jacobean Diamond Pattern.

Fig. 378.—Incised Wall Panel.

Fig. 379.—Modern Design with Jacobean Band.

Fig. 380.—Band and Rosette (Modern).

Fig. 381.—Diaper Pattern (Modern).

effect, this kind of work is pleasing as wall decoration, and can be rapidly done with a keen dividing-tool, for driving which a pewter dummy is better than a mallet. The intricacy of the design matters little when several similar panels have to be carved, as they can all be traced off from one drawing; but this system would not have commended itself to the earlier carvers.

in Fig. 377. The central flower is simply incised work, but to give roundness and relief to the boss there is a slight lowering of the surrounding surface. Fig. 380 has a band somewhat differently disposed and enriched, but worked in the same way; its central rosette is, however, carved in relief in a sunk medallion. The corner sprays, with their stems, are merely incised. In the diaper (Fig. 381) the trellis is dealt with in the same way as the bands in the two last-named patterns. When several panels decorated with such diapers as this are brought together, a very rich effect is gained ; yet, owing to the smallness of the work, it might perhaps be more

The photo was supplied by Mr. J. P. White, of the above works.

Panel by Luigi Frullini

While striving to depict simple designs of flowers, leaves, and fruit, and afterwards figures and groups, Luigi Frullini, the great

Fig. 382.—Ealustrade Panel.

satisfactory to carve this design in lime or pear tree than in oak.

Balustrade Panel

The balustrade panel (Fig. 382) was, with a large number of other panels of a similar nature, carved at the Pyghtle Works, Bedford, for the decoration of a Suffolk mansion. The panels are of walnut, 3 in. thick, carved both sides, there being in the centre of each panel a different design.

Florentine carver, became discouraged in his first resolve to devote himself to wood carving, because he found it impossible to reproduce, with the primitive and meagre supply of tools then in vogue, the desired effects and combinations. Turning to the antique, he found that certain cuts must have been made by certain edges. Led by the study of these works and the hints given by them, and with his own ingenuity, he invented tools which are in use by Italian

Fig. 384.

Fig. 383.

Figs. 383 and 384.—Two Panels. By Luigi Frulini.

wood carvers of to-day. In his studio there were to be found blades and points and edges and files made by himself, at his

Fig. 385.—Litany Desk, Bridgnorth Church. By J. Phillips.

of his works until its nature had been minutely studied from every aspect. Never a flower of his modelling had a petal too many or one too few. He was a man who saw the beautiful and the graceful in all, and with his unerring genius he plucked out, as it were, the heart of his subjects, realistically reflecting the central point without being over-elaborate. He went straight to Nature, and his work-bench was covered with the flowers or leaves which he was reproducing with even more deliberation than a painter. In fact, with more than a painter's attention was every line executed, for from the living model he worked straight upon the final study. And thus he brought the life and movement of his subject into the very fibre of the wood. Frullini worked without design or sketch, following Michael Angelo in cutting immediately into the final material, and he often found that the block from which he worked was not of sufficient size to contain the work of his imagination. Consequently, as has already been remarked, in his studio were numberless figures in graceful poses, one lacking an arm, another a bit of floating drapery. So careful was he of every detail in his work, so conscientious and scrupulous, that he would not, for example, twine primroses and morning glories together, insisting that though they might appear in the

Fig. 386.—Altar Frontal.   By J. Phillips.

own forge, and only finished as far as the necessity of their use demanded. Never did Frullini allow an object to enter one

same panel, they must represent a different set of thought and ideas, for they could not be in bloom at the same time, and there-

Fig. 387.—Panels with Different Treatment of the Same Lines of Design.   By J. Phillips.

Fig. 388.   Fig. 389.   Fig. 390.

Figs. 388 to 390.—Flemish Panels.   From Vaughan Bequest.

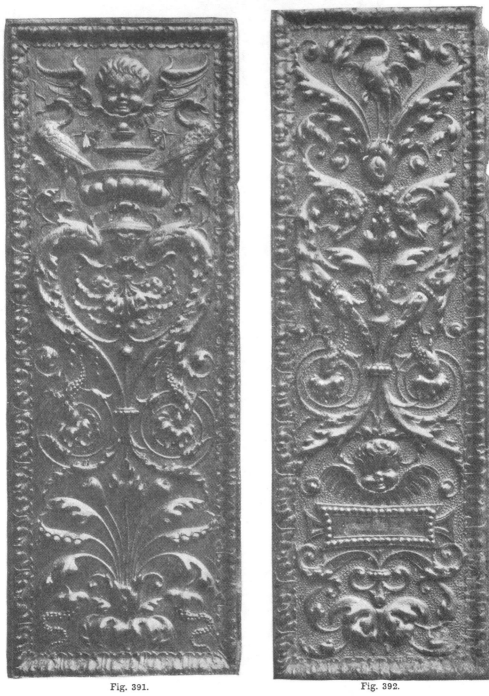

Fig. 391.   Fig. 392.

Figs. 391 and 392.—Flemish Panels (Date, 1540) with Arabesque Ornament.

Fig. 393.

Fig. 394.

Figs. 393 and 394.—French Panels from a Credence.   Period, François I.

Fig. 395.—End of Shutter Panel.   Attributed to Gille-Marie Oppenord.

Fig. 396.—East Indian Panel.

fore could not be copied together, unless one of the two were faded. Frullini specially succeeded in the figures of children. The cupids in his work were so lifelike as to be startling. In the representations given by Figs. 7 and 8 (p. 10), each curve of the plump limbs reveals the true artist and the acute student. Luigi Frullini drew his inspiration from the antique, and extracted from it all the good it had to give, yet he added to its frequent conventionality and absence of life the vibrating realism that is a characteristic of modern

Fig. 397.—Panel with Vine Motif.

art. He has touched a note so long unheard as to create the impression of novelty, and he is in truth the master of his school. Two panels typical of the artist are illustrated by Figs. 383 and 384 (p. 193).

Panels, etc., by J. Phillips

Examples of the work of a modern carver, Mr. J. Phillips, are shown by Figs. 385 to 387 (pp. 194 and 195). It should at once be pointed out that the top rail A of the litany desk (Fig. 385) is intended to be carved right up to the ends. The desk is simple in form but well proportioned, decorated with interlacing stems of vine with occasional leaves

and tendrils, treated so flatly as to be scarcely more than incised. They spring from the foot of the uprights, burst forth and run across the shaped bottom of the surface between, crossing and forming a

Fig. 398.—French Panel with Lilies and Olives Motif.

heart-shaped border to a sunk panel, from the top of which they start again, bracketwise, to support the centre of the shelf, and overflow its edge to form a small oblong panel within it. A sanctuary chair, made with the litany desk, for use in the parish church at Bridgnorth, is treated in a somewhat similar fashion, but the stems which

Fig. 399.—Diamond Panel. By F. L. Schauermann.

Fig. 400.

Figs. 400 and 401.—
Two Panel Designs.
By
F. L. Schauermann.

Fig. 401

start from the foot of each leg in the front stop under the arms, and start again from the curve at the back of each, rising to the corner of the framing and meeting in the centre, the containing curve being of a good shape. A sunk panel in the centre of the back shows an owl seated among ivy leaves. The altar frontal (Fig. 386) makes use of the same kind of motif for stiles and rails, but the panels are occupied by cleverly arranged tracery springing from heart-shaped forms slightly sunk. Two panels are shown by Fig. 387 (p. 195). In these, two spaces are enriched with designs based on the same lines, but treated in quite a different way, and so producing quite a different

Fig. 402.—Geometrical Panel Design. By F. L. Schauermann.

effect. This example was prepared by Mr. Phillips as a demonstration for a class under the Home Arts and Industries Association.

Flemish Panels

Figs. 388 to 390 (p. 195) show Flemish work —three oak panels carved in high relief, in the style of the work on the door of the council chamber in the Hôtel de Ville, Oudenarde. These also form part of the Vaughan bequest to the Victoria and Albert Museum. Further Flemish panels are shown by Figs. 391 and 392. Both are carved in oak, and date from about 1540. Their height is 2 ft., and width 8 in. The ornament is arabesque, scroll work being prominent, and is surmounted in Fig. 391 by a cherub and in Fig. 392 (in which the cartouche will be noticed) by a crane.

French Panels from a Credence

The panels illustrated by Figs. 393 and 394 (p. 197) exemplify French work of the period of François I. They originally formed part of a credence, and the subjects treated are extremely interesting, whilst the carving is of a spirited nature. The panels form part of the collection bequeathed by Henry Vaughan to the Victoria and Albert Museum, South Kensington, London.

Louis XV. Panel

Fig. 395 (p. 198) shows the end of a shutter panel in the Edinburgh Museum. This is attributed to Gille-Marie Oppenord, and is of the Louis Quinze period. It exemplifies the system of interpanelling introduced by the artists of the Regency.

East Indian Panel

In the East Indian panel shown by Fig. 396 (p. 198), the beautiful scrolls have something of a Portuguese character, and there is a distinct Renaissance flavour to the central vase from which the stems proceed, the details of the husks, and some of the leaves. This panel was shown in the Colonial Exhibition of 1886.

Panel with Vine Motif

The panel shown by Fig. 397 (p. 199) is one of four door panels designed by Mr. Watson and carved by Mr. A. Lyon, of the People's Palace. This panel was shown at the East London Trades, Industries and Arts Exhibition, 1896.

Panel with Lilies and Olives Motif

A curious instance of eighteenth-century ornament of no precise period is afforded by Fig. 398, which illustrates a panel from the Peyre collection in the South Kensington Museum. This is French work, and is an example of broad and simple yet delicate treatment of leafage. The lilies have only five petals, this often being the case in ornament.

Designs by F. L. Schauermann

Four designs by F. L. Schauermann are illustrated by Figs. 399 to 402. The first is for a diamond-shaped panel, and the fourth employs a geometrical pattern strongly suggestive of chip-carving; the pattern is set out with compasses and ruler. So as to accommodate Fig. 402 within the page, the right-hand margin has been cut off.

Wall Panelling

It is believed that the method of finishing rooms with wall panelling was first used in England in the thirteenth century. Henry III. ordered a room in Windsor Castle to be panelled, not with English oak, but with Norway pine. Colour, of course, played an important part in the interior decoration of the Middle Ages; and in this case the woodwork was little more than a ground for painting. There was, however, abundance of oak panelling before the Gothic period came to its end, and the panels were carved with tracery of the same character as that in church windows; little of this remains in England, though the work is fairly plentiful in France and some other Continental countries. More abundant is the panel enrichment which succeeded to it, and which was partly moulded and partly carved. This was the " linen pattern," of which a rather elaborate example will be given later in the chapter on " Chests and Coffers." This pattern came into vogue near the close of the fifteenth century, and ceased to be used near the close of the sixteenth. It may therefore be regarded as exclusively a

Tudor decoration. But it was not till that busy era of domestic architecture, the close of the sixteenth and the opening of the seventeenth century, that wall panelling became general; and even in Elizabeth's time, when oak was the recognised material, the wainscot, ready made, was imported from Flanders; but English workmen soon learned to compete with their foreign rivals. By far the greater part of old wall panelling in England dates from 1590 to 1630, and the panels of this period are small, and always of oak. Much of it is comparatively plain, the shallow upper panels only being enriched with the "thumb" ornament (also illustrated in the later chapter above referred to). When all the panels are carved in early Stuart work, the design is generally with some one of the variations of the well-known diamond pattern. Few rooms were panelled in oak later than 1650, for during the second half of the century woven tapestries became the favourite wall covering. In older houses the oak panelling was concealed by the new hangings. In the eighteenth century, wainscot was again used, but the material was now deal; the panels were large and tall; they were painted white, and frequently had gilt decorations.

BELLOWS

THE wood carver on the look-out for some small object on which to show his skill can be recommended to attempt the decoration works of art, and in the Renaissance period they were frequent subjects for the lavish ornamentation of those days.

Fig. 404.—Bellows, carved with Masks, Sirens, etc. Italian. Date about 1550.

Fig. 403.—Bellows, carved with Dolphins, Terminal Figures, etc. Italian. Date, 1500-1520.

Italian Bellows of the Sixteenth Century

of a pair of common wood-sided bellows. Carving shows well on these things, and bellows have a record which makes them respectable. Their shape—the ordinary modern shape—was a settled thing earlier than the Christian era, as is shown by antique

Some excellent examples of Italian sixteenth-century work are shown by Figs. 403 to 406. The bellows side shown by Fig. 403 is carved with dolphins, masks, terminal figures, etc., and, as in the next case, there is a chiselled bronze nozzle. The height is

2 ft. 6½ in., and the width 10½ in., and the original was in the Soulages collection. Fig. 404 illustrates a bellows side of chestnut wood, carved with masks, sirens, cartouche-work, etc.; the height of the original is 2 ft. 3 in., and the width 9½ in. In Fig. 405 the carved ornament takes the form of satyrs, a cupid and a grotesque mask. The height is 2 ft. 6 in., and the width 10¾ in. This is a piece of Venetian work, and was in the Soulages collection. Fig. 406 illustrates a

Fig. 405.—Bellows, carved with Satyrs, Cupid, and Grotesque Mask. Venetian. Date, about 1550.

chestnut wood bellows side, carved in relief with a mask, scrollwork, etc., and gilded. This specimen, at the time the photograph was taken, was in the possession of Holling-worth Magniac, Esq. All the bellows above mentioned represent the best period of the Italian Renaissance — the Cinque-cento. After the passing of the Roman Empire, in 476 A.D., there came a few unsettled centuries, during which art of all kinds was subject to very varying influences; but gradually in the north of Italy arose a style

Fig. 406.—Bellows, carved in Relief with Mask and Scrollwork. Italian. Date, Sixteenth Century.

known now as the Lombardic; this showed a strange mingling of the old Classic style with the traditions of the Longobards, and the symbolisms of the art of the Byzantine Empire. At the same time came the Gothic influence, which although never having the hold upon Italy that it had upon Germany, France, and England, yet was strong enough to influence the art of the country to some considerable extent. Never-

1400 A.D.; (2) the quattro-cento, 1400–1500; (3) the cinque-cento, 1500–1600. The examples of carved bellows shown by Figs. 403 to 406 are from the last period, during which all the decorative arts reached their highest point. One very remarkable feature of Italian carving of this period is the successful adaptation to the purposes of decorative art of life forms based upon the human figure, but appearing generally

Fig. 407.—Modern Conventional Design for Bellows.

Fig. 408.—Jacobean Design for Bellows.

theless, the whole of the period since the break-up of the Roman Empire can be looked upon as a period of transition and of preparation for the greater period which was to follow. This was the Renaissance, the influences of which are felt at the present time.

Italian Renaissance

The Renaissance in Italy is divided into three broad classes : (1) the tre-cento, 1300–

as grotesques, masks, satyrs, centaurs, cherubs, cupids, and sirens. Dolphins, griffins, and similar grotesque forms were also used.

Another feature is the development and use of the scroll, part of whose evolution may be traced in the illustrations given in this volume showing carved bellows, chests, coffers, and brackets, dating from the fifteenth to the eighteenth century.

Notes on Fig. 403

The design shown in Fig. 403 has a good effect. The dolphins ending in terminal figures, the figure on the handle and the mask, give quite sufficient life to the design.

Notes on Fig. 404

In this example the mask and sirens are arranged with great effect. Note the fact that master minds arranged these designs that has prevented a redundant and vainglorious scheme of ornamentation, attendant upon a straining after effect. The scroll with its cross fluting is a prominent feature in this design.

Notes on Fig. 406

In this piece of work the possible objection just mentioned cannot be urged ; only one

Fig. 409.—Acanthus-leaf Design for Bellows.

Fig. 410.—Cinque-cento Design for Bellows.

largeness of the treatment, as well as of the design. This gives strength, appropriate enough in an object of this kind.

Notes on Fig. 405

Fig. 405 is another example of the use of life forms, which here are certainly used in great profusion. It is a question whether the Italians of the sixteenth century did not overdo the use of this class of element. In this pair of bellows there are three masks, two satyrs, and one cupid. It is only the

life form, and that a mask, combined with the scroll, forms the basis of the design ; and the appropriate nature of the mask (which, with open mouth, and wildly waving hair, appears to be energetically supplying the wind for the bellows) is to be commended. This bellows was assisted in its scheme of ornamentation by the addition of gilding ; and it may be remarked that gilding and colouring were largely employed, not only in

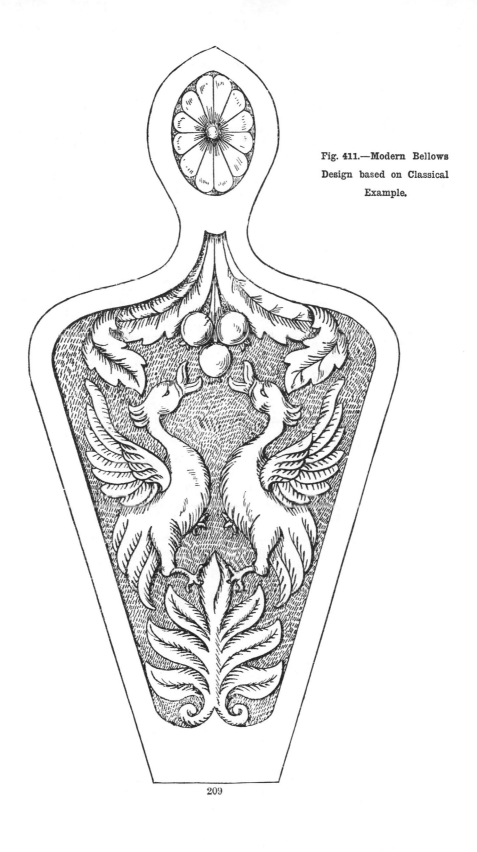

Fig. 411.—Modern Bellows
Design based on Classical
Example.

Italy, but throughout Christendom. Much of the church work in England was coloured, traces of it still remaining even to this day. In this example the drawing is not perfectly symmetrical. The design is intended to be symmetrical, but the draughtsman, or the carver, has not carried out this symmetry quite accurately ; with regard to the scrolls, one of each pair does not correspond exactly to the opposite one. Whilst this may be open to objection, it certainly prevents any suspicion of its being machine-carved. All carving should be so executed that it bears plain evidence of its craftsmanship. Too great precision and accuracy of arrangement is apt to be painfully obtrusive and insistently harsh.

Modern Conventional Design

In the design presented by Fig. 407, the carving is of a simple kind, and such as can be rapidly executed : there is no deeply sunken ground, the sinkings being merely triangular hollows after the manner of chip carving. The five-point star is a pattern capable of being applied in a number of cases with satisfactory effect.

Jacobean Design

In the Jacobean pattern (Fig. 408) the ground is regularly sunk, and worked over with the grounding punch. The central medallion is for a monogram or crest.

Acanthus=leaf Design

In the acanthus-leaf pattern (Fig. 409) also there is a sunken ground ; and the head in this is intended to be kept in very low relief. This design might possibly work out better in hard than in soft wood.

Cinque=cento Design

In Fig. 410 a design is shown for a pair of bellows based on an Italian sixteenth-century example. With all due deference to the designer, it may be suggested that the ornament here appears to be overdone. Such a pair of bellows is better fitted for the glass case of a museum than for blowing the fire ; whilst in Figs. 407 to 409 it will be observed that the aim has been never to carry ornament so far as to interfere with use. Fig. 411 is another design based on a classical example.

BREAD PLATTERS

BREAD PLATTERS are in such common use that everyone knows that they are made of hard wood, that the centre part must be perfectly flat, and that it is usual to keep that part highest by sloping the ornamental border slightly down to the outer rim. It is not advisable to indulge in very high relief.

Hops Pattern

Among the many plants whose beauty of form or colour renders them valuable for decorative purposes the hop must ever take a foremost place. The young vine pushes forward, feeling hither and thither for support; here, tightly clinging to whatever offers—often, if no independent means of support is within reach, several stems will twist together round each other like a many-stranded rope; there, hanging in long festoons from plant to plant in endless graceful curves. The leaves, too, are most beautiful. A well-grown leaf is full of

character, and will amply repay anyone for the time spent in making a careful study

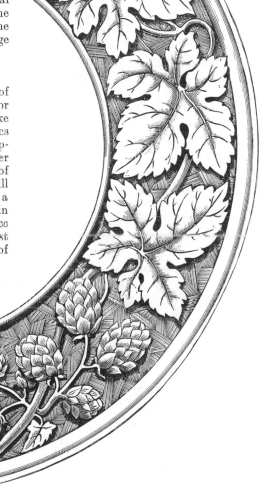

Fig. 412. — Hops Pattern for Bread Platter Border.

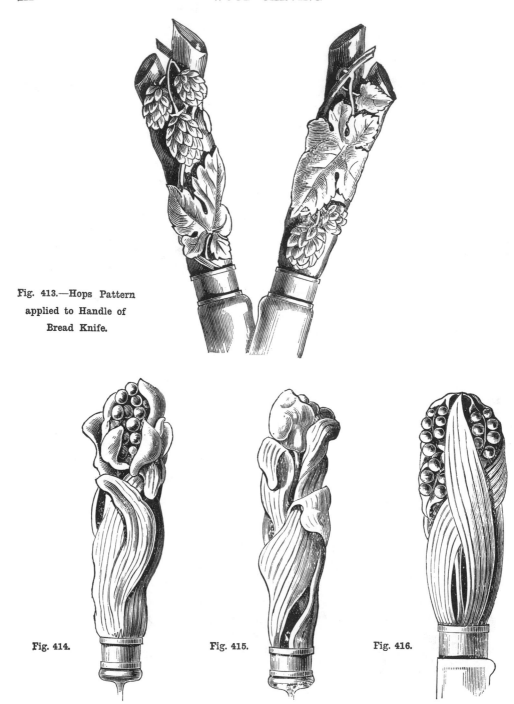

Fig. 413.—Hops Pattern applied to Handle of Bread Knife.

Fig. 414.

Fig. 415.

Fig. 416.

Figs. 414 to 416.—Wild Iris Pattern applied to Bread Knife Handle.

Fig. 417.—Wild Iris Pattern
for Bread Platter
Border.

of it in sepia, for its form and surface modulations, and then afterwards in its natural green. Only a dull green apparently, and yet sorely taxing the artist's skill as it varies with the light from steely blue to vivid, almost yellow green. The flowers, too,

leaves and berries of the wild purple iris have been used as motif. Three views of the handle of the bread knife carved to agree with the platter are presented by Figs. 414 to 416, the platter being shown by Fig. 417.

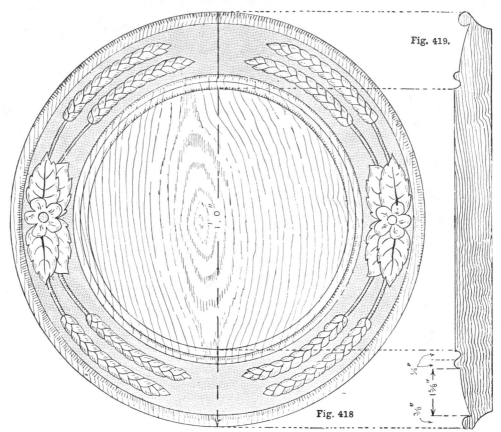

Fig. 418.—Bramble Leaves and Corn Pattern for Bread Platter.

Fig. 419.—Section of Carved Bread Platter.

although individually so insignificant and colourless, have the charm of airy lightness, while the clustering hops are universal favourites, and well deserve their popularity. The design offered by Fig. 412 is based on the hop, and the same motif is employed for the handles of the bread knives (Fig. 413).

Wild Iris Pattern

For the bread platter next shown, the

Bramble Leaves and Corn Pattern

Much less free is the design shown by Fig. 418. This is 12 in. in diameter, and should be made out of 1-in. oak, sycamore, or any other suitable wood, according to the taste of the worker. The carving, which should be in low relief, consists of bramble leaves with flower and ears of corn. A section of the platter is shown by Fig. 419.

SMALL BOXES

Small Carved Box

A SMALL box, as shown in Fig. 420, is often very useful as a receptacle for keys, odds and ends, thimbles and cottons, or even as for the moulded edges, and on that a pattern similar in design is carved. There is no reason why the same pattern should not be repeated in every instance; and a beginner would find that the time would be

Fig. 420.—Small Carved Box.

a gentleman's cuff box. The body of the box consists of four panels of ½-in. oak, each 6 in. by 6½ in., on which a simple design is worked, as in Fig. 420. The extra ½ in. is allowed for fixing the moulding round the base. The cover is 7 in. square to allow well spent in taking that on the cover as a first example, as it is simply a fretted-out exercise. The pattern outlined on the body of the box marks a step forward. Portions of this design overlap or underlie other portions, and the desired effect is produced by cutting down the shaded portions with a suitable firmer chisel. For those who desire something more advanced, an exercise in natural foliage and berries is offered in Fig. 421. It should be cut away fully $\frac{1}{8}$ in., and then slightly modelled as shown in the illustration. Fig. 422 offers a more exacting exercise, being a purely conventional design, with flowing curves and hollows, which demand both knowledge and skill to execute. Carvers do not generally construct the articles they carve; but for those who

Fig. 421.—First Alternative Design—
Natural Foliage and Berries—
for Small Carved Box.

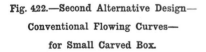

Fig. 422.—Second Alternative Design—
Conventional Flowing Curves—
for Small Carved Box.

desire to construct this box, it may be mentioned that the sides are best joined by rebated secret dovetails; and if the body of the box is to be fastened to a moulded bottom, the panels can be used 6 in. square. An ordinary ogee moulding is very suitable for both the cover and the bottom of the box.

Fig. 423.—Front Elevation of Tea Caddy.

Fig. 424.—Plan of Tea Caddy.

Tea Caddy

Figs. 423 to 425 give a design for a carved tea caddy which can be easily constructed and ornamented. The various sizes are as follows :—Lid, 11 in. long by 8 in. wide by 1 in. thick ; bottom, 9 in. long by 6 in. wide by ¾ in. thick ; two sides, 9⅜ in. long on the top edge by 7⅝ in. long on the bottom edge by 5 in. wide by ½ in. thick ; two ends, 6⅜ in. long on the top edge by 4⅝ in. long

thicknesses ; square and trim the top and bottom to their sizes, and then work the moulded edges. Make the sides and ends ¼ in. wider than the finished sizes, to allow for the subsequent planing of the edges. As the sides and ends are out of the perpendicular, they will require trimming to make the edges level to receive the top and the bottom. The sides and ends, however, can be taken to their correct shapes at first, so that very little trimming is required

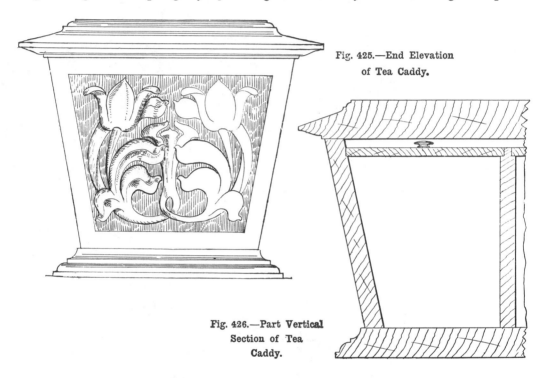

Fig. 425.—End Elevation
of Tea Caddy.

Fig. 426.—Part Vertical
Section of Tea
Caddy.

on the bottom edge by 5 in. wide by ¾ in. thick ; partition, 4¾ in. wide by about 6 in. long, of ⅜-in. stuff (see Fig. 426) ; and two lids about 6 in. wide by 4 in. long, out of ¼-in. stuff. It will be seen that only nine pieces of wood are required. The other items required are one pair of 1½-in. brass butt hinges, one brass box lock, and two small handles or knobs for the lids. The compartments of the caddy should be lined with lead paper.

Constructing Tea Caddy.—To construct the caddy, first plane the wood to the exact

afterwards. They are then prepared for secret dovetailing, which is the strongest method of fixing them together. A groove should be made in each side for the partition, and another groove near the top, in the sides and the ends, for the lids. The partition should also be rebated on each side for the lids. It should then be glued together, the bottom screwed on, the lid hung, and the lock, which should be fixed in the front side before the partition is secured, arranged for easy working. The lead paper should now be fixed to the inside and to

Fig. 427.—Jewel Case.

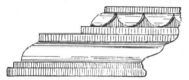

Fig. 428.—Moulded Edge of Jewel
Case Cover.

Fig. 430.—Moulding of Jewel
Case Panels.

Fig. 429.—Part of Panel of Jewel Case
Cover.

Fig. 431.—Part of Panel of Front of Jewel
Case.

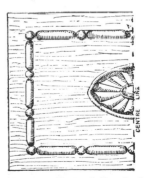

Fig. 432.—Part of Panel of
End of Jewel Case.

the lids by means of starch or prepared mountant.

Finishing Tea Caddy.—The caddy is now ready for the finishing process, and this will depend on the kind of wood used. Oak will be a very suitable wood, and if used, should be fumed and wax-polished. If American walnut is used, it can be oiled

should be done when the sides and ends are dovetailed, and before they are glued up. The top should be carved after the edges have been moulded.

Jewel Case

A jewel case or box which can be constructed in oak, walnut, or any close-grained

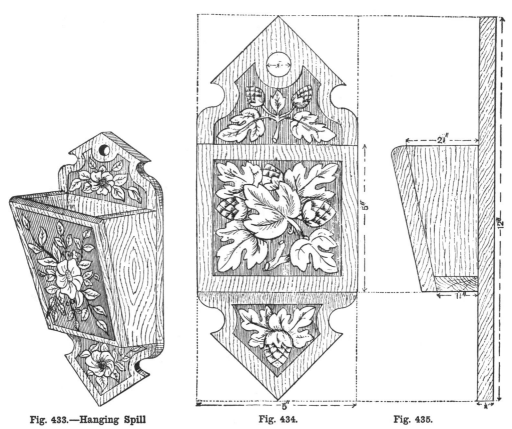

Fig. 433.—Hanging Spill Box.

Fig. 434.

Fig. 435.

Figs. 434 and 435.—Front and Side Elevations of Spill Box.

with raw linseed oil and turps, or it can be french-polished. If of mahogany, it could be french-polished its natural colour, or it could be given a Chippendale colour, obtained by staining with bichromate of potash and afterwards french-polishing. The foregoing methods of finishing apply if the caddy is made without carving. If it is carved, the same description will apply to it, with the exception that the carving

wood, is illustrated by Fig. 427. The size can be about 12 in. long, 6 in. wide, and 6 in. deep. The cover is hinged at the back with ordinary brass butt hinges, and secured at the front with an ordinary box lock of brass, with a little ornamental escutcheon. Fig. 428 gives an enlarged view of the corner of the cover, which is flat, the ornamental panel being fixed on. The outer moulding of the panel can either

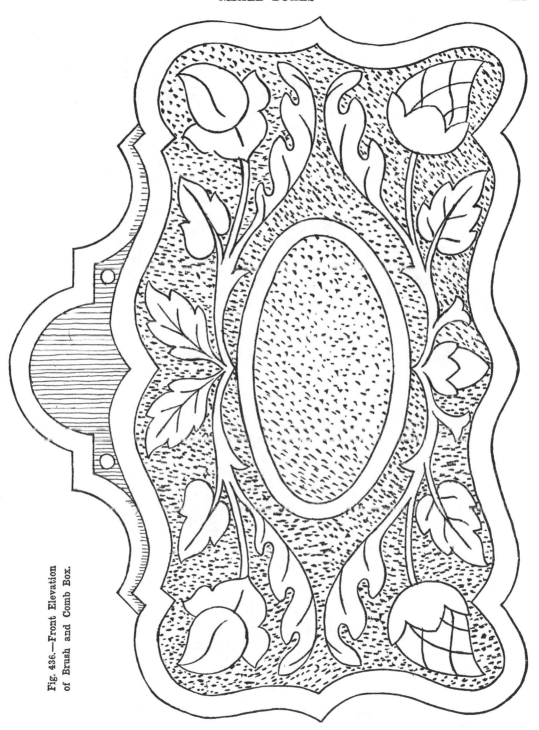

Fig. 436.—Front Elevation of Brush and Comb Box.

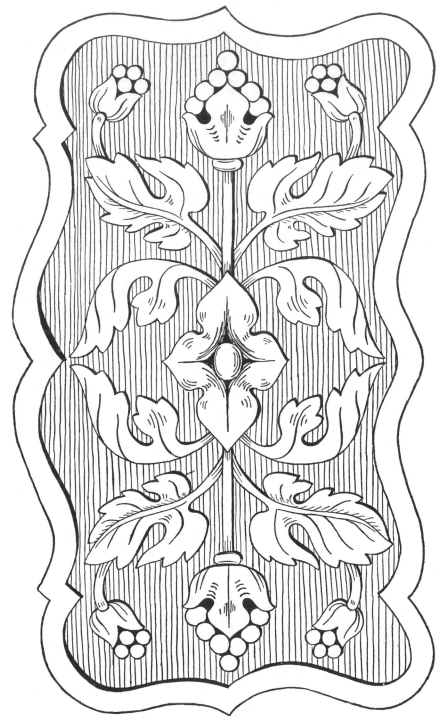

Fig. 437.—Alternative Design (in Incised Carving) for Front of Brush and Comb Box.

be carved as shown, or left plain. Half the panel is shown enlarged by Fig. 429. The carving is raised in low relief above the groundwork of the sunk panel, which should be matted to give a better effect to the ornament. The central pattern is shown with the date of the year carved on it, raised or incised. If preferred, a monogram can be used here with equally good effect. The front of the box (*see* Fig. 427) is shown with a sunk panel having a plain moulding round as seen in Fig. 430. The

plain box of similar size can be arranged by using at the front and top the pattern adopted here for the end only. The woodwork should have a dead finish, the carving being left from the tool. If more ornament is desired, the moulding of the panels can be carved; but, with certain marked exceptions, carved work looks best when enclosed within plain mouldings.

Hanging Spill Box

Figs. 433 to 435 give three views of a

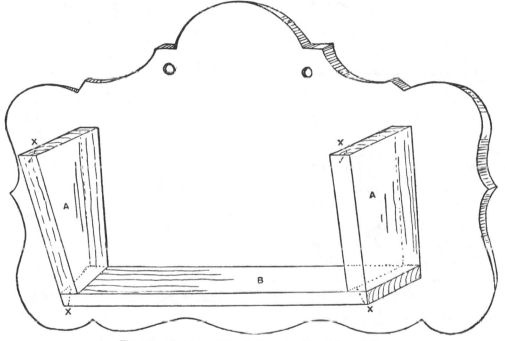

Fig. 438.—Comb and Brush Box with Front Removed.

panel is carved in low relief above the groundwork, which can be left plain ; or, to give a good effect, it can be matted: Fig. 431 shows half this panel of enlarged size, giving the modelling of the carving, which requires careful execution, the scroll lines being well kept. The ends of the box are shown with sunk panels the same as the front, but the carving should be plainer. Fig. 432 shows half the end, to enlarged size. The escutcheon of the keyhole on the front should be of polished brass. From these illustrations a

carved hanging spill box, which may be made of ½-in. oak. Fig. 433 shows a simple pattern of roses and leaf-sprays. Fig. 434 shows both a front and side view of the box with alternative designs, and gives dimensions. These may be enlarged or decreased according to requirements. The design, representing hop-vine and blossoms, looks well when carved about ⅛ in. deep. If in pine, the parts should be secured with light brads. If in oak, the sides and bottom should be secured to the back with ¾-in.

screws, and the front should be held in place with round-headed or fancy-headed brass screws.

Brush and Comb Box

The box shown by Figs. 436 to 438 combines elegance with utility. Fig. 436 gives a front view, with the back board showing

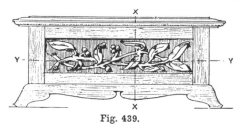

Fig. 439.

Figs. 439 and 440.—Elevations of Handkerchief Box.

Fig. 441.—Plan of Handkerchief Box.

gether. Before affixing the back, screw the front to the carcase by means of four screws, driven in a slanting direction, through the top and bottom corners of A, as shown at x (Fig. 438). Carefully select and drive the screws so that they shall not appear through the front. Then fasten the whole to the back board by screws driven in from behind.

Fig. 440.

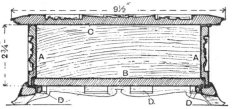

Fig. 442.—Vertical Section of Handkerchief Box (on Line X X).

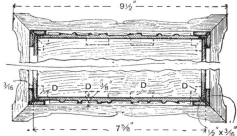

Fig. 443.—Horizontal Section of Handkerchief Box (on Line Y Y).

above the front one. It may be maed of whitewood, stained and varnished, with a simple outline design on it, as shown in the illustration. The front board is $14\frac{1}{2}$ in. long by 8 in. wide, while the back board is $14\frac{1}{2}$ in. by $10\frac{1}{2}$ in. wide. Fig. 438 shows the box attachment, with the front removed. It consists of one long piece $10\frac{1}{2}$ in. long by $2\frac{1}{2}$ in. wide, and two end pieces, each $4\frac{1}{2}$ in. long. They both slope in front from $3\frac{1}{2}$ in. at the top to $2\frac{1}{2}$ in. at the base. To fix, shoot the sides and screw them firmly to-

The design shown in Fig. 436 is simply outlined with a fine fluter, and then the ground punched. For hard woods, the design in Fig. 437 looks well if carved about $\frac{1}{8}$ in. deep and carefully finished in detail. This is an example of incised carving.

Handkerchief Box

A handkerchief box is shown by Figs. 439 to 443. The sides A of the box, $\frac{3}{4}$ in. thick, are dovetailed, the joints being concealed by mock stiles placed down the ends and mitered at the corners. The sides are raggled for the bottom B, which is also ⅜ in. thick. Next run the ogee moulding for the base with the rebate for the box, out of ¾-in. stuff, which moulding should be prepared all in one piece for convenience. When this is done, cut it into the several lengths required for the sides, and it should be mitered at the corners and fretted. The top C is ½ in. thick, with flat ogee and bead moulding round the edge. As an alternative, bevel and cavetto moulding (see Fig. 442) can be used. The material is now ready for carving. The motifs of the design are

Fig. 444.—Plan of Handkerchief Box.

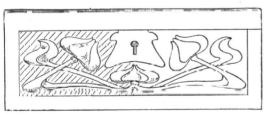

Fig. 445.

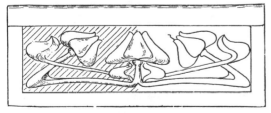

Fig. 446.

Figs. 445 and 446.—Front and Side Elevations of Handkerchief Box.

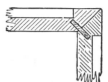

Fig. 447.

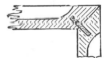

Fig. 448.

Figs. 447 and 448.—Horizontal Sections showing Alternative Methods of Grounding.

Fig. 449.—Centre Vertical Section of Flower.

Fig. 450.—Cross Section of Flower.

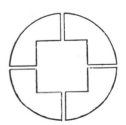

Fig. 451.—Cramping Blocks for Box.

the laurel and oak. The carving is in low relief, the ground being sunk to the extent of $\frac{3}{16}$ in., and left clean from the grounder. In working the monogram, sink the wood gradually from the edge of the circle. When the carving is completed, glue and pin the sides, the bottom, and the stiles. Next fix up the base, setting in the box, and at D glue on blocks 1 in. by $\frac{3}{8}$ in., to bind all together. This done, screw on two 1-in. by $\frac{3}{8}$-in. brass hinges on the side with the

to 450. The material required will be ; One piece, 2 ft. 6 in. by $2\frac{1}{2}$ in. by $\frac{3}{8}$ in., for the front, sides, and back ; one piece, $7\frac{1}{8}$ in. by $7\frac{1}{8}$ in. by $\frac{3}{8}$ in., for the top ; and one piece, 7 in. by 7 in. by $\frac{3}{16}$ in., for the bottom. Plane and gauge the length for the front, sides, and back ($2\frac{1}{2}$ in. by $\frac{5}{16}$ in.), and mark off the length of each (7 in.), leaving a space between them to allow for waste in cutting. From each mark, square across, bevel the edges to a mitre, and square over on the

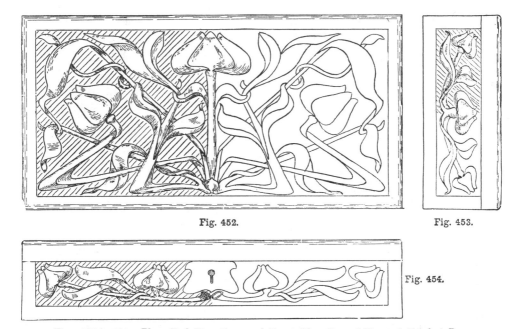

Fig. 452.   Fig. 453.

Fig. 454.

Figs. 452 to 454.—Plan, End Elevation, and Front Elevation of Pin and Trinket Box.

laurel panel, and the box is completed but for the finishing. A lock can be fitted if desired. The following is a list of the material required, finished sizes (allowance for waste must be added when ordering): For the top, one piece $9\frac{1}{2}$ in. by $9\frac{1}{2}$ in. by $\frac{1}{2}$ in. ; sides, four pieces $7\frac{5}{8}$ in. by $2\frac{3}{4}$ in. by $\frac{3}{8}$ in. ; bottom, one piece $7\frac{5}{8}$ in. by $7\frac{5}{8}$ in. by $\frac{3}{8}$ in. ; base, four pieces $9\frac{1}{2}$ in. by $1\frac{1}{2}$ in. by $\frac{3}{4}$ in. ; and blocks, one piece 1 ft. by $\frac{3}{8}$ in. by $\frac{3}{8}$ in.

Handkerchief Box with Tulip Design

Oak, walnut, or mahogany will be suitable wood to use for the box shown by Figs. 444

other side. Plane and square the top and bottom, making the top $7\frac{1}{16}$ in. square, to allow for cleaning off the edges after gluing together. It will be better to do all the carving while the parts are separate, as they can then be held in position more easily, and much more firmly than after being put together. Draw the design, or trace it on the wood by means of black or blue carbon paper, and make a gauge mark on the top border of the carving, and continue over on the other side. This will facilitate the cutting open of the box at a later stage. The ground should be sunk to a depth of $\frac{1}{8}$ in. Care must be taken not to exceed that depth, if the borders of the design are cut square, on account of the tongues in the mitres (*see* section, Fig. 447). By rounding off the borders as shown in Fig. 448, the ground may be sunk $\frac{3}{16}$ in. Little difficulty will be experienced in executing the modelling, the general effect of which is shown by the shaded half of the designs. Sections of the flowers are given, Fig. 449 being a centre vertical section, and Fig. 450 a cross section. If the ground has been sunk only $\frac{1}{8}$ in., it should be punched evenly, and care should be taken not to show the shape of the punch; but if the alternative method has been

clamping up the mitres may be made out of ordinary wood blind sheaves, by cutting them as shown in Fig. 451. The method of using them is to place one block at each corner, pass a piece of Venetian cord round (in the grooves) two or three times, and tighten up by twisting the cord with a nail until all the mitres are drawn tight. It will be better to use two sets of these blocks, one near the top and the other near the bottom. Next fit the bottom in the rebate, and make the top edges of the sides, etc., perfectly level; then fit the top. Smooth and glasspaper the under side of

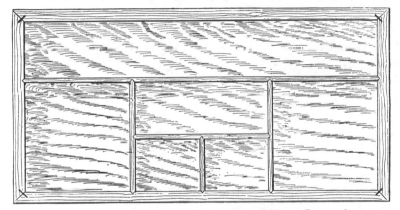

Fig. 455.—Plan of Pin and Trinket Box, with Top Removed.

adopted, the ground should be made as clean as possible with the tools, and left quite plain.

Making Handkerchief Box.—The carving having been completed, the making of the box may be proceeded with. Rebate the bottom edge of the front, sides, and back, $\frac{3}{16}$ in. by $\frac{3}{16}$ in., for the bottom; then cut and shoot the mitres. Make a cut with a tenon-saw at right angles to the mitres, as shown in Figs. 447 and 448, and prepare four slips or tongues to fit in the saw-cut thus made; the grain of these slips should run across, not lengthwise. When the parts are ready, first glue into place one half of each slip; then fit them into the opposite sides of the box, glue all the mitres and the other halves of the slips, and fit the parts together. The insertion of these slips greatly strengthens the mitres. Blocks for

the top and the top side of the bottom, and all other inner surfaces, before joining up the parts. Glue the rebate and the edges of the bottom, and secure together. Now glue the top edges of the sides, etc., place the top on evenly, and cramp together with hand-screws. Leave it in the cramps until the glue has thoroughly set; then smooth off and glasspaper, and slightly round over the top edge. Mark the place for the hinges across the gauge line on the back. This is easier to do before the lid is cut off. A dovetail saw should be used for separating the lid from the box. Cut along the gauge line until it is completely detached; plane the edges, fit them together, and hang the lid. A portion has been left in the carving on the front to allow for the fixing of a lock, which should be let in from the inside; or a fastener may be screwed on the outside. In finishing, the best possible effect is produced if the plane surfaces of the box are skilfully polished and the carving left dull or merely wax-polished.

Pin and Trinket Box with Tulip Design

The pin box shown by Figs. 452 to 455 is designed to match the handkerchief box above described. The material required will be : One piece 3 ft. by 2 in. by $\frac{3}{8}$ in. for the front, back, and ends ; top, $11\frac{1}{8}$ in.

In setting out the **V**-grooves which receive the ends of these partitions, care must be taken not to mark above the gauge line. Cut the partitions, front, ends, and back a trifle longer than required, mark to their respective lengths, and bevel to the mitres as shown in Fig. 455. Square over on the sides, cut and shoot all mitres, and cut the **V**-grooves in the partitions, sides, etc. This done, it may be put together in the same way as the handkerchief box referred to above. The partitions should be put in before gluing on the bottom.

Fig. 456.　　　　　　　　　　　　Fig. 457.

Fig. 458.

Figs. 456 to 458.—Front and End Elevations and Plan of Glove Box.

by $5\frac{5}{8}$ in. by $\frac{3}{8}$ in. ; bottom, 11 in. by $5\frac{1}{2}$ in. by $\frac{3}{16}$ in. ; and a piece for the partitions, 2 ft. 3 in. by $1\frac{1}{2}$ in. by $\frac{1}{8}$ in. It is better to work the lengths before cutting, as far as possible, on account of the great saving in labour, and to avoid the difficulty usually experienced in planing short pieces. The method of construction, as well as the carving, is the same as that of the boxes already described ; but in this case the partitions form an extra consideration in setting out. The line which separates the lid from the lower part of the box should be gauged on both sides of the front, ends, and back ; for this, beside being the cutting line, indicates the height of the partitions.

Glove Box with Tulip Design

The glove box shown by Figs. 456 to 458 is designed to match the handkerchief box and the pin and trinket box described in the two previous paragraphs. One length 3 ft. by 3 in. by $\frac{3}{8}$ in. will make the front, back, and ends ; for the top, a piece 1 ft. $\frac{1}{8}$ in. by $4\frac{1}{8}$ in. by $\frac{3}{8}$ in. will be required ; and for the bottom, a piece 1 ft. by 4 in. by $\frac{3}{16}$ in. The carving is similar in design to that of the other boxes.

Panel for Glove Box

A panel applicable to a glove box and to a variety of other purposes is illustrated by Fig. 459. The motif is found in the leaves and fruit of the grape vine.

Glove Box with Alternative Designs

Hop Design.—The design given in Fig. 460 is suitable for a fancy glove box, and for many other kinds of boxes. Fig. 460

margin all round, but also for an ovolo, ogee, or other moulding to be run around its edges. Thus the box-cover consists of a single solid slab, and good well-seasoned timber should be selected, or a tendency to warp may become apparent. The bottom of the box is an exact copy of the cover,

Fig. 459.—Vine Pattern for Glove Box Cover.

shows its general appearance when put together, and after being carved with a shallow-cut pattern of conventional hop-vine design. The whole box is constructed from $\frac{3}{4}$-in. stuff, worked somewhat thinner in planing true, and it might be darkened by fumigation and then wax-polished, or even left in its natural state to darken with age. The top is really a panel 8 in. by 13 in.; the carving design 5 in. by 10 in.; and this not only leaves space for a 1-in.

minus the carving, and the body of the box is fixed to this by means of glue and screws from beneath. The long sides are each $5\frac{1}{4}$ in. by 12 in., while the ends are $5\frac{1}{4}$ in. by 7 in. The top, sides, and ends have all a 1-in. margin left outside the carving pattern, not only for effect but for convenience in making up. The sides are best secured by a secret dovetail; or the thickness of the wood could be sawn off each end of the shorter pieces with a fine saw, and, after shooting them, the body could be bradded or screwed together. However, this short method detracts from both strength and elegance, as the end grain is noticeable at the ends.

Floral Design.—An effective and flowing floral design is given as an alternate pattern in Figs. 461 to 463. If cut nearly $\frac{1}{4}$ in. in depth, it affords much scope for artistic treatment, but care should be taken not to go too deep in cutting and so to pierce the wood. The design for the cover in Fig. 461 gives four overlapping blossoms as the central idea, and they should be left as prominent as possible, or even gluings may be planted on them to give the top a more imposing appearance. Fig. 462 presents three lapping blossoms on the

Fig. 460.—Glove Box.

Fig. 461.—Alternative Design for Glove Box Cover.

Fig. 462.—Alternative Design for Glove Box Sides.

Fig. 463.—Alternative Design for Glove Box Ends.

long sides, well in keeping with the top, and planted gluings would not be out of place on the whole of the blossoms carved. Fig. 463 has only one blossom on its re-

to the mind the great fact that decoration is simply an accessory art. In the general sketch of a cigar box (Fig. 464) a suggestion is offered of a pattern composed mostly

Fig. 464.—Cigar Box.

Fig. 465.—Alternative Design for Cigar Box Sides.

stricted space, but this is set off by inter-lacing leaves which contrast effectively.

Cigar Box

The slightness of the material used in the construction of a cigar box precludes any idea of deeply-cut work, and brings sharply

from bird form. Figs. 465 to 467 are based on fishes so conventionalised as hardly to deserve the name. This is a gain rather than a blemish from a decorative point of view, and these patterns will be found very effective when worked. If a specially sound and well-finished box is desired, some fret-wood in mahogany, oak, walnut, or other wood could be purchased and made up. The long sides, given in Fig. 465, are 3 in. by 9 in. The ends, shown in Fig. 466, are

fectly square, and round off the edges of top and bottom pieces in a corresponding pattern. When carved, the pieces may be held together by glue and fine tacks ; some

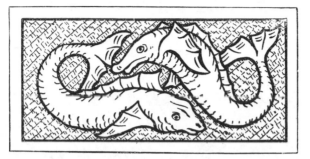

Fig. 466.—Alternative Design for Cigar Box Ends.

Fig. 467.—Alternative Design for Cigar Box Cover.

3 in. by 6 in. The top and bottom, shown in Fig. 467, are $6\frac{1}{2}$ in. by $9\frac{1}{2}$ in. A margin of $\frac{1}{4}$ in. has been allowed around the edges of both sides and ends, while a $\frac{1}{2}$-in. margin has been allowed on top and bottom to permit of their being nosed or otherwise finished off. Before carving, carefully shoot each piece of wood to make sure it is per-

small hinges, of fancy design if preferred, will keep the cover on.

Card Basket

The dimensions of the carved card basket illustrated by Fig. 468 are :—Long sides, $4\frac{1}{2}$ in. by 18 in. ; short sides, $4\frac{1}{4}$ in. by 8 in., all band-sawn or bow-sawn to shape from

$\frac{1}{2}$-in. walnut or oak. The size of the bottom piece is 10 in. by $5\frac{1}{2}$ in.; it is cut from $\frac{1}{2}$-in. stuff, and nosed or beaded to taste. The exact shape of the sides and ends can be better ascertained from Figs. 469 and 470, though their angle at the ends is about 60°. The ends could be planed to a mitre, then glued and screwed together, or they could be rebated in half the thickness of each before gluing and fastening up. As all the sides are on the slant, their base will need to be planed down a little before the bottom piece is fastened on. The addition of small fancy brass legs to the corners imparts

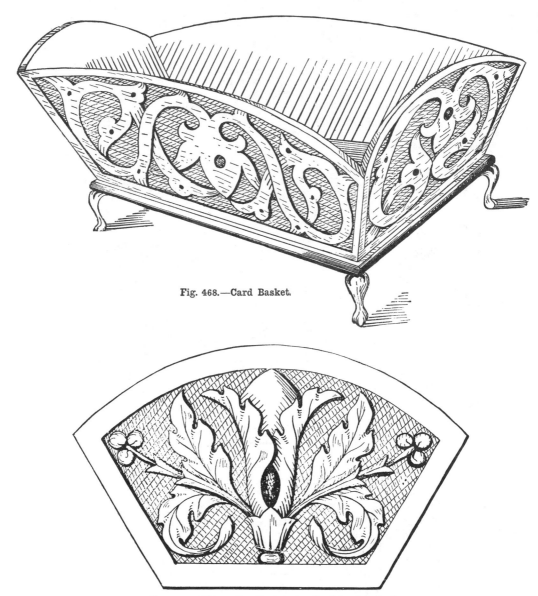

Fig. 468.—Card Basket.

Fig. 469.—Alternative Design for Card Basket End.

lightness and grace to the article. A very simple strapwork design is sketched on the a flowing conventional pattern is given for the side of the basket, and in Fig. 470 a

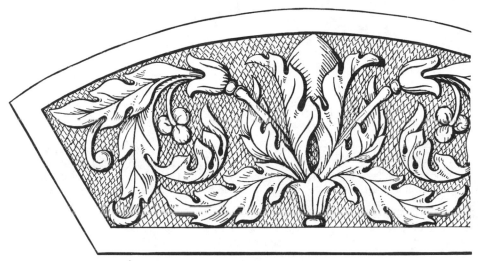

Fig. 470.—Part of Alternative Design for Card Basket Side.

side and end in Fig. 468. Figs. 469 and 470 supply an alternative design of a somewhat more elaborate character. In Fig. 469 similar pattern for the end will be seen. These should be carved not too deeply, and modelled to taste.

BOOK RESTS AND BOOK STANDS

Book Rest

THE book rest, or reading desk, illustrated by Fig. 471 affords an extensive surface for carving, and is simple in construction. Fig. 473 (p. 238) gives all necessary details. The front is a panel of ¾ in. thickness, measuring 10 in. by 14 in. The ledge or shelf on which the book rests is planted on the panel 1¼ in. from the base, and is ¾ in. thick, and not less than 1½ in. wide. The ledge shown is simply a piece of oak picture moulding, with the chamfered rebated edge and one string of surface beadwork planed away. This leaves a surface above the ledge of 8 in. by 14 in.; and, after allowing

Fig. 471.—Book Rest.

Fig. 472.—Alternative Design for Book Rest Panel.

1 in. all round for the plain margin, there
remains a carving surface of 6 in. by 12 in.
An alternative design for this space is provided by Fig. 472. It could be cut with a
V-shaped tool ; or it could be fretted out,
say ⅛ in. in depth, and then slightly modelled
for effect. The supports are two in number.
Their size, shape, and a pattern for carving
on them, are shown in Fig. 474. Care must
be taken to reverse the pattern when carving
the second support, so that the pattern may
show on the outside of each piece. The
panel could remain square-edged or be

Fig. 474.—Design
for Book Rest
Supports.

moulded to taste, but the bottom edge
must be planed to an angle which leaves
it straight with the base of the supports.

The supports should be fitted about 3 in.
from each end. They may be screwed to
the back by using two pairs of brass hinges,

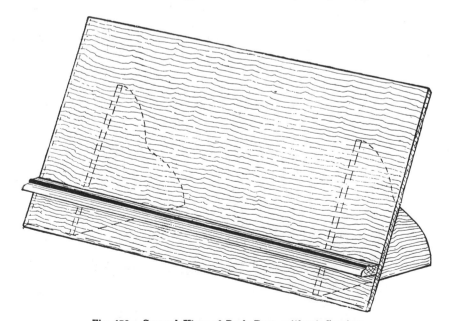

Fig. 473.—General View of Book Rest, without Carving.

in which case they would be folding supports. If fixed supports are desired, a screw may be driven into each from the front on the space covered by the ledge. This would be hidden when the ledge itself is screwed on from behind. Additional screws may be driven in a slanting direction through both top and bottom of each support, or a strip may be fixed on the back, its ends just fitting the supports at right angles.

Book Cradle

A well-executed design for the end of a book cradle for standing on a table is presented by Fig. 475. The book cradle is of telescopic construction, one part sliding

Fig. 475.—End of Book Cradle.

within the other, and is adapted to accommodate any number of books from two or three to ten or twenty.

Table Bookstand

Fig. 476 shows a bookstand for placing on a side table, or a set of shelves for placing on the hall table. The ornamental ends are the principal feature, the other portions being quite plain. The ends are shaped from material 7 in. by 18 in., the wood being 1 in. in thickness in the rough. It can be worked in oak, mahogany, or some softer wood, as yellow pine or basswood. The upper shelf is 5 in. by 26 in., and is made from at least $\frac{3}{4}$-in. stuff. The lower shelf, or base-board, is fairly substantial, say 8 in. by 28 in., and at least 1 in. in thickness. A

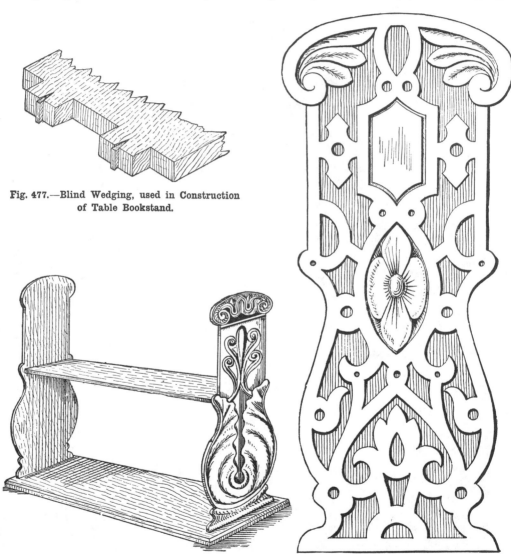

Fig. 477.—Blind Wedging, used in Construction of Table Bookstand.

Fig. 476.—Table Bookstand.

Fig. 478.—Alternative Design for Bookstand Ends.

glance at Fig. 476 shows the position of the upper shelf. In fastening, however, as nails or screws would disfigure the carved face, and a supporting block would be unsightly, some concealed method of securing the shelf in place must be resorted to. This is best done by means of blind wedging. Cut two tenons at each end of the shelf, and corresponding mortices on the insides of the ends. Chisel these latter in rather a dovetail-shaped form, and see that the tenons fit exactly. For the method of blind wedging, make a saw-cut in each tenon, as shown in Fig. 477, and a small wedge for inserting in each cut. It will readily be seen that, when the parts are glued and fitted together, the force necessary to make the joints meet will drive the wedge into the saw-cut, and consequently spread the tenons closely against the sides of the mortices.

After being driven in as shown, the tenon cannot be withdrawn without fracturing the woodwork. But before this is attempted, the lower shelf should be worked up, so that the whole may be put together at the same time. The material of the sides allows for a couple of 1-in. tenons to be cut at the base of each, and corresponding mortices must be cut in the lower board for them to fit into. These tenons can be secured by driving in a couple of wedges at the bottom after the parts have been well glued. A chamfer, beading, or moulding could be worked around the edges of the bottom shelf, in order to give a nicer finish. As the carving shown in Fig. 476 is of a somewhat difficult nature, owing to the modelling required, a simpler yet very effective alternate design, almost without modelling, is presented by Fig. 478.

CHESTS AND COFFERS

In no other form does old oak work so often come to hand complete as in that of the chest. The admirable construction of the seventeenth-century chests, which renders them all but indestructible by fair wear and tear, largely accounts for this; but it is also evident that they must have been made in far greater numbers than any other articles of furniture. Chests have always held an important place among household gear. In primitive times they were seats and tables, as well as almost the sole depositories for valuables; it has even been suggested that the chest was the germ from which various other articles of furniture developed; that the settle was at first but a coffer, to which, for comfort's sake, arms and a back were added; that cabinets and buffets were merely chests raised on legs; and that the chest of drawers (a late development) was simply an expedient for utilising the interior of the chest more conveniently.

Early Chests

Among the Saxons, the earliest chests were dug out from solid logs, and some of these still exist. There is one in the church of Halesowen, and another in Wimborne Minster. In the latter part of the Middle Ages, cypress wood was much in vogue for chests to hold tapestries and costly clothes, as giving security from moths. A few of these still remain, and in the case of one dating from about 1475, the carpentry is rude, but the cypress boards are still sound. It has been covered with finely gilt and tooled leather, and is girthed by elegant iron bands, 4 in. apart, from

end to end, each band having its own hinge; it thus has fourteen hinges in all. Fig. 479 shows the graceful way in which the bands terminate in front, above and below the opening of the lid. This chest is not panelled. Panelled chests were, however, known in England in the thirteenth century; therefore the form of construction above described must not be regarded as a characteristic of the Elizabethan chests.

Linen Pattern

Some of the earlier panelled chests were decorated with Gothic carving, and between this and the Elizabethan Renaissance work is found an intermediate form of panel ornamentation. This was cut with a moulding plane, and is familiar as the " linen pattern " (see Fig. 480). It is usual to assign this ornament almost exclusively to Tudor times—Henry VII. to Elizabeth—and a chest thus enriched is almost sure to be earlier than 1600. The ends of the folds at top and bottom are, of course, cut by hand. Panelled and carved chests which can be dated earlier than the latter years of Elizabeth's reign are, however, not common.

Oak Chest: Date, 1600 to 1610

The example shown in Fig. 481 is as recent as 1600 to 1610. The design is bold and effective, as designs of that time usually were, but the workmanship is by no means accurate or neat. The demi-figures, of which there have originally been three, but of which the central one is now wanting, are to be noted. Such figures became so common on buffets, bedsteads, etc., in the early part of the seventeenth century as to form a characteristic feature ; towards the middle of the century, and later, they were not used. Unlike most early chests, this has preserved its original lock and other ironwork, and shows how complete had been the change of style since the forging of the iron band shown by

and such-like receptacles were almost unknown.

Seventeenth=century Oak Chests

The chests of the earlier part of the seventeenth century are to be distinguished by the greater richness of their carving,

Fig. 479.—End of Iron Band on Cypress Chest. Date, 1475.

Fig. 481.—Oak Chest. Date, 1600-1610.

Fig. 482.—Seventeenth-century Oak Chest.

Fig. 480.—Linen Pattern.

Fig. 479. The ends fasten down with spring catches, so that the contents of the chest, even when it was unlocked, must have been safe except from those acquainted with the secret of certain iron knobs by which the springs were forced back. At one end, close against the lid, is a crib or tray to receive minor articles, a common arrangement in old chests, and one that must have been useful when small drawers

and by being, as a rule, large and heavy. As the century advanced, the chests were made lighter, whilst the carving became flatter. In the latter half of the century the pattern on the panels is often expressed by mere incised lines, with no attempt at relief. Fig. 482 shows a favourable example of a late chest, of which the date is 1670–80. Although apparently richly carved, the panels, which are charged with feeble imitations of the Jacobean cartouche, are in very shallow relief, whilst the mouldings are weak. No lock-plate is to be seen, for by this time chests had ceased to have

throughout the century, but in the earlier work it was usually combined with carving. One or two drawers at the bottom are as common in such chests as they are rare

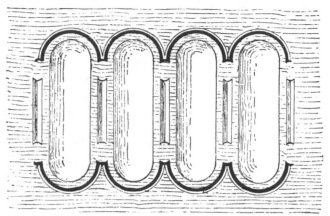

Fig. 483.—Thumb Carving from Rail of Old Chest.

anything of the nature of artistic iron-work.

Thumb Carving

An impression that the chests which have no ornament beyond thumb carving (Fig. 483) on their rails are always of late date is erroneous. Thumb carving was in use earlier than 1600, and remained long in fashion. Its presence simply implies that cheap ornament was desired; the date of the chest bearing it must be judged by general appearance.

Other Details of Seventeenth-century Oak Chests

Dates when found on chests are, if authentic, generally later than 1650, but incised dates are always to be regarded with suspicion. A date in raised figures is, however, generally reliable. Some late seventeenth-century chests are carved on both sides, which would indicate that they must have been intended to serve occasionally as tables. Towards the year 1700, when carving on panelled chests became rare, its place was sometimes taken by appliqué decoration. This consisted of pieces of moulding or split turned ornaments glued on the oak. Appliqué had been more or less in use

in the carved ones. More use, also, is now made of inlaid ornament than earlier. Few large panelled oak chests were made later than 1700. The chest of drawers had then taken its place in public favour, but carved coffers continued to be produced some years later. They are usually of elm, and are formed by simply nailing the front and back to the thicker plank of the ends. The carving is little else than a pattern in incised lines. Initials and dates are frequent on them. The persons for whom these were originally made do not appear to have stood very high in the social

Fig. 484.—Oak Chest, bearing Date 1680.

scale. Under the general heading of chests, some mention ought to be made of the small carved oaken boxes of seventeenth-century work. They were commonly from 18 in.

Fig. 485.—Italian Coffer or Cassone in Walnut Wood. Style, Cinque-cento Renaissance.
(Scale : $1\frac{5}{8}$ in. = 1 ft.)

to 24 in. long, 14 in. or 15 in. wide, and slightly less than 1 ft. deep. It was for the female members of the family that these were specially made, as receptacles for their trinkets and small personal belongings. Fig. 484 shows one bearing a genuine date of 1680.

Italian Coffer or Cassone

A beautiful coffer or cassone is illustrated by Fig. 485. This is of walnut wood, the

art were the scroll and the building of the design (especially frieze designs) on a continuous curved line, the scroll ending in a rosette. In this instance (Fig. 485) there is the scroll and the continuous skeleton line in the panel, the scroll ending in a grotesque animal form of the griffin or dragon kind, instead of a rosette. The " skeleton " or " leading " line is clothed with the same type of acanthus leaf that is seen on the frieze of the Forum of Trajan,

Fig. 486.—Chest, carved in Style of Holbein.

front being carved with a shield supported by winged figures, at the sides of which are griffins and floral scrolls. The whole is enclosed by a raised border of fruit and foliage. The interior of the coffer is fitted with drawers and recesses, and is inlaid with marquetry. The height is 2 ft. 2 in., the length 3 ft. 10 in., and the width 1 ft. 11 in. This coffer is Italian work, and belongs to the cinque-cento period of Italian Renaissance. It exemplifies the manner in which the designs of this period were based on the old Roman sculptures. The principal features of Roman decorative

A.D. 110. The enclosing raised band of leaves and fruits is very characteristic of Italian Renaissance; and English wood carvers will find this of interest, because, 200 years after, it occurs in English work: a similar type of ornament was used largely in Georgian schemes of ornament. The feet are interesting, because they are so admirably carved with a view to subsequent wear and tear. There are no weak projections likely to get broken off. The contrast obtained by the brisier, or cut-up, treatment of the raised border, and the quieter, broader treatment of the

Fig. 487.—Italian Coffer in Walnut. Date, Sixteenth Century. (Scale 2¼ in. = 1 ft.)

scrollwork of the panel, is a feature that is worth noticing.

Chest in Holbein's Style

Fig. 486 shows a chest carved with a feature characteristic of a device favoured by Holbein (1488–1554), an artist of the early Renaissance. This feature is the head within a circle. Above this is the winged cherub, and below are two dragons, whose tails proceed from a shell. The South Kensington Museum contains a panelling series from Waltham Abbey carved in this style. The work is not always well finished, and strikes one as being careless, certainly as regards the application of its design; and it does not in either design or workmanship approach the work of the

Fig. 488.—Flemish Virginal, or Harpsichord. Date, probably Sixteenth Century. (Scale : 1⅜ in. = 1 ft.)

Italian Renaissance as typified by the chest shown by Fig. 487.

Italian Coffer in Walnut: Sixteenth Century

In this chest (Fig. 487) can be seen the spirit of exuberance that stands for so much in Italian work. The outlines, the wealth of moulded edges, the richness and variety of the carving, are characteristic of the furniture of the Italian Cinque-

in which the tones were produced by plucking, instead of striking, the strings. Fig. 488 illustrates a virginal in a walnut-wood case, elaborately carved on the outside with medallions, scrolled cartouches, trophies of arms and musical instruments, animals' heads and other ornament. The lid is decorated outside and inside with flat floral scrollwork, amid which on the outside is an oval medallion enclosing a shield bearing the arms of William, Duke of

Fig. 489.—French Gothic Coffer in Walnut.

cento period. The carving on the prominent lower member of the chest is of a type that became common in various applications during Elizabethan times. The continuous line and the scroll are in evidence in the panel of the chest. The masks at the corners form a very effective finish. Attention is directed to the carved mouldings.

Flemish Virginal or Harpsichord

It is convenient to describe in this chapter a fine example of a virginal—a spinet or harpsichord resembling a piano in the arrangement of keyboard and strings, but

Gueldres, Juliers, Cleves and Berg, and Count of La Marck and Ravensberg (born 1516; died 1592). The whole rests on four turned and carved feet. The virginal is further enriched with colour and gilding, and bears various Latin inscriptions, one of which contains the date 1568. It should be said that, as illustrated, the virginal has been restored. Flemish influence on decorative art throughout Western Europe is past calculation. Flanders was particularly rich in expert craftsmen and masterly designers; and its influence over Germany, France, Spain and England was so powerful as to impress indelibly its character on the

Fig. 490.—Italian Cassone or Marriage Coffer.

art of each country: Of the elements used, (and already mentioned), the scroll cartouche is one that is known in England perhaps the best of all, because it forms such a feature of Elizabethan, Jacobean and Stuart wood and stone carvings. The carved heads are interesting features, and it is instructive to notice how they have been introduced to break the monotony of a long surface of flatter carving. The treatment of the corners by covering them with an acanthus leaf is admirable. Note the delicate carving of the feet, as shown in Fig. 488.

Gothic Coffer in Walnut

An interesting example of the French Gothic is shown by Fig. 489. The Gothic style in France did not develop on the same lines as in England. The fifteenth century Gothic in England is remarkable for its upright mullions, its panel treatment of walls, pilasters, and windows, and its stiffness of ornament. In France, during the same period, the ornamentation ran wild, and finally manifested itself in a style known as Flamboyant, because of the flame-like openings in its tracery. This feature can be seen in the chest shown by Fig. 489. The second panel from the left-hand end shows this peculiarity very distinctly. The tracery of the panel at the right-hand end appears not to have been set out with any regard to the space it is fitted into, which is a decided transgression of the rules of design. The four-leaved flower at the intersections of many of the tracery lines is a characteristic feature of fifteenth-century French Gothic tracery. The interlaced strapwork of the plinth is quite Celtic in appearance, and this and the round-headed arches of the panels, which seem to suggest the coming Renaissance, make this chest a most interesting study.

Italian Cassone or Marriage Coffer

Of the same period as the other Italian examples described in this chapter is the cassone or marriage coffer shown by Fig. 490. The original is gilt, and measures 3 ft. 1 in. high, more than 7 ft. long, and 2 ft. 7 in. wide.

RACKS

Letter Rack

THE letter rack illustrated by Fig. 491 is of quite simple construction. Possibly it would look best in walnut. The base is a piece of $\frac{3}{4}$-in. stuff, 8 in. by 14 in., a piece of $\frac{1}{2}$-in. stuff, 5 in. by $11\frac{1}{2}$ in. ; while the central piece of similar substance should be cut from 7-in. by $11\frac{1}{2}$-in. stuff. As shown in Fig. 493, the ends of all these pieces correspond. But while the middle portions of the outside pieces are depressed, that

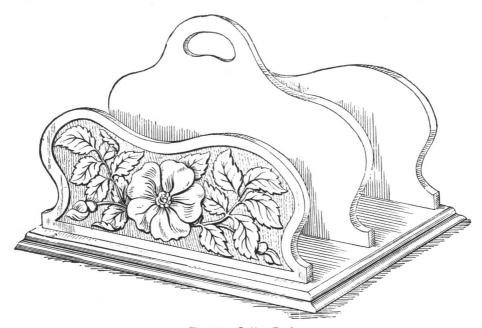

Fig. 491.—Letter Rack.

with a $\frac{3}{4}$-in. moulding run round it. The moulding can be carved if desired. The three uprights are planted on the base at a distance of $\frac{1}{2}$ in. from the plain edge, and a space of 2 in. comes between each. For exact dimensions of all fittings *see* Fig. 492. Each of the outside uprights is shaped from portion of the inside piece rises to form the necessary handle. If these three pieces are cut on the end grain, or with the grain perpendicular to the base, allowance could be made for two or more tenons to be cut on the bottom of each, and corresponding mortices could be made in the base-board in order to receive them. But if the wood is cut with the grain lengthways, tenons are impossible, and two or three screws should be carefully driven into the wood from beneath, with their heads duly countersunk. This would hold the article firmly together. But if there is any looseness or warping of the parts, they could be further secured by

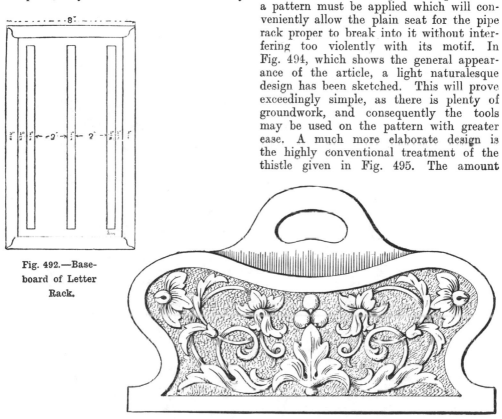

Fig. 492.—Base-board of Letter Rack.

Pipe Rack

For the construction of the pipe rack outlined in Fig. 494, well-seasoned oak, say ¾ in. thick, and measuring 18 in. in length by about 11 in. breadth, will be necessary. It must first be bow-sawn or band-sawn into the required shape. Then a pattern must be applied which will conveniently allow the plain seat for the pipe rack proper to break into it without interfering too violently with its motif. In Fig. 494, which shows the general appearance of the article, a light naturalesque design has been sketched. This will prove exceedingly simple, as there is plenty of groundwork, and consequently the tools may be used on the pattern with greater ease. A much more elaborate design is the highly conventional treatment of the thistle given in Fig. 495. The amount

Fig. 100. Alternative Design for Letter Rack.

shooting two pieces of stuff, each 2 in. by 4 in., and gluing them on each side of the central board, and at right angles to its exact middle. This would not only hold the sides, but would help to keep them square. The two outside pieces could be carved, and the central one left plain. A natural pattern—flower and leaves—is given in Fig. 491, and a design in conventional style in Fig. 493. The treatment of the ground is a matter of taste.

of work this design will take is limited only by the carver's skill and patience, for the figure lends itself to any treatment, from the broadest to the most finical. Still, it is a design that will repay all the labour bestowed on it. In Fig. 496 a design of a more arbitrary nature is offered, one whose flowing lines, deep serrations, and bold relief make it a really valuable exercise in conventional carving. When the style of design has been fixed upon and duly executed, the work that remains to be done presents but little difficulty. A flat is left for the attachment of the shelf. All that is required is to work up a piece of $\frac{1}{2}$-in. oak, 13 in. by 2 in., and to bore half a dozen suitable holes at equal distances apart down its middle ; for the sake of lightness, these may be cut away on a curve to the front, as shown in Fig 494. This done, the pipe rack may be firmly held on its seat by means of two, or at most three, screws driven through the rear of the backboard. For hanging the rack, a couple of ordinary picture eye-screws, or a pair of brass glass-plates, may be used, **as may** be found suitable.

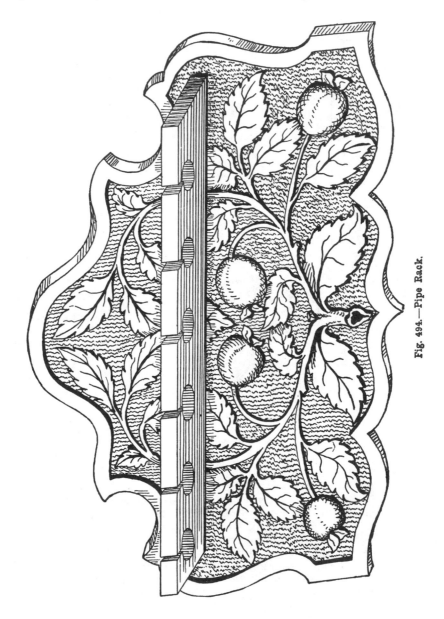

Fig. 494.—Pipe Rack.

Another Pipe Rack

Figs. 497 and 498 are front and end elevations of a rack for five pipes, which are so arranged that the bowls are below, so that the nicotine is prevented from draining into the mouthpiece. The pipe rack is 10 in. long by 8 in. wide by 2½ in. thick, and would look well in oak or walnut. It may be prepared from one piece of wood, when a piece 4⅜ in. wide and 1¼ in. thick may be sawn away above the shelf before the pattern of the carving is traced on it. The lower part, if in two pieces, should be 10 in. by 3⅝ in. by 2½ in., and must be rebated to receive part of the upper piece,

Fig. 495.—Conventional Thistle Design for Pipe Rack.

which would be 10 in. by 5 in. by $1\frac{1}{4}$ in., and would run down behind the shelf $\frac{5}{8}$ in., and be screwed on from the back. The ornament at the top of the pipe rack should be cut right under, so that the stems of the pipes may be put up between it and the backboard, which should be about $\frac{1}{4}$ in. thick.

Hanging Rack for Newspapers or Sheet Music

A simply constructed rack for newspapers or sheet music is shown by Fig. 499. It consists of three parts—the front, the back, and the inner shelf. These can be shaped either by band-sawing or bow-sawing,

Fig. 496.—Conventional Foliage Design for Pipe Rack.

and can be easily put together when the decorative portion is completed. The front may be cut from $\frac{1}{2}$-in. mahogany, 12 in. by 19 in.; the back from $\frac{3}{4}$-in. stuff, $15\frac{1}{2}$ in.

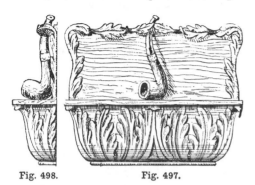

Fig. 498.   Fig. 497.

Figs. 497 and 498.—Front and End Elevations of Pipe Rack.

by $20\frac{1}{2}$ in.; while the inner shelf, of $\frac{3}{4}$-in. stuff, is 12 in. by 2 in., but bevelled on the front edge as shown in Fig. 500. Fig. 499 shows the article completed. The back is left plain, though two $\frac{1}{2}$-in. holes are bored through by which to hang it on the wall, and the patterns on the front board can be worked to taste. The front is fastened to the inner shelf with screws and two small brass hinges, which allow free play to the front. The inner shelf is secured to the back-board with two long stout screws let in from behind. Fig. 500 illustrates the method of securing each piece, A indicating the front, B the inner shelf, and C the back. For carving, either oak, walnut, or mahogany can be used, according to the furniture in the room where the rack is to be hung. Alternative patterns are given in Fig. 501. It will be noticed that each pattern fills only one-fourth of the space, and has to be quadrupled to complete the design.

Music Rack

The music rack shown by Figs. 502 and 503 is strong and simple in design and construction. It consists of six principal pieces and three subordinate pieces of wood, namely, two sides, 2 ft. 4 in. by 1 ft. 4 in. by $\frac{3}{4}$ in.; two ends or legs, 2 ft. 6 in. by 1 ft. 1 in. by 1 in.; two shelves, one 1 ft.

$10\frac{1}{2}$ in. by 9 in. by $\frac{3}{4}$ in., and the other 1 ft. $7\frac{1}{2}$ in. by 8 in. by $\frac{3}{4}$ in.; one partition, 1 ft. 6 in. by 9 in. by $\frac{1}{2}$ in.; and two bearers for shelf. It may be made in figured oak or

Fig. 499.—Hanging Rack for Papers or Sheet Music.

American walnut. If in oak, it should be fumed and wax-polished; and if in American walnut, the plain portions should be french-polished, and the carving either left perfectly plain or simply oiled; or it may be given just one coat of polish. The sides

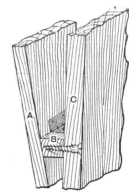

Fig. 500.—Detail of Construction of Hanging Rack.

(Figs. 504 and 505) should first be cut out together, to ensure their being exactly alike, and marked for the dovetail, making the cut narrower at the top than at the

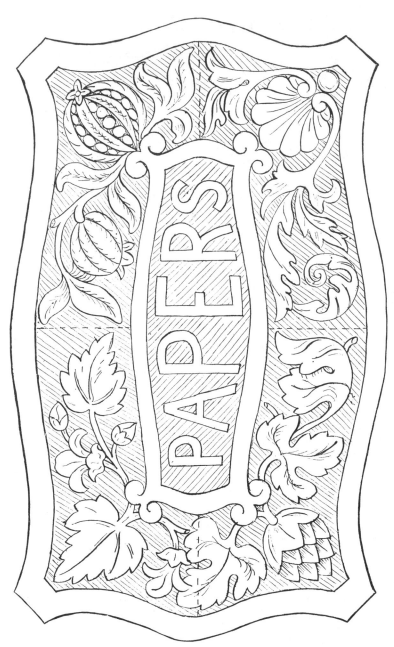

Fig. 501.—Alternative Design for Front of Hanging Rack.

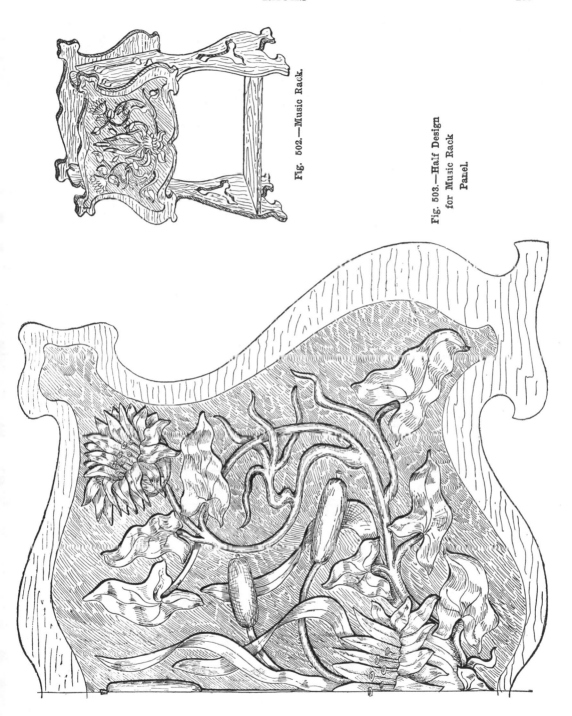

Fig. 502.—Music Rack.

Fig. 503.—Half Design for Music Rack Panel.

bottom. Then prepare the ends or legs by cutting to shape together, and work the dovetail pin on each edge, to fit the hole. Make the groove for the lower shelf, polished. In fixing it, the legs should be slid into the sides, one leg being put into both sides at once ; then the partition should be fixed, next the upper shelf, and after that

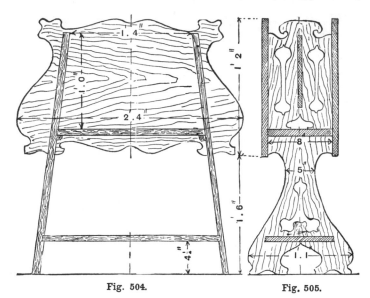

Fig. 504.   Fig. 505.

Figs. 504 and 505.—Sections of Music Rack.

and screw on bearers as a rest for the shelf above, for which also a groove should be made. Now prepare the two shelves and the partition. Before the rack is finally put together the sides should be carved, and the whole bodied in if it is to be the lower. If the joints fit properly, it will only be necessary, owing to its perfect construction, to use glue for fixing the rack together. It can now be polished or otherwise finished off. Fig. 503 shows an enlargement of part of the carving.

BRACKETS

Carved Wall Brackets

First Example.—The carved fancy bracket shown by Fig. 506 is somewhat out of the ordinary style. Its flowing outline may be shaped by bow-saw or band-saw from a piece of ¾-in. stuff about 9 in. by 16 in. It may be worked in any hard wood, as oak, mahogany, or walnut, and stained or polished to taste. In

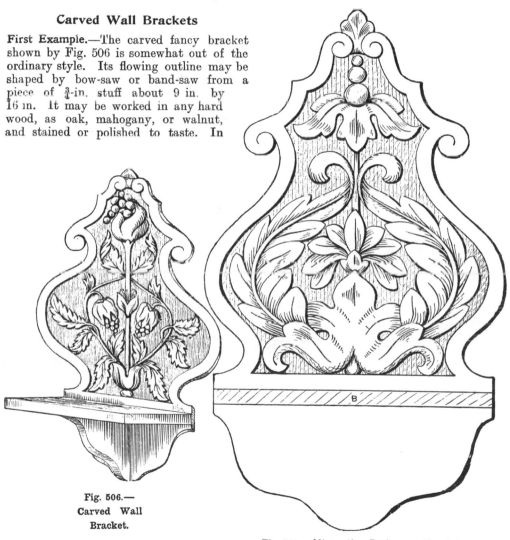

Fig. 506.—
Carved Wall
Bracket.

Fig. 507.—Alternative Design for Bracket.

Fig. 506 its general outline is seen, with a flowing design sketched upon its face. It is finished with a rectangular shelf, fitted at B, as shown in Fig. 507, and having an extra support underneath. The shelf and support may be permanently fixed with screws, the front. The pattern may be outlined as shown in the examples, and a more elaborate form of shelf may be adapted if desired. A very simple pattern is shown in the general view, Fig. 508; but Figs. 509 and 510 are more conventional

Fig. 508.—Bracket with Square Back.

or, if desirable, both pieces can be held in place by a couple of fancy brass hinges.

Second Example.—The simple form of bracket illustrated by Fig. 508 offers an exceptionally large field for work, and is most simple in construction. A square piece of oak, or other hard wood, of a size suitable to the requirements of the worker, may be bordered by a cavetto or other moulding, and a simple shelf hinged on in treatment, and make greater demands on the carver's skill. They also show seats for the shelf and its support, in case the bracket assumes somewhat large dimensions.

Third Example.—Fig. 511 (p. 265) shows an oak bracket; Fig. 512 is a half front view, and Fig. 513 side view. Fig. 514 gives a plan of the shelves, and Fig. 515 is an enlarged section through the top of truss. The carving is simple; the grounding need not be sunk deeper than $\frac{1}{8}$ in. The mouldings are all planted on.

Fourth Example.—Figs. 516 to 518 (pp. 265 and 266) show brackets, which can be

wide. The shelves are 1 ft. 1 in. long by 7 in. wide, and can be cut to either of the shapes shown at Figs. 519 and 520, the outside edges being beaded. They are fixed

Fig. 509.—Conventionally Ornamented Bracket with Square Back.

made of oak and relieved with carving. They can be of wood $\frac{3}{8}$ in. thick, but, if they are intended for the display of heavy ornaments, $\frac{1}{2}$-in. stuff should be used. The backs are 1 ft. 7 in. high by 1 ft. 2 in.

to the backs with screws, and are supported at each end by bracket pieces, suitable shapes being shown at Figs. 521 and 522. These bracket pieces should be dovetail grooved into the shelves, and stump tenoned into the backs, and fixed with screws. They are 6 in. wide and 4 in. high; Fig. 523 shows an end view. The distance from the bottom of the back to

Fifth Example.—The carved bracket represented by Figs. 524 to 526 (p. 267) could be cut in oak, walnut, or mahogany, and is 1 ft. 3 in. long by 6½ in. wide over the

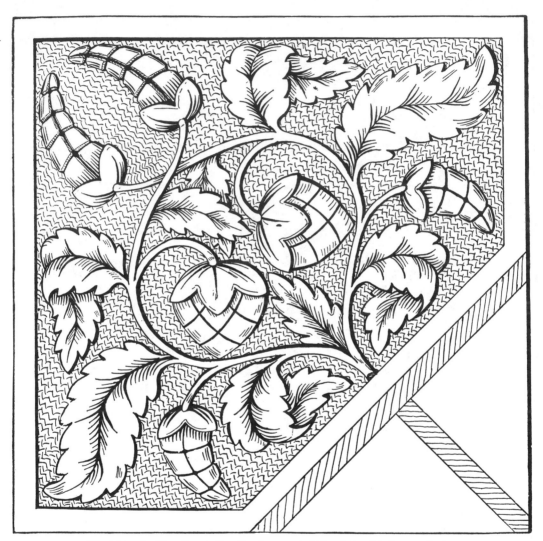

Fig. 510.—Another Conventionally Ornamented Bracket with Square Back.

the top of the shelf is 6 in.; and the distance between the bracket pieces is 8 in. The moulding across the top of the back is made up separately and fixed on. The distance from the top of the back to the top of the moulding is 2 in.

scrolls, and 5¾ in. wide across the centre by 5¾ in. deep. It may be cut out of the solid, or in two pieces, using 4½-in. stuff for the upper part, and 1¼-in. for the lower part, as indicated by dotted lines in Fig. 526, which also shows four dowels for fixing

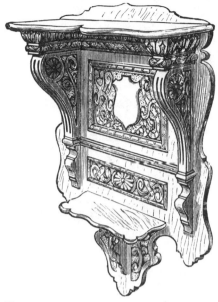

Fig. 511.—Oak Bracket with Trusses and
Two Shelves.

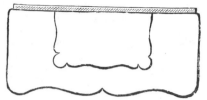

Fig. 514.—Plan of Bracket Shelves

Fig. 515.—Section through Top of Bracket
Truss.

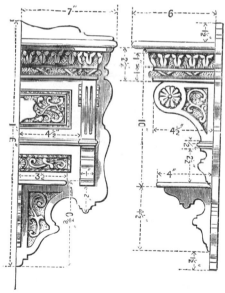

Fig. 512.   Fig. 513.

Figs. 512 and 513.—Half Front Elevation
and Side Elevation of Bracket shown
above.

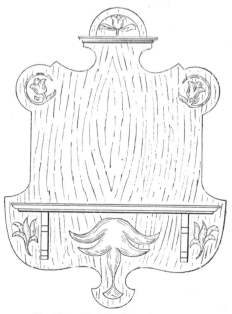

Fig. 516.—Lightly Carved Bracket.

the two pieces together. After having traced on the design, get the outline cut with a band-saw, and then boast in the carving. The leaf ornament should be in about $\frac{1}{4}$-in. relief, and the scrolls must be well undercut. Then, having finished the carving, glue, dowel, and cramp the two parts together.

Sixth Example.—The bracket shown by Fig. 527 is based on a classical design.

Seventh Example.—Fig. 528 shows a bracket which suggests fret-sawing. Indeed, the easiest way to execute it is to cut it out with a fret-saw and then lightly model it with a carving tool.

Eighth Example.—The masks (Figs. 529 and 530) are of an early Italian character, and could easily be elaborated by the introduction of masses of foliage, the mask being the central figure. Fig. 531 is the plan of the top of the masks, and shows the bracket shelf.

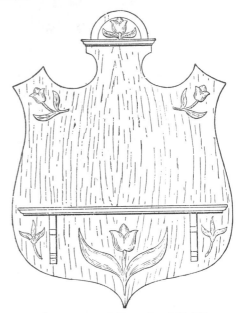

Fig. 518.—Third Example of Lightly Carved Bracket.

Fig. 517.—Second Example of Lightly Carved Bracket.

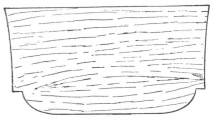

Fig. 520.—Bracket Shelf.

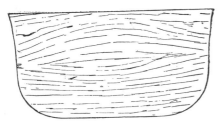

Fig. 519.—Bracket Shelf.

Fig. 521.   Fig. 523.   Fig. 522.

Figs. 521 to 523.—Bracket Pieces.

Brackets Designed by F. L. Schauermann

Two designs for brackets, by F. L. Schauermann, are presented by Figs. 532 and 533.

haps foreshadow, the peculiar development of the scroll which became a prominent feature of the Louis XIV. and XV. periods. Notice, too, the cross fluting on the inner surfaces of the scrolls; this

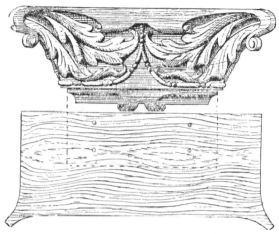

Fig. 524.

Fig. 525.

Figs. 524 to 526.—Front and Side Elevation and Plan of Bracket Carved in the Solid.

Fig. 526.

Having much in common with the second one is the banding or frieze shown by Fig. 531; and this design could be easily worked into the back piece of the complete bracket having side supports of the kind shown by Fig. 533.

Venetian Bracket or Console

An extremely beautiful specimen of Venetian work of the late sixteenth century is shown by Fig. 535. It is carved with two mermaids, scrolls, and shells, and is enriched with gilding. It is possessed of many points of interest, both in the way of design and treatment. The use of the semi-human figures to uphold the shelf is a happy idea, and the figures themselves are arranged most admirably, from both the decorative and constructional standpoints. The arrangement of the scroll shows considerable development as compared with the examples of cinque-cento work previously illustrated in this volume. The scrolls are now used to give the outline, thus becoming an architectural as well as an ornamental feature. Their particular shape and arrangement suggest, and per-

was also used during the Louis periods in a more developed form. The method of scaling is very effective, whilst being

Fig. 527.—Bracket based on Classical Design.

Fig. 528.—Bracket in Lightly Modelled Fretwork.

quite simple; it consists merely of incised cuts the shape of the scale; there is no sinking of the upper part of the scale. This method avoids a cut-up appearance which

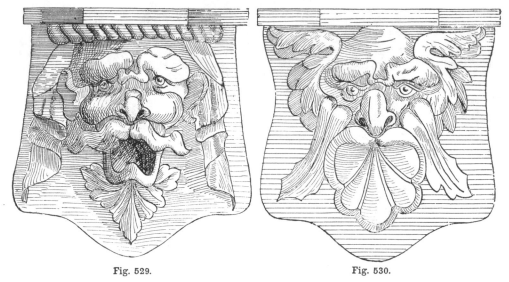

Fig. 529.   Fig. 530.

Figs. 529 and 530.—Brackets with Early Italian Masks.

might easily result from the attempt to
sink the upper part ; and it avoids a great
amount of cutting "against the grain,"
which would be necessary in cutting scales
on the body of a creature having convolutions such as this has. This method

Fig. 531.—Plan of Bracket Shelf.

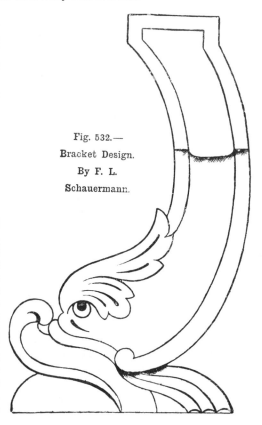

Fig. 532.—
Bracket Design.
By F. L.
Schauermann.

of scale cutting, too, preserves the original
continuous outline of the mermaid's tail.
The pierced and deeply sunk portions of
the work supply the dark shadows, against
which the mermaids, shell, and scrolls
stand out very effectively. Notice, too, that
in the leaf-like terminations of the tails
there is another point of interest to wood
carvers ; that is, that all the veins and ribs
are formed in the wood itself by means of
the tool cuts, and are not cut in afterwards
with a **V**-tool or veiner, as so many pieces
of work done professionally are. The
latter method appears to have been adopted
because of the ease with which it is accom-

plished ; but it is a cheap and nasty way, unworthy of any artist.

Louis XIV. Bracket

The carved and gilt bracket shown by Figs. 536 and 537 dates from early in the eighteenth century, and is of French origin. In it can be seen the ultimate development

this bracket ; what would have been a heavy mass of wood at the top is most ingeniously lightened by piercing from both sides, leaving it as a shelf with four light curved legs or supports. The principle of piercing is carried out very successfully in other parts of the bracket also. The elements used, such as the scroll, acanthus

Fig. 533.—Another Bracket Design.
By F. L. Schauermann.

Fig. 534.—Banding or Frieze Design.
By F. L. Schauermann.

of the scroll noticed in Fig. 535. This bracket is built up of these scrolls, their employment as architectural features being now complete, combined, too, with a refinement of ornamental detail which is very striking. The work of this period reached a very high standard of excellence, the craftsmanship being really magnificent. The designs and the conceptions of the period often overstepped the bounds of reason ; but nothing can be urged against

leaf, and shell, which were used in the bracket shown in Fig. 535, are still in use, but in a more refined form ; and a close comparison of these two brackets will well repay the time taken. In addition, natural flowers are used, as in the swag, to be seen in Fig. 536, the front view ; this is interesting as showing that French and English development proceeded upon similar lines, the date of this bracket corresponding to the period remarkable in

Fig. 535.—Venetian Console, carved with Mermaids, Scrollwork, and Shells.
Date, late Sixteenth Century.

Fig. 536.

Fig. 537.

Figs. 536 and 537.—Front and Side Views of Louis XIV. Bracket.
Date, Early Eighteenth Century.

Fig. 538.—Louis XIV. Bracket in Carved and Gilt
Limewood. Date, late Seventeenth or
Early Eighteenth Century.

Fig. 539.—German Gothic Bracket. Date, Fifteenth Century.

England by the work of Grinling Gibbons, who made an extensive use of natural flowers and fruit.

Bracket with Carved Head, Wings, and Scrolls

Another Louis XIV. bracket—this being of carved and gilt limewood—is shown by Fig. 538. This is an interesting, instructive, and at the same time beautiful, piece of carving. A remarkable feature is the wealth and the refinement of its ornamental detail. No opportunity is lost of adding to its charm, by the use of carved detail, yet at the same time it is by no means smothered with it. Its beautiful outline is kept clear, continuous, and distinctive; and all the ornament employed emphasises the general shape. The use of the crossbanding over the greater part of the upper portion is a good example of the use of simple elements, whose effect depends upon their arrangement, and the manner of their repetition. The superimposing of the carved ornament upon this crossbanding is a bold proceeding that can only be justified by its ultimate success, which in this case is certain. In the carved scrolls which form the outline of the bracket the sunk carving in one or two instances reminds one of the strapwork of a century before; and the husks employed are the same as those in use during the eighteenth century in English furniture. The use of the head completes the scheme in a thoroughly artistic manner, and the arrangement of the wings is noticeable. Their treatment appears to be careless; but this is not a fault, as, by this means, they avoid that clean cut, staringly accurate cutting which is not the correct treatment for feathers.

German Gothic Bracket

In Fig. 539 is illustrated a bracket, in pierced German Gothic carving, of the fifteenth century. German Gothic carved ornament was naturalistic, and this bracket exemplifies it. Such a bracket most certainly should be placed where there is no risk of the corners being broken off; it presents many points, which though attractive enough so far as the design is concerned, yet should be avoided as a general rule in pierced work. The feature of this work is the continuous " line " arrangement upon which it is built; it is a study in perfect radiation. The tool work is perfect; this was always characteristic of the German wood carvers of Gothic and Early Renaissance times; their technical ability very often exceeded their capacity as designers. Notice in this example that, even when an extreme point overlies another portion of the leaf, the work is most delicately and perfectly carved. Notice, too, how the veining tool is used to emphasise the beauty of these curves by sinking a slight vein along the centre of the leaves—a feature well illustrated in Fig. 539.

CUPBOARDS AND CABINETS

THE same period which produced the great carved bedstead also brought into vogue the carved buffet and cabinet. Such things were a natural outcome of the changed times. Through the Gothic period, when the normal state was one of warfare and uncertainty, receptacles of the chest kind—things easy of removal when danger threatened—were chiefly in favour. But in a period when life and property were comparatively secure, as they were under the Tudors, more permanent and convenient receptacles were preferred. It has been suggested that cabinets and allied furniture developed originally from chests mounted on legs ; but it is more probable that the buffet and cabinet are rather derived from the " dressoir "—in modern English " dresser " —which was in use in royal and baronial halls in Gothic times. It appears to have been a kind of panelled cupboard below, whilst above were ranges of shelves for the display of plate. The transition from this to the buffet or the cabinet is easy. South Kensington Museum contains a most elaborately carved and inlaid cabinet, made, as would appear from its heraldic devices, for Henry VIII. This is early sixteenth century, but, though probably made in England, is obviously the work of foreign craftsmen, and can scarcely therefore be properly called an English cabinet. The English series proper of such things begins some years later. In assigning dates to such articles, one point to be considered is the front supports. If they have heavy bosses, the work will not be much earlier or later than 1600. In short, they will follow much the same fashions as regulate table-legs

and bedposts. Figure subjects, large heads carved in panels, and portions of figures in other parts, may be taken as indications that the work, if not late sixteenth, is early seventeenth century. English-made oak articles of this class later than the Restoration are not abundant ; when found, they are without representations of the figure, and are flat and weak as regards ornamental carving. The reproduced photographs in this chapter show English, French, and other examples.

Seventeenth-century Court Cupboard

The seventeenth-century court cupboard illustrated by Fig. 540 (p. 276) is the property—or was, at the time the photograph was taken—of C. H. Woodruff, Esq. Court cupboards were common during the late sixteenth and early seventeenth centuries. The enormous corner pillars in the example shown appear to be most unwieldy ; but they form an integral part of the complete conception, and the cupboard would certainly lose in value if they were omitted. They provide scope for carving which, however, does not interfere with their outlines, and the ornament is sufficiently subdued to give it a subordinate position in the general scheme. The top frieze is reminiscent of Elizabethan strapwork, and is of a common pattern. The same can be said of the centre frieze, at the end of which are two projections bearing a slight resemblance to grotesque heads. The deep mouldings of the panels are carved, and the panels themselves left untouched. The ovolo edges of the frieze mouldings are carved, but their contour is not interfered with thereby. The plinth of the cupboard is ornamented with incised carving, which is particularly suitable for such a position, where there is the risk of projecting ornament being kicked off. Nearly all Jacobean

mended to wood carvers for anything else than their suitability of design. Their treatment could certainly be improved with great advantage to the ultimate effect.

Fig. 540.—Seventeenth-century Court Cupboard.

carving is either incised or in low relief. The execution of the carving in the present example appears to be hurried and crude, as though the craftsman attempted to get the greatest possible amount of effect out of the design at the least possible expense. This is evident from an examination of the enlarged views of the pillars (Figs. 541 and 542); and these carvings are not recom-

Sixteenth-century Cabinet

In the cabinet shown by Fig. 543 (p. 278) is seen the influence of classic architecture as shown through the Renaissance. The new spirit began to influence decorative art first in the details of ornament, and not until some years had gone by did it gather enough strength to alter the character of the buildings and furniture. In this cupboard, made during the latter half of the sixteenth century, the architectural character of the conception is more in evidence than anything else. The proportions of the details are good, but the work is unsatisfactory because natural construction has been sacrificed to decorative necessities. For example, the door when it opens takes with it the pillars with their plinths, bases,

Fig. 541.   Fig. 542.

Figs. 541 and 542.—Top Left-hand and Bottom Right-hand Pillars of Court Cupboard.

and capitals, which appear, when the door is shut, to support the entablature. This cabinet is in pearwood, and affords an excellent example of the combination of classic five orders were used, shown here by the carved capitals, fluted columns, entablature, mouldings, and Roman semicircular arch.

Fig. 543.—Sixteenth-century Cabinet, showing Influence of Classic Architecture.

carving and inlay work. The carved panels represent battle scenes, and the inlay has for its elements the rose, portcullis, and the Tudor arms. The cabinet well illustrates the elements in use during the period 1550–1600 ; thus, all the details of the

Henry II. Cabinet in Walnut

The walnut cabinet shown by Fig. 544 (p. 279) is the property of T. Foster Shattock, Esq. It has two stages, the upper of which contains three cupboards, whose

Fig. 544.—Henry II. Cabinet in Walnut.

Fig. 545.—Sixteenth-century Walnut Cupboard, Carved and Inlaid.

Fig. 546.—Henry III. Cabinet in Chestnut.

fronts are enriched with strapwork, masks, and grotesque figures, and are separated by four terminal figures with baskets of fruit on their heads ; below the central cupboard is a drawer carved with interlacing leafy stems. At the top is a broken pediment surmounted by two dragons, and having a mask in the centre. The lower part consists of a cupboard with two doors, separated by a terminal figure, and enriched with architectural and floral ornament ; above this cupboard are two drawers, each ornamented with a cartouche between grotesque heads. The sides of the cabinet are decorated with strapwork. The cabinet is French work, in the style of Jacques Androuet *dit* Du Cerceau (b. probably 1510 or 1520 ; d. about 1580), and dates from the middle of the sixteenth century. The Henri Deux and Henri Quatre period, 1547–1610, to which this example belongs, is characterised by interlaced strapwork, delicate reliefs, and the cartouche. These are shown in Fig. 544 ; note the delicacy of the carvings as distinct from English work, which was stronger and more vigorous. The caryatides are excellent examples of the kind ; and the griffin seen on the side edge of the upper part gives a welcome variation to the outline, as do also the griffins on the broken pediment, the latter being a feature much used during this period. Despite the delicacy of the carvings of the period, a great effect was obtained by the judicious variation of surface—a thin stalk rising from $\frac{1}{32}$ in. above ground level to $\frac{3}{8}$ in. or more, and at the same time swelling out to a considerable width, giving a remarkable play of high lights and deep shadows. The lower panels are ornamented with a device much used for wall tablets during the century following, and many examples of which may be seen in English churches and cathedrals.

Walnut Cupboard, Carved and Inlaid

A cupboard of about the same date as the one above described is shown by Fig. 545 (p. 280). Again can be seen in the pediment a gradual rise of the element from a thin stalk lying on the ground to a full thickness and width. The broken pediment is used again, but extended in the centre, to get

in the finely carved mask, from whose mouth the floral ornament springs. This part is a fine example of the acanthus employed as a decorative termination of a life form. The mask represents the human face distorted by various phases of mind— in this case by laughter, light-heartedness ; and the acanthus is used to represent the tossing hair with good decorative effect. The acanthus is used again, with a remarkably subdued but happy effect, for the lower half of the side pilasters ; at the upper part is the laurel on an interlaced basis, together with a winged cherub's head, quite a familiar feature of the period. The eagle on the upper part of the panel is finely conceived and executed ; and the griffins below show Roman, not to say Egyptian influence. Note the leaves falling gracefully over their backs ; the graceful curves of the wings ; the way in which they serve as supports for the ornament hanging from the eagle's mouth ; and the decorative effect produced by the arrangement of the tails. The moulding scheme is worthy of attention ; the succession of flat surface with narrow suites of mouldings has a fine effect, which is emphasised by the cut-up surfaces of the carvings.

Henry III. Cabinet in Chestnut

A chestnut-wood cabinet, in two tiers, is illustrated by Fig. 546 (p. 281). The upper part has two cupboard doors carved with emblems enclosed with a framework of strapwork, masks, and birds ; the stiles between are decorated with terminal figures. The lower part has also two cupboard doors ornamented with masks within a similar framework. The whole is supported on four legs, the front two of which are carved in openwork with masks and scrolling bands. It is French work of the period of Henri III., and bears date 1577. It is interesting to note the resemblance between the French carved ornament of Francis I., Henri II., III., and IV., and that of Elizabeth in England. At this period of wood carving, cartouches, strapwork, caryatides, grotesque masks, are the principal elements employed. The splendid cupboard shown by Fig. 546 illustrates this resemblance well. The strapwork in the panels of the doors of the lower portion is in fairly good relief, giving high lights and deep shadows. The broad, clean treatment gives an opportunity to the carver for bold, firm work to be done with a flat tool. The quicker gouges are not required for strapwork of this kind ; and the clear surfaces produced by the flat gouges and straight tools reflect a large amount of light, giving a clean, strong appearance.

Fig. 547.—Seventeenth-century French Cabinet.

Fig. 548.—Rubens Cabinet in Ebony, Flemish Work.   In Royal Collection, Windsor Castle.

Fig. 549.—Interior Recess and Carved Doors (one open) of Rubens Cabinet.

Seventeenth-century French Cabinet

Sixty years later than the previous example is that shown by Fig. 547 (p. 283).

suggest the cabinet illustrated by Fig. 543 (p. 278); but a great difference of treatment and arrangement is observable. There is no severe adherence to the architectural

Fig. 550.—Left-hand Panel of Rubens Cabinet.

Its architectural character, evidenced by its columns with their carved capitals, the frieze, and the lower pilasters and frieze,

type or model. The present example is more like a cabinet; the other is like a building. The ornament now begins to lose the vigour and boldness given by the strapwork and cartouches, and to become daintier, more refined, and more characteristically French. As an instance, note the figure standing in the shell, in the centre of the upper portion. Notice the bases of the pillars, and how they are carved for a part of the way up their height. The central figures of the panels are enclosed in cartouches; but their treatment is softer and more refined. The "pyramid" ornament is there, but it is truncated. Swags of fruit and flowers appear, and these were largely used towards the end of the seventeenth and the beginning of the eighteenth centuries. The diminished pilasters, typical of Elizabethan ornament in England and that of the time of Henri II. in France, are still retained, with a diminished ornament, however.

"Rubens" Cabinet in Ebony

The imposing ebony "Rubens" cabinet shown by Figs. 548 to 550 forms part of the Royal Collection in Windsor Castle. It is carved with numerous reliefs, and is, indeed, a monument of patient and artistic work. The motifs are partly Biblical and partly classic, and in either case somewhat obscure; but the chief concern here is the amazing skill with which the obstinate ebony has been carved. The comparative flatness of the design, when compared with the massive sculpturesque dressers and cupboards of the sixteenth century—such as those of the Burgundian school and that of Lyons—was no doubt dictated by the material. When, however, one considers the modelling of the figures in the niches, or the complete relief of some of the detail on the twisted columns of the base, the conclusion is that the men who carved this cabinet did practically what they pleased with their material. The conscientiousness and completeness with which this work is finished cause constant surprises. Most people would have thought that the elaborate decoration of the outside doors, with their fluted Corinthian columns, would have been sufficient. The inside surfaces of these same doors are carved with designs almost as elaborate, though, as was necessary, in lower relief. The flower and scrollwork is done with a

veiner, and is almost like engraving. One of the panels in the centre represents an annunciation, in which Henrietta Maria is the principal figure; the other illustrates the presentation of his son to Charles I. by

Fig. 551.—Modern Cabinet, showing Italian Renaissance Influence.

the queen. These panels, in which the likeness of the king at least is striking, are sufficient evidence as to the approximate date. The inside of the cabinet contains six large drawers on each side, all with elaborate figure reliefs and brass head handles. The insides of all these drawers

Fig. 552.—Modern Cabinet in Ash.

are completely veneered with various woods in geometrical patterns. Below these, again, are to be found on the one side a chessboard, on the other a backgammon board. It will be seen that there is an interior recess, with two elaborately carved

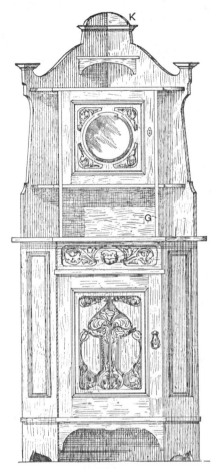

Fig. 553.

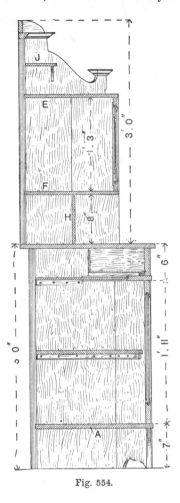

Fig. 554.

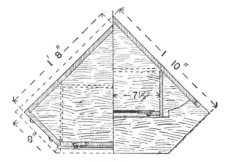

Fig. 555.

Figs. 553 to 555.—Front Elevation, Vertical Section, and Two Half Horizontal Sections of Corner Cabinet.

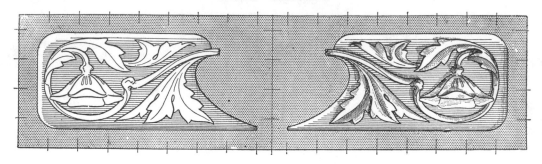

Fig. 556.—Drawer Front of Corner Cabinet.

Fig 557.—Door Panel of Corner Cabinet.

doors, disclosing the tortoiseshell and gilt columns and mirrors generally found in these cabinets (*see* Fig. 549). The floor is laid with squares of ivory and ebony, running back in artificial perspective. The

Modern Cabinet showing Italian Renaissance Influence

In Fig. 551 (p. 287) a modern cabinet is illustrated, showing the influence of the

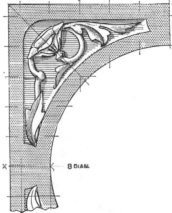

Fig. 560.—Carving round Circular Mirror of Corner Cabinet.

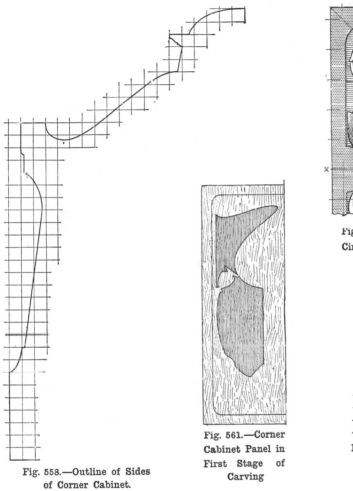

Fig. 561.—Corner Cabinet Panel in First Stage of Carving

Fig. 558.—Outline of Sides of Corner Cabinet.

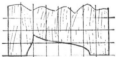

Fig. 559.—Bottom End of Side of Corner Cabinet.

backs of these interior doors are inlaid with ivory. There are several drawings on the doors and in the recess. These are signed " Clérisseau fecit Romæ, 1763," and are typical of this artist, who had a great vogue. Charles Louis Clérisseau was an architect and painter in water colours, and died in 1828. The above description is due to the "Magazine of Art."

Italian Renaissance in its carved ornament. This cabinet was exhibited at the Chicago exhibition by Messrs. Collinson and Lock.

Modern Cabinet in Ash

Fig. 552 shows a cabinet of carved ash, stained green, picked out in red, and enriched with mirrors and copper mounts. It was designed by Edmund Farago, of

Hungary, and was exhibited at the Paris Exhibition, 1900, by the Musée Commercial Royal Hongrois. It formed a part of the Donaldson gift to the Victoria and Albert Museum. It is quite modern, both in conception and execution. The carving is, perhaps, based to some extent upon fourteenth-century Gothic, as far as its treatment goes; but otherwise it may be said to be quite different, and to be wholly

Fig. 562.—Bracket for Cabinet (shown on End).

Fig. 563.

Fig. 564.

Figs. 563 and 564.—Elevation and Horizontal Section of Cabinet for Crucifix.

apart from historical influence. The "New Art" has produced many abortions which their creators have termed "quaint" furni-

Fig. 565.—Small Jacobean Cabinet.

ture. This example, however, is not one of them. The carving is neither too lavishly

applied to furniture. This tendency to exclude carving from modern furniture may be a protest against its undue, extravagant, and useless application, characteristic of much nineteenth-century furniture; but considered as a serious phase of furniture design it is somewhat foolish. In this cabinet the ornament is applied restrainedly, and with an evident view to emphasise

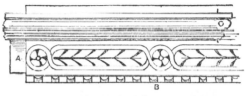

Fig. 566.—Middle Rail of Jacobean Cabinet.

and to support the general conception of the cabinet.

Corner Cabinet

Illustrations of a corner cabinet are presented by Figs. 553 to 561. The construction is illustrated clearly in Figs. 551 and 555, in which A indicates a shelf; E and F shelves housed into the sides G (Fig. 553) and screwed through from the back; H

Fig. 567.

Fig. 568.

Figs. 567 and 568.—Front and End Panels of Small Jacobean Cabinet.

put on nor altogether ignored. The latter is often the case, as though wood carving is not of sufficient decorative value to be

a board nailed to the back of the sides G to form a rectangular space for books (see the dotted lines in Fig. 555); and J a small shelf to hold a vase or other ornament. Fig. 558 shows the outline of the sides of the cabinet, the shaped bottom end being shown by Fig. 559. The designs for the panels (Figs. 556 and 557) should be drawn out full size, and the lines on the illustrations, being 1 in. apart, will enable this to be easily done. The outside line of Figs. 557 and 560 represents the inside edge of the moulding, so extra widths must be added to the panels to allow for tongueing, etc. The constructional work should be done before any carving is attempted, or the design transferred to the wood. Fig. 560 is the design for carving round the mirror; the design is transferred to each corner, being turned over at about the line x. The depth of the ground for Figs. 556 and 560 should be $\frac{3}{16}$ in. and $\frac{1}{4}$ in. respectively, and is concave round the edges. The panel (Fig. 557) is grounded to two depths, that round the carving being $\frac{3}{8}$ in. deep and the spaces $\frac{1}{8}$ in. deep. This will be understood from the numerous sections on Fig. 557. The plain spaces would be first to house-out or ground, these being $\frac{1}{8}$ in. deep; and the panel after this first stage is shown at Fig. 561. Having got the groundwork fairly true (these spaces form part of the design and must, therefore, be left plain), the next step is the grounding round the carving to a depth of $\frac{3}{8}$ in. Before beginning to carve, study the design well. It is important to select the primary masses, keeping them high, the secondary masses and so on being subordinate to these. In this case the flowers will be primary. Any method that will emphasise the stalks is to be commended, and they should not be rounded. Treat them squarely, or hollow them down one side and bevel the other (see sections in Fig. 558). The stalks enclosed by the bottom leaf husks should be kept fairly low, otherwise they will appear rather wiry. The grounds should not be punched just to hide bad work, as, apart from other reasons, punching tends to separate the pattern from the groundwork.

Carved Bracket for Cabinet

It is usual to construct bric-à-brac cabinets with a number of shelves supported by pillars and brackets, although very often the support afforded by the brackets is more apparent than real. The brackets, however, give a finish to the work, and generally look better than the square edge of the shelf alone. A suitable design for a bracket is illustrated by Fig. 562, this representing a conventional treatment of simple foliage and fruit.

Cabinet for Crucifix

A Gothic cabinet for a crucifix is illustrated by Fig. 563. Fig. 564 is a section on line A B. The cabinet is built on a flat backboard c, to be screwed to plugs in the wall. The dotted line at D shows the dimensions of the top and bottom pieces. Lines at E indicate the position of the bracket which supports the bottom of the cabinet. Double doors, as shown at F F, will look best. The diagonal side pieces G G, to which the doors are hinged, owing to their peculiar form, should be of thicker board than the rest. The carving may be in quite low relief—the outlines cut well in with the dividing tool, but the ground only slightly lowered. The depth of the carving is, however, rather a matter for individual judgment. The wheel tracery in the upper part of the backboard is intended to be pierced with the fret saw. The mouldings around this board should be hollow ones, run out with the gouge.

Small Jacobean Cabinet

The cabinet illustrated by Fig. 565 includes turned work as well as carving. The turned pieces are, however, only five in number, namely, the two front uprights and three of the foot-rails. Of these the most important are the uprights: they must be pieces of oak 3 in. square and 3 ft. 8¼ in. long. The back uprights, which are of the same length, not being turned, will need to be only 2 in. square; and, indeed, the extra thickness of the front pair will be only required at the places where it is wanted to form the large Jacobean bosses; elsewhere it will be seen that these pieces are cut down to 2 in. square, like their fellows behind. The cabinet is but a small one. Exclusive of the overhanging top and the projecting ornamental mouldings, it is only 21 in. wide and 12 in.

deep; its height is 3 ft. 9 in. Its top measures 24 in. by 13½ in. It is regularly framed after the Jacobean manner with mortices and tenons. Three tiers of rails let into the uprights with inch tenons hold the latter together, and give that strength and solidity which are characteristic of the furniture of the Jacobean period. At 3½ in. from the ground-line are foot-rails, which are features of the style; they are always present in tables, chairs, and all other articles which have legs, and contribute not a little to their powers of endurance. Besides the turned work on their lower parts, the front uprights are ornamented in those portions which come opposite to the door with some slight carving. They have small rosettes in sunk medallions, and flutings cut with the gouge in the manner technically known as "thumb carving." The rosettes are similar to those shown on a larger scale in Fig. 566. The sides of these uprights are left plain. The back uprights are plain throughout.

Foot-rails.—The foot-rails are cut from stuff 1¼ in. square; that at the back is left plain; the three others are turned to a ball pattern, as shown in Fig. 565. In cutting these, as well as the rails of the higher tiers, allowance will have to be made for the length of the tenons—all the front and back rails will be 17 in. at sight, and 19 in. inclusive; all the end rails, 8 in. at sight, and 10 in. inclusive. At A (Fig. 566) the tenon of a middle rail is shown.

Middle Rails.—Fig. 566 (scale, 2 in. = 1 ft.) gives a part of the front middle rail, which, like all the rails of the two upper tiers, is made of ¾-in. board, and is 5 in. wide. The design with which it is carved, including the guttæ B, which enrich its lower edge, is from a genuine Jacobean example. This rail is partly covered by the ornamental moulding which lies upon it, and of which the section is shown at C. This moulding is carried round the end rails and mitered at the corners. The small ornamentally shaped piece which is shown in Fig. 565, below the rail, is no part of it, but is a strip of panel inserted in grooves sunk for it in the lower edge of the rail and in the uprights. The end middle rails are 11 in. wide, for they rise as high as the end panels

which are let into them. These rails are carved with the same pattern as the front, but there are only two rosettes on each.

Upper Rail and Concluding Details.—The front upper rail is plain; its width is 2¼ in. Along its upper part lies a moulding 1¼ in. wide, which serves as a cornice beneath the overhanging top. The edges of the top, which is of ¾-in. board, are ornamentally moulded, as shown. The end upper rails are 5¼ in. wide. As the aim has been to keep this cabinet as simple and easy as possible, it has but a single door, and this is 19 in. high by 17 in. wide; the panel which forms its centre is shown in larger scale by Fig. 567. The design with which it is carved is on well-known Jacobean lines; the decorative band which forms one of its more prominent features is made by cutting two parallel incised lines with the V-chisel, and hollowing the space between with the gouge (the conventional leaves are in incised lines only); whilst the central rosette has its petals slightly hollowed with the gouge. For the ornamentation of the side panels a less elaborate design will be sufficient—that adopted is given on the larger scale in Fig. 568. The interior is large enough to afford a useful space for fitting with small drawers, or otherwise, as may be preferred. Of the illustrations, Fig. 565 is, as regards the front, about ⅔ in. to the foot; Figs. 566 to 568 are 2 in. to the foot.

Large Jacobean Cabinet

The Jacobean cabinet in carved oak shown by Fig. 569 contains, in addition to drawers for small curios, two sets of shelves for bric-à-brac. These last are obtained by providing the cabinet with canted sides, an arrangement not unfamiliar in Jacobean work, and one which produces a satisfactory effect. Though oak would be the more correct material to use for the cabinet, walnut, chestnut, or even teak may very well be employed. The cabinet is 5 ft. 2 in. high, 4 ft. 4 in. wide, and 1 ft. 2 in. deep; the two last dimensions do not include mouldings. It is framed together on four upright pieces, which, owing to the sloping of the sides, are somewhat unusual in shape. They are shown in section at A A, B B

Fig. 569.—Large Jacobean
Cabinet.

Fig. 570.—Horizontal Section of Jacobean Cabinet above
Bottom Rails.

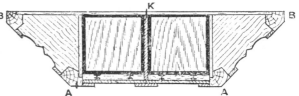

Fig. 571.—Horizontal Section of Jacobean Cabinet through
Inside Shelves.

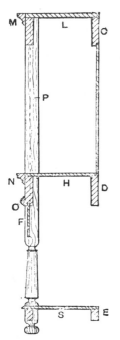

Fig. 572.—Vertical
Section of Large
Jacobean Cabinet.

Fig. 575.

Fig. 576.

Fig. 577.

Figs. 575 to 577.—
Sections of Upper, Middle,
and Lower Mouldings of
Cabinet.

Fig. 573.—Door of Large
Jacobean Cabinet.

Fig. 574.—Running Pattern for Rails and
Uprights of Cabinet.

(Figs. 570 and 571), and are 5 ft. $1\frac{1}{4}$ in. long; they should be cut from a 3-in. plank. Fig. 572 shows how the leg portions of the two front ones are turned. The back legs are shown plain, but this is merely a matter of taste. The uprights are framed together with three tiers of rails mortised into them, the latter being shown in section at c, d,

$2\frac{1}{2}$ in. above the ground line. The tenons by which all these rails are mortised into the uprights should be about $1\frac{1}{4}$ in. long. Before the skeleton is framed together the pieces F (Fig. 572), forming the flat arches beneath the middle rails, should be inserted. They are merely strips of $\frac{1}{2}$-in. panel, 6 in. wide, slipped into rebates cut for them in

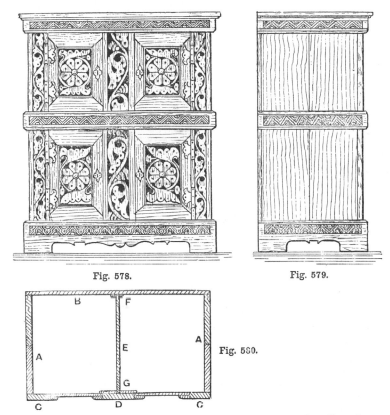

Fig. 578.

Fig. 579.

Fig. 580.

Figs. 578 to 580.—Cupboard Carved in Flat Relief on Sunken Ground.

and E (Fig. 572). For the sake of strength, and especially as the bearing at the back is a long one, they are cut from $1\frac{1}{2}$-in. stuff. The upper rails c are $5\frac{1}{4}$ in. wide, and their upper edges are on a level with the tops of the uprights, whilst their outer faces come flush with the faces of the uprights. The middle rails d are $5\frac{1}{2}$ in. wide, and their upper edges are $24\frac{1}{2}$ in. below the bottoms of the upper rails. The lower rails E are only 2 in. wide, and their bottom sides are

the uprights and in the lower edges of the rails. They are set $\frac{1}{2}$ in. back from the faces of these pieces. The back, between the top and middle rails, is boarded up with $\frac{1}{2}$-in. stuff, rebates being cut in the back uprights, as shown in Fig. 571, and also in the top rail, as at c (Fig. 572), to receive the ends of the boards, which are 4 ft. long, and, together, are 2 ft. 1 in. wide. The foot shelf may now be cut; the upper side of it is shown in Fig. 570. It rests on the lower rails, is made of ½-in. board, and projects ½ in. at the front and at the sides, the projections being worked with a simple moulding. The shelf is 4 ft. 1 in. long and 14 in. wide, and is marked s in Fig. 572.

Fig. 581.—Lower Door Panel of Cupboard.

Fig. 582.— Carved Moulding of Cupboard.

The floor of the cabinet (H, Fig. 572) is of the same thickness as the shelf, but is 1 in. less in width, as it does not project beyond the front rail; it is screwed down on the middle rails, and space has to be left at the back of it for the backboard. Before proceeding with the top of the cabinet it will be well to fit the two sides and the partition down the middle (K, Fig. 571). These are all of ½-in. wood, and stand 29½ in. high—that is to say, ¼ in. higher than the uprights and upper rails. The reason for this is that V-shaped grooves, ¼ in. deep, have to be scored in the underside of the top to receive the upper ends of these pieces; the ¼ in. at the top of each has therefore to be cut to fit the grooves. The grain in the middle partition K should be upright. This partition is 12 in. wide, and is fixed by screws driven into it through the floor and the backboard. The grain in the sides should run horizontally, and from back to front these pieces should measure 11½ in. only, a rebate being cut in each front upright, as shown in Fig. 571, to receive their front ends. The sides are screwed in these rebates, and screws are also driven into them through the floor and the backboard. The top L (Fig. 572) may now be put on,

having first cut the V-grooves in it. It is of ¾-in. board, and rests on the uprights and upper rails, with which its edges come flush. Inside the cabinet there is a set of small drawers on each side of the partition; they are shown in Fig. 571. The triangular ends are fitted with shelves for bric-à-brac placed at convenient heights, as shown in Fig. 569. The shape of these shelves is seen in Fig. 570; they are of ½-in. board, and are fixed by screws driven into them through the sides and the backboard. Fig. 573 shows one of the doors of the cabinet on an enlarged scale. The doors are made of two layers of ½-in. panel screwed together, this being by far the easiest way for the inexperienced workman to make them. The carving on the larger panel, which forms the inner side of the door, is executed in incised lines only, but the smaller panels on the outside are carved in relief with a sunk ground. The easiest way to cut out the arch piece is to use a fret-saw. The fluting

Fig. 583.   Fig. 584.

Figs. 583 and 584.—Centre and End Uprights of Front of Cupboard.

of the pilasters is run out with a small gouge, like thumb carving, but with relatively greater depth. The ornamental fronts to the corner shelves are similar to the front layers on the doors, except that, instead of the cross pieces at the bottom, the pilasters are carried down to the floor. The running pattern on the bands of carving that surround the doors and bookshelves is shown

middle rails, indicate the front edges of the mortices by which the tenons of these rails enter the uprights. A little study of the illustrations will make this clear.

Fig. 585

Fig. 586.

Figs. 585 and 586.—Front and Side Elevation of Cabinet to be Supported by Stand.

enlarged in Fig. 574, and is used alike on all the three faces. It is on the six rails, twice on each of the front uprights, and once on the back ones, and must of course be executed before the upright and rails are framed together. It only remains now to ornament the front and sloping sides of the cabinet with their mouldings. Three suitable sections of Jacobean character are shown in Figs. 575, 576, and 577, which are intended for M, N, and O respectively in Fig. 572. It may not be possible to procure mouldings that exactly follow these sections, but some sufficiently near to them may always be obtained. Referring to Fig. 572, it should be observed that the dotted line at P indicates the back edge of the door, whilst the dotted lines that appear to be continuations of it through the upper and

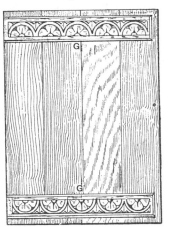

Fig. 587.—Inner Side of Cabinet Door.

Cupboard Carved in Flat Relief on Sunken Ground

For the carved cupboard illustrated in Figs. 578 and 579 the best material is oak, 1 in. thick, but pine is cheaper and more easily worked. If pine is used, it will look best stained and finished to an old oak colour. The cupboard is 3 ft. 9 in. high, and is 2 ft. 10 in. wide (without the mouldings), and 1 ft. 8 in. deep. In making, first cut out the side pieces A (Fig. 580), each of which is formed of two lengths of 1-in. board 3 ft. 8 in. long, and together $18\frac{1}{2}$ in. wide. These are dowelled together, and are further secured by two ledgers screwed to their inner sides; the top of one ledger is 5 in. and that of the other $25\frac{1}{4}$ in. above the ground line. These ledgers may be of $\frac{3}{4}$-in. board, and $1\frac{1}{2}$ in. wide; their chief purpose will be to support the floors of the lower and upper cupboards. The lower of

in $18\frac{1}{2}$-in. lengths; the lengths are fitted into grooves formed by fixing slips of board to the back and front. Narrow slips as at F will suffice at the back, but those at the front G should be 3 in. wide, so that the doors may close against their projections beyond the upright D, and to exclude dust. For the lower cupboards these slips should be $19\frac{1}{4}$ in. long, and for the upper cupboards 18 in. The horizontal bands of moulding which tie up on the front and ends of the cupboard are all of 1-in. board. The upper band, which forms a cornice beneath the top, is $2\frac{1}{2}$ in. wide, and has its lower front edge chamfered off. The middle band is

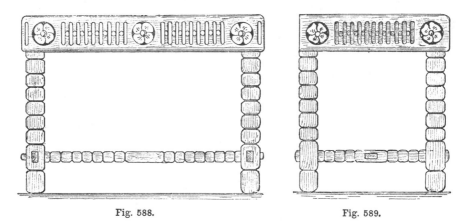

Fig. 588.　　　　　　　　　　Fig. 589.

Figs. 588 and 589.—Front and Side Elevations of Stand for Cabinet.

these floors should be of 1-in. board, and the upper floor of $\frac{3}{4}$-in. board. Their dimensions are 2 ft. 8 in. by 1 ft. $6\frac{1}{2}$ in.; the boards are screwed down to the ledgers, screws also being driven into them through the end pieces. The back can then be boarded up with $\frac{1}{2}$-in. stuff, as at B (Fig. 580). In the front of the cupboard, at each end, there is an upright piece of 1-in. board (C, Fig. 580) 4 in. wide, forming a hingetree for the doors; and in the centre is an upright piece D, 6 in. wide, against which the doors close. These three pieces are of the same length as the sides, namely, 3 ft. 8 in. They are screwed to the floors, and the narrower ones to the side pieces also. Fig. 578 shows the uprights carved. The partition E (Fig. 580) is of $\frac{1}{2}$-in. board

3 in. wide, and has its edges chamfered both above and below. The lower band is 6 in. wide, with its upper edge chamfered; it is shaped below to form legs. The ends of the bands mitre with the front pieces, and are screwed to the pieces beneath. The top is of 1-in. board, 3 ft. $1\frac{1}{2}$ in. long by 1 ft. $9\frac{3}{4}$ in. wide, which allows it to overhang the cornice by $\frac{3}{4}$ in. at the front and the ends. A hollow moulding along its lower edge to lighten its appearance is screwed down to the upright pieces and to the cornice. The doors of the cupboard are 10 in. wide; the lower ones are 17 in. high, and the upper $15\frac{1}{2}$ in. high. For each door a $\frac{1}{2}$-in. panel of the above dimensions is required. One of these panels is shown enlarged by Fig. 581. Four slips of board

of the same thickness are screwed on each panel, the transverse lips being 3 in. wide and the upright slips 2 in. wide. These should be shaped as shown in Fig. 578, and chamfered off on their inner edges, thus leaving a sunk panel for decoration. The carving for the cupboard should be kept in flat relief upon a sunken ground.

Cabinet and Stand

The Cabinet.—A hard, close-grained wood should be used for the cabinet shown in front elevation by Fig. 585; for though the carving is not deep, it has much detail that will require careful working out. Mounted on its stand, it is 3 ft. $0\frac{1}{2}$ in. high; the

Fig. 590.—Oak Cabinet Carved with Scrollwork.

The various patterns are shown enlarged. Fig. 581 is a design for the carving for the lower doors. The design for the upper doors is similar, except that the conventional leaves are compressed to bring them into the shorter space. Fig. 582 shows the simple ornament which runs round the bands of moulding, whilst Figs. 583 and 584 give the decoration of the central and side uprights of the front.

width is 1 ft. 7 in., and the projection 1 ft. The cabinet and stand are made separately, the stand being 1 ft. 3 in. high and the cabinet 1 ft. 10 in., $\frac{1}{2}$ in. of the height of the latter being sunk into the rebate, which holds it in place on the stand. The dotted line A B (Figs. 585 and 586) shows how far the cabinet enters into the rebate. Fig. 586 is an elevation of one of the sides. The board forming each side is 1 ft. $9\frac{1}{2}$ in.

by 10¾ in. by ¾ in., and is lightly planed down. A ledger, ¾ in. square by 10¾ in., is screwed on its inner side flush with the upper edge, to serve as a means of fixing

bottom of the door, thus forming the necessary stop. At the sides, the bottom is screwed down to the ledger. The bottom strip E (Fig. 585) is cut to 1 ft. 2 in. by ¾ in.

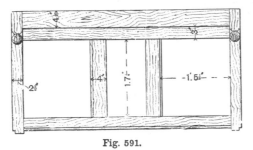

Fig. 591.

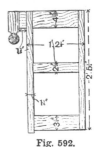

Fig. 592.

Figs. 591 and 592.—Front and End Elevations of Top Framework of Cabinet.

the cabinet top. A similar ledger, screwed with its upper surface 1½ in. above the lower end, will serve to support the cabinet bottom. The back boards, which are screwed to the sides and bottom, are of ½-in. stuff, and laid horizontally. From top to bottom they measure 1 ft. 9½ in. and from side to side 1 ft. 7½ in. They thus project ¼ in. beyond the sides at each end, as shown at c (Fig. 585), where they are rounded off. The carved side strips in Fig. 585 are of ¾-in. stuff, of the same length as the sides, and 3¼ in. wide. The extra ¼ in. projects beyond the sides, and is rounded off. These strips are secured to the sides and bottom with round-headed brass screws. The

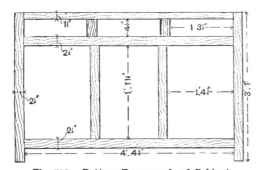

Fig. 593.—Bottom Framework of Cabinet.

cabinet bottom is of ¾-in. board, 1 ft. 5½ in. by 10¾ in. It rests on the lower ledgers already mentioned, and is so placed that its upper surface is ½ in. higher than the

Its ends are mortised or halved into the carved side strips, with which its face comes flush. The strip F above the door is of the same thickness, but only 1 ft. 1 in. long and 1 in. wide. At its back is screwed a strip of board 1 ft. 5½ in. by 1½ in. by ½ in., which, being also screwed from within to the carved strips, holds the top piece F in place. The cabinet top is 1 ft. 8½ in. by 1 ft. 0¾ in. by ½ in., and overhangs the front and sides by ¾ in. It is secured with screws driven upwards through the small ledgers at the sides, and similar ledgers fixed at the front and back. The door is of ¾-in. board, slightly planed down, and measures 1 ft. 6 in. by 1 ft. 1 in. As will be seen, it is rather elaborately carved. Some strengthening is needed at the back to prevent warping or splitting, and this is provided by the cross pieces G (Fig. 587). These are of ½-in. wood, and are lightly carved. The internal fittings of the cabinet will be arranged according to requirements, this design being most suitable for a cupboard. As the inside height is about 1 ft. 7 in., there would be room for two or three shelves if desired.

The Stand.—The stand is shown in front and side elevations by Figs. 588 and 589. The legs are 1½ in. square and 1 ft. 2½ in. long. The ball-like enrichment is worked by making a cut round the four sides with the tenon-saw, trimming slightly with the chisel, and smoothing with the file. The ties at the bottom are similarly ornamented, but are only 1 in. square ; those at the

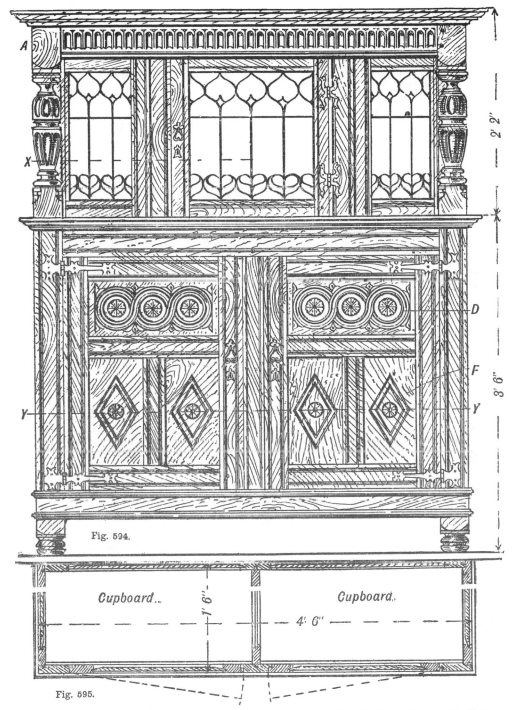

Fig. 594.

Cupboard.

Cupboard.

Fig. 595.

Figs. 594 and 595.—Front Elevation and Horizontal Section of Oak Cabinet with Leaded Glass
Door and Panels

Fig. 596.—Side Elevation of Oak Cabinet with
Leaded Glass Door and Panels.

cabinet. They are secured to the legs with round-headed screws. The back strip differs from these in being quite plain and only $2\frac{1}{2}$ in. wide ; it is halved where it fits against the backs of the legs. The cabinet, when in place, rests on the back strip, on the tops of the legs, and in the rebate. The illustrations are reproduced to a scale of $1\frac{1}{2}$ in. = 1 ft.

Fig. 597.—Detail of Moulding and Carving
of Cabinet at A (Fig. 594).

Oak Cabinet Carved with Scrollwork

An oak cabinet carved with scrolls is illustrated by Fig. 590. Front and end elevations of the top framework are presented by Figs. 591 and 592, whilst the bottom framework is shown in front elevation by Fig. 593.

Oak Cabinet with Leaded Glass Door and Panels

The front and side elevations of a carved oak cabinet with leaded glass door and similar front and side panels are presented by Figs. 594 and 596, and Fig. 595 is a horizontal section on line Y Y. Fig. 597 is an enlarged detail of the moulding and

ends are mortised into the legs, whilst the cross-bar is mortised into the end ties. The legs are cut away $\frac{1}{4}$ in. on their front, end, and back sides, for a depth of $2\frac{1}{2}$ in., to receive the ornamental strips at the top. These strips are of $\frac{3}{4}$-in. board, 3 in. wide ; and in their top edges, on the inner side, is cut a $\frac{1}{2}$-in. by $\frac{1}{4}$-in. rebate, to receive the

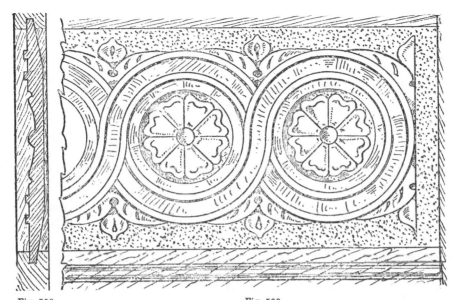

Fig. 598.   Fig. 599.

Figs. 598 and 599.—Detail of Cabinet Panel (see D, Fig. 594).

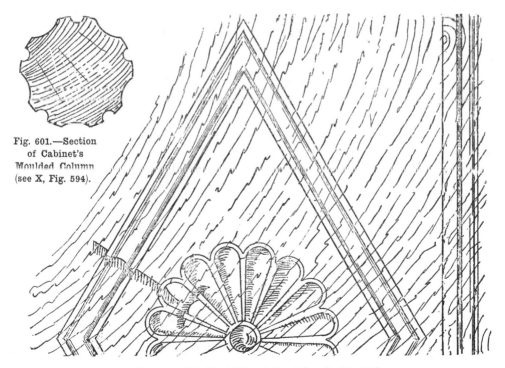

Fig. 601.—Section
of Cabinet's
Moulded Column
(see X, Fig. 594).

Fig. 600.—Detail of Cabinet Panel (see F, Fig. 594).

carving at A; Figs. 598 and 599 show the carving on panel D; and Fig. 600 the carving on panel F. Fig. 601 is an enlarged section of the moulded column, on line X.

successfully. The bold, effective lines, of but slight depth, can be cut with the simplest tools, but the work must not be left in a rough state, but given as high a finish

Fig. 602.—Bureau in Elizabethan Style.

Bureau in Elizabethan Style

A bureau carved in the Elizabethan style is shown by Fig. 602. There is no undercutting, and all the work is bold and free, and of a kind that the beginner can do

as possible, whilst not destroying the vigour and robustness which characterised the mediæval craftsmen. It will be noticed that two doors take the place of three long drawers, but drawers can easily be fitted behind the doors. Even if the doors are

Fig. 603.—Alternative Design for Pateræ in Bureau Lid Frame.

Fig. 604.—Alternative Design for Pateræ in Bureau Lid Frame.

Fig. 605.—Corner of Lid Frame of Elizabethan Bureau.

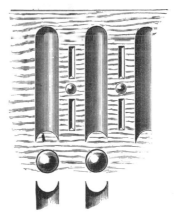

Fig. 606.—Detail of Carved Panel of Elizabethan Bureau.

dispensed with, the drawer fronts need not be carved all alike, as such a course tends to monotony ; the details of the rosettes or pattern may be varied. Fig. 602 gives only a general idea of the front of the

Fig. 607.—Detail of Carving on Drawers of Elizabethan Bureau.

bureau. The lid may be made with the panel flush or sunk. As the panel is rather a large surface to carve, it may have a bevelled edge with advantage to those who do not wish to bestow too much labour on it. The framing around the panel may be left plain, or be carved as shown. The pateræ in the lid frame may be as in Fig. 603 or Fig. 604 ; the corner pattern is shown by Fig. 605. The frame may be left uncarved, like the door frames, if pre-

ferred, and, it is almost needless to add, the latter may be carved in a similar manner. It will be noticed that the long rails, those at the top and bottom, are moulded on the inner edges. To be in character with the style of decoration these mouldings should, strictly speaking, be worked on the solid : that is, instead of gluing them to the framing they should be cut on the framing ; but with care a very serviceable job may be made with mouldings stuck on. The carving on the panel itself is represented by Fig. 606, while that on the drawer fronts is shown by Fig. 607. The door panels are carried out much as the other carving, and no minute description is therefore necessary. Each door has three panels, the middle one being the principal, with fluted carving arranged in circular form, instead of being straight as on the lid. As the flutes converge towards a centre, they, of necessity, assume a tapering form. The top and bottom panels are simply flutes similar to those on the lid, but shown of a simpler form, with the addition of pateræ on the bottom panel. The door framing should be fastened with the ordinary mortice and tenon joints, the two intermediate rails being tenoned into the stiles. If the lower part is to have drawers behind the doors, it is better to hinge the latter on the ends, instead of within them, as shown in Fig. 602. To do so, of course, the end pieces must be cut away to the thickness of the door framing, and the doors themselves be correspondingly wider. By hingeing the doors on the ends, it will be seen that the drawers can be the full length of the inside of the cupboard part ; but if they are hinged within, the ends must be lined up, or thickened, that the drawers may work clear of the doors.

FRAMES

Sixteenth-century Italian Frame

THE architectural tendency in the planning and construction of frames is well illustrated in Fig. 608, which shows an admirable example of late sixteenth-century Italian, enriched with carved figures, painting, and gilding. It is interesting to note the way in which the mouldings are broken round the oblong sight, being taken upwards at the top to leave a clear space ornamented with colour and gold. The broken pediment at the top is a well-conceived ornament; the edges remind one of the scrolled strapwork, typical of Elizabethan wood carving in England, with which it was, of course, contemporaneous. The carved scroll on the frieze is very similar to the string course in St. Paul's Cathedral, executed by Grinling Gibbons about one hundred years later. But the principal source of interest lies in the finely carved female figures flanking the frame. These caryatides are carved with great spirit; the breasts are, perhaps, too strongly developed, although even that may be looked upon as being an example of " artist's licence."

Another Sixteenth-century Italian Frame

Fig. 609 shows a type of frame which is interesting because it marks a decided attempt to get away from the architectural character that had previously dominated the style; further, there are in the scrolls the forerunners of a style that culminated in the elaborate carved work of Louis XIV. and XV., and of which a developed example is shown later in this chapter. There are the caryatids at the side, as in the previous

frame. The pediment is arranged upon the plan of the broken pediment in that example, but the frieze is omitted; and the introduction of pierced carving considerably lightens the frame, as does also the omission of the plain moulding. Practically the whole of the surface of this frame is ornamented with carving. The caryatids are not carved with the spirit and power of the frame shown by Fig. 608. The breasts are poor and small; the faces are unexpressive and vague. The decorative carving is good, and attention is directed to the carved moulding immediately surrounding the picture space; this was very prevalent during the sixteenth century, and in England was certainly characteristic of Elizabethan carved ornament.

Walnut Frames: Italian Sixteenth Century

In somewhat similar style are the frames shown by Figs. 610 and 611. They have been carved to practically the same design, although evidently not by the same artist. The outlines of the frames differ somewhat, but the carved ornament is to the same design. The greater refinement in the arrangement of the design in Fig. 611 suggests that this one was carved after the other. The side panels are enclosed in a cartouche, and the moulding below the picture or mirror is reproduced below the side panels in the second frame. Notice, too, the different expressions on the masks, carved on the frieze. The arrangement of the hair of the female heads on the side panels, too, is of a better type. The cartouches, cupids, and masks are very similar to the type of ornament in use in England about the same time, and show

309

Fig. 608.—Italian Sixteenth-century Frame.

Fig. 609.—Another Italian Sixteenth-century Frame.

that the Renaissance spread its influence very rapidly over Europe.

scheme of ornament is worthy of close study. If the frame is intended for a mirror, then

Fig. 610.—Walnut Mirror Frame: Italian, Sixteenth Century.

Sixteenth=century Oak Frame flanked by Statuettes of Adam and Eve

In Fig. 612 is illustrated a really remarkable piece of work, built up and conceived from the architectural standpoint, and its

nothing much might be urged against such an elaborate scheme; but the frame is not suitable for a good picture—the two would clash and detract from the value of each other. Apart from this, nothing but admiration can possibly be expressed for this remarkable frame, both in its conception and its execution. The figure carving is of the highest excellence : the pose of the figures, the character expressed on their faces, the spirit that characterises the cutting of the bodies—all these are most noteworthy. The arrangement of the frame is on an architectural basis, a fact that is made insignificant by the quality of the figure sculpture. Note how the lower suite of mouldings—those below the opening—are so arranged as to fall in with the scheme of ornament. Every part appears, on close examination, to have been so thoroughly well thought out in relation to every other

Fig. 611.—Walnut Mirror Frame : Italian.   Sixteenth Century.

Fig. 612.—Sixteenth-century Oak Frame, flanked by Statuettes of Adam and Eve.

Fig. 613.—Venetian Mirror and Stand.   Sixteenth Century.

Fig. 614.—Mahogany Frame. English. Early Eighteenth Century.

part; and nothing appears to be superfluous to the design, or to have been added because the space it occupies simply wanted "filling up." This is a test of a good design. Nothing can be taken away from a ornament of mediæval times. This is true of all the European nations throughout the Gothic and the Renaissance periods. The mirror and stand shown by Fig. 613 is a typical example. The framework of walnut is

well-arranged design without disturbing the symmetry and balance of the whole; every part of a good design is essential to it.

Venetian Mirror enriched with Mother=of=Pearl, etc.

It has been said that gold and colour played a very large part in the schemes of bevelled inwards and inlaid with plaques of mother-of-pearl enriched with painted and gilt floral scrolls; on each of the four sides is a pediment-shaped ornament containing two sunk shaped compartments with a mother-of-pearl plaque in each, and a central oval compartment with gilt floral scrolls on a green ground. The rest of the

Fig. 616.—Top Half of Grinling Gibbons
Frame.

Fig. 617.—Bottom Half of Grinling Gibbons Frame.

319

surface is enriched with gilt floral scroll-work on a black ground. The stand, also of walnut, is carved with two voluted scrolls, having an oval boss between, and a moulded capital and base; the sunk portions are decorated partly with mother-of-pearl plaques painted and gilt with scrollwork, and partly with gilt scrolls upon a green ground. The rest of the surface, including the turned bosses on the scrolls, is enriched with gilt scrolls on a black ground. The glass is bevelled. The work is Venetian, sixteenth century. The height of mirror and stand together is $22\frac{7}{8}$ in.; height of mirror without the peg 15 in., width $12\frac{3}{8}$ in.; height of stand $7\frac{7}{8}$ in., width $9\frac{5}{8}$ in. This style of ornament was known as "Pietra-dura." There is nothing in the carving of this example that calls for special comment.

Early Eighteenth-century English Frame

More than a hundred years separates the sixteenth-century Italian frames from the example shown by Fig. 614, and the development that has taken place in the interval is remarkable. The original architectural basis is no longer apparent; the scroll has been so far developed that the result is a frame with beautifully curved outlines, instead of the square, uncompromising lines of the picture opening of the earlier frames. This frame is English, and is symmetrical. In France, during the Louis Quatorze period, the tendency to curved lines ran riot, and produced the "Rococo" and the "Baroco" styles; and a similar style or development known as the "Rocaillo." These had no symmetry, but a prodigal profusion of curves, built upon a peculiar plan. In this example (Fig. 614) some such curves are found in the scrolls, but they are arranged with admirable restraint. The leaves, based on the acanthus, are carved with a much greater refinement, and the scrolls are very clever examples of skilful wood carving. These particular scroll terminations were largely and cleverly used during Elizabethan and the later Stuart times, but the scrolls in this frame show a developed genius in their inventiveness. The mask is well done, and the face flows out into the acanthus leaf terminations in an interesting way. The

balance existing between the plain portions and the carved work brings about economy of effect.

Walnut Frame Attributed to the Barili

The frame shown in Fig. 615 is exactly what a frame should be—that is, a border dividing the mirror or picture from the surrounding wall space. The carved border is based upon the Roman scroll, a characteristic feature of which is the flower in the centre, terminating the scroll. The cupids are beautifully conceived and carved, being full of joyous and bounding life. Designs of this type are of the kind that is now most generally known as Italian Renaissance, and are characterised by the thin stalks, kept low on the ground, not more than a hair's breadth from it, in many cases, by the beautifully and delicately modelled leaf work; and by the scroll as already mentioned, terminating in a flower. The kind of wood employed influenced the style of carving. Italian walnut is a wood capable of being carved in a most delicate manner. The Barili (uncle and nephew), to whom this frame is attributed, worked in Siena or Rome early in the sixteenth century.

Mirror Frame in Limewood by Grinling Gibbons

Figs. 616 and 617 show a magnificent example of the work of Grinling Gibbons, that great master of the late seventeenth and eighteenth centuries (see also Fig. 343, p. 163). Whatever can be said about the characteristic arrangement of the elements of ornament, typical of Grinling Gibbons' work, it must be admitted that his executive powers were on the very highest plane. As can be seen by this example, he drew his elements very largely from natural sources, especially flowers, foliage, and fruit; and the lightness, grace, and naturalness of his work are truly wonderful. The lower part of the frame consists of shells of all kinds, carved with a really remarkable similitude to the natural form. There is no groundwork to most of Gibbons' examples, the whole block of wood being made to do duty as a field for ornament. This frame shows in the general arrangement of its masses a knowledge and an application of architectural effect. Notice, too, how the outline is formed by the arrangement of the leaves and flowers.   Such beautiful work as this is always worth the attention and close study of earnest wood carvers.

Mirror Frame in Seventeenth-century Italian Renaissance Style

The design presented by Fig. 618 is a free adaptation of a good and well-preserved specimen of a seventeenth-century mirror

Fig. 618.—Seventeenth-century Italian Renaissance Mirror Frame.

Fig. 619.—Oval Mirror Frame.

Fig. 620.—Mirror Frame with Rectangular Opening.

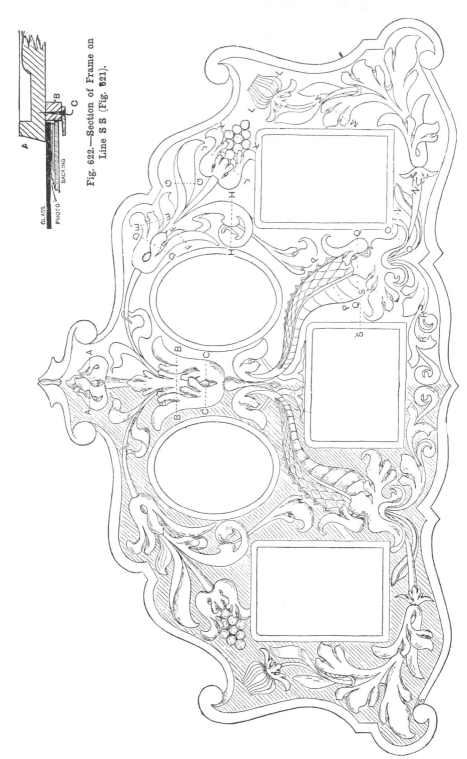

Fig. 622.—Section of Frame on Line S S (Fig. 621).

Fig. 621.—Frame for Five Cabinet Photographs.

frame. Work of this character is difficult, and should be attempted only by those who have passed the initiatory stage. The carving must be executed with precision and crispness, and, at the same time, there must be a freedom and springing quality about it, in order to give the sensation of the lines flowing from a common centre and being continuous throughout. Broken-backed curves and disconnected lines ruin the entire effect. On looking at a good speci-men of seventeenth-century Italian carving, one can imagine the craftsman taking a soft,

due to the different planes (or depths) in the work, and the back scrolls that support the front ones should be, say, 1½ in. thick; and allowing for the parts in highest relief the wood ought to be from 3 in. to 3½ in. thick. Two pieces 1½ in. thick when planed might be glued together, the lower piece for the back scrolls and the oval frame itself, and the upper piece for the work in highest relief. Make a careful enlargement of the design as far as the main lines go, and paste this down on the wood; be careful to strike the oval correctly. The wood should first

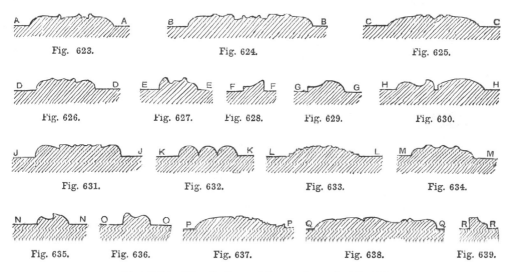

Figs. 623 to 639.—Sections of Frame shown by Fig. 621.

yielding material, and by dexterously guid-ing his tools, executing the long flowing curves that make up the design, in a few sweeps of his gouge. Actually, this effect is obtained by time and labour, and the finished work suggests that it was wrought in the first freshness of the day, when the nerves are vibrating and the energy is elastic. There should be no feeling of labour about wood carving. If the work is for gilding, good pine can be used, but if the wood is to show, American walnut, oak or mahogany is better. The thickness of the wood depends upon the amount of under-cutting. This class of design does not look well in too low relief. The effect is largely

of all be pierced, and the outside or outline of the design should also be cut round; now ground out to the depth of the back scrolls; if two pieces were glued together, ground out to the depth of the upper piece. This gives a fair idea of the "masses" of the design. The real difficulties begin with the carving itself. In Fig. 618, the light and shade indicate the general disposition of the principal curves, and intelligence and artistic perception must do the rest. The scrolls resting on the oval frame should be, say, ½ in. deeper than the frame itself, that is the full depth of the wood through where two pieces are glued together. As already said, the lower piece should be for the frame and back scrolls; but where the wood is solid, the oval frame itself might be 2 in. deep, the back scrolls 1½ in., and the foremost ones the full depth, 3 in. This gives three planes, and subtler gradations can be introduced as the work progresses, so that one plane loses itself or sinks into

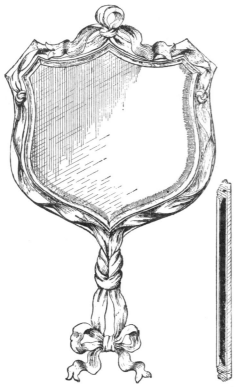

Fig. 640.—Hand
Mirror.

Fig. 641.—Section
of Hand Mirror.

the one below it, for it should not be apparent how many planes there are.

Oval Mirror Frame

The fancy-shaped mirror shown by Fig. 619 is cut with a bow saw out of a nice piece of American oak, 11 in. by 18 in. The oval for the mirror is about 7 in. by 9 in. A rebate is worked from the back about ½ in. in depth for glass and back, and about ¼ in. wide. The pattern is of purely conventional style, very freely curved. Both inner and outer edges are worked on a bevel; while

the head and tail pieces are boldly and deeply carved.

Hanging Mirror Frame with Rectangular Opening

Fig. 620 represents an original design for a hanging mirror to be made out of a single piece of oak, but would look equally well in walnut or in darkened mahogany. The wood is 24 in. by 12 in., and about ¾ in. thick. The outline can be band-sawn or bow-sawn. If bow-sawn, it should be carefully finished with the file. The cut-out centre space for receiving the bevelled mirror is about 13 in. by 4 in. This is cut away with the bow saw and finished with the file. It is rebated at the back about ⅔ in. The margin at the centre and the edges is about ½ in. all over. Beyond being bevelled both inwards and outwards to disguise the thickness of the wood, the margin is left plain with the exception of the knobs, which are slightly worked out. The ornamental tags or bosses at the top, bottom, and sides are more elaborately carved. The pattern looks well if cut ¼ in. deep.

Frame for Five Cabinet Photographs

The Construction.—The design for the frame shown by Fig. 621 should be carried out in oak, walnut, or mahogany, for preference ; but sycamore, kauri, or canary wood may be used if desired. The piece for the front carved portion of the frame should be 2 ft. 9 in. by 1 ft. 6 in. by ⅝ in. The wood should be thoroughly seasoned, and have a close, straight grain, which should run from the right to the left of the board when placed in position for carving. If possible, it will be better to have the wood in one piece, as a joint is liable to break whilst being carved. The front surface should first be planed true and then gauged up as thick as it will work ($\frac{9}{16}$ in.). For cutting out the openings, use a brace and bit to make a hole for the insertion of the compass or keyhole saw. The accurate cutting of these openings will be rather difficult, especially in the ovals, for all the cuts run at an angle as at A (Fig. 622) ; and the exact amount of bevel is difficult to find. The best way to avoid mistakes is to cut square through ⅛ in. within the line, and bevel the cut down to the line afterwards by means of chisels, gouges, and spokeshaves. The outside curves should be cut square through as near the line as possible, and trimmed up with the same tools as for the inside, and all the curves finished off with rifflers and glasspaper. To make the frames at the back, five strips of wood B (Fig. 622), each 2 ft. long by $\frac{3}{8}$ in. wide by $\frac{5}{16}$ in. thick, are required. Each

frames. It will be advisable not to screw on these frames until after the carving is finished, for the material must be perfectly flat and firmly fixed on the bench or table to avoid splitting it.

The Carving.—Should the work be done on a table which is in everyday use, ordinary carving cramps must be used. Used on the frame itself, they are apt to make a nasty

Fig. 642.—Photograph Frame in Incised Carving.

strip is sufficient to make one frame ($6\frac{5}{8}$ in. by $4\frac{1}{4}$ in. inside measure), which should be mitered, glued, and nailed together with fine wire nails. When the glue has set, the frames should be smoothed off and a hole bored through the centre of each of the four sides, through which passes a $\frac{1}{2}$-in. screw C, attached to a small brass button, to fasten them to the back of the carved portions of the frame. The backs, made out of ordinary picture backing, may now be fitted in, and the glass cut $\frac{1}{8}$ in. less than the size of the

mark on the finished edges ; while the wood may warp if not continually held in place until the carving is finished. This can easily be avoided by getting three pieces of deal 1 ft. 6 in. by 1 ft. by 1 in. and screwing them temporarily on the back of the frame, taking care that the screws do not enter more than $\frac{3}{16}$ in. into the wood of the frame. If the work is carried out on a bench, all the better, as it may then be left in position. Should there be no objection to making screw-holes in the top of the bench, little wood clamps

(A, Fig. 84, p. 36) may be attached, half a dozen of these effectually preventing the frame moving. The frame being properly fixed, the grounding out of the carving should be proceeded with. The ground when finished should be $\frac{1}{4}$ in. deep, but in the first instance it must be made a shade less than this, to allow for cleaning off when the carving is finished. The longer curves had

to them lowered slightly, and, generally, they should be subordinate to the dolphins. The central husk above should be rather prominent, as also should the flower rising from it. A careful examination of the sections (Figs. 623 to 639) will give an idea of the different curves employed. The narrow border round the frame could be relieved by slightly lowering the shaded por-

Fig. 643.—Another Photograph Frame.

better be done with a **V**-tool, as it gives a cleaner cut and makes a more graceful sweep than is possible when the curve is " set in " the full length with gouges. When the ground has been cut fairly even, the details may be added to the wooden masses. The modelling will require careful consideration. As will be seen, the dolphins are the principal figures, and consequently ought to stand out boldly. All leaves in close proximity to them should have the side nearest

tions. The punching of the ground may be left to the discretion of the carver. If a good finish can be obtained without punching, it will be advisable to do without it.

Hand Mirror

Fig. 640 illustrates a carved hand mirror which should be cut with a fret saw, and rebated to receive glass. To fix the frame for carving, mount it on a piece of pine with very thin glue, with brown paper between, and fasten the pine to the bench. To remove the frame, insert a thin knife between it and the paper. The back, which is about ⅛ in. thick, is of shield shape, and does not run behind the handle or the ribbon at the top ; it is secured with small brass screws, with paper between it and the glass, as shown in Fig. 641. The mirror frame should be about

to shape with an ordinary saw or a fret saw. The inner edges of the central opening should be moulded as shown, and a rebate made for the glass and photograph. A back board of thin wood should be screwed at the back to keep the glass and photograph in position. The carving is of a simple character. The design should be

Fig. 644.—More Advanced Photograph Frame.

1 ft. by 6½ in., of ⅜-in. stuff, and would look well in brown oak, walnut, or mahogany.

Three Photograph Frames

First Example.—Fig. 642 shows a frame of simple construction, the size being according to the photograph to be framed. The wood suitable is oak, walnut, mahogany, or any hardwood, and may be finished dull or polished. If required black or ebonised, the softer woods should be used. The wood should be ½ in. thick, and should be cut

drawn out and traced on the wood, and worked with a half-round carving tool to form the incised leaves. Care should be taken to keep the points of the leaves sharp. The lines of the stems and the rings should be also worked with this tool. The lines round the edge of the frame are worked with a small **V**-shaped tool, taking care that they are true and straight. This design may be simplified by dispensing with the upper ornaments, and substituting the side ornament with circles at each corner.

Fig. 645.

Fig. 646.

Figs. 645 and 646.—Frames with Open-work Foliage.

Second Example.—Fig. 643 shows a design of a frame which requires greater skill in working, the construction being much the same as before. The work adopted generally is incised or sunk, the face of the ornament being flat and of the same surface. This ornament should be sunk about $\frac{1}{8}$ in. below the face surface. The corner ornaments and the circular roses at the feet may be treated in the same way, or they may be treated as shown in the design, by having the leaves slightly shaped and modelled. The groundwork of the small panels should be dotted or lined, so as to show up the lines of the ornament, and thus give a better effect.

of this kind is better left from the tool, only rubbed smooth. It will be readily seen that various flowers may be adapted for a design of this kind. The ordinary lily, the bluebell, the Canterbury bell, the wild rose, and many others are suitable for the purpose.

Frame with Open-work Foliage

The frame shown by Fig. 645 is the work of Mr. James Marr. It is 22 in. long by 20 in. wide, and is made of satin-walnut and stained American walnut, with a $\frac{3}{4}$-in. gilt slip inside. The wood is 1 in. in thickness, which is quite sufficient to give a wonderful relief effect ; of course, it is principally cut

Fig. 647.—Section

of Frame on Line A B

(Fig. 646).

Fig. 648.—Florentine Open-work Frame.

The circular beads at the side may be omitted if desired, and the edges left square.

Third Example.—The frame shown by Fig. 644 is of a more ambitious pattern, the working of which will require greater skill in the manipulation of the tools. The frame is constructed in a similar way as described for Fig. 642, but thicker wood will be required, say $\frac{3}{4}$ in., or even thicker if the leaves and flowers are to be in bold relief. This design must be carefully drawn on the wood so as to keep the lines of the stems and leaves graceful in outline. The groundwork is then cut down to the depth required. The flowers, buds, and leaves must then be carefully worked with suitable tools, so that the most natural effect is given to them. Work

through, and shaped away towards the outside and down to the back.

Another Open-work Frame

The mirror frame, illustrated by Fig. 646, may be cut from 1-in. oak or walnut. The outside measurement is 1 ft. $11\frac{3}{4}$ in. by 1 ft. $7\frac{1}{2}$ in., the sight line 1 ft. 2 in. by $\frac{7}{8}$ in. by $10\frac{11}{16}$ in., and the width of moulding $4\frac{3}{8}$ in. First work the two sides to 2 ft. by $4\frac{3}{8}$ in. by 1 in., and the top and the bottom to 1 ft. 8 in. by $4\frac{3}{8}$ in. by 1 in., and rebate them on the back and front and bevel the edge on the face side. Next cut and shoot mitres to the required size and dowel together as shown by Fig. 647. Do not glue up until the carving is finished. Now take the frame apart and carefully trace on the design, fret or drill through the groundwork, and begin carving by carefully roughing out all four pieces, modelling the work well in the round, and keeping a nice finish. The veins should be raised by gouging on each side. Do not finish the corner leaves close to the mitres, as they can be made to correspond better when glued together. When glued together, undercut the parts that stand in high relief ; care must be taken not to do this before the ornament is thoroughly

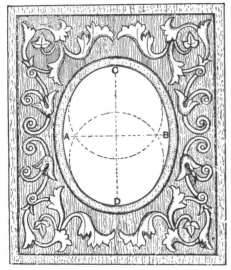

Fig. 649.—Simple Frame with Oval Opening.

worked up, as it cannot be lowered afterwards. Carefully finish all the ornament with very sharp tools, and finally chamfer the work from the back to take off any rough edges that may be seen from the front.

Florentine Open-work Frame

A frame in Florentine open-work is illustrated by Fig. 648. Such frames generally are carved in soft yellow pine, and gilded. This frame illustrates those principles of ornament known as regularity, order, and rhythm, besides in an incidental way those of repetition and alternation. The leaved scroll is introduced here with good effect, this effect being obtained by its reduction to

order and regularity. The eye can follow many lines along these scrolls, and can make the frame assume various shapes because of this. There is not much piercing, but it is quite sufficient. The breaking of the straight outline is small, and does not hinder the eye from travelling round the frame easily and taking in the oblong shape.

Simple Photograph Frame

Walnut, oak, or canary wood is suitable for constructing the photograph frame illustrated by Fig. 649. It should be about $\frac{3}{4}$ in. or 1 in. thick, and $10\frac{3}{4}$ in. long by 9 in. wide. The outside margin is $\frac{3}{8}$ in. ; the size of the inner oval, from A to B, $4\frac{3}{8}$ in. ; from C to D, $5\frac{3}{4}$ in. ; and the outer oval is $\frac{3}{8}$ in. larger all round. The oval could be made larger or smaller, to suit the photograph ; the dotted lines show the method of construction. The design is simple and plain, and easy to mark on the wood. If the lines A B and C D are continued to the outer edges of the wood, they will divide it into four equal parts, and if one part of the design is sketched and taken off on tracing paper, it can be applied to each corner.

Oak Overmantel

The overmantel illustrated in front and side elevations by Figs. 650 and 651, and in plan by Fig. 652, should be made in oak, and carved. The frame is 3 ft. 9 in. wide by 2 ft. $11\frac{1}{2}$ in. deep, the two stiles and top rail being 4 in. wide, and finishing $\frac{7}{8}$ in. thick ; the bottom rail is $4\frac{3}{4}$ in. wide, and shaped as shown in Fig. 650. The rails are stump-tenoned into the stiles. Fig. 653 is a section through the pediment, shelf, and frame. The rebate for the moulding is made by gluing and bradding strips of pine inside the frame, setting them back $\frac{3}{8}$ in. from the face side. The glass is secured with wooden wedges about 3 in. long, also glued and bradded. The pillars (Fig. 654) are 2 in. square, and are placed cornerwise. They may be reeded on the two face sides, as shown in Fig. 655, or left plain. To reed them, mark with three pencil lines, and carefully hollow these with a carver's parting or V-tool ; then, removing the sharp edges with a long thin paring chisel, finish with fine glasspaper. A small patera is carved on each face side at the bottom, and at the top three grooves are made with a ¼-in. gouge. A square pin is left at the bottom of each pillar, this fitting into a square hole

shape of the shelf is shown by Fig. 652; it is ¾ in. thick, and overhangs each end of the frame 1½ in.; a moulding is worked on its under side at the front and ends. The moulding on the pediment (*see* Fig. 653) is

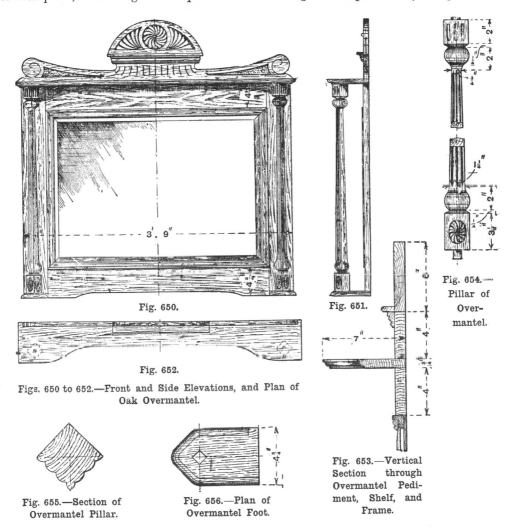

Fig. 650.

Fig. 651.

Fig. 652.

Figs. 650 to 652.—Front and Side Elevations, and Plan of Oak Overmantel.

Fig. 654.—
Pillar of
Over-
mantel.

Fig. 655.—Section of
Overmantel Pillar.

Fig. 656.—Plan of
Overmantel Foot.

Fig. 653.—Vertical
Section through
Overmantel Pedi-
ment, Shelf, and
Frame.

in the shaped foot (*see* Fig. 656). A round pin ¼ in. long is left at the top, a corresponding hole in the shelf being made to receive it; it is then secured with a screw driven in from the top. The shaped feet (Fig. 656) are 4¾ in. by ¾ in. A moulding is worked on the top outside edge, stopped on the inside level with the face of the frame. The

a short length of the same section as that used for the frame, with an additional piece glued to its top. The top carving should be made separate, the joint being level with the top of the moulding. A thin pine backboard should be screwed to the back of the overmantel in the usual way to protect the glass.

Frame Carved with Strapwork Pattern

The frame shown by Fig. 657 is carved to an effective strapwork pattern in oak, walnut, or mahogany moulding. The outside size of the frame is 15½ in. by 17½ in. ;

great significance. The pattern may be repeated to any extent.

Gothic Boss Corner for Picture Frames

The two designs presented by Figs. 659 and 660 are very simple in character. The

Fig. 657.—Frame Carved with Strapwork Pattern.

Fig. 658.—Section of Frame.

the inside measurement is 8 in. by 10 in. A section of the moulding (Fig. 658) shows it to be 3½ in. wide, made from 2-in. stuff, but bevelled inwards to 1 in. The two saw-kerfs indicate the width of the carving ground and the depth of the cutting. The shaded portions of the relief work show where it has been depressed by a straight firmer. The corners should be finished off after the frame is jointed and set. The size of the material or of the frame is of no

first (Fig. 659) is an adaptation of a tolerably familiar pattern used in the bosses or Gothic wooden roofs, and consists of two double leaflets interwoven, and forming the termination of the twisted stem that occupies the rest of the frame. It would be easier when the frame is mitered and glued up to glue an extra piece, say, ¼ in. or ⅜ in. deep, at each corner, so that the corners are in higher relief than the stems running along the four sides. The four bosses can then

Fig. 659.—Gothic Boss Corner for Picture Frame.

Fig. 660.—Hispano-Moresque Corner for Picture Frame.

be carved out of the pieces glued on, the grounding out being taken to the depth of the pieces glued on, and not to the depth of the flat upon which the twisted stems lie. The corner is illustrated full size. Having grounded out, carve away the leaves as they approach the edges of the bosses, so that the centre is the highest part of the corners, and the edges of the leaves only slightly higher than the thickness of the pieces glued on. Let the veining be simple and in the direction of the way of the leaf. Get the contour of the leaves sharp and angular (*see* p. 178), and let the carving be crisp and

Fig. 661.—Top Half of Frame: Designed by W. Harry Rogers.

executed in a broad, free manner. The stem running along the sides of the frame should be about $\frac{1}{8}$ in. in relief. The length and height must be divided up so that the twist or knob comes at regular intervals. The stem should not be smooth, but have a sort of bark-like surface running the lengthway of the stems. The background would look well if worked over with a punch instead of being left plain.

Hispano-Moresque Corner for Picture Frames

Fig. 660 is adapted from a Hispano-

Fig. 662.—Bottom Half of Frame: Designed by W. Harry Rogers

Moresque piece of carving, and is only intended to be like a fret upon the flat. Consequently the grounding out should not be taken deeper than ⅛ in. Some portions of the design should be lower than the others. Be very careful to get the curves correct, and not broken, as the beauty of these designs is their flowing, interwoven character. The rest of the frame can have the double arabesque running the whole length of the frame, and terminating at each corner. Such designs as these Moorish

centre, literature is represented, a monogram of the owner being worked in the ornament. On the bottom rail is a pair of doves nestling in clusters of Italian leaf foliage and bearing a ribbon with the words, " A Thing of Beauty is a Joy for Ever."

Frame Carved by Miss Muriel Moller

A modern frame showing a late tendency of carved ornament is shown in Fig. 663. This is the work of Miss Muriel Moller, well

Fig. 663.—Frame Carved by Miss Muriel Moller.

arabesques would make good fretwork designs, and, in fact, a frame might be decorated in this way by cutting the design out as a fret and gluing it on the flat.

Frame Designed by W. Harry Rogers

Figs. 661 and 662 show a frame designed by the late W. Harry Rogers and carved in boxwood by the designer's father, the late W. G. Rogers. It was lent by the late Baroness Burdett-Coutts for exhibition at the Royal Albert Hall in 1880. This is an example of a mixed style producing a successful result, it combining Renaissance, natural flowers, and foliage. It is 20 in. high, and the corner roundels bear emblems of music, poetry, sculpture, and the plastic arts. At the top

known during the last few years as a successful exponent of modern naturalistic ornament. The " new art " has had many stages. Begun by William Morris in the most earnest spirit as a protest against the continually stereotyped reproduction without life and character of the work of past centuries, it developed later a tendency to " quaint " detachment of parts and a curious heterodoxy of shape and outline. But more recently there has developed a saner method of expression, and it is to be hoped that we are now at the beginning of a new style that will eventually vie with the greatest periods of past historic ornament. The modern phase of carved work, it may be remarked, is based principally upon natural forms.

Photograph Frame

The frame shown by Figs. 664 and 665 has been designed to hold a cabinet photo 4 in. by 5½ in., but the design could be altered to suit any size required. The width of the frame at the bottom is 8 in., and the height from the bottom to the top over all is 9 in.

the top and ¾ in. wide at the bottom. It is fixed to the back with a 1-in. butt hinge. The leg is kept in position, when open, by a piece of tape.

Early Frames

Prior to the Italian Renaissance, frames were not generally in use for pictures; and

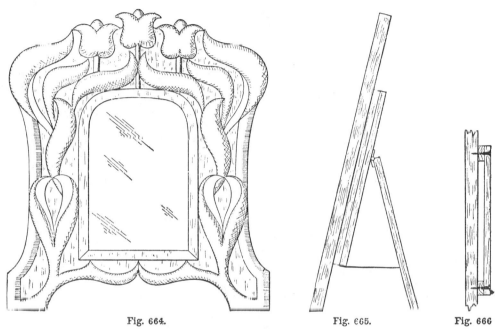

Fig. 664. Fig. 665. Fig. 666

Figs. 664 and 665.—Front and Side Elevations of Photograph Frame.
Fig. 666.—Part Cross Section of Frame.

It can be made of either oak or mahogany ⅝ in. or ¾ in. thick, and if it is enamelled, soft wood could be used. A cross section of the frame is shown at Fig. 666. Strips of wood ¼ in. thick are fixed to the sides and bottom; and the back, which is ¼ in. thick, is fixed to them and the frame with screws. The glass and photo are dropped in from the top. The leg is ¼ in. thick by 1 in. wide at

even for mirrors they were not at all common. The first frames were mainly architectural in character, and in this respect the development of the frame is a reminder of the evolution of the cabinet (*see* pp. 276 to 278, and especially Fig. 543, p. 278). As already shown, colour was freely used; also gold; and the ornamental details were in " gesso " and in carved work.

CHAIRS

CHAIRS and stools have not always been in such common use as they now are. In olden times, even amongst civilised nations, a reclining position was adopted when resting, thus rendering somewhat superfluous the use of an individual seat, such as a chair. This article was more largely used as a throne, or for very important persons, even when its use became more common; whilst stools were reserved for persons of lower rank. In the evolution of the chair first came that most primitive of all manufactured seats, the three-legged stool, made of wood. Later, it was adorned with velvet and other stuffs, or was painted or stained or enriched with carved ornament. It is astonishing, considering the really simple essential nature of a chair, into what curious shapes it has developed, as will be evident from a comparison of the chairs shown in this section, dating from the ninth to the twentieth centuries.

Norwegian Armchair : Ninth or Tenth Century

The copy of an old Norwegian chair of the ninth or tenth century is illustrated by Fig. 667 (p. 341). These chairs kept for many years to the same type, a chair of the thirteenth or fourteenth century in Dr. Figdor's collection in Vienna being constructed on exactly the same plan and general arrangement. A most interesting type of ornament has been adopted in the example shown by Fig. 667 as a basis for the carving. Scandinavian ornament is based upon the legend of the dragon Fafni. The peculiar nature of the ornament is its extensive and typical interlacement, largely corresponding to that of the Celtic races. This much

can be observed in the front panel of the chair (Fig. 667), and in the side stretchers below the side panels. In the side panels is portrayed a battle scene, the combatants being depicted in a vigorous and decorative manner. The wood sculpture of the Scandinavians was not remarkable for its refinement; but it was always full of life and close to truth. The terminals of the arms of the chair remind one very strongly of the prows of the Viking ships. Plant forms are not found in Scandinavian ornament until the twelfth century, before which period the ornament consists almost wholly of the dragon; and the value of the spiral arrangement of the scroll is shown on the front panel and on the terminals of the arms, the latter corresponding closely to the Ionic volute. The whole arrangement of the ornament shows a considerable advancement in the knowledge of the art of ornamental planning, and exhibits a fine appreciation of decorative effect. The actual chair shown by Fig. 667 was carved in pine by J. Borgerson, of Christiania, and is a copy of an old chair formerly in Blaker Farm, Lom, in the district of Gudbrandsdalen, and now in the Museum of the University of Christiania.

Modern Norwegian Armchair

An armchair in carved pine, by C. G. Christensen, is illustrated by Fig. 668 (p. 342). This was shown at the Paris Exhibition of 1900, and formed part of the Donaldson gift to the Victoria and Albert Museum, London. The chair is painted red, blue, green, and yellow. The value and importance of tradition in the conception and planning of ornament is evidenced in this example.

Fig. 667.—Armchair, Carved in Pine by J. Borgerson.
Copied from Ninth- or Tenth-century Norwegian Chair.

Fig. 668.—Modern Norwegian Armchair.   Made by C. G. Christensen.

There is the same kind of square pillar at each corner as in the previous example, acting as leg and arm support ; and although the panels are omitted, yet the general outline and plan are the same. After the lapse of 1,000 years, the ornament, although differing in details, is yet of the same general type, being based upon the same dragon *motif*. The application of colour to carving is not so much in favour at the present time as in mediæval ages, it being thought better to

king, archbishop, noble, and judge when on their journeys, each chair being sacred to the use of its owner. These chairs folded either from back to front, as in the case of a Glastonbury chair ; or from side to side, as in the type of chair here illustrated. The form of an animal's foot has in all ages been adopted as an ornamental feature of the feet of chairs, it being found in Egyptian, Assyrian, Grecian, and Roman furniture, and from time to time throughout the whole

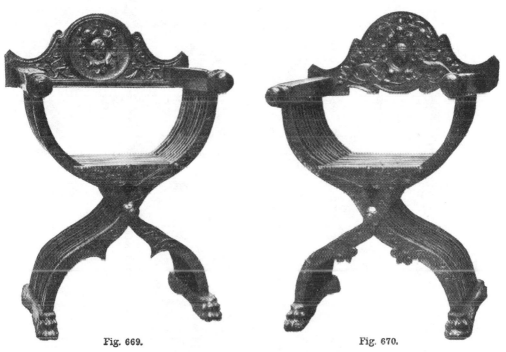

Fig. 669.   Fig. 670.

Figs. 669 and 670.—Oak Folding Armchairs.   Italian.   Date : about 1550.

allow the carving tool to play the most important part in giving effect to the work. If colour is thought necessary, stain would be the better medium, as it does not fill up the cuts made by the carving tool.

Sixteenth=century Folding Armchairs

In Figs. 669 and 670 are shown two similar chairs of a type that became common during the sixteenth century. The prototype of this class of chair was, without doubt, the folding stool. Backs were added as time went on. These folding chairs always accompanied

of the Christian era up to the present century. Figs. 669 and 670 show examples.

Sixteenth=century French Chairs of State

First Example.—In addition to the feet of animals, their heads were used very extensively to form the arms of chairs, in all historic periods. This is the case with the chairs shown in Figs. 671 to 674 (pp. 344, 345, 346, and 347). These chairs are very important pieces of work, being, in fact, thrones or chairs of State, rather than chairs

Fig. 671.—Walnut Chair of State.   French.   Late Sixteenth Century.

Fig. 672.—Panel from Back of Chair of State (see Fig. 671).

Fig. 673.—Another Walnut Chair of State.   French.   Late Sixteenth Century.

Fig. 674.—Panel and Stiles from Back of Chair of State (see Fig. 673).

for ordinary use. The first chair is of
walnut and was made at Lyons, France, in
the second half of the sixteenth century.
The panel of Fig. 671, which is enlarged in
Fig. 672, is of the greatest interest to the
wood carver. The careful evidence of the
original planning of furniture upon an architectural basis is afforded by the dentilled
pediment at the top of the panel. It rests
upon moulded abaci supported by a square
carved capital resting upon the heads of
two winged satyrs. Observe the conventional way in which the wings are curled
up to form a scroll. The treatment of the
foliage throughout the whole of the panel
is admirable ; the way in which the small
leaves are made to twist, and the way in
which they are cut to break the reflection
of light, and so to cause a succession of
high light and deep shadow, are especially
worthy of notice. Foliage of the type forming the base of the design is often spoilt in
its treatment by being too much cut up by
gouges ; but in this case the treatment is
restrained and dignified. In contrast to
the free, effective treatment of the main
design, the carving on the mouldings seems
somewhat poor and mechanical ; but in all
probability this is a studied attempt to
enhance the effect by means of contrast.
There is much carving on the chair, but
its judicious arrangement prevents its claim-
ing too great a share of attention. The
level cornice is now becoming very familiar,
through much of the modern work.

Second Example.—Very similar in type
is the chair illustrated in Fig. 673 (p. 346),
the panel and stiles of which are shown on
larger scale by Fig. 674. This example is
of the same origin and date. Here the arms
are solid, those in Fig. 671 being open ; but
the same arrangement has been carried out,
whereby the upper edge of the arm is quite
clear of projections, thus not interfering
with its proper use as an arm rest. Noteworthy are the convex frieze, its admirably
planned moulding, the dentilled cornice,
and, in particular, the whole suite of carved
mouldings. These two chairs are perfect
studies of carved mouldings. Notice in
Fig. 674 the arrangement of the two carved
mouldings round the panel. The plain
mouldings form a perfect foil to the carved

mouldings. In the caryatids at the side,
notice the terminal foot, the fluted column,
the strength and vigour of the carved heads,
and the carved mouldings. The ox's head
at the lower part of the panel is reminiscent
of the similar heads originally sculptured
on Roman tombs ; the cartouche surrounding it was further developed during the
century following the date of construction ;
and the corn and fruit and flowers, and
the head in the centre swathed in drapery,
were for one hundred and fifty or two hundred
years common elements in the carved ornament of Europe, as witness the next example.
Both of the chairs above described are the
property of Mr. J. Pierpont Morgan.

Oak Armchair

The oak armchair shown by Fig. 675 (p.
349) is used by the Masters of the Worship-
ful Company of Brewers. It dates from
about 1720, and has a high back and scrolled
top, surmounted by a grotesque mask. It is
carved with the company's coat-of-arms,
drapery, and festoons of fruit and ribbons.
It has massive arms, square back legs, and
baluster shape front legs. There is a solid
seat with stuffed cushion covered with
leather. The ornament is of the Grinling
Gibbons style. Fruit, flowers, laurel and
olive branches, ribbon and drapery were
the staple elements in use, together with the
scroll. The grotesques on the arms do not
interfere with the use of the arms. It is
not so much the choice of any particular
element that characterises a period, as it is
the particular manner of its manifestation.
Thus, drapery as an element of ornament
has been in use in all ages ; but the particular manner adopted by the Grinling Gibbons
school, of which the drapery on this chair is
a good example, is peculiar to this period.
This chair is also referred to on p. 171.

Dutch Armchair with Cane Seat

Dutch furniture of the sixteenth and
seventeenth centuries was of a heavy character, and this is evidenced in the chair
shown by Fig. 676 (p. 350). The carved
ornament, however, is derived from the
Italian Renaissance, although of a heavier
type. The scroll and conventional acanthus
leaf, together with the lily and the calyx,

Fig. 675.—Oak Armchair used by Masters of the Brewers' Company.
Date : about 1720.

Fig. 676.—Dutch Armchair with Cane Seat.   Date: 1640.

are the principal elements used in this chair. Round the ovals is a kind of "scaling" often used during this period ; but, in this case, it is of poor quality, and evidently used to produce an effect at a small expenditure of labour ; it is the result of a very obvious use of the quick gouge.

Chairs of Turned and Carved Walnut

The chairs shown in Figs. 677 and 678 (pp. 352 and 353) show Dutch influence in the heavy pierced scroll-work on the back splats and lower stretcher. In the case of Fig. 677, the scroll-work front legs came from Holland or Flanders, and this class of leg eventually developed into the shape made familiar by the chairs of Thomas Chippendale (*see* Fig. 680, p. 355). In the chairs here shown, the carved work forms an essential part of the construction.

Venetian Armchair of Carved Walnut

Often there is met with work that has been obviously designed with the express intention of "showing off" the carving. The chair illustrated in Fig. 679 (p. 354) is obviously an example of this ; there is no restraint, and although the result suggests magnificence, the general impression is one of dissatisfaction, owing to the fact that the ornament has been allowed to occupy the first place in the planning of the chair, instead of planning the construction first and leaving the arrangement of the ornament until afterwards. Venice has produced some of the finest wood carving the world has ever seen, and the chair under consideration is proof of this. It requires more than average ability to carve ornament of this kind from the solid block, and the earnest and studious attention of the wood carver is directed to this as being a worthy example of such a form of carving.

Chippendale Armchair in Mahogany

Fig. 680 (p. 355) shows a familiar example of the great eighteenth-century cabinet-maker, Thomas Chippendale, who utilised the various kinds of ornament fashionable in his day to produce his well-known style of furniture. He combined chiefly three styles, the Louis, the Chinese, and the Gothic.

In this example, which shows French influence, the ornament consists of the acanthus, on the knees of the legs and on the arms ; the claw and ball-foot, developed through Dutch influence ; the beautiful ribbon-work in the back, common during the Grinling Gibbons period ; the carved moulding round the edge of the chair, immediately under the upholstered seat ; a scroll development that was so characteristic of the Louis XIV. and XV. styles across the Channel. Whatever may be said about the strength of the back splat, there can be no question as to the grace and beauty of the ribbon-work. The carving does not break into the outline of the form which it decorates. Thus, the legs do not have their outline broken into by the carving ; it simply breaks what would otherwise have been a blank, heavy surface. The same can be said respecting the carved moulding ; the scroll-work on the open back actually helps to form the outline ; and this application of ornament cannot have too much attention called to it.

Empire Chairs

A few years after Chippendale achieved such success, events in France moved forward with the most alarming rapidity, culminating in the creation of an Empire with Napoleon at its head. A minor result was the creation of the "Empire" style of furniture, of which two examples are shown by Figs. 681 and 682 (pp. 356 and 357). One marked feature of this development is the way in which certain great historic styles were drawn upon to form it. Thus, contributions are taken freely from the Egyptian, Assyrian, Grecian, and Roman periods of ornament. The throne chair shown by Fig. 681 is of gilt wood, winged griffins forming the arms and front supports. The back is solid to the ground, elaborately carved in relief with foliage ornament and rosettes. The back inside and the seat are stuffed and covered with red velvet. The date is about 1820, and at the time of taking the photographs the examples here described belonged to the late Queen Victoria. The second example (Fig. 682) is of painted and gilt wood, the semicircular back and sides being solid and continuous, and being surmounted by a rail carved with wreaths and

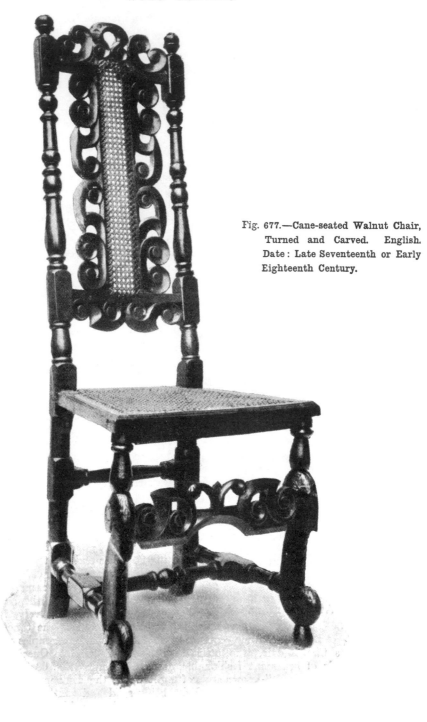

Fig. 677.—Cane-seated Walnut Chair,
Turned and Carved. English.
Date : Late Seventeenth or Early
Eighteenth Century.

Fig. 678.—Rush-seated Walnut
Chair, Turned and Carved.
English.   Date :   Late
Seventeenth or   Early
Eighteenth Century.

Fig. 679.—Venetian Seventeenth-century Armchair of Carved Walnut.

Fig. 680.—Chippendale Style Mahogany Chair.   Date: Second Half of
Eighteenth Century.

gilded. In front are two carved bands carved with leaf ornament, and terminating in lions' heads, and further enriched with black and gold. At the back are two similar bands. The whole rests upon four curved (Fig. 681) has not only heads and feet, but the entire bodies of griffins in addition, their wings being well arranged to form first the arms, and then supports for the back. Notice how the wings are worked into scrolls

Fig. 681.—Throne Chair in Empire Style. Date: about 1820.

legs, similarly decorated, ending in lions' feet; and in front is a carved and gilt rosette. The back and sides are covered inside and out with red velvet, as is also the stuffed seat. The date is supposed to be about 1800. The laurel leaf used as a band and the leaf bands encircling the legs were features of the period. The throne chair at their upper terminations. The feathers of the wings are full of life, and the bodies are well thought out and executed. The tails terminate in a rosette, Roman style. Griffins are generally grotesque, having the body of a lion and the head of an eagle; but in this case two beautifully carved female heads, in Grecian style, complete the figure.

Modern Hungarian Chairs

Designed by Edmund Farago, and exhibited at the Paris Exhibition, 1900, by the Musée Commercial Royal Hongrois, the chair illustrated by Fig. 683 (p. 358) is decorated with three strips of leather (*see* Fig. 683). A noticeable feature is the way in which the carving is subordinated to the general scheme of construction and to the essential idea of a chair; compare Fig. 683 with the Venetian chair shown by Fig. 679

Fig. 682.—Armchair in Empire Style. Date: Early Nineteenth Century

an instructive example of modern Hungarian work. This chair is part of the Donaldson gift of "New Art" furniture to the Victoria and Albert Museum, London. It is made of ash, stained green; the seat is covered with leather stained purple, and fixed by brass-headed nails, the back being (p. 354). In the former there is no attempt at magnificence, but rather a desire to produce a useful, as well as a pleasingly decorated, chair. The ornament is small and not obtrusive; the chair legs are strengthened by means of the rail and yet lightened by the introduction of pierced carving.

Fig. 683.—Modern Hungarian Chair of Ash.   Designed by Edmund Farago.
Date : 1900.

Chairs in Old Oak Style

Elizabethan Chair.—In the earlier days of Elizabeth there were, it is said, in the palaces of the great nobles, chairs of which the seats and backs were of rich velvet. Probably these chairs came from overseas, or else were made at home by foreign workmen. The first chairs to be claimed as English, and as belonging to old oak style, had wooden seats and backs, and owed any gay colour or comfort to movable cushions.

Fig. 685.—Cromwellian Oak Chair.

still in existence. The material is almost invariably oak.

Cromwellian Chair.—The next marked type of English oak chair is known as the

Fig. 684.—Elizabethan Oak Chair.

They were armchairs, for while the bench or stool was as yet sufficient for the ordinary person, the chair was a seat of dignity. Fig. 684 (above) may be taken as the type of a really English chair in Elizabeth's reign, though it is probable that most of the examples of that pattern still remaining were actually made in early Stuart times. Of these Elizabethan chairs—so to call them—the arms or legs were not usually carved, but much work was lavished on the back, which was ornamentally shaped and elaborately carved. They were so strongly framed together that it is easy to understand how it is that considerable numbers of them are

Fig. 686.—Dauphin Oak Chair.

Cromwellian (*see* Fig. 685, p. 359), so called from the period when it was most in favour. It was, however, in use earlier than Cromwell's Protectorate, for in a woodcut of 1650 chairs of this kind are shown. There are armchairs which may fairly be considered as

Dauphin Chair.—During the reign of Charles II. the chairs became more elegant but less solid. The Dauphin chair (Fig. 686, p. 359) is of about 1670–75 ; as well as its name, it doubtless derived much of its character from France. It suggests the

Fig. 687.—Armchair in Carved Oak.

Cromwellian, but for the most part these chairs are without arms, whilst hard wooden seats and backs are now discarded. They are, however, still strongly framed, foot-rails running all round within an inch or two of the floor, as well shown in Fig. 685. Some of the Cromwellian chairs are constructed of oak, but they are, perhaps, more often of walnut or chestnut.

walnut chair shown by Fig. 677 (p. 352), and is of the same date and general style. Several points in connection with this chair should be specially noted. Foot-rails, though not yet abandoned, are no longer carried all round the bottom, which indicates a tendency towards weaker construction. The uprights of back, legs, etc., show the double twist, which is said not to have been introduced into England till this reign, whilst of the single twist there are abundant earlier examples. Also, the seat and back are of plaited cane, which is also said to have been

of the seventeenth century that high-backed chairs are to be assigned; the legs and front bar are generally carved in scroll patterns (*see* Fig. 677, p. 352), as are also the ends of

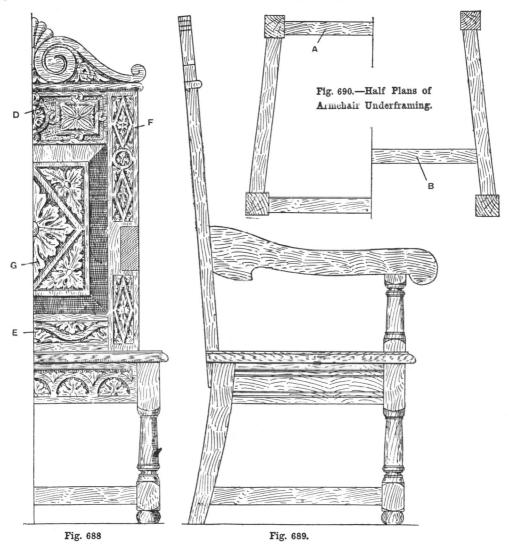

Fig. 690.—Half Plans of Armchair Underframing.

Fig. 688   Fig. 689.

Figs. 688 and 689.—Half Front Elevation and Side Elevation of Armchair.

first used in England under Charles II. It was, however, no modern application, for ancient Egyptian chairs thus seated are in existence. Chairs of this type are frequently in walnut. It is to the last twenty-five years

the arms, if arms are present; their seats, and a thin strip running up the middles of their tall, narrow backs, are of cane. Such chairs are more frequently made of soft wood, stained black, than of oak;

16

Armchair in Carved Oak

The armchair illustrated by Fig. 687 is suitable for a large entrance hall. A half front view, with the arms omitted, is given at Fig. 688, and a side view at Fig. 689. The main dimensions are as follow : height of seat from floor, 1 ft. 5 in. ; width outside the legs, across the front, 1 ft. 11 in. ; depth outside back and front legs, at the seat, 1 ft. 6 in. ; height of arms from seat, measuring over the front supports, 9 in. ; width of chair back, 1 ft. 8 in. ; height of back, including shaped pediment, 2 ft. 7 in., the latter being 7 in. high. The back is $3\frac{1}{2}$ in. out of the perpendicular, measuring from the back of the seat, and the back legs splay outwards $1\frac{3}{4}$ in. The thicknesses of the various parts are as follow : Seat, 1 in. ; front legs and arm supports, $2\frac{1}{4}$ in. square ; back legs, 2 in. square ; seat rails, $1\frac{1}{2}$ in. ; lower rails, $1\frac{1}{2}$ in. ; arms, 2 in. ; chair back, $1\frac{1}{4}$ in. ; panel, 1 in. ; shaped pediment, $1\frac{1}{4}$ in. The underframing and seat should be put together first. The rails are connected to the legs with mortice-and-tenon joints, care being taken that the tenons do not go right through the legs. To obtain the correct angles of the shoulders of the rails and tenons, a full-size plan should be made, as in Fig. 690, the right half showing the lower rails and the left half the seat rails. The back rail A stands in $\frac{3}{4}$ in. from the outer face of the legs, and the front and side rails $\frac{1}{4}$ in. The lower cross rail B is set back $4\frac{1}{2}$ in. from the face of the front legs. The seat projects 1 in. at the front and sides, but is kept level with the chair back behind (see Fig. 689) ; it should be cut away along the back edge to enable the back to rest against the seat rail. As an alternative to cutting the seat away to receive the back, short pieces c (Fig. 687) may be glued to the seat. This continuation piece is shown in section at Fig. 691, which is a sectional view of the lower corner of the back secured to the rail. A thumb moulding, shown enlarged at Fig. 692, is worked on the front and side edges of the seat. To fix the seat to the underframing, drive screws in a slanting direction through the rails. Bead mouldings are worked on the upper side rails (see section, Fig. 693). The chair back is framed together, the top and bottom rails D and E (Fig. 688) being tenoned into the side uprights F. The tenons must not go quite through the uprights. The carved centre panel G is bevelled, and fits into grooves ploughed into the rails and uprights (see section, Fig. 694). Between the shaped pediment and the framing is a strip of 1-in. stuff rounded on the front and ends. This is secured with screws and glue, while the pediment is fixed with dowels passing through this 1-in. strip into the chair back. The bottom of the chair back is secured to the back rail of the seat with screws. A centre-bit hole, $\frac{1}{4}$ in. deep, is first bored at H (Fig. 691), then the hole for the neck of the screw. When the screw has been inserted, the centre-bit hole is filled up with a circular plug of wood running the same way of the grain as the rail, this being afterwards levelled with the plane. Another way is to fill up the hole with a turned button similar to that shown at Fig. 695. Fig. 691 shows how the chair back is cut away at the bottom corners to enable it to pass between the back legs. The chair back will have to be bevelled at the bottom, so as to give the necessary pitch backwards. The turned columns over the front legs are butted between the seat and the under sides of the arms and secured with wooden dowels, say four dowels, $\frac{3}{8}$ in. in diameter, in each. The arms may be similarly dowelled to the back, or secured with stopped screws in the same way as the back is secured to the seat. The arms are slightly rounded on the top and down the face of the scrolls. The outer faces of the arms are level with the outside edges of the chair back and the turned supports. As the arms are thinner than the supports, the projection left on the top of the latter must be bevelled, as shown in Fig. 687. The carving, of course, should be done before the various parts are glued together. The design on the front rail of the seat consists of a series of semicircles enclosed in a rectangle, forming the surface of the rail, the leaves being cut in low relief. The rectangles and leaves in the centre panel of the chair back are carved in the same way. An enlargement of the side of the chair back is given at Fig. 696. In carving the top rail, shown enlarged at Fig. 697, the surface is retained at J, but to give an outline to the connecting circles, the surface is slightly bevelled down. The design on the bottom rail is a variation of that on the seat rail. The dotted or roughened ground is sunk about $\frac{3}{16}$ in. In carving the pediment, the surface is retained in the scrolls, and the rest carved in low relief.

Another Armchair in Carved Oak

Of very similar construction to the last example is the chair shown by Figs. 698 to

needed. The construction of the chair is simple, only five pieces of wood being used. The seat slab is $16\frac{1}{2}$ in. long by 11 in., and into it are mortised the back, 20 in. by 11 in., the front leg piece, 17 in. by 13 in., and the back leg piece, 21 in. by 13 in., the two last pieces being braced together by a cross spar, $15\frac{1}{2}$ in. long by 2 in. wide. Fig. 707 shows the mortices by which the back and leg pieces are let into the seat; they are 1 in. wide only, and the tenon A (Fig. 705) of the back leg piece, after passing through its

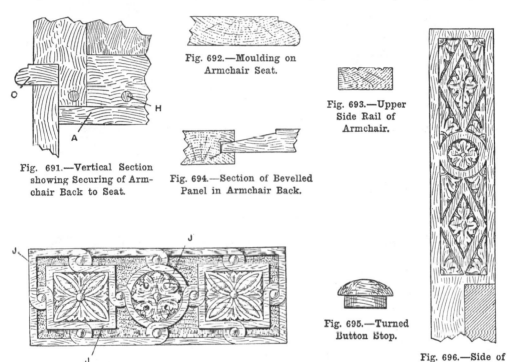

Fig. 692.—Moulding on Armchair Seat.

Fig. 693.—Upper Side Rail of Armchair.

Fig. 691.—Vertical Section showing Securing of Armchair Back to Seat.

Fig. 694.—Section of Bevelled Panel in Armchair Back.

Fig. 695.—Turned Button Stop.

Fig. 697.—Top Rail of Armchair.

Fig. 696.—Side of Armchair Back.

700. The carved pediment is illustrated by Fig. 701; the carving of the top rail by Fig. 702; and the carving of the back legs by Figs. 703 and 704.

Hall Chair

The chair shown in Figs. 705 and 706 must be of stout material. For the seat, a 2-in. slab, slightly planed down, is recommended, and for the other parts a thickness of not less than $1\frac{1}{2}$ in. after planing is

mortice, is splayed off and screwed to the back piece, to which it thus gives considerable support. Below the seat the back leg piece is like the front one in outline, but plain. The cross spar B, which is mortised into the front and back leg pieces, is carved alike on both sides; but it is on the back that most carving appears, and here the thickness of the material allows this to be done boldly and effectively. The rows of dots, seen both on the back and on the front

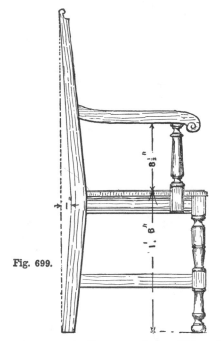

Fig. 699.

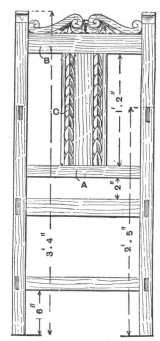

Fig. 700.

Figs. 699 and 700.—Side and Back Elevations of Another Armchair.

Fig. 698.—
Another
Arm-
chair.

Fig. 701.—Carved Pediment.

Fig. 702.—Carving on Top
Rail of Armchair.

Fig. 703.

Fig. 704.

Figs. 703 and 704.—Carving on Back Legs of
Armchair.

legs, are intended to indicate brass studs, which will greatly add to the appearance of the chair. The scale of the illustrations is 1 in. to the foot.

Quattro-cento Hall Chair

Figs. 708 and 709 show a design which, as regards construction and general form, is they take but little room, and they are fine subjects for the display of wood carving. The old Italian chairs, besides being elaborately carved, were usually gilt. The chair here illustrated is not meant for gilding, and the style of carving shown upon it is different, it being made to approach more nearly to the English manner of the carved oak

Fig. 705.

Fig. 706.

Fig. 707

Figs. 705 to 707.—Side and Front Elevations and Seat Plan of Hall Chair.

modelled on some of the chairs of the Italian quattro-cento period. These chairs do not appear to have been intended for ordinary living-rooms, but rather for halls or large corridors. As regards comfort they are not equal to modern requirements, but they sufficed for occasional use, and seats on the same plan may well serve for the halls of modern houses. They have good points: they are simple and strong in construction, period. Oak, chestnut, walnut, or some other hard wood not liable to split, should be the material. The old Italian chairs were made of thick plank, thus allowing for much depth and relief in the carving; but probably sufficient strength and effect would be gained by using 1½-in. board for the seat and 1-in. board for the four other pieces. The plank for the seat (see plan, Fig. 710) is 12 in. wide and 16 in. long. Its middle is slightly hollowed, and two pairs of mortices are shown for the tenons of the front and back legs; there is also a longer mortice for the tenon of the back piece. The leg mortices are represented as being cut quite through the slab; this gives greater

edges. It is on the chair back that carving will show to most advantage. The ornament in Fig. 708 may by its style recall to the reader some of the English high chair backs of the time of Charles II., and it is suggested that the crown and acanthus scroll should be

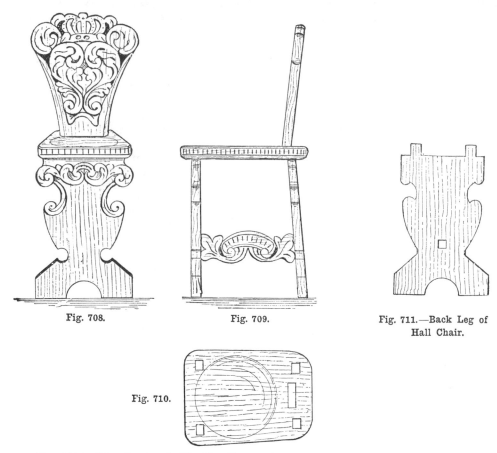

Fig. 708.   Fig. 709.   Fig. 711.—Back Leg of Hall Chair.

Fig. 710.

Figs. 708 to 710.—Front and Side Elevations and Seat Plan of Quattro-cento Hall Chair.

strength, but is not absolutely necessary, and if the appearance of the tenons above is thought unsightly, the mortices might be cut 1¼ in. deep only. The mortice for the back piece will be carried right through in any case, and the tenon of that piece should be made so long as to project beyond the lower surface far enough to be secured with a couple of pegs. The appearance of the seat is lightened by chamfering off its under

treated much in the same way that they are in those " Restoration " chairs. The vacant spaces, which are in the illustration left unshaded, should be pierced through, and, to lighten the appearance of the edges of these openings, they should be chamfered off behind—more or less, according to circumstances. The chairs just mentioned are generally in walnut or chestnut, both good woods for the purpose. The board needed for the back will be 13 in. wide and 19 in. long ; this length includes the tenon, which is 3 in. long. A chair of this kind should be somewhat high in the seat ; this is 19 in. above the floor line. The two boards which form the front and hind legs are 12 in. wide and 19 in. long, the upper 1½ in. being cut into tenons, as shown in Fig. 711. The cross rail, seen in Fig. 709, which binds the legs together in their lower parts, is 3 in. wide and, including its tenons, 14 in. long. Inch board will be none too thick for it, for as it runs under the middle of the chair and shows equally on both sides, both sides must alike be carved. It may be that some readers who are aware that the above form of chair was in fashion in the fifteenth century may think that the term quattro-cento has been used inadvertently ; but they are asked to remember that with the Italians what in England is called the sixteenth

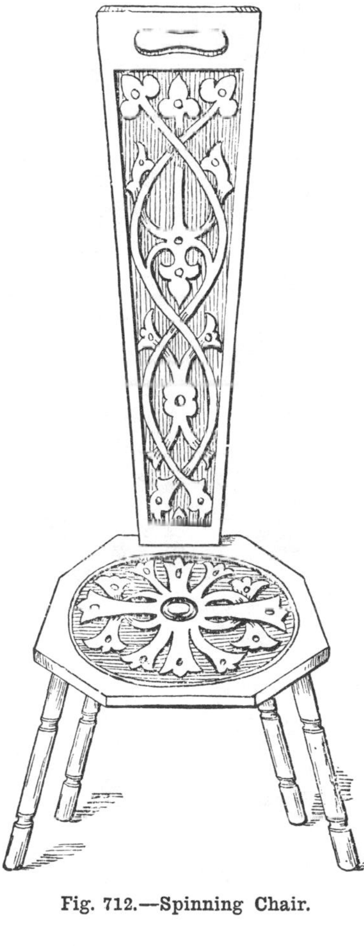

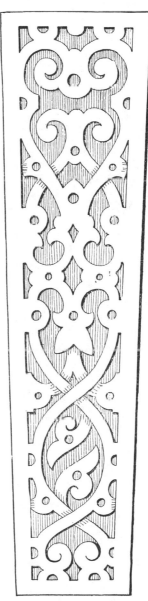

Fig. 712.—Spinning Chair.

Fig. 713.—Alternative Design for Back of Spinning Chair.

century is called cinque-cento; our fifteenth-century is their quattro-cento; and so on.

Spinning Chair

A spinning chair is shown by Fig. 712. The seat is 1½ in. thick, and the back 1 in. thick, American oak being a suitable material. The back is 26 in. long, tapering from 6 in. at the top to 4½ in. at the bottom. The legs are 12 in. long and are turned in oak. A simple strapwork design for the chair back is shown by Fig. 713, and one for the seat by Fig. 714.

Fig. 714.—Alternative Design for Seat of Spinning Chair.

STOOLS

Designs for Stool Tops

THREE designs for stools are represented by Figs. 715 to 717. That given in Fig. 715 is simply a flat pattern first grounded out, and then the idea of the parts overlapping imparted by cutting away the wood over

the depressed portions. The rosette in the centre is a matter of choice, and may be worked in various ways. The design in Fig. 716 is more exacting than Fig. 715, and it possesses possibilities for advanced carving. The skilful workman will see that the leaves may be hollowed, rounded, or curled in many

Fig. 715.—Simple Strapwork Design for Stool Top.

Fig. 716.—
Conventional Floral
Design for Stool
Top.

Fig. 717.—
Tulip Design for
Stool Top.

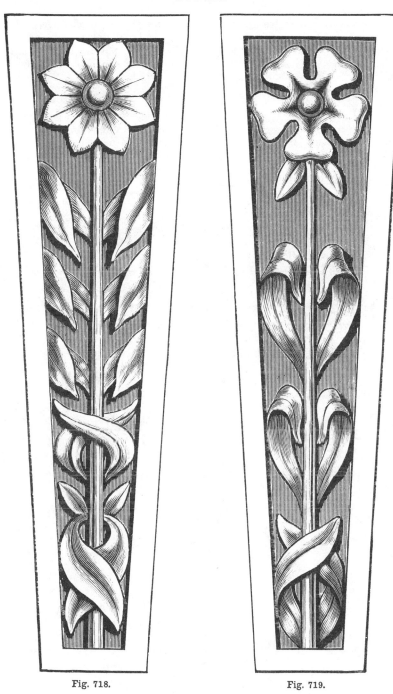

Fig. 718.   Fig. 719.

Figs. 718 and 719.—Conventional Floral Designs for Chair Backs.

ways, while the flowers and stalks are open to further artistic treatment. The execution may vary from a flat pattern to a finished relief carving. The natural design of tulips and leaves in Fig. 717 affords more advanced pupils scope for their skill.

Spindle Chairs

By the addition of a back (*see* Figs. 718 and 719), the stool becomes a small spindle chair. Though Fig. 718 requires more work,

it is not the more effective of the pair, as the greater distance between the various parts of the pattern in Fig. 719 is a means of imparting additional lightness and grace to the work.

Another Stool Top

Another design for a circular stool top is presented by Fig. 720. This does not need any words of description, design and treatment being quite conventional.

Fig. 720.—Design for Round Stool Top.

Fig. 724.—
Leg of
Stool.

Fig. 722.—Seat Plan of Stool.

Fig. 721.—Oak Stool with Detachable Back.

Fig. 723.—Method of Securing Detachable Back
of Stool.

Fig. 725.—Detachable Back for Stool.

Oak Stool with Detachable Back

In the carved oak stool illustrated by Fig. 721, the detachable back is mortised through the seat and fixed underneath with a wedge. The seat (Fig. 722) is octagonal

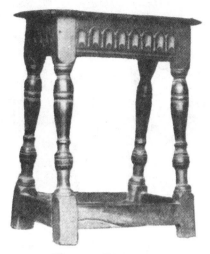

Fig. 726.—Joint-stool.

in shape and $1\frac{3}{4}$ in. thick, with a sash moulding run round the top edge (*see* Fig. 723). The under edge is bevelled all round to give the seat a light appearance. For the legs, holes at a suitable angle should be bored with a $1\frac{1}{4}$-in. bit, and the legs rounded at the top to fit tightly. The legs (Fig. 724) are octagonal in section, and one side only is carved. They are tapered from $1\frac{5}{8}$ in. at the bottom to $1\frac{1}{4}$ in. at the top. The back (Fig. 725) is $\frac{7}{8}$ in. thick, and is tenoned and rebated to enter a mortice in the seat A (Fig. 722), $2\frac{1}{2}$ in. long and $\frac{5}{8}$ in. wide, which is bevelled to the angle of the back. A mortice is made in the tenon of the back B (Fig. 725) for the wedge D (Fig. 723), which is $1\frac{1}{4}$ in. by $\frac{3}{4}$ in. When the back is inserted in the seat, the wedge is driven in firmly, making the whole rigid. A sash moulding is run on the edge of the back, which is also fretted at c (Fig. 725), thus forming a convenient means of lifting the stool. The carving of the stool is comparatively flat, with little or no grounding, but looks very effective when finished.

Joint-stools

Joint-stools are a characteristic feature in the furniture of the time of James I., as well as somewhat before and somewhat after it. Their primary office was to serve as seats at the festive board, in which duty they succeeded rude benches. The joint-stool is scarcely a luxurious seat; it is inconveniently high, and uncomfortably hard, yet it allowed each guest a seat to himself, and when not in use, the joint-stools were ranged in two rows beneath the great table, dormant. Carved joint-stools are numerous, but the carving is generally poor, either a flat strap or the thumb pattern. Ordinarily, the legs of joint-stools are as shown at *a* (Fig. 729, p. 377), but sometimes they have bosses. Perhaps the earliest mention of these things is in a list of the bedroom furniture of Henry VIII. But whether the joint-stool there spoken of was identical with those of the Jacobean age is open to question, since any stool framed or joined together might be called a " joint-stool " to distinguish it from the rude three-legged stools of earlier times. Shakespeare mentions the joint-stool in *King Lear*. A curious error is prevalent in some parts as to the original

Fig. 727.—James II. Stool.

use of joint-stools, namely, that they were intended as rests for the coffin in churches during the funeral service. This doubtless arose from the fact that in country churches they are often devoted to that use; but they were not so employed earlier than

Fig. 728.—Stool in Carved Pearwood.
Made by E. Baguès, and Exhibited at the Paris Exhibition, 1900.

the eighteenth century, the recognised support for the coffin in the seventeenth century being of quite another kind. A typical joint-stool is shown by Fig. 726. Few of the joint-stools still so abundant in rural districts are later than the Commonwealth, for about the middle of the century lower tables came into vogue, and chairs more or less assimilating to the Cromwellian type superseded joint-stools. Of course, stools for independent use continued to be made, many following more or less the lines of the true joint-stool, but they are easily distinguished from it. Fig. 727 shows a stool of the reign of James II. Though framed together like the joint-stool, it differs from it in shape. The turned legs are characteristic of the time which produced this stool. Note the heavy foot-rails shown in Figs. 726 and 727.

Modern French Stool

Fig. 728 shows a stool of carved pear-wood, with gilt brass mounts, and a yellow velvet-covered seat. This forms part of the Donaldson gift to the Victoria and Albert Museum. It is the work of E. Baguès, and was shown at the Paris Exhibition of 1900. The construction of this stool is good, and is not sacrificed to any ornamental purpose. It should always be remembered that wood carving is an attendant art only, being subordinate to constructive requirements. In this stool—a noteworthy specimen of modern work—those requirements are in evidence first, the ornament being added afterwards to complete the whole scheme. Thus the stool is artistically, as well as constructionally, sound.

TABLES

TRESTLE-BOARDS were apparently introduced about the time of Henry III., planks fastened to uprights fixed in the floor having been usual in early Gothic times. From illuminations found in MSS., it seems that chests frequently served the purposes of small tables. The reign of Henry VIII., however, saw the origin of an ordinary type of modern table—one with two leaves supported by sliding bars which pull out from under the central part. The nominally movable but ponderous form of dining table, known as "Jacobean," seems to have come into use in great houses in the early part of Elizabeth's reign. Writers of that age sometimes speak of it as the "table dormant," thus contrasting it with the easily removed trestle-boards. In the times of James I. and Charles I. these tables had become general, even in middle-class houses. They rested on four, six, or even eight massive supports, which, in such fine examples as were made near the year 1600, were turned from huge logs of wood, and bulged out into great bosses, carved with rude acanthus foliage. Others, of less ambitious design, had tapering pillars with raised bands, in form somewhat similar to *a* (Fig. 729), and of great strength and weight. These supports were always connected at the bottom by a massive framework, and beneath the top frequently ran a carved cornice. Frequently, the table could be lengthened by means of a double top, the under portion of which drew out at the ends, and was supported by an ingenious arrangement of rails. A remarkably fine example of a carved Jacobean table, with bossed pillars, is to be seen at Naunton Court, Worcester-shire, now a farmhouse, but formerly a seat of the Littletons. These tables are a great feature in the old oak work of the end of the sixteenth and of the early part of the seventeenth centuries.

Charles I. Table

Small tables that can be dated earlier than 1600 are rarely met, but many may be

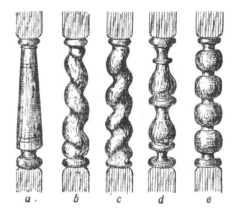

a.   *b*   *c*   *d*   *e*

Fig. 729.—Legs of Seventeenth-century English Oak Tables, and of some Stools and Chairs.

found of the reigns of James I. and Charles I. Fig. 730 shows a frequent type. Such tables as this, though light, are strongly framed together, and have foot-rails. Those which are most prized by collectors have twisted legs, and the twist is always a single one, as shown. This table is 2 ft. 6 in. by 1 ft. 4 in., and 2 ft. 6 in. high. Of almost the same period were more heavily made round tables, often with carving running round their frames. They stand on four legs, on three of which one half of the top is fixed, whilst the other half, which folds down as a leaf, rests, when raised, on the fourth leg. This type of table may generally be assigned to the reign of Charles I.

Gate-legged Table

Whilst the great Jacobean table was by far the most important feature of the first half of the seventeenth century, the gate-legged table is the table of the second half. The sizes vary from 2 ft. to 8 ft. in the longer diameter, for they are generally oval, though the smaller ones are sometimes round. Fig. 731 shows their construction, in which

b is seen in the small early Stuart tables, and in chairs and cabinets of Charles I. Tables with legs of these types may therefore be concluded to be as early as 1650, or very little later. The double twist *c* and the vase pattern *d* belong usually to the reign of Charles II. The ball pattern *e* is a late form, and may be found on tables some of which are as recent as 1700. The gate-legged tables are generally oak throughout, but the legs, when twisted, are sometimes in walnut or chestnut, these woods being more easily worked. The absence of carving on the frames of these tables does not imply either that they are of very late dates, or

Fig. 730.—Charles I. Table.　　　Fig. 731.—Gate-legged Table.

the strong framing of the foot-rails must not be overlooked. The only ornaments are their twisted or turned legs, for they are never carved. Occasionally an example may be seen that is plainly later than 1700, whilst some few such tables are as distinctly earlier than 1650. It may not be possible to lay down positive rules by which to date them, yet the ornamentation of the legs will afford some guide. In Fig. 729 several varieties of these are shown, and these types may also be found useful for reference when similar forms occur in other articles, such as chairs and joint-stools. The pillar *a* occurs frequently on joint-stools and early chairs, and on a large scale is found in the plainer Jacobean tables. The single twist

that they were made for meanly furnished rooms only. The best of these tables were doubtless intended to be draped.

Oak Table with Circular Top

The table illustrated by Fig. 732 is 2 ft. in diameter by 2 ft. 5 in. high; but these dimensions may be altered as desired. The table top, for instance—shown enlarged at Fig. 733—could be made of greater diameter. The carved design is a combination of chip and stamped carving. The framing of the table is hexagon in plan, with the outer faces of the legs, which are $1\frac{3}{4}$ in. square in section, standing in $2\frac{1}{2}$ in. under the top, and the top and bottom rails $\frac{3}{16}$ in. from the faces of the legs. The top rails are about

7 in. deep over all by 1 in. thick, and the bottom rails $1\frac{3}{4}$ in. wide by $1\frac{1}{4}$ in. thick, and about 7 in. from the ground. To get the correct measurements and angles for the rails, it is advisable to make a full-size drawing of the plan (Fig. 734). Fig. 735 is an elevation of one side of the table; while Fig. 736 is an alternative design, in which the legs, instead of being turned, are ornamented with chip carving. The top should be taken in hand first; this is made with 1-in. or $1\frac{1}{4}$ in. boards, jointed with a trying plane, and dowelled and glued together. In gluing up the dowelled joints, cramps will be required. If iron cramps are not available, make wooden ones as follows: Get some pieces of deal about 1 ft. longer than the table top, and about 3 in. wide, and screw cross pieces on them at each end, thus forming a double-ended **T**-square. To cramp up, place one outer edge of the top against

Fig. 732.—Oak Table with Circular Top.

Fig. 733.—Circular Table Top

one of the **T** ends, and between the opposite edge and **T** end drive wooden wedges and tighten up. The ordinary straight rubbed and glued joints are suitable for soft woods, with one shoulder on the face side). If the legs are to be as in Figs. 732 and 735, they will have to be turned. This is best done after the legs are mortised. The framing and

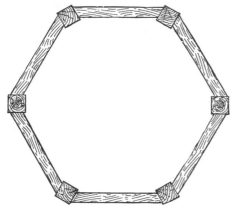

Fig. 734.—Underframing of Circular-top Table.

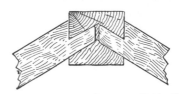

Fig. 737.—Method of Mortising Table Rails to Legs.

Fig. 738.—Moulding on Table Top.

Fig. 735.—Elevation of One Side of Table.

Fig. 739.—Detail of Alternative Design for Table Leg.

Fig. 736.—Alternative Design for Side of Table.

such as pine or deal, but are not strong enough for oak and other hardwoods. The legs should next be squared to thickness, and mortised to receive the tenons of the rails (*see* Fig. 737, which shows the tenons the legs should be put together dry, and each rail marked, so that when knocked apart for carving they may be put back in their right places.

The Carving.—The table top should now

be cut to its circular shape, and the moulding either turned or carved by hand to the pattern shown in Fig. 738. Before drawing the design on the top, rub the latter with chalk so that the pencil lines may be more clearly seen. The outlines connected with the spotted ground must be sunk about $\frac{1}{8}$ in. deep with chisels or gouges. The other outlines are formed by bevelling down from the surface. The spotted parts are sunk about $\frac{1}{8}$ in., the ground being roughened with a blunt-pointed punch. The semicircular patterns in the top rails are treated in the same way as the top, and the lines of the panels in Figs. 732 and 735 are made with a gouge about $\frac{1}{4}$ in. wide. The ornamentation on

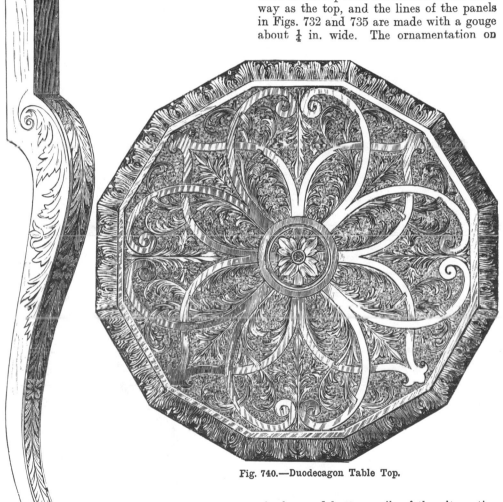

Fig. 740.—Duodecagon Table Top.

Fig. 741.—Scroll Leg for Table with Duodecagon Top.

the legs and bottom rails of the alternative design (Fig. 736) is shown enlarged in Fig. 739; this is chip carved in the usual way by bevelling from the surface. (Full instructions on chip carving are given later.) The centre of the table top is done in the same way. The inside faces of the legs

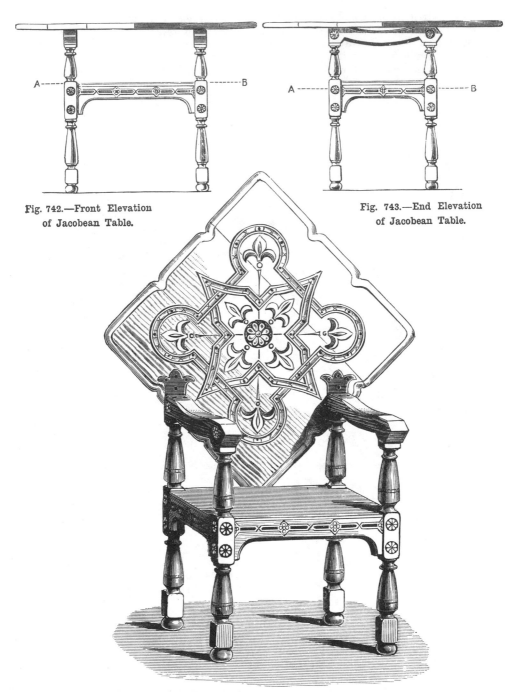

Fig. 742.—Front Elevation
of Jacobean Table.

Fig. 743.—End Elevation
of Jacobean Table.

Fig. 744.—Oak Jacobean Table Convertible into Hall Seat.

should also be carved if the time can be spared. When the whole of the carving is done, the framing should be glued together. The top may be fixed by driving slanting screws from the inside of the rails into the top ; or by means of buttons, $2\frac{1}{2}$ in. by $1\frac{3}{4}$ in. If this method is adopted, $\frac{1}{4}$-in. grooves must be ploughed in the rails, $\frac{3}{4}$ in. from the top edges. The button is provided with a tongue at one end, to fit in the groove. The advantage of this method of securing the top is obvious, as it allows for shrinkage

moreover, when not wanted as a table, this article is both serviceable and ornamental as a seat for the hall (*see* Fig. 744). The design is an original one, but it is based on an idea as old as the reign of James I., and in style and decoration the taste of that period has been pretty closely adhered to. The carving is not elaborate ; that on the frame is little beyond mere gouge-work. As a table, the article stands 2 ft. 4 in. high and has a top 2 ft. 6 in. square, its frame measuring 2 ft. by 1 ft. 6 in. As a chair,

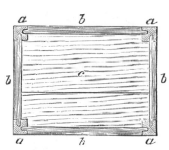

Fig. 745.—Horizontal Section of Jacobean Table on Line A B (Figs. 742 and 743).

Fig. 746.—Jacobean Rosette.

Fig. 747.—Under Side of Top of Jacobean Table.

Fig. 748.—Part Section of Top of Jacobean Table.

in the top, which is almost sure to take place, unless the wood is absolutely dry.

Table with Duodecagon Top

Fig. 740 shows the top of a table made in red oak by W. Gladman, and exhibited by him at the Herts Arts and Crafts Exhibition, St. Albans, in 1894. The table top is only 2 ft. 6 in. in circumference. One of the four scroll legs, 2 ft. 5 in. high, and carved in shallow relief, is shown by Fig. 741.

Oak Jacobean Table Convertible into Hall Seat

As an occasional table, the piece of furniture shown by Figs. 742 and 743 has a strength and solidity not to be attained by the ordinary pillar stands, and if used as a writing-table or a work-table the chair-seat beneath it forms a decided convenience ;

the seat is 1 ft. 6 in. high, the arms 1 ft. $11\frac{1}{4}$ in. high, and the back about 4 ft. 9 in. The legs a (Fig. 745) are turned from stuff 2 in. square ; their length is $24\frac{1}{2}$ in., exclusive of the tenon for entering the mortice in the arm, which demands an additional $1\frac{1}{2}$ in. There is a little ornament on the legs—two rosettes on the outer sides of each, which are carved in sunken medallions ; these are of a very ordinary Jacobean type, but at Fig. 746 is one shown on a larger scale. These rosettes figure on all the legs alike, since all are alike supposed to show when the article is in use as a table. Each leg has mortices $\frac{1}{2}$ in. wide, $\frac{3}{4}$ in. deep, and 3 in. long, to receive the tenons of the cross-pieces, as shown in Fig. 745. These cross-pieces b (Fig. 745) are of 1-in. stuff, $4\frac{1}{2}$ in. wide ; those for the back and front are 20 in. ; those for the ends 14 in. long, exclusive of the tenons, which are ¾ in. long at each end. There is a line of gouge-work ornament running along them. The lower edge of each cross-piece in the part hollowed out has a hollow moulding worked with the gouge. On the cross-pieces rests the seat *c* (Fig. 745), which is of ½-in. wood. The Jacobean way of fixing this down to the

ward objectionably. The arms, on which the table top rests when turned down, are cut from stuff of the same thickness as the legs, namely, 2 in., but in depth they are 2¾ in. They are, as shown in Fig. 743, hollowed on their upper face ; this adds to the comfort of the chair, and the table top is rendered more firm by resting on four

Fig. 750.

Fig. 751.

Figs. 750 and 751.—Side Panels of Occasional Table.

Fig. 749.—Occasional Table.

Fig. 752.—Side Panel of Occasional Table.

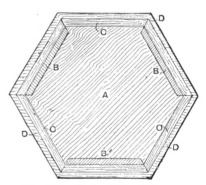

Fig. 753.—Under Side of Top of Occasional Table.

cross-pieces would be with wooden pegs. As illustrated, the seat comes just flush with the frame (24 in. by 18 in.), and is slightly rounded off on its upper edge, but some might choose to gain a little relief by making it project ½ in. on every side and finishing off with a moulding ; this would need a seat 25 in. by 19 in., and it would be desirable to cut away the projection in the centre of the back where the turned-up table top touches against it, or, when in use as a chair, the upper part of that member will tilt for-

points only. Below, a corresponding curve is given, and the edges of both the upper and lower curves are chamfered off. These arms are 19¼ in. long, their front ends projecting 1¼ in. beyond the general line of the frame. The rosettes carved on the outer sides of the arms are similar to those on the legs, and are shown full size by Fig. 746. On its under side each arm has a mortice 1¼ in. long by ¾ in. broad, and 1½ in. deep to receive the tenons of the legs. The shape and ornamentation of the table top on its under side are shown in Fig. 747. The top is of ¾-in. board, and is 2 ft. 6 in. square. The moulding round its edge is alike above and below, as is shown in the section (Fig. 748), in which is also indicated something of the depth to which the carved decoration should be cut. The carving here shown is

arm by ornamental hinges, and these should be let in so as to come flush with the surface of the wood.

Occasional Table

For the occasional table illustrated by Fig. 749, the three side pieces forming its

Fig. 754.—French or Italian Sixteenth-century Table.

mere surface decoration, an adaptation of the band-work so often met with in seventeenth-century panels. The interlacing bands are marked out by a line on each side incised with the V-chisel, whilst down their centres a shallow hollow is run with the gouge, which hollow is afterwards enriched by using the grounding-punch at intervals, or by dots or markings made with other gouges, as the fancy of the carver may direct. The top is shown to be fixed to the

legs are of ¾-in. oak, 10 in. wide and 1 ft. 11½ in. long, the height of the table when fitted with its top being 2 ft. The lower part of each side piece is shaped with the frame-saw, and thus far all three pieces are alike. The carved sunken panels above are, however, all different, and are shown to scale in Figs. 750 to 752. In all of them the ground is roughened with the grounding-punch. The table is adapted for home making, all its parts being screwed together.

The upper ends of the side pieces are screwed to a false top which fits within them, as may be seen in Fig. 753, which shows the under side of the top. The false top A is of ¾-in. deal, and openings are cut in it to receive the side pieces B, the corners of which

false top. At 1 in. less than half-way down is a shelf, shown in Fig. 749, which gives such further connection to the side pieces as is required. It is of ½-in. oak, and screws are driven into its edges through the side pieces. The heads of these screws are hidden

Fig. 755.—French Sixteenth-century Walnut Table.

are trimmed to fit. A circle of 10-in. radius will touch the angles of the false top. Round them and the false top, and coming flush above, run strips of moulding C, ¾ in. high and 1 in. wide. On these pieces rests the true top, which is of ½-in. oak, and its angles would touch a circle of 12-in. radius ; its edges D are neatly rounded, and it is fixed by screws driven into it through the

by a ½-in. moulding, which appears in the same figure.

Sixteenth-century Carved Table

The table shown by Fig. 754 is a typical example of the spirit of ornament that ran riot during the sixteenth and seventeenth centuries. Notice how every part of the table is utilised for the purposes of orna-

Fig. 756.—End of French Sixteenth-century Table.

Fig. 757.—Genoese Console Table.   Date : 1700.

Fig. 768.—Oak Altar Table.

ment, the supports in the centre being most gracefully turned, whilst every other part of the table is carved. The feet are carved in the form of a creature with a lion's body and a woman's head and breasts. The strained position of the heads is rather unnatural; yet every part of the foot is perfectly solid and secure and quite unlikely to be kicked off—a very admirable form of treatment for a foot. The principal end pillars are carved with a free, running orna-

on the wings and neck should be noticed, the wings being evidently kept narrow in width to prevent a heavy, clumsy appearance. There is an echo of Grecian tradition in the Ionic volutes at the head of the central pillar. The body treatment is free and forceful, being conventionalised only so far as the limits of the material demand. The table was made at Lyons, France, in the second half of the sixteenth century, and at the time the photograph here reproduced

Fig. 759.—Modern Hungarian Table. Designed by Edmund Farago.

ment that was commonly applied in England during the seventeenth century. The table is either Italian or French work, dating from about 1550. Its height is 2 ft. 11 in., length 4 ft. 1 in., and width 2 ft. 6 in.

French Sixteenth=century Table in Walnut

An admirable use of griffins is demonstrated in the table shown by Figs. 755 and 756. A griffin is a creature consisting of a combination of eagle's head and neck and a lion's body. In this case the griffin has wings, and the two legs are those of the lion. The conventional treatment of the feathers

was taken, it was the property of Mr. J. Pierpont Morgan.

Genoese Console Table

Fig. 757 illustrates an Italian (Genoese) console table, dating from 1700, very richly ornamented with carving and gilding. The top is a marble slab. The height is 3 ft. 3 in., length 4 ft. 3 in., and the width 1 ft. 8 in. This is a most interesting example from the wood carver's point of view, showing in unmistakable fashion the lengths to which furniture designers and makers eventually went in their attempts to express themselves in ornamental terms. Ornament here gets out of bounds and becomes too insistently obtrusive. A "magnificent" effect is undoubtedly obtained, but with it a complete subservience of construction to ornament. The latter should be subordinate to the former. This extravagant use of the scroll dominated furniture making for the greater part of the eighteenth century, it being reserved for Sheraton about 1780 to introduce a saner and sounder type of furniture, in which carved ornament was placed in its proper position.

Oak Altar Table

A fine example of the restrained use of carved ornament, influenced largely by fourteenth-century Gothic treatment, is illustrated by Fig. 758. The question as to which part of framed work should be carved —the panels or the framing—is a much disputed one. Some authorities say the framing ; others the panels ; and others, again, say both. Whatever the right opinion is, there can be little question that a very fine effect is obtained by the spirit of restraint that is shown in this work. Natural foliage,

it will be noticed, forms the basis of the ornament—a modern tendency of quite the right kind. The table here shown was carved at the Pyghtle Works, Bedford, for St. Saviour's Church, Poplar, the photograph reproduced on p. 389 being supplied by Mr. John P. White.

Modern Hungarian Table

Austrian artists in furniture designing have undoubtedly done much to encourage an interest in modern furniture. There is little wood carving in the example shown by Fig. 759, the general modern tendency being to employ carved ornament as little as possible, which is a somewhat regrettable feature of present-day furniture design. Whatever is used in this table, however, is admirably planned, and is of a kind suitable to its purpose. This example was designed by Mr. Edmund Farago, is believed to have been on view at the Paris Exhibition of 1900, and it is included in Mr. George Donaldson's gift (1901) of " New Art " furniture to the Victoria and Albert Museum, London, S.W.

SETTLES

Oak Settle

FRONT and end elevations of a carved oak settle for the hall are shown by Figs. 760 the front and end framing; they are also grooved between the mortices for the ends of the panels. The top and bottom rails of the front frame are $2\frac{1}{4}$ in. deep by $1\frac{1}{4}$ in.

Fig. 760.—Front Elevation of Oak Settle.

and 761. The seat is hinged at the back, thus forming a chest suitable for storing odd articles (*see* Fig. 762). The two front posts are $2\frac{1}{4}$ in. square, turned at the top and bottom, and mortised to receive the rails of thick. Two muntins of the same width divide the front into three panels. The rails and muntins are grooved for the panels, the bottom rail being checked to a depth of $\frac{5}{8}$ in. on the under edge for the bottom. The rails are kept $\frac{3}{8}$ in. from the front posts. The back frame is of $1\frac{1}{4}$-in. stuff, mortised and tenoned together, the rails and muntins being $2\frac{1}{4}$ in. deep, except the middle rail, which is $4\frac{1}{4}$ in. deep. Fig. 763 is a section of the back frame, giving the positions of the rails. There are no muntins below the middle rail, the panel being in one length ; it may be of pine stained to match the oak. The bottom can

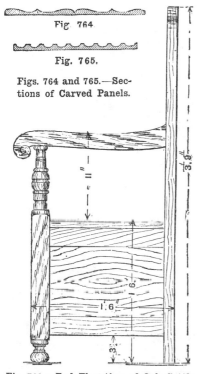

Fig. 764

Fig. 765.

Figs. 764 and 765.—Sections of Carved Panels.

Fig. 761.—End Elevation of Oak Settle.

bored in the under side at the front, into which the pin, turned on the top of the post, is fitted tightly, and glued. Each arm is fixed at the back by two screws through the back. A piece 3 in. wide by 1 in. thick, with a thumb moulding run on the outside edge, is glued on the top edge of the ends, and further secured by blocks glued on the inside (*see* A, Fig. 762). This allows the lid to

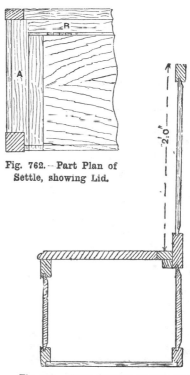

Fig. 762.—Part Plan of Settle, showing Lid.

Fig. 763.—Cross Section of Oak Settle.

be match-boarded or lining, also stained and put in across from back to front. The end stiles of the back are left longer at the top and finished with the ornament shown in Fig. 760. The top and bottom rails of the ends are tenoned to the posts at the front and the stiles of the back frame, the tenons being wedged at the back. The stiles of the back frame are carried down to the floor to form feet. The carved pediment should be 1 in. thick, and dowelled to the top rail. The arms, shaped as shown in Fig. 761, are 2 in. thick. A hole, 1 in. in diameter, is

clear the posts. A 2-in. piece B (Fig. 762) is fixed to the back rail by screws and blocks, and the lid is hinged to it, a bead being run along the edge to break the joint. The lid, 1 in. thick, has a thumb moulding worked on the front edge, and to keep it flat is cross-headed at the ends. The carving is simple and bold, and should not be too finely finished, the tool marks being left prominent. The two end panels in the back are ornamented with the linen pattern, a cross section being shown in Fig. 764. A section of the two end panels of the lower front is shown in Fig. 765. Each of the front and back frames is cramped together, and the two are then cramped to the ends, and the bottom is added, the arms being fixed on after the job is put together. The designs for the panels are roughly suggested in Fig. 760, but enough is shown to enable the carver to draw them out full size.

Settle, carved by Miss Gertrude White

Fig. 766 illustrates a settle exhibited at the Herts Arts and Crafts Exhibition, held at St. Albans in 1894, the maker, Miss Gertrude White, being at the time an instructor under the Herts County Council. It is well

Fig. 766.—Settle, Carved by Miss Gertrude White.

Fig. 767.—Settle, Carved by Joseph Hetherington.

constructed and highly finished, and is of solid English oak. The eight panels are richly carved in somewhat low relief in a conventional manner, the design being admirably adapted to the purpose to which it is applied. The seat acts as lid to the lower part, thus forming a chest; this is ornamented with five panels, three in front and one at each end, the same design being used throughout, slightly altered to accommodate the different panels. The three front panels in the lower part of the settle are of the same design, the two end ones larger and the three at the back of the seat higher and arched. The lid forming the seat is ornamented with a carved moulding. The length of the settle is 3 ft. 3 in., and its height 3 ft. 8 in. The details are carefully carried out, and the effect is most striking.

Another Settle

The settle shown by Fig. 767 is the work of Joseph Hetherington, and was a prize exhibit at the Arts and Crafts Exhibition held at Carlisle in 1895. It will be noticed that the principle of repetition has been greatly relied upon, and that in carrying that principle into execution a good balance has been attained. Apparently, the lines of construction, as well as the designs for some of the panels, were suggested by Miss White's settle, illustrated on p. 394.

BEDSTEADS AND OTHER BEDROOM FURNITURE

Bedsteads

TILL the close of the Gothic period it was rather in rich hangings and coverings than in the woodwork of bedsteads that luxury was displayed in England. In the houses of rich nobles, costly draperies were usually embroidered with heraldic devices. But the great "monumental bedstead" of carved wood does not appear till the Renaissance period. Some bedsteads of quite the early part of the sixteenth century have arrangements for entirely closing in the bed with panelling, sufficient openings only being left for getting in and out. The typical form, however, of the great Elizabethan and early Stuart bedstead (*see* Fig. 768) was much the same as that of the four-poster of recent

Fig. 768.—Elizabethan Bedstead of Carved Oak.

397

Fig. 769.—Foot-post of Elizabethan Bedstead. Date : 1610.

times, and was furnished with curtains to draw round it in the same manner; the head and tester were, however, entirely of wood. The head was usually deeply moulded, and had richly carved panel-work—the panelling being often recessed in arcades. Demi-figures most frequently divided the panel-work into compartments. The foot-posts, turned from huge logs of oak, swelled out in places into enormous carved bosses (*see* Figs. 768 and 769). The tester, which was of lighter panelling and less elaborately carved, had commonly decorations in appliqué work, which included pendants at the intersections of the panelling, and would be bordered by a massive carved cornice. The post shown by Fig. 769 is from a bedstead (date 1610) formerly at Cumnor Place, and now at Sudeley Castle.

The Great Bed of Ware

This is a bedstead of the above class, but of earlier date, and instead of having the

Fig. 771.—Centre Panel of Carved Oak Bedstead.

great turned bosses, the upper parts of the foot-posts rise from a kind of square arcade.

Fig. 770.—Footboard of Carved Oak Bedstead.

The date 1460 is painted on this bedstead, which is, of course, incorrect, for it is not earlier than 1560. Little is, however, known of its history. Its real dimensions are 10 ft. 9 in. square by 7 ft. 6½ in. high. Such bedsteads as the above were, of course,

Fig. 772.—Appliqué Chest of Drawers.
Date : About 1690.

" state " bedsteads, but there were humbler forms, also decorated with carving. Among these one of the most noteworthy was the " Stump," the head of which was shaped into a pediment. Two of these are in the Goodrich collection, one of them being dated 1628.

Stuart Bedsteads

The carved bedsteads of the later Stuart times are characterised by foot-posts of slighter and more uniform girth ; by the carved decorations of their heads being more architectural in design, and being without figures ; and by having their panels more frequently inlaid than carved. Comparatively few great " monumental " bedsteads are, however, later than the Restoration; for rich hangings now began to resume the favour which they had formerly held as the chief vehicles for display about beds.

Old Oak Bedstead

Illustrations of parts of a carved oak bedstead exhibited many years ago by

Messrs. Hewetson, Milner, and Thexton, Ltd., are presented by Figs. 770 and 771. This is considered to be a truly magnificent specimen of work, and was discovered in an old house near Tonbridge, where it had been for about 150 years. It is a solid structure with canopy, and is ornamented with most elaborate carving, covered at the time it was discovered with sixteen coats of paint.

Chests of Drawers

Mention has already been made (*see* p. 244) that somewhat earlier than 1700 large panelled chests ceased to be made, being superseded by the chests of drawers. The change was, however, gradual. Drawers were first introduced in the bottoms of the old-fashioned chests of late make, and their convenience being obvious, they presently usurped the whole of the interior. This change occurred at a period when oak carving was already virtually a thing of the past. Thus there is no authentic carved chest of drawers. At that day the rich and fashionable affected foreign furniture ornamented with marquetry and veneers of handsome exotic woods, and more homely households were content with coarse inlay and applied ornament.

Fig. 773.—Iron Hinge. Date : about 1600.

Fig. 774.— Brass Drop Handle. Date : about 1690.

Appliqué Chests of Drawers

Thus Fig. 772 is not a bad example of the style of appliqué work in which the ornament consists of rectangular patterns formed of mouldings. The date is about 1690. The carved feet on which it stands are not the original ones, which were of turned work only. These earliest chests of drawers have a peculiarity which the collector should note—the drawers do not, like modern ones, slide on their bottoms, but on runners, arranged for that purpose, halfway up the sides. Another distinctive feature is their brass furniture. The furniture of panelled chests, and of articles of the carved period generally, is of iron ; and in earlier examples this ironwork is often highly artistic, as in the hinges (Fig. 773), which shows a characteristic form of about 1600. Early chests of drawers have brass key-scutcheons and drop handles (Fig. 774), the latter often being seen in pieces of furniture of this period. It is to be regarded as the characteristic handle of the time, and is to be found on these articles of furniture as early as 1685 and as late as, or possibly slightly later than, 1715.

Fig. 775.—Dressing Chest.

Only a few of these appliqué chests of drawers are to be found later than 1700.

Queen Anne Chest of Drawers

There is, however, a form of chest which may, perhaps, be considered typical of Queen Anne's time. It stands on six turned legs rather more than 1 ft. high, which are ornamentally framed together. On these rest a kind of plinth surrounded by a bold

ran to absurd extremes in shaping, carving, and gilding, the inclination of the unfashionable classes leaned still more and more towards simplicity and plainness, and appliqué work died out as carving had died before it. The graceful drop handle disappeared, and gave place to handles of the form still in use. These were at first mounted on large pierced-work plates, to which there were corresponding scutcheon plates. These produced an

Fig. 776.—Upper Part of Dressing Chest.

Fig. 777.—Drawer Front of Dressing Chest.

moulding, and containing a single shallow drawer. On this plinth, as on a platform, to which it is not attached, stands the main square chest of drawers, which is considerably shorter than the plinth. Such chests of drawers, though often of quite plain oak, have from their outline a distinctly pleasing appearance.

Early Eighteenth-century Chests of Drawers

Although in the earlier part of the eighteenth century the furniture of great houses—following the fashion of France—

ornamental effect without which the square, inartistic oak furniture of the earlier Georges would have been quite unworthy of notice.

Dressing Chest

A dressing chest enriched with carving is illustrated by Fig. 775. This is of original design in general, although the elements, of course, are drawn from early examples of carved work. The top roll (see also Fig. 776) contains the date when the chest was constructed, as well as the initials of the maker's name—T. H. Roberts. A drawer front is shown enlarged by Fig. 777.

SIDEBOARDS

THE sixteenth century might reasonably be said to be a golden age of wood carving. Not only was furniture very profusely ornamented with it, but the choice, conception, and execution of subjects were of the very highest possible degree of merit. Most clearly is this illustrated by the examples about to be presented.

French Sixteenth-century Walnut Sideboard

In Fig. 778 one is amazed at the number of varying elements of which the designs are built up, and yet more at the harmony that exists in spite of this. The moulded top is supported in front by an arcading, decorated with two male and two female terminal figures, which are enriched with masks and floral ornament, and have baskets of fruit on their heads. The central arch is surmounted by a mask and olive branches, and above the side arches are panels with sphinxes. Behind the arcading is a table supporting a cupboard and resting in front on four turned columns; it is fitted with three drawers. The fronts of drawers and cupboard are decorated with monsters, grotesque masks, and scrollwork. The back is divided into panels decorated with bosses, scrolled cartouches and guilloche ornament; the remaining spaces are similarly enriched. This sideboard is in the style of Jacques Androuet *dit* Du Cerceau (born, probably 1510 or 1520; died about 1580). At the time the photograph was taken the sideboard was the property of Mr. T. Foster Shattock. To English craftsmen this sideboard is particularly interesting, because it foreshadowed that style known as Eliza-

bethan in England. The influence of the Renaissance spread rapidly from Italy, through France, Germany, Flanders and Spain to England. Speaking generally, English ornamental art was influenced more directly by that of France; and this example supplies a typical instance. The round-headed arches, the pilasters with the terminal figures, the masks, monsters, and scrollwork; the cartouches, bosses, and the guilloche pattern, are all indicative of that new spirit of ornament which came to England in the opening years of the sixteenth century, and had by the end of the century entirely ousted the characteristically English Gothic ornament.

French Three-tier Sideboard

Another French sixteenth-century walnut sideboard is shown by Fig. 779. At the time of taking the photograph it was in the possession of Mr. George Salting. The top panel (*see also* Fig. 780) is carved with a shield bearing the arms of the family of Guyrod d'Annecy, between two female monsters terminating in floral scrollwork. On each side of this panel is a satyr with a basket of fruit on his head, surmounted by a projecting cornice. Below are two cupboards (*see also* Fig. 781) the doors of which are carved with two representations of Laocoon and his two sons killed by serpents; three terminal monsters occupy the centre and the two sides. Under the cupboards are two drawers, the fronts of which are carved with masks and leaf ornament. The whole is supported at the back by a panel carved with flat floral scrollwork, and in front by two female monsters with wings

Fig. 778.—French Middle Sixteenth-century Walnut Sideboard.

Fig. 779.—French Sixteenth-century Three-tier Walnut Sideboard.

Fig. 780.—Panel in Top of French Sixteenth-century Sideboard (see Fig. 779)

Fig. 781.—Middle Part of French Sixteenth-century Sideboard (see Fig. 779).

Fig. 782.—Detail of Figure at Lower Part of French Sixteenth-century Sideboard (see Fig. 779).

Fig. 783.—Gothic Style Sideboard, Carved by Crace, from Design by A. Welby Pugin.

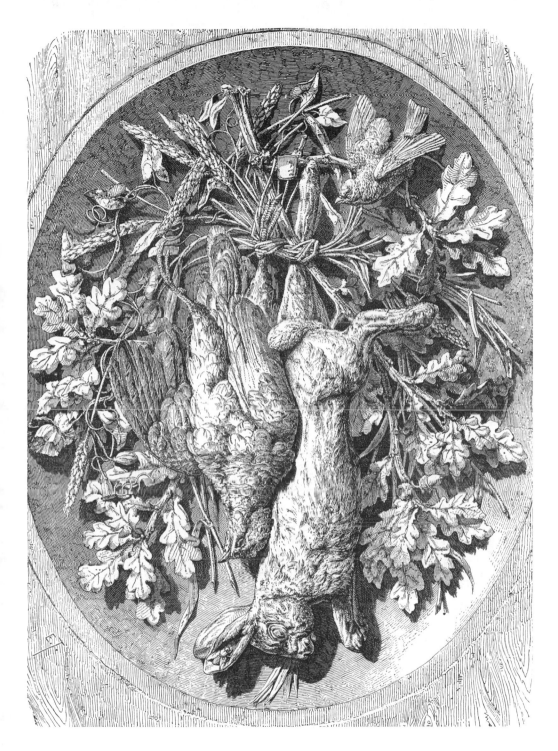

Fig. 784.—Panel for Sideboard.

Fig. 785.—Modern Sideboard of Conventional Design.

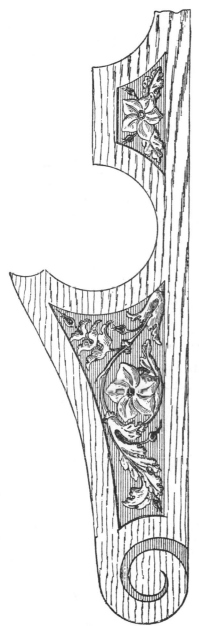

Fig. 786.—Pediment over Centre Cornice of Sideboard.

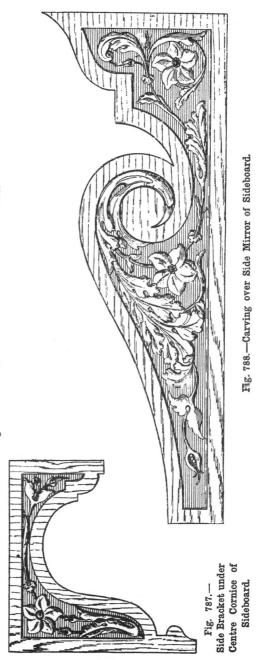

Fig. 788.—Carving over Side Mirror of Sideboard.

Fig. 787.—
Side Bracket under
Centre Cornice of
Sideboard.

terminating in floral scrolls (*see also* Fig. 782). The base is ornamented with carved mouldings. In this example, the exuberant variety and almost splendid extravagance of the ornamental details is yet more typically emphasized. The grouping or arrangement of the ornament is very fine, the value of the mouldings as elements of ornament being very well brought out. Just as in the sideboard previously shown, the harmonious effect produced by the use of such a variety of elements is most wonderful. The panel shown in detail by Fig. 780 is worthy of more than passing notice. It is a study in design, the conception and arrangement of its parts being admirable; and it is equally valuable as a study in execution, its general treatment, and its tool work, being extremely good. But it should be said that the fine parallel gouge cuts on the foliage are not altogether good to copy, a plainer surface, formed by a flat tool, being much to be preferred. The detail shown by Fig. 781 gives, perhaps, the finest piece of work both in

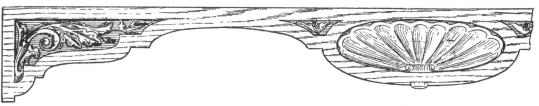

Fig. 789.—Part Detail of Carving under Centre Cornice of Sideboard.

Fig. 790.—Panel under Side Mirrors of Sideboard.

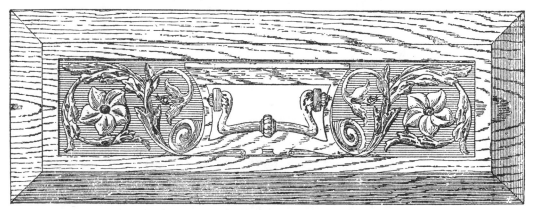

Fig. 791.—Drawer Front of Sideboard.

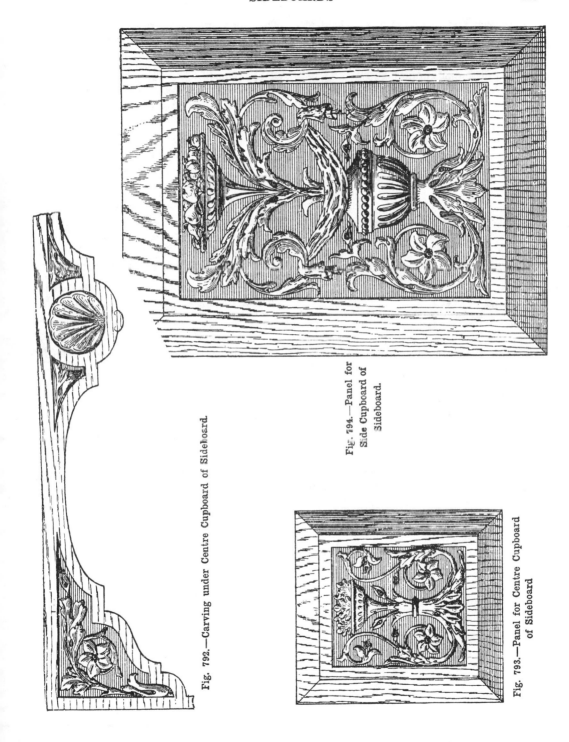

Fig. 792.—Carving under Centre Cupboard of Sideboard.

Fig. 794.—Panel for Side Cupboard of Sideboard.

Fig. 793.—Panel for Centre Cupboard of Sideboard

conception and in execution. The Greek character of the panels is quite evident in the poses and in the treatment of hair and muscles of the human figures. The less important ornamental details, too, are of the greatest interest; notice the grotesque masks in the lower band of carving, and how the surfaces of the mouldings are cut so as to get a perfect balance of light and shade. In the detail at Fig. 782 the supports of the sideboard are shown. This is a wonderful study in " carving in the round," into which pierced carving is introduced. The treatment of the hair on the breast is extremely vigorous. The feathers on the wings, as well as the outline of the wings, are executed with most admirable effect. The terminal scrolls of the tail end in the well-known Roman rosette, showing well the source of inspiration.

Gothic Style Sideboard

The sideboard in the Gothic style carved by Crace from a design by A. Welby Pugin (*see* Fig. 783) marks a period in the nineteenth century when a very serious and determined attempt was made to revive Gothic architecture and ornament. Whatever its success may have been in directly influencing contemporary architecture and ornament, the movement, to say the least, stimulated interest in the work of the great period of Gothic art, and has helped in preserving, and in many cases restoring, many of the gems of the twelfth, thirteenth, fourteenth and fifteenth centuries.

The sideboard shows sixteenth-century influences in the panels, while fifteenth-century carving dominates the rest of the work. The open-work " brattishing " at the top is characteristic of many a West-country fifteenth-century oak rood-screen, as also is the frieze border of grapes and vine leaves. The four-leaved flower, typical of fifteenth-century ornament, is a prominent feature in the scheme, too ; whilst the finials at the top are reminiscent of the " poppy-heads " found so largely in the Midlands and the Eastern counties.

Panel for Sideboard

Some few years ago one of the most popular styles of panel for a dining-room sideboard was that shown by Fig. 784, which is the outcome of the Grinling Gibbons sytle, already illustrated by Figs. 616 and 617 (pp. 318 and 319) and Fig. 675 (p. 349). Such panels generally show a profusion of fruits, fish, birds, hares, etc., and whilst they are often open to the objection that their projecting parts are easily knocked off, there cannot be any doubt as to the suitability of their motif.

Modern Sideboard of Conventional Design

A sideboard of modern conventional style is shown by Fig. 785, full details of the whole of the carving designs being given by Figs. 786 to 794. Description of these figures is unnecessary, as in every case the inscription to the illustration clearly shows the application of the design.

FIGURE CARVING

THERE are, perhaps, not a hundred good figure carvers in England. Most carvers can produce good decorative woodwork, such as foliage, geometrical tracery, etc., but it seems that a really good figure sculptor must be born. Although hard work and industrious application are necessary to the very best and highest work, yet it is extremely doubtful whether a figure carver may be produced by their means. There is a wide chasm between decorative carving and figure work. Then, too, with respect to figure carving itself, there are men who are good at drapery, others at carving the hands, limbs, and the figure generally, and others who are specially expert with faces. Comparatively few there are who can combine the whole, and execute a figure in its entirety with perfect skill and genius.

Idealisation

In carving a figure, the object should not be so much to carve it exactly true to life in every particular, but to use it in expressing some idea; that is to say, it should be idealised. Much of the figure carving of the past has been associated with the religious life of the nations, and has therefore lent itself to idealisation. The statue of St. John the Baptist (Fig. 795) is a good example of this; so is that of St. John the Evangelist (Fig. 796) and the figure of the Archangel Gabriel (Fig. 797). The carving of each figure admirably shows how the ideal can be made manifest in the real; that is, the aims, intentions, and lifework of each of these characters can be traced in the pose of the statues, the expression on the faces, and even in the drapery. It is this percep-

tion of the ideal which is the only reality; and the power and ability to crystallise it in the material used constitute the great artist in wood. It is largely this knowledge and use of symbolism that distinguished the wood carvings of the Gothic period from the work done by the artists of the Renaissance. The latter is remarkable for its beauty of line and form—naturally enough, seeing that the Renaissance is a development, or rather a continuation, of Grecian traditional art. This consideration of beauty of line is illustrated in the group of figures shown in Fig. 798.

Drapery

Drapery is a phase of the wood carver's craft that should receive the greatest attention. Wooden figures are rarely clothed in anything other than drapery. The very earliest carved wooden statue—that known as the "Sheikh-el-Beled," which is 6,000 years old, and is carved in sycamore, as were nearly all Egyptian statues and other carved woodwork—is clothed in this way; and all through the Gothic period this was the case. In the illustrations accompanying this section, drapery is very much in evidence, and some remarkably good examples of it are shown. That of the Archangel Gabriel (Fig. 797) is of a most refined and delicate type, the folds being treated in a most artistic manner and reminding one very much of the "linen-fold" pattern so commonly employed during the fifteenth and sixteenth centuries. The drapery of St. John the Baptist and St. John the Evangelist in Figs. 795 and 799 is of a much more rugged character; it is not so delicately

Fig. 795 -St. John the Baptist.
German Statue.   Date : about 1500.

folded as that of the Archangel Gabriel, but it is characteristic of a suitable treatment for wood. Any piece of carved work should show evidence that it has been freely and honestly done by means of wood-cutting tools, and is not the result of a series of gymnastic exercises on the part of the carving tools, rifflers, glasspaper, etc. All good work comes clean from the tool and shows nothing but the tool cuts. Oak especially should be allowed to remain as it comes from the tool. The value of drapery as a decorative feature of statuary will be understood by comparing the draped figures already mentioned with that of St. George and the Dragon (Fig. 800). After the graceful folds of Gabriel, and the rugged drapery of the St. Johns, this group appears to be very angular, and, however lifelike it may be, it cannot be said to be the embodiment of grace and beauty. Even modern clothing is preferable to this angular armour of mediæval times. Drapery is most certainly the best medium for the expression of beauty, because of the continuity of treatment necessitated. In the Archangel Gabriel (Fig. 797) some of the lines of the drapery follow the course of the whole length of the figure, and give it an unbrokenness of effect the value of which cannot well be over-estimated.

Difficulty with Drapery

One difficulty experienced in the carving of a draped figure is the necessity that exists for preserving the contour and proportions of the figure beneath. Especially is this so when the drapery is thin, and is not so full in nature as those shown in the illustrations here presented. Sometimes nearly a whole limb has to be shown covered tightly with drapery ; and in such a case much thought has to be given and care taken in getting the true proportions of the limb. Sometimes drapery is treated in a way that is almost entirely decorative. This is so in the case of some of the figures in Fig. 801, the skirts or tunics being treated so that elevation and depression, hollow and round, follow one another with the order and regularity that are always associated with purely decorative work. This group, it will be noticed, is in oak, painted and gilded ; and

Fig. 796.—St. John the Evangelist.
French Half-length Figure.   Date : Sixteenth Century

attention is called to this, because colour has played such a great part in the schemes of carved ornament in the past, from Egyp-

Fig. 798.—Group: "Hercules carrying off Deianeira from Achelous." Italian. Date: Sixteenth Century.

tian and Abyssinian ornament to the days of the later Renaissance.

Less Important Kinds of Figure Carving

To make a figure live, one has to be able to catch and fix the appropriate expression;

Fig. 797.—Archangel Gabriel. Italian Figure. Date: Fifteenth Century.

Fig. 799.—St. John the Evangelist. German
Statue. Date : about 1500.

Fig. 800.—Group : "St. George and the Dragon."
French. Date : Fifteenth Century.

Fig. 801.—Two Groups: "Legend of St. Hubert." French.   Date : Late Fifteenth Century.

and this needs the artist who is born, not made. But for representations of the human figure such as satyrs, griffins, cupids, caryatids, masks, and so forth, such a highly developed ability is not so necessary. Caryatids, as shown in many illustrations in this book (particularly, *see* Fig. 804, p. 423,

period in England, so much so as to make them a typical feature of it.

The Proportions of the Human Figure

It is important for the figure carver to know the proportions that the different

Fig. 802.—Bust of "Virgen de los Dolores." Attributed to Montañés. Spanish. Date: Seventeenth Century.

of this chapter), have been a common representation of the human figure in history. The most famous example is the portico of the Erectheum at Athens, B.C. 420. Caryatids were extensively used in the Elizabethan

parts of the human figure bear to one another. The adoption of some standard of proportion is necessary as a basis to the correct representation of the human figure. At the same time, this should not be taken as being an absolutely unalterable standard. It gives what might be termed a basic knowledge; but as there are many types of beauty, and as the art of symbolic expression requires alterations of proportion, many variations will be found necessary. Measurements taken from the antique show that the is exactly the same height as when seen in front, but is only half the length. The ear is equal in width to the length of one eye, and in length to that of two eyes nearly. The hand is the same length as the face, and its width is equal to one half. The foot in profile is nine eyes in length and three in

Fig. 803.—Flemish Carving: "St. Christopher bearing the Infant Christ on his shoulder."

mouth is equal in width to the length of one eye and a half, and its height to one half. In profile it is the same height, but only half the width, the upper lip projecting more than the lower. In width the nose is equal to the length of one eye, and in height to the length of two eyes, measuring parallel to the eyebrows; and the eyebrow is situated above the eyelid about one-third the length of the eye. In profile the eye width. Taking the general proportions of the human figure, the height of a man is about nine times the length of the face, measuring from the root of the hair on the forehead to the tip of the chin; but taking the whole head in height, the proportion is as 7 is to 1. As is generally known, the height of a man is about equal to the measurement from finger tip to finger tip of the arms stretched horizontally. The width of the neck seen in front is equal to the length of two noses. Twice the length of the head is equal to the width of the shoulders, front view. Further, it should be stated that the length of the forearm is equal to seven and a half nose lengths, measuring from the tip of the fingers to the point of the elbow. The width of the wrist, front view, is equal to one and a sixth nose lengths; and the width of the knee, front view, is equal to one and two-third nose lengths; in profile, two nose lengths. From the knee to the heel is three face lengths. These principal proportions will be sufficient to serve as a guide. Because of the grouping of the parts of the human figure and the poses of the trunk, head, and limbs, the real proportions can be obtained only by actual sketches from the life, or by a very keenly observant and accurately discriminate eye.

Position of Work in Carving

The actual carving of a figure should not be done on the bench. The work should be done as it will eventually stand when in its final position. A plank of suitable size stood in an upright position, and fixed to the floor and the beams above, should serve as a support, to which the block to be carved can be screwed.

Jointing Wood Together

A difficulty that is met in large statuary, or in any with extended arms or legs, is the size of the material. Big blocks of oak can be obtained, of course; but to get a block big enough to take in an extended arm only is to cause waste of material and consequent expense. This difficulty was got over by the Egyptian artists, who carved the statue of the "village sheikh," already spoken of, by mortising one arm into the main block, which was sufficient to carve the body, head, and the other limbs out of; and this is one way of arranging for any extra width required. Another way is to glue, with a dowelled joint, two or more blocks together. With high-class craftsmanship this is excellent, but the joinery has to be good or the joints will open and ugly gaps appear. A figure in a prominent church in London has a gap of this sort which runs for part of its length down the face of the figure, and, of course, presents a very unsightly appearance.

" Roughing-out "

It might easily be assumed that the most valuable wood carver is the one who can finish off well. " To put the finishing touches

Fig. 804.—Truss in Italian Walnut, for Chimneypiece.

on " is a phrase suggesting that the greatest ability lies with the person who can successfully put them on ; but this is by no means so. The one who can "rough-out" the block is the person who determines the true proportions of the figure, who really decides the position and the pose of the limbs, trunk, and head, and who is responsible for the occurrence of the various thicknesses, the increases and the diminutions of the wood where they are the most required. Then when all this, the really important and essential part of the work, is arranged for, the "finishing touches" may be put on ; but this part of the work is child's play to the "roughing-out," as anyone who has tried it will readily realise.

The Illustrations to this Section

St. John the Baptist.—Fig. 795 shows German work of the late fifteenth or early sixteenth century.

St. John the Evangelist.—Fig. 796, illustrating French sixteenth-century work, should be compared with Fig. 799, illustrating German work of the late fifteenth or early sixteenth century. The French half-length figure is painted and gilt.

Archangel Gabriel.—Fig. 797 shows a figure from a group of the Annunciation, said to have formerly stood in the cathedral at Pisa. It is Italian work of the fifteenth century.

Group: "Hercules Carrying off Deianeira from Achelous."—A group depicting this is shown by Fig. 798 (p. 418). The original is painted, and is an example of the Giovanni da Bologna school, it being Italian work dating back to the second half of the sixteenth century.

Group: "St. George and the Dragon." —This group (Fig. 800, p. 419) is French fifteenth-century work, enriched with paint and gilding. It will be noticed that St. George wears a wreath and no helmet, and that his sword and shield are missing.

Groups: "The Legend of St. Hubert." —French late fifteenth-century carving is illustrated by Fig. 801 (p. 420), the originals being painted and gilt. St. Hubert, Bishop of Liége, born in 656, is the hero of the legend. He is "startled into repentance when hunting on Good Friday by the sudden appearance of a stag bearing between his horns a radiant crucifix." The crucifix is missing from the head of the stag.

Bust: "Virgen de los Dolores."— This bust (Fig. 802, p. 421) is probably the work of the Spaniard, Montañés, during the seventeenth century.

"St. Christopher bearing the Infant Christ on his Shoulder."—Fig. 803 (p. 422) shows a fine example of Flemish work. Note the expression of wonder in the saint's face at the weight of his burthen. The upturned face is most artistically treated. The original carving is about 3 ft. 6 in. high.

Truss.—The truss, shown in front view by Fig. 804, was carved in Italian walnut for a large chimneypiece at Sudborne Hall, Suffolk. The carving was executed at the Pyghtle Works, Bedford, and the photograph here reproduced was kindly supplied by Mr. John P. White.

MISERERE OR MISERICORD SEATS

Miserere Seats

MISERERE, or more properly "Misericord," seats are found in most cathedrals and churches. Their origin was the result of necessity, and their subsequent ornamentation a fine illustration of the irresistible way in which the spirit of ornament seizes any and every opportunity of expressing itself. Originally, the clergy had to stand during the long church services; but during the eleventh century sitting had partially

Fig. 805.

Figs. 805 and 806.—Miserere Seats at Exeter Cathedral.
(*Photos: Frith & Co., Reigate.*)

Fig. 807.

Fig. 808.

Figs. 807 to 809.—Miserere Seats at Exeter Cathedral.

(*Photos: Frith & Co., Reigate.*)

Fig. 810.

Fig. 811.

Figs. 810 to 812.—Miserere Seats at Exeter Cathedral.

(*Photos: Frith & Co., Reigate.*)

427

come into vogue, and the ingenious idea occurred to some of the early builders to hinge the seats of the stalls, so that they could be raised. The block fixed under each seat would act as a support for the standing

grotesquely secular subjects, such as a goose giving a monk a penny, and so on. Besides the purely grotesque, there were carved seats having a subject that was amusingly and often bitingly satirical. Thus in the

Fig. 813.

Figs. 813 and 814.—Miserere Seats at Exeter Cathedral.
(*Photos: Frith & Co., Reigate.*)

clergyman. Generally the ornament found on these seats is of a grotesque and often ridiculous kind, as shown by illustrations herewith. In Beverley Minster, for example, out of sixty-eight seats, most of them dating from 1520, sixty-six are concerned with

beautiful fifteenth-century church of St. Mary at Beverley there are a few seats which are carved to show wolves and foxes attired in friars' garb, preaching to the people. This satire was directed against the friars as a body, because although they

Fig. 815.

Fig. 816.

Figs. 815 to 817.—Miserere Seats at Exeter Cathedral.

(Photos: Frith & Co., Reigate.)

Fig. 818.

Fig. 819.

Figs. 818 to 820.—Miserere Seats at Exeter Cathedral.
(*Photos: Frith & Co., Reigate.*)

430

had no settled church, they were allowed privileges which were considered to be the prerogative of the monks who possessed monasteries and churches of their own. The purely grotesque character of the seats is in all probability due to the grotesque books, called the " Bestiaries," which were circulated at that time, and which contained illustrations of the strangest and most fabulous animals and creatures the human mind could possibly imagine. The miserere seats illustrated in this section are from Exeter and Ripon Cathedrals and Ludlow Church.

Fig. 821.

Figs. 821 and 822.—Miserere Seats at Ludlow Church.

(Photos: Frith & Co., Reigate.)

Miserere Seats at Exeter Cathedral

Those from Exeter (*see* Figs. 805 to 820) are amongst the most remarkable misericord seats in the world. As they are, they are practically the entire original set, fifty in number, made, carved and fixed in the early part of the thirteenth century by Bishop Bruere (1224–1244), and are as sound now as when placed in position nearly 700 years ago. The distinguishing features of the Early English period of Gothic ornament are the three-lobed foliage and the dog-tooth ornament. In the seats at Exeter the former is very much in evidence, the ornament of some of the seats being based entirely

Fig. 823.

Figs. 823 and 824.—Miserere Seats at Ludlow Church.
(*Photos : Frith & Co., Reigate.*)

upon this conventional element (refer to Figs. 806 and 811), whilst nearly all the terminal ornaments are of this kind. The influence of the Crusades is shown, too, in this series of seats. Notice in Figs. 813 and 815 the figures of the mythical creature known as a centaur, being a horse's body with a man's head. The elephant was then only just becoming known, as will be quite evident when referring to Fig. 820 ; for the hocks of the elephant are shown at the back as in the horse, whilst in reality they should be at the front. The seat in Fig. 817 reminds one very strongly of the legend of

Fig. 825.—Miserere Seat at Ludlow Church.
Photo: Frith & Co., Reigate.)

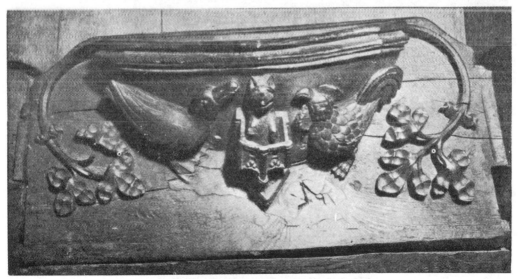

Fig. 826.—Miserere Seat at Ripon Cathedral.

Fig. 827.—Bench End and Miserere Seat of Mayor's Stall at Ripon Cathedral,
showing Keys of St. Wilfred.

Fig. 828.

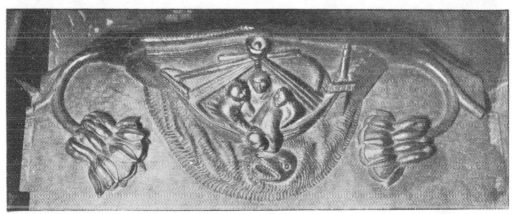

Fig. 829.

Figs. 828 to 830.—Miserere Seats at Ripon Cathedral.

435

Fig. 831.

Fig. 832.

Figs. 831 to 833.—Miserere Seats at Ripon Cathedral.

Lohengrin ; the sea, by the way, is introduced with extremely decorative effect, and is admirably suited to expression in wood. Much of this carving is crude, in the sense that it is not mechanically and mathematically perfect. But the seats are much better than this, inasmuch as they successfully depict what the artist intended ; the impression conveyed is that of life, and strong, vigorous, and virile life at that. Refer to any of the seats that have life figures as a subject, and this will be found to be true. It is useless to get a perfect form of expression if there is nothing to express ; but, on the other hand, given something to express, and a determination to express it, then the result is vigorous work such as has been shown in these seats. The original and somewhat humorous treatment of the lion's mane in the seat shown by Fig. 807 is worth attention. Usually, the mane is treated in long curves to suggest strength and power ;

Fig. 834.

Figs. 834 and 835.—Miserere Seats at Ripon Cathedral.

here it is done in short curls, that remind one to some extent of a negro's woolly pate.

Miserere Seats at Ludlow

Miserere seats at Ludlow Church are illustrated by Figs. 821 to 825. The grotesque nature of these seats is further evidenced by the amusing example shown in Fig. 821. Again, it must be said how keen an eye and how true an aptitude for expression had these old wood carvers, whatever their shortcomings might be, when viewed from the point of view of clean workmanship and perfectly moulded form.

Miserere Seats at Ripon

These are shown by Figs. 826 to 838. The decorative character of the wings of the pelican in Fig. 834 is well worthy of attention, as is the treatment of the well-known

Fig. 836.

Figs. 836 and 837.—Miserere Seats at Ripon Cathedral.

story of Jonah in Fig. 829. Notice how the sea is treated to represent the storm. The treatment of the vine leaves and grapes in is taken and lines cut in across the bunch at right angles to each other. The succeeding squares are then rounded off, and

Fig. 838.—Miserere Seat at Ripon Cathedral.

Fig. 832 is subject for comment. The way in which the grapes are formed is very instructive. The bunch of grapes is blocked out and roughly rounded ; then the **V** tool the grapes are made. This is quite a simple, rough-and-ready way, but yet, withal, extremely effective and well suited to the material.

CHIMNEY-PIECES

Italian Renaissance Mantelpiece

Such a mantel as is shown by Fig. 839 would be best suited for execution in American walnut, or mahogany with very little figure in it. The plainer the figure of the wood for the carvings and mouldings, the better; although in the plain surfaces of the base, etc., some little figure would not come amiss. The wood should be of a very close grain, in order that the delicate lines of the carvings may not be interfered with. It is well to get the pilasters carved before the making of the mantel is begun. Each pilaster measures 4 ft. 2 in. long by 6½ in. wide, and is 1 in. thick. At the top end, a space of 4 in. is covered with the bed moulding under the mantelshelf, and at the lower end 7 in. will be covered with the base, so that the rest of the surface is what will be seen after the mantel is finished. The pilaster is not set in as a panel, observe, but is placed against the framing of the mantel-jamb. There is, therefore, 3 ft. 3 in. clear space left for carving; and in Figs. 840 and 841 is given the design for one pilaster, the other being of a slightly different pattern. This is an agreeable feature—this balancing of pattern without necessarily having one feature a duplicate of its corresponding one. These two figures overlap each other by about ½ in. The cutting is, in this style, very flat, or in " low relief "; the ground will not be more than ¼ in. down from the face of the wood. As much modelling as possible may be put into the work, but it always is very flat, and the ground should not be punched, but left quite smooth. The corresponding pilaster should be of a different design, but the leading forms or lines should be kept similar in them both. In Fig. 842 is given three portions which may be used in place of some parts of Figs. 840 and 841. For instance, the top part of Fig. 842 takes the place of the top part of Fig. 841. The connecting scrolls being exactly alike, there need be no fear of an awkward joining. The central portion of Fig. 842 takes the place of a portion of Fig. 841 near its lower end, where the outline is the same but the detail in the centre of pilaster is quite different, and the enclosing leaf is much lighter in mass. The lower portion of Fig. 842 is set in immediately above the scrolls which rest on the vase in Fig. 840. With these three portions incorporated with the first pilaster design, the two will then be sufficiently like, and yet unlike, one another. With these pilasters carved, the mantel proper may now be started. An end elevation is given to the scale of 1 in. = 1 ft., in Fig. 843. An enlarged plan of the jamb is shown in Fig. 844, while a section through the frieze in centre is given in Fig. 845. If possible, get the size of the actual grate that will be put in; but if, as is not uncommon, that cannot be determined, the next best plan is to make the opening of the mantel of a size such as will most likely suit the grate when it is placed in position. A usual opening to work to in such a case is that taken in this instance, namely, 3 ft. 4 in. wide, and 3 ft. 2 in. high. The moulding round the opening is fastened separately, so that it may be fixed to suit the grate, ½ in. further in or out. The mantelshelf should stand about 4 ft. 3 in. from the floor. The jambs are formed with a frame as in Fig. 846, which will measure 4 ft. 2 in. long, reaching from the floor to under side of shelf. Each stile or upright is 2½ in. broad by 1 in. thick, and the breadth of the frame finished is 10 in. These stiles are of walnut, but the three rails will be quite covered up, so they may be of deal, 4 in. broad and 1 in. thick. Against this frame is placed the carved pilaster, which overlaps the edges of the stiles by ½ in., leaving 1¾ in. of their surface seen. The pilaster is screwed fast from

Fig. 839.—Italian Renaissance Mantelpiece.

Fig. 840.

Fig. 841.

Figs. 840 and 841.—Mantelpiece Pilaster, shown in Halves.

behind, through the three pine rails, and is blocked up the sides of the stiles as well (*see* Fig. 844). On the outer side of each jamb is now placed a piece of wood the whole length, by 3 in. wide and 1 in. thick. This is glued and blocked fast, and the jamb now looks as shown in Fig. 847—ready for the base and other mouldings and carvings to be planted in their positions, and ready also for the deal rail behind the carved frieze, which connects the two jambs together.

Mouldings, etc.—The moulded base is 7 in. high to top edge of moulding, and is $\frac{7}{8}$ in. thick ; it is mitered round pilaster and jamb, butting against the wall at the one side, and the moulding (to be afterwards fixed) round the grate. The piece on the front of the carved pilaster is carved ; before

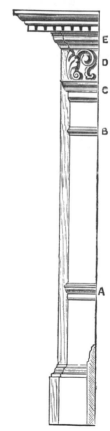

Fig. 842.—Alternative Designs for Parts of Mantelpiece Pilaster.

Fig. 843.—End Elevation of Italian Renaissance Mantelpiece.

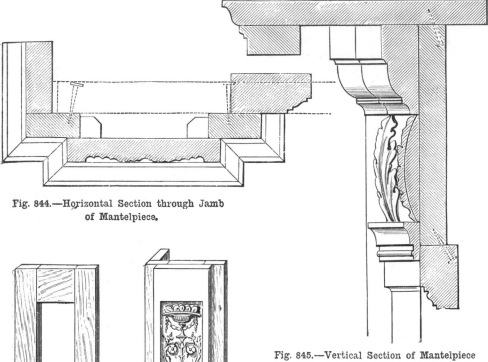

Fig. 844.—Horizontal Section through Jamb
of Mantelpiece.

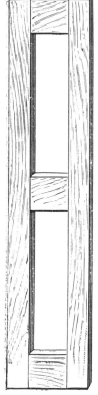

Fig. 845.—Vertical Section of Mantelpiece
Frieze and Shelf.

Fig. 846.—Framing
of Mantelpiece
Jamb.

Fig. 847.—
Mantelpiece Jamb
with Pilaster.

fitting and gluing it round the base, the
carving should be wrought. The detail of
this carving will afterwards be given. The
next moulding is the surbase A (Fig. 843).
It is mitered round the jamb, butting against
the wall at one side and the grate moulding at the other side, exactly as the base
did; but it also butts against the side of
pilaster, instead of mitering round it like the
base (see Fig. 839). The pilaster is 1 in.
thick, and as this moulding has less than that
of projection, it will stop nicely against its
edge. The neck moulding B (Fig. 843) is
fitted in the same way as A. The next
moulding, C, is also fitted in the same
way. After marking the position of mouldings B and C, the little flutes (shown in Fig.
839) should be worked, after which the
mouldings may be made fast—excepting the
inner parts of C, which must be mitered to the
moulding carried along the frieze, and as the
other mouldings above this are also mitered
along the frieze, the deal rail before mentioned should now be fastened in position.

This rail is entirely covered with carving and mouldings planted on its face; hence it need not be of walnut. It measures $9\frac{1}{2}$ in. by 1 in. thick, and is long enough to extend behind the framing of jamb, so that it may be screwed to both stiles of framing (*see* dotted lines in Fig. 844). If any blocking connecting the outer gable with this frame is in the way of this rail, it should be removed where the rail interferes; it may, of course, be put in again on the top of the rail. A rough spar, about 3 in. by 1 in., should be secured temporarily at the bottom of the jambs in the same way as this top rail is, to keep everything square until the job is finished. The bed-moulding E (Fig. 843), $4\frac{1}{8}$ in. wide, is next mitered round all the breaks of the pilaster and along the frieze. The portion of moulding on the front of the carved pilaster is carved also. After being fitted, and before being fastened, this carving should be done, as it will be more easily handled than when fastened in its place. The moulding C (Fig. 843) was left unfastened to allow of its being mitered along the frieze. This is only partly carried along the frieze; the lower part stops against the grate-moulding yet to be put on. In Fig. 845 this is clearly indicated, where also is shown the moulding projecting below the bottom edge of the deal frieze-rail. When this moulding is properly fitted and fixed, the convex frieze D (Fig. 843) is prepared. It is of wood 1 in. thick, and of sufficient breadth to fit accurately between mouldings C and E. It is convex, as shown in Fig. 845, the greatest thickness being 1 in., and the least $\frac{5}{8}$ in. In fitting this frieze, the centre piece should butt right between the framing of jambs. This part of the frieze must then be carved—or, at least, have the ground set down at each end before the adjoining parts of the frieze can be fitted; for they are scribed against it. This frieze is mitered round the jambs, and, when fitted, the different parts are carved and then fastened in their positions. The moulding round the grate, shown in Figs. 844 and 845, extends behind the framing sufficiently to be screwed firmly to it, and it is pocket-holed, to be screwed to the frieze-rail (*see* Fig. 845). In order to get this moulding put on, the temporary rail at the foot must be

Fig. 843.—Part of Mantelpiece Frieze.

removed, and afterwards fastened on behind this grate-moulding, until the mantel is fitted up in its place. This prevents any unnecessary strain being put upon the

front and ends. It is secured by driving in half a dozen screws from the underneath side.

Some Details of the Carvings.—Illus-

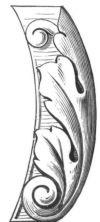

Fig. 849.　　　　　　　　　　　Fig. 850.　　　　　Fig. 851.

Fig. 849.—Foliage for Mantelpiece Frieze.

Fig. 850.—Top of Carved Pilaster.

Fig. 851.—Carving round Break of Mantelpiece Jamb.

Fig. 852.—Carved Moulding above Mantelpiece Pilasters.

fastenings of the frieze-rail while the mantel is being handled—in polishing, etc.

Mantelshelf.—The mantelshelf is the only thing required to complete the cabinet-making part of the job. The shelf itself is 11 in. broad and 1 in. thick, and has a clamped moulding $2\frac{1}{2}$ in. by $1\frac{3}{8}$ in. along its

trations showing the carvings for the different portions of mouldings, etc., already mentioned, will now be referred to. The central portion of the frieze is given in Fig. 848. The left-hand vase and fruit may be used at both ends. The other pattern may be used for the two centre vases, but reversing the spiral, or twisted, fluting in vase, and re-arranging the apples, plums, etc., on top. The upright leafage in Fig. 848 in the centre of the frieze, and the arrangement in Fig. 849, may be used at the two other intervals between the vases. The dotted curved line at the left-hand end of Fig. 848 represents the position of the adjoining piece of frieze which butts against this, and which consequently must be left clear of carving for that purpose, of course retaining the same

inner semicircles, and that on the other for the other inner one. The base of the pilasters is carved as in Fig. 853. If much cutting were put on this base, lying as it does, it would constantly be catching dust. Fig. 854 is a full-size detail of the dentils in the clamp on the shelf. They are cut in the plain band, which is carried uninterruptedly all the way along. Three patterns are given ; these should be cut in groups of three —three of the first design, three of the

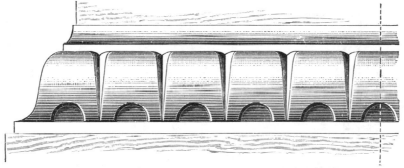

Fig. 853.—Detail of Ornament at Base of Mantelpiece Pilaster.

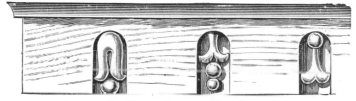

Fig. 854.—Dentils in Clamp on Mantelpiece Shelf.

curve as the rest of the ground has. This ground should be taken down to a bare $\frac{1}{8}$ in. at each side. This allows $\frac{1}{2}$ in. of wood for carving, which is enough for the purpose. The little piece of frieze at each side of the carved pilaster is shown in Fig. 850, and the piece round the break of the jamb in Fig. 851. The outside gable (Fig. 843) is carved similar to Fig. 850, but the scrolls, etc., are extended to fill up the larger space. The moulding E (Fig. 843), carved above the pilasters, is shown full size by Fig. 852. There being four semicircles of carving above each pilaster, the two end ones may be as the left-hand pattern in Fig. 852, while the right-hand pattern is shown with two arrangements—that on one side being for one of the

second, three of the third ; three of the second, three of the first, and so on.

Chimney-piece with Overmantel

Well-seasoned oak should be used for the chimney-piece shown in elevation by Fig. 855. A horizontal section through the mirrors of the chimney-piece, and a plan of the lower shelf, are represented in Fig. 856, while Fig. 857 gives a vertical section through the middle. The chimney-piece is 9 ft. $2\frac{1}{2}$ in. high by 7 ft. $4\frac{1}{2}$ in. wide, and its greatest projection is 1 ft. $1\frac{3}{4}$ in. The top framing is prepared from $1\frac{1}{2}$-in. stuff. The top shelf is worked in the solid from 4-in. stuff, and is $5\frac{3}{4}$ in. wide in the widest parts, over the pilasters, and $4\frac{1}{4}$ in. wide where set back.

Fig. 855.—Front Elevation of Chimney-piece with Overmantel.

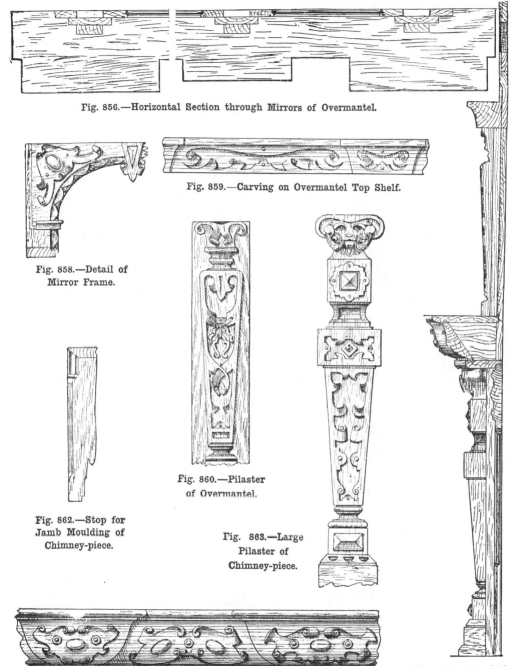

Fig. 856.—Horizontal Section through Mirrors of Overmantel.

Fig. 859.—Carving on Overmantel Top Shelf.

Fig. 858.—Detail of
Mirror Frame.

Fig. 860.—Pilaster
of Overmantel.

Fig. 862.—Stop for
Jamb Moulding of
Chimney-piece.

Fig. 863.—Large
Pilaster of
Chimney-piece.

Fig. 861.—Breast Moulding of Chimney-piece.

Fig. 857.—Vertical
Section of Over-
mantel.

Fig. 864.—Swag for Frieze over Chimney-piece, at Bedale Hall, Yorkshire.

The upper part of the overmantel is mortised to receive the tenons of the two outside pieces, which are partly covered by, and screwed on to, the pilaster backs. The arches, or mirror frames, made up of spandrel, key-block, etc., are set out clearly in Fig. 858. These are grooved and tongued together as the dotted lines indicate. The joints are covered (when the framing is screwed into position) by the pilaster backs, and the small cap moulding, which is housed in and glued. The key-block, after being carved, is also cut into the top rail and glued. The rails and stiles are rebated to receive the back of the mirror and the beads necessary for fixing the glass. The carved moulding, of which a section is included in Fig. 858, is simple, yet gives a richness to these frames, and is quite in harmony. A portion of the upper shelf is shown to an enlarged scale in Fig. 859. The carving is sunk in this as in the pilasters. Fig. 860 shows an enlarged detail of the capitals and pilasters of the overmantel, which are fixed with screws driven through the $1\frac{1}{4}$-in. backs. The capitals are somewhat plain, but will be effective if freely cut. The design for the carving on the pilasters is of rather unusual character, and will be found effective. The strapwork in these would look well if undercut a little. The construction of the lower shelf, with the bold breast moulding supporting it, is shown in Fig. 857. The breast moulding is tongued into the shelf, and the $1\frac{1}{4}$-in. moulding below it is blocked with dry pine blocks, and screwed. Fig. 861 shows, to an enlarged scale, the carving, which stands out from the moulding about $\frac{1}{2}$ in. The strapwork panels on the part of the moulding that is set back, with two ovals in each, represent an unusual arrangement, which, however, is of excellent effect. There is a bold and free design on the rail that is tenoned into the jambs. The moulding on the jambs is stopped as shown in the enlarged detail (Fig. 862), while Fig. 863 is an enlarged illustration of the pilasters and capitals that support the lower shelf. These may be prepared in three pieces, and are mounted on $1\frac{1}{2}$-in. backs and screwed from behind. The capitals are much richer than those of the overmantel, and this design is carefully drawn and reproduced, so that it

Fig. 865.—English Chimney-piece. Date: about 1750.

Fig. 866.—Chippendale Style Chimney-piece.   Date : Second Half of Eighteenth Century.

may render efficient aid to the carver. An end elevation of these capitals is shown clearly in Fig. 857. The greatest projection of the pilaster is $3\frac{3}{4}$ in. The plainness of the base moulding is relieved by semi-elliptical sinkings, set in square, and grounded out to a suitable depth. The opening of the chimney-piece is 4 ft. by 3 ft. It should be fumigated or stained a rich brown and wax polished.

Swag for Chimney-piece Frieze

A swag carved in limetree wood for the frieze over a chimney-piece at Bedale Hall, Yorks., is shown by Fig. 864. The work was executed at the Pyghtle Works, Bedford, and the photograph was kindly supplied by Mr. J. P. White. In this example, the influence of Grinling Gibbons can be plainly seen. Fig. 864 should be compared with Figs. 616 and 617 (pp. 318 and 319).

Eighteenth-century Chimney-piece

A chimney-piece with a characteristic broken pediment is shown by Fig. 865. This was carved in pine, and was discovered in a house in Carey Street, Lincoln's Inn Fields, London. It is English work, and dates from about 1750.

Chippendale Style Mantelpiece

The Chippendale style has already had its salient features described (see p. 351). Now, a mantelpiece in this style is illustrated (see Fig. 866). It consists of a mirror in an elaborate openwork frame of carved pine, beneath which are similarly decorated lintel and jambs, with plain marble slips surrounding the fireplace. It was formerly in Winchester House, Putney, and dates from 1750–1800.

STAIRCASES

Carved and Panelled Staircase in Hardwood

THE short flight of stairs, with suitable panelling for the hall, illustrated by Figs. 867 to 869, is in the style known as Jacobean, its characteristics being distinctive of the architectural period that coincided with the reign of James I. of England (1603-25). Elevations of handrail, balusters, newels, and string are given in Fig. 867. The handrail is moulded, and the outside bead may be enriched as represented in Figs. 870 and 871. This arrangement will leave, on the inner side of the rail, a convenient moulding on which the hand may slide. Fig. 868 shows

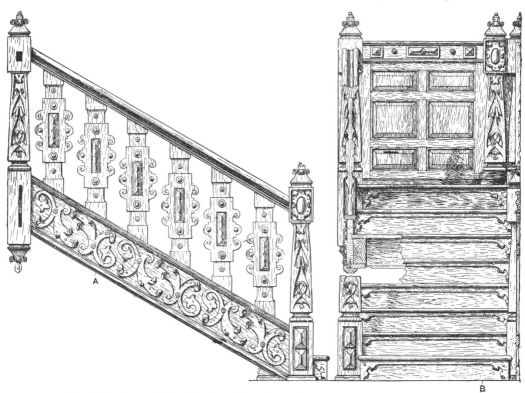

Figs. 867 and 868.—Side Elevation, Front Elevation, and Part Section (through A) of Staircase.

Fig. 873.

Fig. 874.

Fig. 872.—Part of String of Staircase.

Fig. 870.—Part of Handrail (shown on end).

Fig. 871.—Plan of Carving on Handrail.

Fig. 875.

Fig. 876.

Figs. 873 and 874.—Alternative Designs for Small Panels.

Figs. 875 and 876.—Alternative Designs for Large Panels.

Fig. 877.—Newel of Staircase.

Fig. 869.—Part Section of Staircase (through B, Fig. 868) and Elevation of Panelling.

a front elevation of the staircase, and a part section taken at A (Fig. 867) through the handrail, baluster, string, and soffit The balusters are carved on both sides. The panelling of the soffit corresponds to that shown on the landing (Fig. 867), and is screwed on to the string, the joint being covered by the moulding as indicated in section. The treatment of the risers is somewhat richer than in the usual designs, in which the plainness is relieved simply by a small moulding under the nosing. The introduction of strapwork design is a great improvement to the staircase. Fig. 869

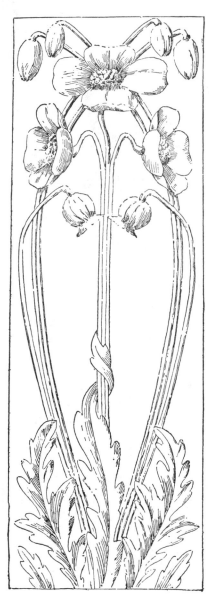

Fig. 878.—Poppy Design for Baluster.

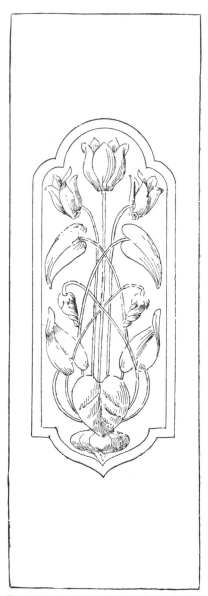

Fig. 879.—Cyclamen Design for Baluster.

represents a section through B (Fig. 868), showing, besides the method of construction, the panelling above and below the stairs, and the dado carved with the simplest and most characteristic ornaments found in Jacobean work. The stairs are strengthened with bracketed carriage pieces, the treads and risers being screwed and blocked together, and housed into the strings in the usual way. An enlarged detail of the carving on the wall string is given in Fig. 872. The carving for the hall panelling will have a good effect if arranged as illustrated. The panels are prepared from $\frac{3}{4}$-in. stuff, and the stiles and rails from 1-in. stuff, mortised and tenoned together, and rebated to receive the panels, which are fixed with strips of wood bradded at the back. Figs. 873 and 874 represent alternative designs for the small panels, while Figs. 875 and 876 show other designs for the large panels. The design shown by Fig. 876 is somewhat less severe than the others. Fig. 877 represents an enlarged elevation of a newel, showing the carving in detail.

Carved Baluster

A few suggestions as to the decorative filling of an upright panel in a square-turned baluster are given below. Fig. 878 is taken from the poppy, Fig. 879 from the cyclamen, and Fig. 880 from the narcissus. Fig. 881 (a rosette) and Fig. 882 (a lion's head) are merely hints as to a very simple means of ornamenting a given space by a single spot in the middle. This idea is somewhat elaborated at Fig. 879, though this design might be easily adapted to fill the whole panel.

Staircase at Aston Hall, Birmingham

When the feudal system passed away and the country, as a whole, became more united in its aims—social, political, and religious—there came a marked development of family life. The great fortified castles gave place to the unfortified mansions, so characteristic of the sixteenth and seventeenth centuries. One result was the setting apart, for the exclusive use of the family, of various apartments, which were often on the first floor and so necessitated the construction of a grand staircase. Thus,

in the great Elizabethan mansions, the oak staircase was an important ornamental feature. This is well illustrated in the Aston Hall staircase shown in Fig. 883. The handsomely carved newels with their finials, the carved pierced balustrading, and the handsome suites of mouldings all combine to make of the staircase a very striking feature. The ornament of this period was, of course, based upon the Italian Renaissance ; but inasmuch as England was longer

Fig. 881.—
Rosette for Baluster.

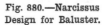

Fig. 880.—Narcissus
Design for Baluster.

Fig. 882.—Lion's Head
for Baluster.

than other countries in fully accepting the new style, it follows that the Elizabethan style is curiously composite. Later, in the Stuart phase of Renaissance development, staircases were sometimes simply fitted with turned balusters. In the Aston Hall staircase, note the distinct traces of Classic ornament in the Ionic volutes on the finials, and the scrolls on the newels and in the pierced balustrading. The strap ornamentation of the last named is typical of Elizabethan carved ornament. It is about the width of a leather strap and about the same thickness, on flat carved work, but assumes larger proportions in pierced carving, especially when in important positions. It is

Fig. 883.—Grand Staircase at Aston Hall, Birmingham.

(Photo: Frith & Co., Reigate.)

458

Fig. 884.—Staircase at Dunster Castle.

(Photo: Frith & Co., Reigate.)

interlaced, often in grotesque patterns, and on its surface are carved representations of nail heads and rivets, as if the strapwork was fastened with them. This is clearly discernible in Fig. 883. Sometimes, as at Aldermaston, in Berkshire, carved figures stood on the carved newels.

Staircase at Dunster Castle

As time went on, the newer influence became stronger and the ornament became more purely Renaissance, losing the simple strapwork, the flat scrolls, and stiff foliage that characterised the Elizabethan, and becoming more flowing in form, and much more florid in character. An example is to be found in the staircase at Dunster Castle (see Fig. 884). The details of the mouldings and the smaller carved bands are more refined in character. The ornament of the pierced balustrading is based upon the Roman scroll, terminating in a rosette. In the eighteenth century, festoons of fruit and flowers were largely used, tied with ribbons, as in the face of the terminal newel shown in Fig. 884. Notice, too, the egg and tongue and the bay leaf carved moulding, showing on the upper part of the staircase ; both exemplify the tremendous influence exerted by the Grecian and Roman styles through a period of 2,000 years—an influence, too, which is still active.

Flemish Eighteenth-century Newels

The eleven illustrations of Flemish eighteenth-century newels shown by Figs. 885 to 895 possess many interesting features. They clearly show the influence of that characteristically French development of the Renaissance known as " Rococo " on the sturdy, somewhat heavy, but always sound ornament of the sixteenth- and seventeenth-century Flemish style.

Newel surmounted by Ram's Head.— In Fig. 885, the leaf ornament and its manner of application, the hanging drapery, and the repeating band ornament above the scrolled leaf, are all reminiscent of French ornament of the eighteenth century ; but the head terminating the newel is typically Flemish.

Newel Carved with Large Floral Scrolls. —Tradition stands for much in the con-

tinuity of architecture and ornament, and the older mode of expression takes a long time to die out, under the influence of the incoming spirit of the newer ornament. Such is the case in this series of newels, and it is well illustrated in the one represented by Fig. 886. There are the details of the newer French influence, but they are arranged on a much more solid and heavy basis than the French would have employed. The oval arrangement of the scroll on the base is typical of the Louis XIV. style. The newel is carved with a rosette, pendant of laurel leaves, and large floral scrolls.

Turned Newel with Acorn Finial.—The newel in Fig. 887 is a fine example of carving applied to turned work. The guilloche pattern is a heritage of the ages before history began, coming down through Assyrian, Grecian, and Roman times, and, later, through the whole of the Renaissance. In this particular case it is a reminder of the Flemish sixteenth-century work. Notice how the turned member on which the guilloche is worked is bellied out to get the centre of the flower to project.

Newel surmounted by Bust.—The newel shown by Fig. 888 is square in section and tapered in elevation. The bust, although admirably done, is not very cleverly made to grow out of the newel. It is too suddenly applied, and a turned or shaped neck between the bust and the flat abacus would have lightened the effect. The newel is carved with a rosette, a pendant of leaves and berries, and a gadrooned oval boss.

Newels Carved with " Money " Ornament.—The newel shown by Fig. 889 illustrates the " Rococo " influence in the curved scroll, which is raised at its termination. The " money " ornament is interesting as showing what an effect can be obtained by the repetition of a single element which in itself possesses but little decorative interest or value. However, some difficulty is attached to the cutting of this ornament, extreme accuracy being necessary to give this pattern its full value. Fig. 890 illustrates a newel carved with " money " ornament, leaves and scrolls, above being the voluted end of the handrail.

Newel Carved with Rococo Ornament.— Fig. 891 shows the application of previous

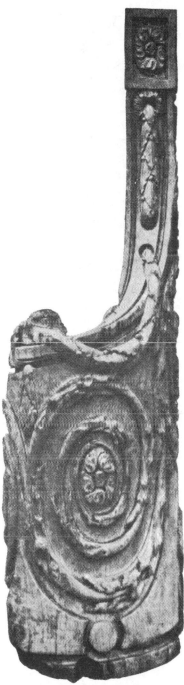

Fig. 885.—Newel with
Ram's Head.

Fig. 886.—Newel with Large
Floral Scrolls.

Fig. 887.—Turned Newel
with Acorn Finial.

Fig. 888.

Fig. 889.

Fig. 890.

Fig. 888.—Newel with Bust.

Figs. 889 and 890.—Newels carved with "Money" Ornament.

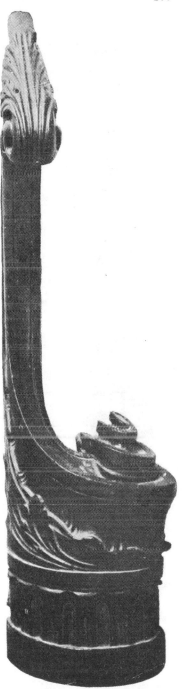

Fig. 891.—Newel with
Rococo Ornament.

Fig. 892.—Newel with
Lion's Head.

Fig. 893.—Newel with
Volute.

Fig. 894.—Newel with
Acorns and Volute.

Fig. 895.—Newel with Laurel
Leaf Pendant.

Fig. 896.—French Newel with
Vase Finial.

remarks concerning the influence of the French Rococo phase of Renaissance ornament on such a solid style as the Flemish. Here are French elements treated with the traditional heaviness of the Flemish craftsman, yet with his perfect mastery of the tool. In somewhat the same way did his English contemporaries work when the Renaissance was first introduced, the Gothic training of the wood carvers causing them to give a heavy, solid feeling to the lighter motifs of the Italian Renaissance.

Newel Carved with Lion's Head.—In Fig. 892 the scroll is given extreme prominence, and its parts are greatly increased. From the wood carver's point of view it is of interest, as it raises the question of whether these scrolls and other figures of a geometrical nature have been properly drawn out, or whether they are the product of the carver's "eye," or natural sense of symmetry of curve and judgment of proportion and balance. The latter is most generally the case, because, as a rule, the carver relies very little indeed upon rules and compasses. If he did, the work would partake too much of the mechanical; a freer treatment gives it life and strength, and, therefore, character.

Newel with Volute.—A point of interest in Fig. 893 is that the emphasis of eleva-tion given to each ring of the scroll shows the use of the gouge in cutting them. It might be, and often is, assumed that they are carved by vertical and horizontal cuts, meeting at a sharp angle. But the use of the gouge gives a softer finish, more in keeping with the work of a carving tool.

Newel Carved with Acorns and Volute. —Fig. 894 shows an oak newel carved with leaves, a bead moulding, pendant of oak leaves and acorns, and a volute.

Newel Carved with Pendant of Laurel Leaves.—The side of an oak newel shown by Fig. 895 is carved with a pendant of laurel leaves, a bead moulding, and leaf ornament, above being the voluted end of the handrail.

French Newel

An interesting feature of the newel shown by Fig. 896 is the added vase acting as the terminal ornament. This vase is of the classical type, dates from late in the eighteenth century, and is, most probably, the result of the opening up of the ruins of Herculaneum and Pompeii, an event which very largely influenced European ornament, both in architecture and furniture. The remainder of the newel shown dates from early in the eighteenth century, the finial dating from late in the same century.

CHIP CARVING

CHIP CARVING is a fascinating hobby, and by its means many useful articles can be decorated that are not suitable for any form of relief decoration. It has been said to belong to the childhood of the world, because it forms such a large part of the ornamental art of savage, or semi-savage, peoples.

columns. Chip carving, as an educational agent, emphasises the value of, and gives very great opportunities for, the development of accuracy and precision, whilst introducing the student gradually to the difficulties to be met with in cutting wood. A thorough and systematic course of the art

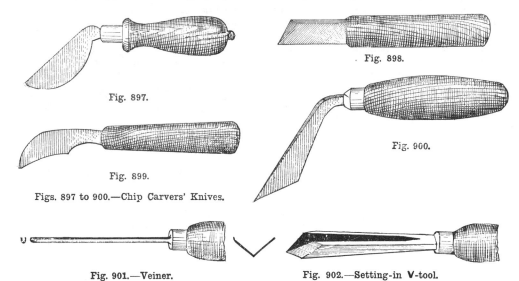

Fig. 897.

Fig. 898.

Fig. 899.

Fig. 900.

Figs. 897 to 900.—Chip Carvers' Knives.

Fig. 901.—Veiner.

Fig. 902.—Setting-in V-tool.

Weapons, oars, paddles, domestic utensils, spear handles, and similar articles may be seen in museums, belonging to these peoples, occurring in all ages, and spreading over a large area. It was introduced to the British Isles by the Scandinavians, and traces of it can be found in carvings in Norman churches, principally on the abacii and the capitals of

assists in laying a foundation for future work in the higher branches of relief carving.

Chip Carvers' Tools

Chip carving consists in forming designs by means of the chips that are taken out, leaving edges on the surface, which form the design. These chips are taken out in various ways. Some workers use a knife only; others use a setting-in tool, commonly known as a "skew chisel," and a veining tool only; others add to these a **V**-tool, or gouges. The shapes of the **V**-tools used vary, some workers

Knives

Figs. 897 to 900 show four kinds of knives, the first one being perhaps the most used, and giving surprising results in the hands of

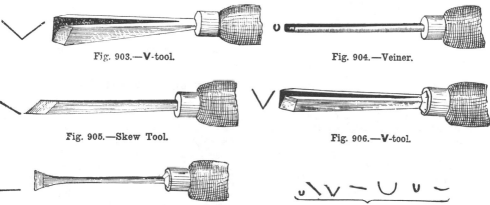

Fig. 903.—**V**-tool.

Fig. 904.—Veiner.

Fig. 905.—Skew Tool.

Fig. 906.—**V**-tool.

Fig. 907.—Straight Spade Tool.

Fig. 908.—Sections of Set of Seven Tools.

preferring wide and others narrow tools. Many chip carvers use an ordinary skew tool for setting-in, whilst others employ a **V**-tool with a long point. Figs. 897 to 908 show chip carving tools arranged in sets.

an expert craftsman. Fig. 909 shows it in use. Chip carving by this method consists of two operations only, setting-in and cutting out. The knife is shown in the act of cutting out after the setting-in operation. It is

Fig. 909.—Ordinary Chip Carving Knife in Use.

worked down to the setting-in cuts with a slicing motion. In chip carving, cut with the grain, and this is always possible when using the knife. Designs with large constituent parts may be executed with the knife;

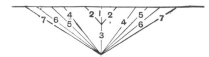

Fig. 910.—Diagram showing Successive Stages in Cutting Out Chips.

by taking the cuts down in stages, any depth may be obtained. In these wide pieces, the greatest difficulty is to get the surfaces sufficiently smooth and level.

Exercise with the Knife

In cutting the piece shown in Fig. 909, a cut is first made down the centre of the space. Then, holding the knife at an angle

enabling the last named to be taken to a greater depth—*see* No. 3 (Fig. 910). Then, holding the knife at a less angle than 45°, take off another chip on each side; then another, and as many more as are necessary to get a surface that extends from the lowest part of the central cut to the outermost limit of the element. Fig. 910 gives a section of this cut, showing the successive operations in executing it each cut being marked 1 to 7 respectively.

Veining and Setting-in Tools

Figs. 901 to 903 show a set of three tools which are in use in some parts of the country. They consist of a veiner and two wide V's (No. 45 in the Sheffield list). One of these V's is used as a V-tool; the other is ground to a long point, and is used for setting-in purposes. It is, in fact, a double "skew chisel." Veining cannot be done with the knife; it consists in going over

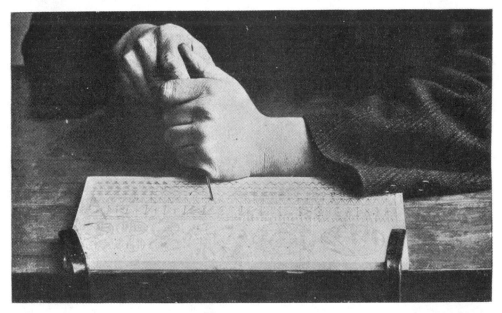

Fig. 911.—Use of Veiner in Chip Carving.

of about 45° to the surface of the wood, a small chip (No. 2 in Fig. 910) is taken off, the direction of the stroke being towards the first central cut. Then take off a similar chip on the other side of the central cut, thus

the lines of the design with the veining tool very lightly, in fact, just skimming the surface, with the result that all the upstanding ridges are traversed with a slight cut showing a double line, and dividing the sunk parts of the design from one another, as well as emphasising the actual outline of the design, which is, of course, formed by these upstanding parts. In carving with the knife, these ridges are taken to a sharp and well-defined edge. Fig. 911 shows the veining tool in use. The V-tool used for setting-in is now brought into use. It is held quite perpendicularly, and simply pressed in far in use, and clearly shows the method of holding the tool.

Advantages of the V-tool

The V-tool (shown in use by Fig. 913) is a great economiser of labour, as it represents at least three of the knife cuts at one stroke, and probably more. With the knife, three cuts have to be made—namely, the central

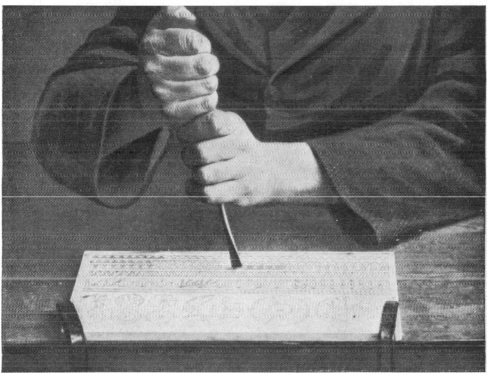

Fig. 912.—Use of Setting-in Tool in Chip Carving.

enough to make it extend to the limits of the element. This limits the depth to the actual ability of the tool, which is restricted to its size. It can be made with a longer or a shorter point, as may be desired , but, once having got it ground to a shape, this shape sets the gauge for the depth of the whole piece of work. It is also limited in cutting the width of the element; that is, each element of the design will be made of no greater width than this tool will cut at one stroke. Fig. 912 shows the setting-in tool cut and at least two side cuts ; these are all done at one stroke with the V-tool. One objection to its use is that, when cutting obliquely across the grain, one edge of the V-tool is always cutting against the grain, and great care must be exercised not to split the corners. A rough surface here and there can scarcely be avoided, unless a flat tool is used to go over these again from the other end of the cut. Nevertheless, because of the great economy of labour, and, with the smaller cuts the greater ease with which clean cutting can be obtained, the **V**-tool should be included in a representative chip carving set.

Useful Set of Four Tools

Figs. 904 to 907 show a set of tools which are largely used, it consisting of a veiner, skew tool, **V**-tool, and a straight spade tool about $\frac{1}{4}$ in. or $\frac{3}{8}$ in. wide. Each tool repre-

sidered either as a complete set or as a basis for the addition of supplementary tools. The difference between this set and the last-mentioned set is that the setting-in tool is a single skew tool, instead of a double skew, otherwise a **V**-tool; also there is added a straight tool to cut, or to smooth, any surface that the **V**-tool cannot successfully manage. The advantage of a single skew

Fig. 913.—Use of **V**-tool in Chip Carving.

sents one particular and distinctive operation, and the set as a whole represents the four essential processes in chip carving. These processes are : (1) Veining, done by the veiner ; (2) setting-in, done by the "skew" tool ; (3) **V**-tool work, done by the **V**-tool ; and (4) cleaning off, done by the straight tool. The whole craft of chip carving practically consists of these processes, and, to an experienced worker, the tools mentioned appear to be the best, con-

is that any depth, width, or angle of cut can be made. But this is not so when using a double skew tool. The veining, setting-in, and **V**-tool work are illustrated in Figs. 911 to 913. The cleaning-off process does not need illustration. This set may be added to, and the scope of chip carving very much extended, by the use of gouges, both flat and narrow, and by the addition of straight tools of greater width, to deal with particularly large surfaces.

Fig. 914.—" Scaling " in Chip Carving.

Fig. 915.—
Chip Carving Design
for Execution with
Knife.

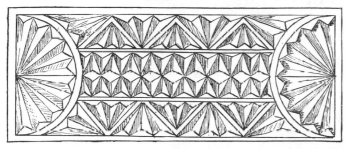

Fig. 916.—
Chip Carving Design
for Execution with
Veiner and **V**-tools.

Fig. 917.—
Chip Carving Design
for Execution with
Veiner, Skew Tool,
V-tool, etc.

Fig. 918.—
Chip Carving Design
for Execution with
Gouges and Other
Tools.

A Seven-tool Set

Fig. 908 shows the outline of a set of seven tools, consisting of the four just mentioned (Figs. 904 to 907), with the addition of three gouges, one of which is of the quick, deep kind known as a "fluter." With these, circular cutting can be introduced with much effect, and the scaling (Fig. 914), peculiar to some kinds of Scandinavian carving, can be done. Circular studs, or beads, can be left in the centre, between two abutting cuts instead of the square- or diamond-shaped piece usually left in;

Punches

In addition to the above tools, various forms of punches are often used to obtain a matted surface, which can be made to form a very pleasing contrast to the remainder of the work. The ordinary single or four- or eight-pointed punches are the most suitable. Fancy-shaped punches should be avoided.

Shallow Reilef in Designs

The introduction of a slight amount of shallow relief, in the shape of a monogram, or some such piece of work, is often of dis-

Fig. 919.—Floral Chip Carving Design.

or rows of these beads may be formed as borders. In addition, a form of carving, illustrated later in Fig. 918, and resembling incised relief carving, can be executed.

Practice Designs

Designs suitable for execution by the various sets of tools described above are given in Figs. 915 to 918. Fig. 915 is suitable for the knife, and Fig. 916 for execution by the three tools shown in Figs. 901 to 903. Fig. 917 can be more easily carved by the set of four tools shown in Figs. 904 to 907, whilst Fig. 918 is especially suitable for cutting by means of the set which contains the gouges (see Fig. 908).

tinct advantage to the general effect. But, as a rule, the combining of the two styles should be strictly avoided. Most of the designs used for chip carving are of a geometrical type, as in Figs. 915 to 917. But they need not be necessarily confined to this type, although much can be said against the use of the floral kind of design (see Fig. 919).

Geometrical Drawing

A fair knowledge of geometrical drawing is essential to the setting out of a design for chip carving; but such knowledge must be gained outside the pages of this book, there being no space available here in which to deal adequately with such a subject.

EXAMPLES OF CHIP CARVING

Ornamenting Edge of Bookshelf

CHIP CARVING decoration suitable to the edge of a bookcase shelf is shown by Fig. 920. This is essentially a horizontal treatment. Fig. 920 is very simple, and does not require much explanation as to its setting out; the line round the semicircles is marked in with the veiner. The student, of course, must fit in the pattern to the length of the shelf. This is easily done by finding the centre of the shelf. Supposing the shelf to

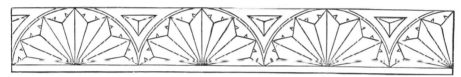

Fig. 920.—Chip Carved Edge of Bookshelf.

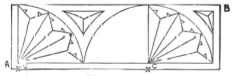

Fig. 921.

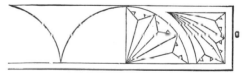

Fig. 922.

Figs. 921 and 922.—Methods of Setting Out Fig. 920.

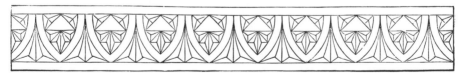

Fig. 923.—Another Design for Edge of Bookshelf.

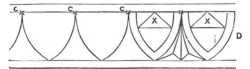

Fig. 924.—Method of Setting Out Fig. 923.

be 2 ft. in length, the centre line would be 1 ft. from either end. On this line will fall the centre of the semicircle; then describe the others on both sides until about ½ in.

from the end; and if there is no room to finish with a semicircle, as at B in Fig. 921, or with the quarter as at A, the space must be filled up with what are known by chip carvers as "fans," which can be made to fill any sized space, as at C (Fig. 922). The small triangular spaces are left in the surface of the wood, with little nicks cut out on each side. Fig. 923 is set out as in Fig. 924, the triangles x x being left solid. All that has been said about starting from the

Fig. 927.—Chip Carving Design for Box End.

centre of the shelf and finishing at its ends applies equally to this pattern. Both these patterns would look just as well reversed. Fig. 925 shows a decoration suitable to a vertical treatment, though it may also be used horizontally. For the skeleton or working lines, see Fig. 926. It will be better to start the setting out from the end instead of the centre, and to make the last fan either slightly longer or shorter than the others, if the space needs it. With c as centre, describe the quarter-circles and insert points

Fig. 925. 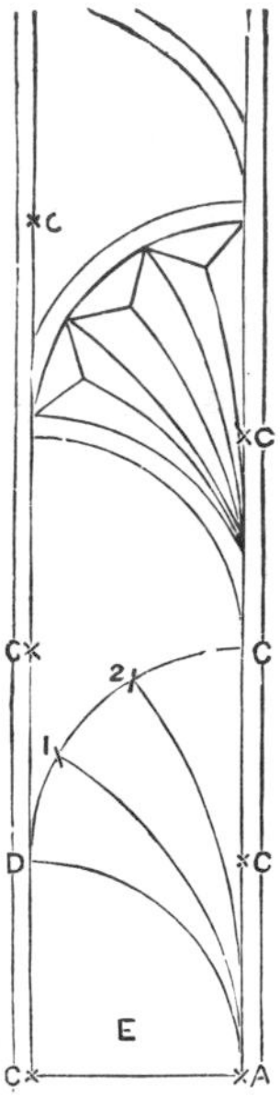   Fig. 926.

Figs. 925 and 926.—Chip Carved Vertical Edge of Bookshelves.

Fig. 28.—Half Design for Box Front.

1 and 2. The lines must then be drawn in freehand or with French curve from these points to their meeting-point A. In this

and lower triangles are solid, and the centre one is sloped towards them, leaving two ridges. No. 2 has only one ridge in the

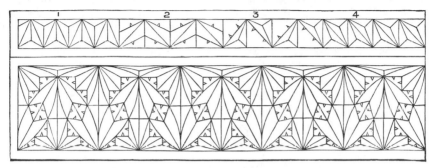

Fig. 929.—Another Half Design for Box Front.

pattern the small triangles may be left solid with the little "nicks" taken out of the side, or else cut into pockets as shown in the pattern.

Boxes: Chip-carved

Fig. 927 shows the end of a box. The pattern should be started from the centre lines of the box—namely, A B and C D, and the circles should be divided into six parts. Fig. 928 shows the long side of a box. Patterns 1, 2, 3 on the border of the lid show three different patterns which are all set out on the same lines. In No. 1, the upper

Fig. 930.—Design for Box End in Chip Carving.

Fig. 931.—Half Design for Box Top.

centre. In No. 3 the squares in the centre are solid, and the upper and lower sets of triangles sloped down to them. In setting out the pattern on the side, start from the centre of the box. Fig. 929 shows a treatment for the front of a box where no plain bands are left. The setting out does not need explanation, being simply a series of semicircles interlacing with little solid triangles and squares. Fig. 930 is another design for the end of a long box, or for all the sides of a small box. One half is left without detail, and shows the way to set out the pattern. In Figs. 931 and 932, which

top of the box. Fig. 935 shows the setting out of the quatrefoil, the half of which is shown to the extreme left in Fig. 931, and Fig. 936 the setting out of the decagon or double pentagon shown in the complete circle to the right of Fig. 931. Both the quatrefoil and the pentagon or decagon have plain bands; but the bands of the quatrefoil are left without any marking whatever, and those of the pentagonal design have a vein or line running along the centre of the bands, and taken out with the veining tool.

Setting Out the Patterns.— In these elab-

Fig. 932.—Another Half Design for Box Top.

show decorative work in chip carving for the tops of boxes, two methods of treatment are illustrated; that in Fig. 931 has plain bands, whilst that in Fig. 932 is without any bands at all. They are both somewhat elaborate, and so in Figs. 933 to 936 are shown the best methods of setting out the principal parts of the design. Fig. 933 is founded on an octagon or eight-sided figure, and exhibits the ornamentation of the circle to the left in Fig. 932. Fig. 934 is based on a hexagon (six-sided), or on a dodecagon (twelve-sided) figure, and shows the principle of setting out the ornamentation of the semicircle to the extreme right in Fig. 932, which, indeed, when repeated, would form the central part of the whole design for the

orate patterns, after ruling the centre lines on the boxes themselves, it will be well to set out the patterns on paper, as in the case of the pentagon here shown; the centres of some of the arcs come far from the figure itself, and cannot be found on the box. Now measure off the points required from the paper on to the wood, and trace the curves, as A B, from centre C in lower right hand corner of Fig. 936, on to a little piece of tracing paper with a black pencil, and then, reversing the paper so as to get the pencil side on the wood, go very carefully over the curves with a pointer or tracer; but, whenever possible, get the centres on the wood so as to do the arcs with compasses. The star in the centre of the pentagon is a decagon or ten-pointed one, obtained by dividing the pentagonal divisions into two.

Paper-knife Handles

Figs. 937 and 938 are paper-knife handles, which would look very well if worked to

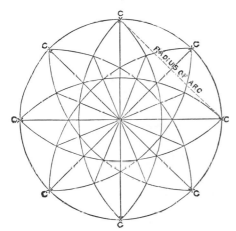

Fig. 933.—Setting Out Octagon (see Fig. 932).

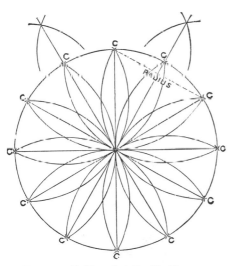

Fig. 934.—Setting Out Double Hexagon (see Fig. 932).

a larger scale. The first is quite simple, and needs no explanation; and the second, also, though it looks more elaborate, is easily set out.

Photograph Frames

Three designs of frames are presented by Figs. 939 to 942. In Fig. 940, which is a

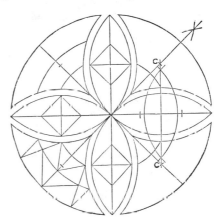

Fig. 935.—Setting Out Quatrefoil (see Fig. 931).

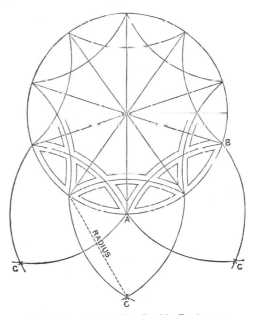

Fig. 936.—Setting Out Double Pentagon (see Fig. 931).

cross-section through the centre of Fig. 939, is shown a method of putting these frames together which prevents warping or splitting, and which also gives a rebate in which to

Fig. 937.

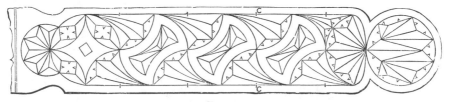

Fig. 938.

Figs. 937 and 938.—Paper Knife Handles.

Fig. 939.

Fig. 940.

Figs. 939 and 940.—Elevation and Section of Photograph Frame having Rectangular Opening.

place the photograph, glass, etc., with little trouble. Each frame is made of two layers of panel glued together, and crossing each other in grain, the opening in the back one being cut larger than that in the front one.

Bellows

It has already been pointed out (*see* p. 205) that a bellows side, made of cheap white wood, is an excellent thing for the beginner

nut. The carving is shown enlarged in Figs. 945 to 948. The following is the method of the construction. The sides and ends should first be prepared and gauged down to 4 in. wide. They are dovetailed together. The top overhangs the sides and ends $\frac{1}{2}$ in., and is made up in three pieces. The centre piece is $1\frac{1}{2}$ in. wide, and is fixed to the top edge of the sides with a screw from the top as shown at Fig. 949 ; the end

Fig. 941.—Star or Diamond Photograph Frame.

to carve. A design is now presented (*see* Fig. 943) for a bellows side in chip carving.

Cigar Box

The chip-carved cigar box illustrated by Fig. 944 is 8 in. long over the ends, 6 in. wide over the sides, and 5 in. deep over the top and bottom. It stands on four small turned feet, and has a handle at the top. The top is made up in three pieces, the end pieces open, being hinged to the centre piece, which is fixed to the sides, and to which the handle is fixed. Smooth, straight-grained wood $\frac{1}{2}$ in. thick, which will not need staining, should be used, preferably oak or wal-

pieces of the top are hinged to the centre piece with 1-in. brass butt hinges. The handle extends the whole width of the box, the ends covering the heads of the screws which fix the centre piece of the top. The handle is fixed with screws from underneath, as shown at Fig. 949. A partition may be fitted to the inside of the box, dividing it into two equal portions ; it should be of wood $\frac{1}{4}$ in. thick **V**-grooved into the sides. The bottom overhangs the sides and ends the same distance as the top, and is fixed with screws from underneath. The small turned feet on which the box stands are $\frac{1}{2}$ in. deep by $\frac{3}{4}$ in. in diameter, fixed to the bottom as shown in Fig. 950. The box should first be fixed together temporarily, and then taken apart for carving. The edges of the top and bottom are moulded as shown in Fig. 944.

Casket

The shrine shape, a form in which numberless chests and caskets were made in the Middle Ages, is one in which chip carving can be shown to advantage. The casket illustrated by Fig. 951 is 11 in. long by 7 in. wide, and 6 in. high in the sides, above which the gabled lid rises $2\frac{3}{4}$ in. The height is

Fig. 942.—Round Photograph Frame.

further increased $\frac{3}{4}$ in. by the feet on which it stands. It opens along the ridge, the lids falling in two flaps. Prepared panel of some hard, smooth-grained wood which will not need staining is recommended for its construction. It is fixed together with screws, and those that show should be round-headed brass ones. From the general view (Fig. 951) it will be seen that the chief ornamentation of the sides and ends is diaper-work, and these panels are shown enlarged by Figs. 952 and 953. In the ends the diaper is precisely the same as in the central panels of the sides (Fig. 952), only that here the panels are of double width. Fig. 954 shows a portion of the running

border above the panels of the sides, the line x x being the centre of this border. The smaller zig-zag border which runs below and between the panels and at their ends is similar to that which appears at the ends of the flap in Fig. 955. This same zig-zag is also used below and at the sides of the end panels. The larger border which runs between the panel of the end and the tympanum is shown at full length in Fig. 956 ;

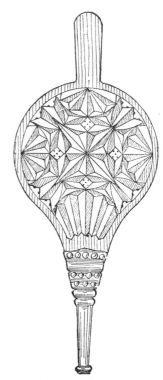

Fig. 943.—Bellows.

the carving of the tympanum above it is shown in Fig. 957.

Constructing the Casket.—Fig. 955 shows a part of one flap of the lids, the centre being marked by the line Y Y. These flaps fold and lock together at the ridge, and are hinged to the sides. As they are of $\frac{1}{4}$-in. panel only, they should be strengthened near their ends with ledgers. These may be of the same thickness as the flaps, and from 1 in. to $1\frac{1}{4}$ in. wide. In the section (Fig. 958) where they are marked A they are shown inside the flaps, from the ends of which they should be $\frac{3}{8}$ in. distant. Like the edges of the flap, their ends must be splayed off to the angle required to fit the edges of the side pieces and of the opposite flap. They are fixed in position with screws. It may be thought that a better effect will result from keeping these ledgers outside the flaps, in which case the carving of the zig-zag border

the grain running vertically. These pieces should be fixed to the bottom with brass round-headed screws, and the side pieces should be fastened in like manner to the bottom and to the ends. The side pieces, which are of $\frac{1}{4}$-in. panel, measure 11 in. by 6 in. The feet are cut from 2-in. squares of $\frac{3}{4}$-in. stuff as is seen in Figs. 959 and 960. Each foot is fixed to the bottom with two

Fig. 944.—Cigar Box.

Fig. 948.—
Half of Cigar Box
Handle.

Fig. 947.—Half of Cigar
Box Top or Cover.

Fig. 945.—Half of Cigar Box
Side.

Fig. 946.—Half of Cigar
Box End.

Fig. 949.—
Fixing Cigar
Box Handle.

Fig. 950.—
Fixing Cigar
Box Feet.

will be on the ledger and not on the flap. If placed outside, the ledgers should not reach the edges of the flap at each end by $\frac{3}{4}$ in., and they should be fixed on with round-headed brass screws; $\frac{1}{2}$-in. stuff should be used for the bottom of the casket. This is $10\frac{1}{4}$ in. long by $6\frac{1}{2}$ in. wide. The two ends are of $\frac{3}{8}$-in. panel, $6\frac{1}{2}$ in. wide ; at their sides they are 6 in. high, whilst to form the gables they are $2\frac{1}{2}$ in. higher. If the wood from which they are cut should be so loose in its grain as to suggest any danger of splitting, it will be best to cut them with

screws, and projects $\frac{3}{4}$ in. beyond the sides and ends. The inside of the casket can be fitted to meet requirements, but a good ordinary arrangement might be as shown in the cross section (Fig. 958). There is a well at the bottom $2\frac{1}{2}$ in. deep, and above this and resting on the slips B, which are fixed to the side pieces, are two short trays measuring externally $1\frac{3}{4}$ in. deep, $5\frac{1}{4}$ in. long, and $6\frac{1}{2}$ in. wide. On these rests a single tray $10\frac{1}{4}$ in. long and $6\frac{1}{2}$ in. wide, the sides being $1\frac{1}{4}$ in. high, whilst the ends and a middle partition rise to within $2\frac{7}{8}$ in. of the gable, as

shown at c. The trays should be of prepared panel of the same wood as the casket,
the ends and middle partition being $\frac{1}{4}$ in.
thick, and the sides and bottoms $\frac{3}{16}$ in.
thick. The best way of fastening them
together is with small screws.

Fig. 951.—Casket.

7 in., excluding the ornamental projections.
Fig. 962 shows the top, Fig. 963 being a

Fig. 952.   Fig. 953.

Figs. 952 and 953.—Middle and Outer Panels
of Side of Casket.

Fig. 954.—Border above Side Panels of
Casket.

Fig. 956.—Border above End Panel of
Casket.

Fig. 955.—Lid Flap of Casket.

Trinket Casket

Fig. 961 is the front elevation of a casket
which will form an elaborate subject for the
chip-carver's art. It stands 6 in. high, and
has an outside measurement of 11 in. by
longitudinal section through the centre.
The material should be solid panel of any
smooth-grained hardwood. The more important pieces—the top and bottom, the
front, back, and ends—are of $\frac{3}{4}$-in. stuff; the
carved ledger-strips, which form a marked

feature in the decoration, are of $\frac{1}{4}$-in. stuff; while both $\frac{1}{4}$-in. stuff and $\frac{3}{16}$-in. panel are used in the interior fittings. The construction is arranged for simply screwing together, so that only ordinary skill and care are required to make the casket, the material being of such thicknesses as may be bought ready planed. The bottom A (Fig. 963) is a plain piece of the thicker panel, $11\frac{3}{4}$ in. by $7\frac{3}{4}$ in.; its upper edges are rounded off as shown. The front and back pieces are of the same material, 11 in. by $4\frac{1}{4}$ in. The back is left quite plain. The design for the front is shown on a working scale in Fig. 961; in this figure A B marks the centre, the design

of the casket; the dotted lines at B B (Fig. 963) indicate the projection of the end strips. If it is desired to hide the mode of attachment, they may be fixed by screws driven from within; but if small round-headed brass screws are used outside, they will be ornamental rather than otherwise. A screw might be driven through each of the four quatrefoils down the central line of the strip. The lid (Fig. 962) is $11\frac{3}{4}$ in. long by $7\frac{3}{4}$ in. wide; it overlaps the ends and front by $\frac{3}{8}$ in., but behind it comes flush with the back piece. Its upper edges are rounded off equally all round. The lid has two ledger-strips, 7 in. by $1\frac{1}{2}$ in., which are

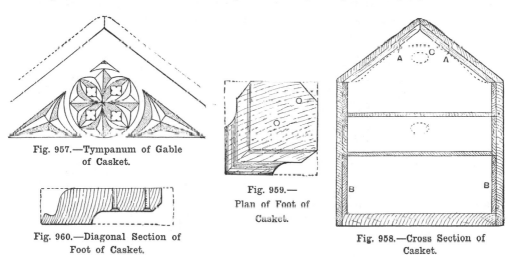

Fig. 957.—Tympanum of Gable of Casket.

Fig. 959.— Plan of Foot of Casket.

Fig. 960.—Diagonal Section of Foot of Casket.

Fig. 958.—Cross Section of Casket.

on each side of the line being the same. The end pieces, which are of panel of the same height and thickness, are $6\frac{1}{4}$ in. long. The pattern carved upon them is the same as the central portion of the front, between C D and E F (Fig. 961). All four pieces are fixed to the bottom by screws driven from underneath, while the corners are fastened together by screws driven through the front and back into the ends. The heads of the screws in the front will not show, as they will be hidden by the ledger-strips. These strips, of which there are two on the front and two at each end, are of $\frac{1}{4}$-in. panel, $1\frac{1}{4}$ in. wide by $4\frac{1}{4}$ in. long. Their outer edges are lightly rounded off. When fixed, their outside edges will come flush with the corners

both useful and ornamental, as they prevent warping. They differ from those below in being carved to another pattern, and in being wider by $\frac{1}{4}$ in. They are fixed 2 in. from the ends of the lid, as shown in section at C (Fig. 963). The feet D are cut from $\frac{3}{4}$-in. board, a square of $1\frac{1}{4}$ in. being needed for each. They are screwed to the bottom. The arrangement of the inside fitting is a matter of individual taste. In Fig. 963 is shown a single tray having a cross division in its middle, with a finger-hole E for lifting out. The bottom and sides of the tray are of $\frac{3}{16}$-in. panel, and the ends and partition of $\frac{1}{4}$-in. stuff, which is also used for the middle partition F of the well, and for the lining G on which the tray rests at each end. Figs.

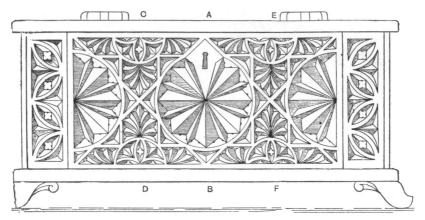

Fig. 961.—Front Elevation of Trinket Casket.

Fig. 962.—Top of Trinket Casket.

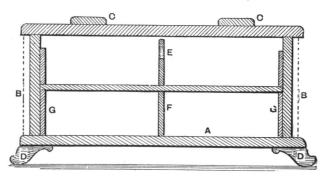

Fig. 963.—Longitudinal Section of Trinket Casket.

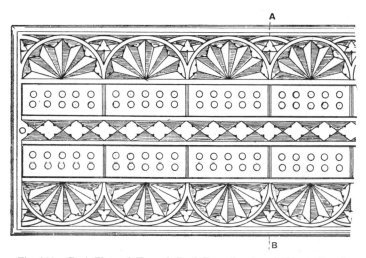

Fig. 964.—Part Plan of Top of Card Box, showing Cribbage Board.

Fig. 965.—Part Side Elevation of
Card Box.

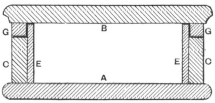

Fig. 966.—Section of Card Box on
Line A B (Figs. 964 and 965).

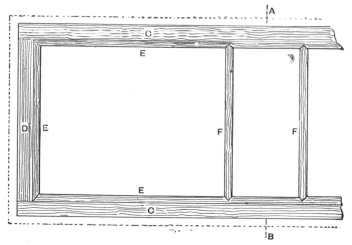

Fig. 967.—Horizontal Section of Card Box.

961 and 962 are reproduced to a scale of one-third full size, and Fig. 963 one-quarter full size.

Playing=card Box with Cribbage Board

The material to be used for the playing-card box shown in part by Figs. 964 and 965 will be solid panel of some smooth and firm-grained wood suitable for chip carving.

section through the central line A B (Figs. 964 and 965), and Fig. 967 a horizontal section through the middle of the box. The bottom and lid, A and B (Fig. 966), $10\frac{3}{4}$ in. long by $4\frac{3}{8}$ in. wide, are each formed of a piece of the thicker panel. The lid, as will be seen from Fig. 964, forms the cribbage board. The sides c (Figs. 966 and 967) are also of the thicker panel, $10\frac{1}{3}$ in. long by 1 in. wide. The ends D (Fig. 967) are of the

Fig. 968.—Front Elevation of Corner Cupboard.

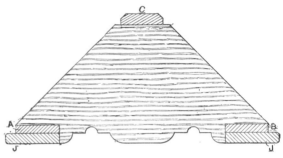

Fig. 969.—Section of Corner Cupboard at Foot Shelf.

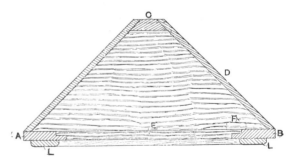

Fig. 970.—Section of Corner Cupboard at Bottom of Lower Cupboard.

Two thicknesses will be needed : $\frac{3}{8}$-in. panel for the top, bottom, sides, and ends, and $\frac{3}{16}$-in. for the lining and partitions, both slightly planed down. Many East Indian tea chests are made of a kind of cedar admirably adapted in both grain and colour for this class of work ; the thin boards can be easily planed down to the required thickness. The box is made of a length to hold two packs of cards, with a smaller compartment between them. Fig. 966 is a vertical

same thickness and width, and, if it is intended to dovetail the corners, 4 in. long. Dovetailing, however, is not necessary ; and, being rather difficult, a simpler method may be adopted. The ends are cut $3\frac{1}{3}$ in. long, and merely screwed together at the corners with a couple of brass screws. This must be done neatly, and the holes for the screws countersunk to bring the heads just flush with the surface. The bottom is fixed to the sides and ends with ordinary screws driven from below ; the holes for these will need to be rather more deeply countersunk, to prevent the box scratching any polished surface on which it may be placed. The lining E (Figs. 966 and 967) is of the thinner panel, and is $1\frac{1}{4}$ in. wide. The corners are mitered, and the whole glued inside the box. The partitions F (Fig. 967) are of the same thickness and width, and are glued, as shown, into V-shaped grooves in the lining, thus forming a handy compartment for cribbage

wide. These strips should be strongly screwed to the top. Although the cribbage board can be used whilst on the box, it may be taken off and used on the lower level if desired. The hollow moulding round the under edges of the top may be easily struck out with a gouge.

Corner Cupboard

The corner cupboard shown by Fig. 968 is so arranged that its constructional parts

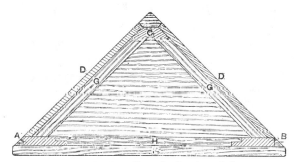

Fig. 971.—Section through Cornice of Corner Cupboard.

Fig. 972.—Cornice of Corner Cupboard.

Fig. 974.—Lower Door of Corner Cupboard.

Fig. 973.—Side Strip of Corner Cupboard.

pegs, whist markers, counters, etc. The chip carving on the sides of the box is illustrated by Fig. 965 ; the pattern on the ends will be the same, but there will be room for only one whole rosette and two halves. The pattern of the top, as regards the chip carving, is one easily set out. The dark lines which surround the different groups of cribbage holes are merely incised, being struck out with the dividing-tool. The small strips G (Fig. 966), which run beneath the top, and which close over the lining when the box is shut, are of the thicker panel, $\frac{1}{4}$ in.

can be put together independently of those which are ornamental, so that the carving can be executed at leisure, and screwed on afterwards. The pieces to be carved are also of small and handy sizes, except the two side strips, which, if desired, can be sawn in two, and the halves worked separately. The material recommended is pine, to be stained to a dark brown, or ebonised. The cupboard stands on three legs A, B, and C (Figs. 969 to 971) ; these are 5 ft. $5\frac{1}{2}$ in. long and 4 in. wide. The front ones, A and B, are of $\frac{3}{4}$-in. board, but the back one, C, is of 1-in. stuff.

The space between the two front ones is 16 in., which gives a width to the cupboard front of 2 ft. The legs are held together by being screwed to the half-dozen triangular pieces which come between them. The lowest of these, the foot shelf, is shown in plan by Fig. 969. It is of ¾-in. board, placed with

board, but they measure only 9½ in. from back to front—*see* Fig. 970, which is a section through the bottom of the lower cupboard. The floor of the cupboard above is just the same. The back-boarding is lettered D; E is the lower front cross strip, which is 3 in. wide, and has its ends, which are halved,

Fig. 975.—Locker-stool.

Fig. 978.—
Border round Top of
Locker-stool.

Fig. 979.—
Top Centre Ornament for
Locker-stool.

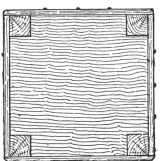

Fig. 976.—Section above Bottom of
Locker-stool.

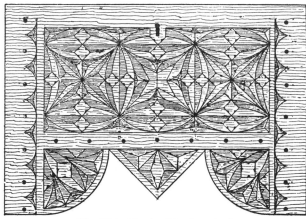

Fig. 977.—Front of Locker-stool.

its upper surface 3 in. from the ground. As there is no back-boarding to this lower part, the shelf goes back to the wall between A C and B C, and projects farther in front than the others by ¾ in. Its depth from back to front is 11 in.; its front edge is shaped ornamentally, whilst the fronts of the others are plain. The floors of the upper and lower cupboards and the shelves are also of ¾-in.

let and screwed into the backs of the legs A and B. In front, it comes flush with them. The upper edge of this strip is 19½ in. above the ground line, the upper surface of the cupboard floor being ½ in. higher; a sufficient ledge is thus given against which the bottom of the door closes. To give a similar bearing for the front edge of the door, a strip is screwed against the inner side of the leg B;

the place of this strip is indicated by the dotted lines at F (Fig. 970). The shelf of this lower cupboard is 12 in. above its floor. The cross strip between the lower and upper doors is only 1½ in. wide, otherwise it is the same as that below. The shelf in this upper cupboard is 10 in. above its floor. The doorway is surmounted by a cross strip H (Fig. 971), 5½ in. wide, the top of which comes level with the tops of the legs ; it is fixed in place like the others. The ½-in. back-boarding D (Fig. 970) is 15 in. wide, and 3 ft. 10¼ in. long on each side. The pieces reach from the level of the tops of the legs to that of the bottom of the lower cupboard floorpiece. They are screwed to the various triangular pieces and to the legs, the back leg being cut away on either side to receive them. Fig. 971 is a plan of the under side of the top. For this, ½-in. board serves ; it should measure 13½ in. from back to front. Along the top of each back board is screwed a 1-in. square strip of wood G (Fig. 971), to which the top is screwed, as well as to the legs and cross strip H. From Fig. 968 it will be seen that the lower part has a front casing which forms a plinth 18 in. high ; parts of it are shown in section at J (Fig. 969). It is of ¾-in. board and in three pieces. The large horizontal one, in which the ornamental arch is cut, is 25 in. by 9 in., and is screwed to the legs and lower cross strip. The two smaller pieces are 9 in. by 4¾ in. ; they are screwed upon the legs. This, except the doors, completes the carcase, and thus far no carved part has been introduced. Of the ornamental work, the cornice (Fig. 972) and K (Fig. 971) is of ¾ in. board, 25½ in. long by 6 in. wide, its lower edge being chamfered off for ½ in. When fixed, its top comes flush with the top of the cupboard. The side strip (Fig. 973) and L (Fig. 970) are of ½-in. board, 2½ in. wide and 3 ft. 6 in. long. They are, when carved, fixed down the middles of the front legs ; round-headed screws should be used for the fixing, black if the work is ebonised, and brass if it is brown. The upper door is 18 in. high by 16 in. wide ; it has a glass panel, the upper cupboard being intended for bric-à-brac. Its frame is made of two layers of strips, 2 in. wide. The inner layer is of ¾-in. board, its cross rails are 16 in. long, and its upright stiles 14 in. Round their

inner front edges is worked a ¼-in. rebate to hold the glass, which is put in with a little putty, and held in place by the outer layer. The glass is 14½ in. by 12½ in. The outer and carved strips are of ½-in. wood, the rails being 12 in. long and the stiles 18 in. ; the two layers, which thus cross at corners, are screwed together. The lower door, shown on a larger scale in Fig. 974, is 21 in. by 16 in. In this is an inner layer of ¾-in. board of the above dimensions, the grain lying horizontally. The outer layer is of 2 in. strips, ½ in. thick, the stiles running the whole height (21 in.). This door is further strengthened by the diamond-shaped centre piece, in which also the grain is perpendicular.

Locker=stool

The locker-stool illustrated by Figs. 975 and 976 has legs which are 18 in. long and 2 in. square at the top, their inner sides being tapered down to 1¼ in., the taper beginning 7 in. from the top. The four side pieces (see Fig. 977) are screwed to the legs as shown in Fig. 976 ; they are of ½-in. board, 9¾ in. wide, the front and back ones being 14 in. long, the end ones 13 in., owing to overlapping ; as the corners are rounded this will be found better than mitre joints. Four screws are used at each end, the intervening dots (see Figs. 975 and 977) being simply holes slightly sunk with a small gouge to complete the pattern. The carving will, of course, be done on these pieces before they are finally fixed, but it will be better to put them temporarily in position with screws to see that they fit before beginning to carve. For the permanent fixing, use roundheaded screws, either brass or black, as they will be an ornamental feature. The locker is 6 in. deep. The section (Fig. 976) is taken immediately above the piece forming the bottom ; ¾-in. board, 13 in. by 13 in., is used for this, 2-in. openings being cut at the corners for the legs. It is fixed in place by three screws driven into it through each sidepiece (see Fig. 975). Lastly, the top or lid is of ¾-in. board, 16 in. by 15 in. The details of its ornament are shown in Figs. 978 and 979, the former being the border ornament and the latter the centre ornament. If pine or other easily-splitting wood is used, it will be well to screw upon its under side two small ledgers, $\frac{1}{2}$ in. thick, $\frac{3}{4}$ in. wide, and 14 in. long, placing them so as to fall just outside the side-pieces; these will not only be a precaution against splitting or warping, but will also help to exclude dust from the locker. The top is hinged to the back side-

1 in. thick, 10 in. wide, and 4 ft. 6 in. long. This can be covered with cloth or velvet, with a deep fringe to hide the stonework beneath. The height and width of the overmantel are both 4 ft. In the centre is a looking-glass 1 ft. 8 in. by 1 ft. 3 in. It

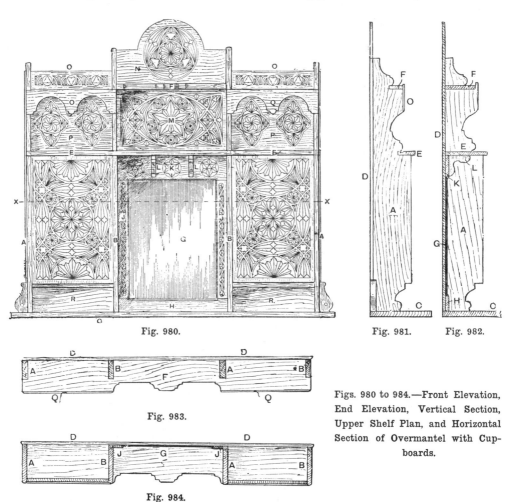

Fig. 980.

Fig. 981.   Fig. 982.

Fig. 983.

Fig. 984.

Figs. 980 to 984.—Front Elevation, End Elevation, Vertical Section, Upper Shelf Plan, and Horizontal Section of Overmantel with Cupboards.

piece and fitted to the front one with a lock, the pattern being arranged to give a place for the keyhole.

Overmantel with Cupboards

For the chip-carved overmantel, illustrated by Figs. 980 to 984, the mantelboard can consist of a plain piece of deal board about

has two shelves respectively 7 in. and 5 in. wide for bric-à-brac, and beneath the lower and wider shelf are two shallow cupboards. The material may be pine or any smooth-working wood suited for chip carving. The parts to be carved, including the upper half of the backboard, should be selected free from knots. The overmantel is supported and held together by the uprights A and B (Fig. 980), which stand on the mantelboard C, to which, however, they are dowelled, so that the overmantel can be taken down without disturbing the mantelboard C, which must be firmly fixed in position before the overmantel is set on it. These uprights are of $\frac{3}{4}$-in. wood, $6\frac{1}{2}$ in. wide; the two outer

shelves are $\frac{5}{8}$ in. thick when planed down; the upper one F is ornamentally shaped in its middle part, as shown in Fig. 983. Figs. 981 and 983 show how the shelf is cut so that the front half of it rests on the uprights, to which it is screwed down; behind it is fixed with screws driven into it through the backboard. The lower and wider shelf E is fixed

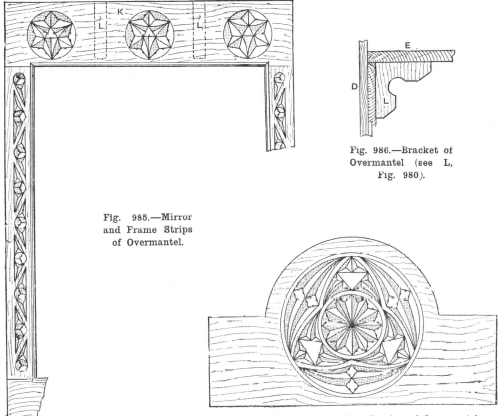

Fig. 985.—Mirror and Frame Strips of Overmantel.

Fig. 986.—Bracket of Overmantel (see L, Fig. 980).

Fig. 987.—Central Top Chip Carving of Overmantel.

ones A are 3 ft. 6 in. high, and the inner ones B 3 ft. $7\frac{1}{2}$ in. high. To these is screwed the backboard D, which is of $\frac{1}{2}$-in. stuff, 4 ft. high; its length is 4 ft. $0\frac{1}{2}$ in., as its ends project $\frac{1}{4}$ in. beyond the upright, where they have their front edges rounded off. The lengths which form the backboard are placed horizontally, and must be neatly jointed, since above the shelf E the greater part of their surface will be carved. The two

in the same manner. The central division of the overmantel is 1 ft. 6 in. from upright to upright, and the lower panel, containing the mirror G, is 2 ft. 2 in. high. The glass is 1 ft. 8 in. by 1 ft. 3 in., and at sight is, when fixed, 1 ft. $7\frac{1}{2}$ in. by 1 ft. $2\frac{1}{2}$ in. It is held in position by strips of $\frac{1}{2}$-in. board, on the inner edges of which $\frac{1}{4}$-in. rebates are worked to receive the glass; they are secured with small screws driven into them through the backboard. The vertical and horizontal sections (Figs. 982 and 984) show the arrangement. The bottom strip H is 2½ in. wide, and is left plain ; an enlarged detail of this panel is shown by Fig. 985. The side strips J are 1¾ in. wide, and have each a narrow line of carving. The top strip K is 4 in. wide, and fixed on it are two brackets L to support the shelf above. One of these is shown separately in Fig. 986. The brackets are fixed with dowels to the shelf, and with screws driven into them through the backboard and strip. This top strip has, as shown in Fig. 985, a little carving in three medallions. The panel M (Fig. 980) of the central division between the two shelves, being a part on which the eye will chiefly rest, is carved throughout. Its ornamentation is shown in Fig. 988. The carved medallion, which decorates the space N above the upper shelf, is shown enlarged in Fig. 987 ; and the spaces O at the top of the side divisions have their

Fig. 988.—Central Panel of Overmantel.

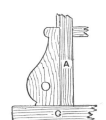

Fig. 991.—Angle Piece at Foot of Over- mantel.

Fig. 989.—Chip Carving over Side Divisions (O, Fig. 980) of Overmantel.

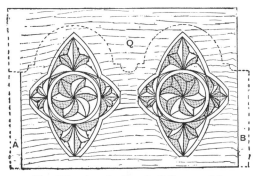

Fig. 990.—Arcade Panel of Overmantel.

Fig. 992.—Cupboard Door of Overmantel.

ornament given in Fig. 989. Some variety is introduced in the side panels P by the arches shown at Q, and indicated by dotted lines in Fig. 990. Each pair of arches is cut from a strip of $\frac{1}{4}$-in. board, and is fixed to the uprights and upper shelf with small round-headed brass screws. The panels beneath the arcades are carved as shown in Fig. 990. The angle formed by the uprights A where they meet the mantelboard is relieved by the small pieces of 1-in. board, shown in Fig. 991.

Cupboards.—Fig. 992 shows the design for the cupboard doors. As seen in the section (Fig. 984), these cupboards are (exclusive of the space taken up by the door) 1 ft. $1\frac{1}{2}$ in. wide and 6 in. deep. They are 1 ft. 9 in. high, leaving a space between them for the nooks R, which are $4\frac{3}{8}$ in. high. The cupboard bottoms are $\frac{5}{8}$ in. thick, and may either be mortised into the uprights, or merely fixed with screws driven into their ends through the uprights. Round-headed brass screws should be used. The doors shown in Fig. 992 are of $\frac{1}{2}$-in. stuff, and are strengthened with $\frac{3}{8}$-in. ledgers screwed to their backs at the top and the bottom. A false top and bottom of $\frac{1}{4}$-in. board should be fixed within each cupboard, for the door to close against. One of the cupboards might be fitted as a smoker's cabinet, with pipe racks at the sides, a deep drawer at the bottom for cigars, and a small shelf near the top for match-boxes, etc. The other cupboard could be fitted with two or three small shelves for minor articles, and with one, or perhaps two shallow drawers at the bottom. Figs. 980 to 984 are drawn to a scale of $\frac{3}{4}$ in. to the foot, and Figs. 985 to 992 are 2 in. to the foot.

CARVING FOR INDUSTRIAL PURPOSES

Carved Foundry Patterns

WOOD CARVING occupies a very definite place amongst the industrial arts, and one of its important applications is in the productions of patterns for ornamental castings, columns, capitals, arches, friezes, pattresses, terminals, finials, brackets, pilasters, panels, balustrades, palisading, doors, staircases, mantels and overmantels, tables, seats, cresting, rainwater pipes and heads; all these suggest themselves very readily as being more or less common building and furnishing materials, which are produced

With regard to the choice of material, if, for instance, the casting will be in a prominent position, forming part of an architectural scheme embracing elaborate ornament, it must be cast in a fine metal. This means that the metal should be free from impurities that would prevent it flowing easily and freely into the mould formed in the sand by the carved pattern, it being then possible to introduce a more delicate type of design, such as that of the Italian or French Renaissance, with the certainty that the design carved in the pattern will be faithfully reproduced in the casting. An essential to

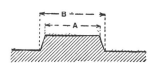

Fig. 993.—Diagram showing Taper of Foundry Pattern.

Fig. 994.—Carved Pattern.

by casting metal in moulds made from wooden patterns. Brass, copper, and bronze ornaments also are sometimes cast from wooden patterns.

Limitations

In wood carving applied to industrial purposes, limitations are imposed which bind the worker to a certain definite treatment of the designs, and which also limit the choice of these designs. These limitations are : (1) The material of which the casting consists, and (2) the particular methods necessarily employed in making the casting.

success in metal casting is that both the pattern and the casting shall leave the sand easily and cleanly. To do this, a slight amount of taper is necessary ; all those surfaces which lie parallel to the plane of the direction in which the pattern is to be drawn out are cut at a slight angle to it, the inclination of these surfaces always being in the direction of a point lying beyond the face of the carving. Thus, in the wooden pattern, the " walls " of the design will incline from the groundwork to the surface. Across the line A, in Fig. 993, the measurement will be slightly less than along the line B, which, of course, means that each wall inclines slightly. The process of moulding the sand consists in preparing a box, into which the carved

when complete, will also probably destroy the mould in the same way. Thus, the pattern for the casting is made to taper from

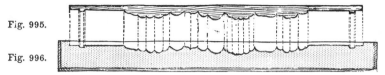

Fig. 995.

Fig. 996.

Figs. 995 and 996.—Section of Wood Pattern and Sand Mould.

pattern is pressed until it has made a cavity that exactly corresponds to the pattern, the last named being carefully withdrawn. But if it is undercut, or has walls at right angles to the surface, it binds on the walls of the sand mould throughout the whole of its

the ground up to the surface. This applies to every part of the carving. Figs. 994 and 995 show a panel for casting, together with the section and the taper allowed to clear the sand mould, and Fig. 996 shows a section of the sand mould after it has been prepared

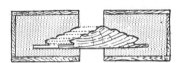

Fig. 999.—Section of Undercut Pattern in Mould

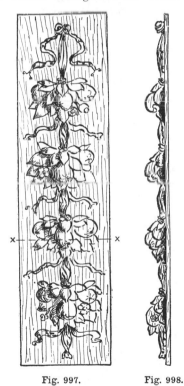

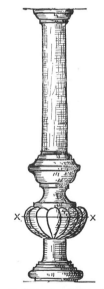

Fig. 997.   Fig. 998.

Figs. 997 and 998.—Front and Side Elevations of Undercut Pattern.

Fig. 1000.—Pattern for Pillar, Turned and Carved.

depth. The result invariably is that some part of the mould is scraped off, and this is difficult to work up again. The casting,

for the casting. Clean, accurate cutting is essential in carving foundry patterns. There must be no ragged edges, or chips not quite clearly cut, or cuts not meeting, or cuts taken against the grain and the surface left rough, or the many other small defects that may often be overlooked in ordinary carvings.

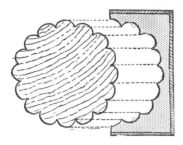

Fig. 1001.—Section of Pillar, showing Excessive Projection.

Undercutting in Foundry Patterns

It is evident that undercut work is, as a rule, not suited for foundry patterns, although it is possible so to arrange the undercutting that it is either all on one side or on opposite sides, and to have all the lines of clearance parallel to one another. In this case the result would be an undercut casting. This possibility is shown in Figs. 997 to 999, which give a front view, side view, and section of a pilaster design, which could be cast standing on its edge. In this case a double box is required for casting it in, and this is shown, one part at each side, together with the dotted clearance lines, in Fig. 999. The design (Fig. 997) is an example of slight

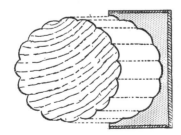

Fig. 1002.—Section of Pillar, showing Proper Projection.

undercutting. But a complete undercut casting is not so easy, although it is merely an extension of the methods employed in casting Fig. 997.

Foundry Pattern for Ornamental Pillar

To cast the circular column (Fig. 1000) in a double box is not an easy matter, special consideration having to be given to the clearance lines. Figs. 1001 and 1002 give sections on x x, and show a series of rounded falling ornament. By following the course of the lines of clearance it will be found that the amount of projection that can be given these elements to make them all uniform in projection is determined by the two outside

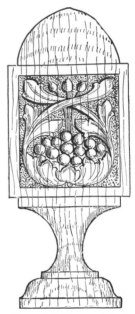

Fig. 1003.—Carved Pattern made in Sections.

lines but one. These are the lines which proceed to the inner junction between the projections; and in order to get a clear road for this line the amount of projection must be small. Fig. 1001 shows excessive projection; Fig. 1002 indicates the right amount. This applies to all the ornament placed on the pillar. This fact is emphasised in all carving done on foundry patterns; all clearance lines must be free from any projections that will prove obstacles to the successful preparation of the mould. All clearance lines should always fall outside the limits of the carving.

Pattern made in Sections

It is possible, however, to ignore the limitations imposed by the lines of clearance respecting the amount of relief that is possible, by means of a division of the pattern. Thus, in casting a head similar to that in Fig. 1003, which is square in plan as shown in Fig. 1004, but carved on all the four sides, it is obviously impossible to cast it if the pattern is a solid piece, because the sides cannot clear the mould. It is, therefore, arranged in sections as in Fig. 1004, which

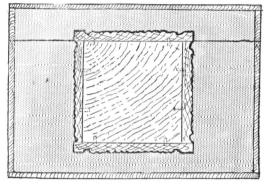

Fig. 1004.—Section of Pattern of Ornamental Block, in Mould.

gives a section of the head, and also the box in which it is cast. In this case the pattern is taken out of the mould in sections. The top piece is lifted carefully off and the centre removed. Then the side pieces are pulled sidewise, leaving the sides of the mould intact and perfect, and then the lower piece is carefully withdrawn. A mould like this

can be used only for one casting, and has to be remade for each subsequent piece required, as the cast itself cannot be in sections, but must be in one solid piece. The rule respecting the tapering of the pattern is also followed in this piece.

Allowance for Shrinkage

Another important point to remember is that metal shrinks in cooling. Therefore, the pattern should be made larger than the required casting, in the proportion of $\frac{1}{8}$ in. to 1 ft. for brass, and $\frac{1}{10}$ in. to 1 ft. for iron. Disregard this for castings less than 1 ft. long, the rapping of the pattern by the moulder usually sufficing.

Other Forms of Carving for Industrial Purposes

There are other forms of carving for industrial purposes. Boxwood moulds for butter making, and wheels for similar purposes, come under this heading. They differ from relief carving, inasmuch as the design is cut into the wood, and is not raised in relief. Then when the mould is placed on the butter, the raised impression of the carving is left in relief. Moulds for casting composition sprays and scrolls are also often carved in similar manner in solid blocks. Moulds, too, for bakers, to form ornamental surfaces to gingerbread, pies, cakes, etc., come under the same heading. In all these cases, make the edges quite sharp, even to the extent of emphasising their sharpness, because the nature of the dough always tends to soften them eventually, and proper allowance for this must be made.

CARVING CLASSES

THE encouragement given to woodwork generally by educational authorities has caused a widespread interest in the crafts. In this section will be given some hints as to the formation, equipment, and management of wood carving classes. Students in these classes require a different course of study from that of the ordinary carving apprentice. The latter serves an apprenticeship of five to seven years, and acquires his knowledge of the craft entirely on " practical " lines. His principal business for the first two years is to keep his eyes open, although, also, he may be given a little, unimportant work to do. After this he is given work suited to his expanding ability ; but, in any case, his training is a matter of many years. Thus, his knowledge of the practical side of the work is sure, because of its slow development. On the other hand, the class student has to pick up his knowledge in the evening, and has not the opportunity of becoming so sure and so sound a craftsman, so far as the technique is concerned. Then, another aspect of the case is the consideration of the educational possibilities that lie in the teaching of all the crafts ; and it is this that dominates the measures taken to construct any craft class, and determines the kind of tuition that is to be given. This, of course, practically decides the choice of teacher, general construction of class schemes, and choice of apparatus and equipment. There are thus two sides—the recreative and the educational—to the consideration of wood carving as a class subject. The evening classes cater more largely for those who look on wood carving as a hobby ; to these, the recreative side of the craft will

appeal. On the other hand, its introduction into secondary schools depends entirely on the educational advantages that will result from its practice. It will be apparent that, although it undoubtedly will be of advantage as a means of recreation, this value is only incidental, the dominating factor being that of its value as a means of drawing out, unfolding, and gradually developing the constructive and artistic qualities of the student. It follows, naturally, that the schemes applicable to these two different sets of classes will vary, and this difference will receive due attention in the course of this section.

Evening Classes

These classes are for students above the age of fourteen, who are not earning a grant in a day school ; and the classes have to be held after four o'clock in the afternoon, except by special permission from the Board of Education. As the classes are public, it follows that it is possible for them to have a most varied constitution, especially in a comparatively small provincial town. Members of all professions, trades, and occupations form the personnel of these classes, and because of their widely varying character they make the task of laying down and planning a working scheme a matter of the greatest difficulty. Some students wish to do their own designs ; others consider themselves of sufficient standing to be quite outside any course that may be planned ; and others, again, do not wish to study the theoretical side of the subject. These are, of course, questions of discipline ; but the chief difficulty is caused by the varying degrees of progress attained by the more advanced students. Some are really too far advanced to come within the working limits of an ordinary scheme. With a secondary school the students can be split up into forms of a more or less equal stage in development and in age. But an evening class presents no possibility of such grading. The students must be taken together. The hours during which a class like this may be held will naturally vary. From 7 to 9, or 7.30 to 9.30, will be found most generally suitable. The duration of the class will depend somewhat on the numbers, and it may be assumed that one teacher cannot possibly take more than

Equipment

The matter of equipment—benches, tools, and other apparatus—for an evening class is largely governed by the room and money available. A permanent class in a room reserved specially for it should have the following equipment. The room chosen should be well provided with artificial light, electric preferred. For an evening class, the matter of daylight is not of importance ; but for day classes, consideration should be given to the amount and disposition of the window space. The electric light should be counterpoised, so that it may be lowered or raised

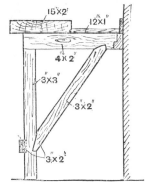

Fig. 1005.—Section of Carver's Bench to go against Wall.

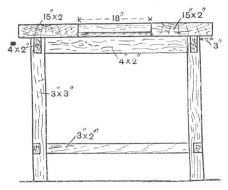

Fig. 1006.—Section of Square Centre Bench.

six students to each hour. Thus, twelve students with one teacher would mean a two-hours' class. As a matter of fact, a wood-carving class should not be of less duration than two hours. A shorter time means that as soon as a student has got into the swing of the work, and has come into touch with its spirit and its purpose, the time to lay down the tools has arrived. This constant starting and finishing, without any adequate length of time between, is detrimental to good work. This applies to practice, too ; as much time as possible should be devoted to practice between the lessons. If eighteen students form the class, it should either be divided into two portions of two hours each for nine students, or an assistant should be obtained for at least one hour for the one class—a matter to be judged in each case according to circumstances.

as required. The benches should be high enough to stand to, should be ranged round the walls under the windows, and should have the electric lights immediately over them. They should be 3 ft. 3 in. high and of a section similar to that shown in Fig. 1005. If there is sufficient space in the centre of the room, a few benches of the shape shown in Fig. 1006, to accommodate four students each, may be fixed. These benches allow the student to get round the work instead of being always on one side of it. Also, a light can be hung over the centre, thus avoiding all shadows. Reserve space for a blackboard, diagrams, sketches, and illustrations, photograph boards, models, and other practical, illustrative apparatus. The blackboard should be placed on a platform raised about 6 in. from the ground, so that it and the teacher can be easily seen from all parts of the room. Fig. 1007 is a plan of the suggested arrangement of a wood-carving classroom, giving the principal objects and their positions, but leaving out details, such as drawers, shelves, etc. Under the benches there should be one drawer and one shelf to each student. Provide a chest of drawers, to contain drawing, tracing, and carbon paper, extra tools, sharpening slips, strops, oil, designs, drawing-pins, pencils, rubbers, punches, and other carving requisites. Cupboard room, too, is never superfluous.

3 (on Sheffield Tool List), 1 in. wide; 3 No. 3, $\frac{1}{16}$ in.; 3 No. 5, $\frac{1}{4}$ in.; 3 No. 5, $\frac{5}{16}$ in.; 2 No. 6, $\frac{1}{4}$ in.; 2 No. 8, $\frac{1}{8}$ in.; 2 No. 8, $\frac{3}{4}$ in.; 3 No. 10, $\frac{1}{2}$ in.; 2 No. 7, $1\frac{1}{2}$ in.; 1 No. 11, $\frac{1}{8}$ in.; 2 No. 21, $\frac{3}{16}$ in.; 2 No. 27, $\frac{1}{4}$ in.; 2 No. 25, $\frac{3}{8}$ in.; 2 No. 40, $\frac{5}{16}$ in.; and 2 No. 23, $\frac{1}{2}$ in. Of course, other tools may be added as required. The handle of each tool should be stamped with the number of its set, and each drawer should be numbered, the tools and apparatus being numbered to correspond. Other apparatus required for a class of twelve students is as follows:

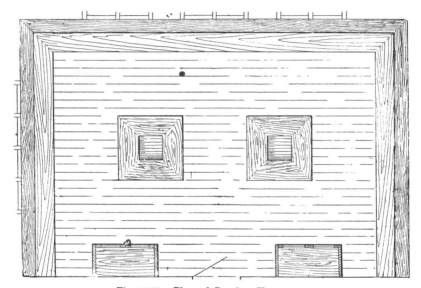

Fig. 1007.—Plan of Carving Classroom.

Tools

A set of tools suitable for general use is given on p. 39. For class use this list may be modified to effect economy. Some of the tools are used continually by the students, whilst others are required only occasionally. For a class of twelve students the following tools for each are necessary: No. 1 (on Sheffield Tool List), $\frac{1}{2}$ in. wide; No. 3, $\frac{1}{8}$ in.; No. 3, $\frac{1}{4}$ in.; No. 3, $\frac{3}{8}$ in.; No. 5, $\frac{3}{16}$ in.; No. 5, $\frac{1}{2}$ in.; No. 7, $\frac{3}{8}$ in.; No. 8, $\frac{1}{4}$ in.; No. 39, $\frac{5}{16}$ in.; and No. 21, $\frac{1}{8}$ in. Other tools, for occasional use only, may be included in a special class set, which, to begin with, may consist of the following: 2 tools No.

12 mallets, 12 pairs cramps, 6 carvers' screws, 12 cases or boxes for the tools, 1 or more cases for the class tools, 12 punches or ground stamps, 2 oilstones in cases, 3 Washita slips, 3 Arkansas slips, 1 oil-can, 3 strops, 6 2-ft. rules, 1 grindstone, and 6 bench brushes. In addition, such things as drawing-pins, carbon, tracing, and drawing paper should be provided; pencils and rubber are generally found by the students. If, say, two instantaneous grip vices are fixed to the benches at one end of the room, they would be of advantage for carving in the round. The foregoing refers to a room used exclusively for instruction in carving, and forms a basis to work on.

Makeshift Classrooms

Unfortunately, such rooms as above described are in a minority, and wood-carving instructors generally have to put up with a makeshift arrangement. In public schools the desks very often have to do duty as benches. A class can sometimes have the use of a manual training room, with its joiners' benches. Whether benches or desks, however, they are only makeshifts; they are not high enough, and the desks, generally, are not firm enough.

The Lighting of the Classroom

For a day class the room requires lighting at one end and one side at least. Cross lights obviate the necessity of continually moving the work to see the effect under a different lighting arrangement, because one light can always be cut off by means of blinds, if necessary. A long room, having one bench along one side, with windows coming down to the bench level, lends itself well to carving. No top light is required, this destroying all shadows. A north aspect is the best, this avoiding direct glare from the sun, which is bad for both the workers and the work. Blinds should be fitted to the windows in any case. For evening work, reference already has been made to the choice and position of the artificial light necessary. The same general rule of no top light is to be observed. If gas is used, jointed brackets, with three or four arms fixed low down, are to be preferred. Oil lamps must be used in many country districts; the kind with reflectors to fix flat on the wall is the best, except in the case of centre tables, when hanging lamps may be used, with a reflector at the top to throw the light downwards.

Schemes and Arrangement of Work

The training of wood-carving students differs very much from that of the professional wood carver. The latter is trained to execute with perfect technique any piece of work specified. But in the case of the student, wood carving has to be considered as a definite factor in a scheme whose object is to widen his general knowledge and ability; it is not to be regarded so much as a means of increasing a certain special ability

in one defined channel. Thus it is that the teaching of wood carving in a day or evening class greatly differs from the method by which an apprentice to the craft gains his knowledge. The study of wood carving in all its aspects is so correlated to the study of other subjects as to make it impossible to continue it without having some acquaintance with them. Thus, successfully to study wood carving, the student must give attention to history, in considering its growth and gradual development; architecture, to which wood carving should ever be subordinate; manners and customs of different peoples and their development, in tracing the evolution of the craft in different countries; geographical, climatic, and geological characteristics of these countries, all crafts depending on the products of the country for their extent and nature of their development. A case in point is that of Chaldea, which, having no timber of native growth, has no wood carving to speak of; the whole character, too, of its architecture, as well as of its industrial arts, is influenced by this lack of timber. These remarks are intended to show, to some extent, the points that have to be considered in arranging a scheme suitable for the highest development of the individual ability of a wood-carving student.

Course of Study for Evening Class

A course suitable for an evening class of both sexes and all ages is here outlined, the lessons, from twelve to twenty-four in number, to be of two hours each. The scheme is divided thus: (a) The practical and technical, (b) theoretical and literary. (a) Practical and technical. This includes a knowledge of various woods in common use for wood-carving purposes, namely, oak, black American walnut, satin walnut, mahogany, kauri, pear-tree, limewood, and yellow pine. The botanical points and distinctions are not essential; but a study of botany, with special reference to timber, makes a more generally capable student. The differences in the grain of the various woods, their individual characteristics, and their suitability for different kinds of work should be taught. Prominence will be given to the tools, their various shapes and makes, how to sharpen them and keep them in order ; various kinds of oilstones and slips, and their use ; the uses of strop and grind-stone, and the right bevel to adopt in grind-ing the tools ; various kinds of mallets and the wood of which they should be made ; cramps ; punches ; cases and boxes to store the tools. Finally, how to use the tools. (*b*) Theoretical and literary. Every scheme of wood carving should devote much time to this side of the subject. The planning may take various forms, but it should in-clude : Some reference to the history of wood carving, and especially to the Gothic and the Renaissance. Visits should be ar-ranged to churches, mansions, museums, and other places, where actual examples of the various styles are to be seen. Students should be encouraged to bring photographs and sketches of work bearing on the subject matter of the lessons and of the visits to the places of interest ; and also to bring actual examples of wood carving, both old and new, on which useful comments may be made by the teacher. Experience has shown it to be a good plan to have boards covered with paper, and labelled, " Early English Gothic," " Norman," " Early Renaissance," " Tudor," etc., and to pin the photographs and sketches to them, so that they may be easily studied. These photographs and sketches need not be confined to wood carv-ing ; they should have reference, also, to the history of architecture, the teacher emphasis-ing the subordinate place to be occupied by wood carving in relation to architecture. The reasons that exist for the various pro-cesses necessary to the production of a piece of wood carving are covered, to some extent, by what has been said in the sub-section, " Practical and technical," but, in addition, it should be said that the grain of the wood should receive special attention. Thus there are at least four methods of determining the direction to be taken by the tool, so that it may always be cutting " with the grain." The reasons for grinding the tools to a cer-tain shape should be carefully set forth. The division of the whole process of wood carving into various distinct stages should be taught —namely, outlining, setting-in, grounding, modelling, etc.—and the reasons why only certain tools should be used in the various stages. The following is suggested as a suitable course for the elementary part of an evening class. For the first twelve lessons, all the students should work together at four exercises, which should be as follow : (No. 1) This should consist of lines, both straight and curved, providing exercise in the use of the **V**-tool only. The size of the board for both this and the subsequent exer-cises should be about 12 in. by 9 in. (No. 2) A similar exercise, of simple design (incised carving), showing the value of the **V**-tool as a modelling tool. (No. 3) A design intro-ducing groundwork, and allowing of a little simple modelling. Not more than six tools should be used for this exercise. (No. 4) A more intricate design, introducing all the stages in the whole process of wood carving, the full set of ten tools being used. After these exercises are completed, the students should work separately and be allowed to make progress at their own rate, so giving them greater interest in their work. The exercises should suit the developing ability of each student. During the whole of the period devoted to the exercises, continual reference should be made to the blackboard, which should aid in correcting mistakes and giving advice. It is of some service occa-sionally—not every lesson—to give questions to be answered during the week. This quickens the students' perception and tends to develop their reasoning powers.

Design and Drawing.—A class course cannot be considered complete without including tuition in design. It being im-possible to teach design fully and thoroughly in the little time at a teacher's disposal; the best that can be done is to give useful hints, to prepare graduated exercises, to stimulate interest in it, to emphasise its im-portance, and to advise and direct students in their efforts to become masters of it. A suitable way of dealing with the subject is to give a few notes each week, either dic-tated or on the blackboard, on the elements and principles of ornament ; the way to build up designs for both high and low relief ; how to plan regular and irregular spaces ; and so on, similarly. Each set of notes should be supplemented by a few minutes' talk about design, illustrated by an actual ex-ample bearing on the notes. During the week the students should prepare a design on similar lines. Remember, most of all, that correct drawing cannot be expected from a class the members of which have probably done little or no drawing of any kind ; but latent in every one is the power to plan, to arrange, and to group elements to form a complete design ; and to cultivate this ability should be the object of attention. The work of teaching design will be very materially assisted by the simultaneous talks on the history of wood carving and architecture.

Spacing of the Lesson Hours.—To get all that has been already outlined as being necessary in a wood-carving class scheme in a two hours' lesson is a work of some considerable difficulty. One of the possible arrangements, and one which has been adopted with good results in a large evening class in the north of England, is to give twenty minutes to the teaching of design and theory, ten minutes to a talk on the history and literature of the craft, and one and a half hours' practical work. The time devoted to design and history may be varied as each evening's work demands ; but one and a half hours is the minimum for practical work. Advanced students require individual treatment respecting their practical work, and the teacher will be expected to regulate their work so that it is proportioned to their ability ; reasonably to curb their ambition, and to give advice on their choice of work.

Course of Study for Day Class

A course suitable for pupils at day schools will differ from the evening school course, but it certainly may be based on it. The great difference is in the number of the exercises. Here it is possible to have a graduated course spread over a period of two years, consisting of from thirty to fifty exercises. The whole class will work together, and the whole course of study, both for the practical and the theoretical work, will be framed with the definite intention of developing latent talent, both artistic and constructive ; of widening the students' knowledge by touching on the many subjects interwoven with the study of wood carving ; and of developing character. The study of the historical side must be emphasised, although it must be presented in a simpler and easier form than for an adult class. The study of design will, too, be modified ; but it can be carried on in conjunction with the pupils' own special design and drawing classes. Indeed, it is advisable to consult the drawing-master, with a view to framing jointly a scheme by which the instruction given in the carving class may be supplemented in the class for drawing. It should be said that wood carving in schools as a means of training mind and character is of much more value than is generally supposed, and most certainly deserves greater attention and encouragement from educational authorities than it at present receives. It trains the eye and the hand ; it develops the gifts of form, proportion, and balance ; it quickens the artistic sensibilities ; it enlarges the student's stock of direct knowledge by its kinship with architecture, history, ethnology, geography, botany, and art ; and it trains character because of the necessity for the practice of perseverance, patience, determination, and energy to attain anything like success.

APPLIQUÉ DECORATION

THE special period for appliqué ornament in old English furniture was the close of the seventeenth century and the beginning of the eighteenth. It had been used earlier in connection with carving, but, at the time named, carving had virtually passed out of fashion, and this method of decoration —the sticking of pieces of wood on the surface so as to form designs—for a short time prevailed in its stead. Sometimes the ornament consisted chiefly of sections of turned work, but oftener of pieces of plane-struck moulding arranged in geometrical patterns.

Cabinet in Appliqué Work

The design shown by Figs. 1008 to 1010 is arranged to be carried out without the help of lathe or moulding-plane, a neat effect being produced by merely chamfering off the edges of the applied pieces. Those who possess moulding planes will, however, readily see how they may use them to good purpose. As regards construction, this cabinet will be found sufficiently simple. First make four upright pieces 2 in. square and 5 ft. 11¼ in. long. The back pair will be left quite plain; but, as seen in Figs. 1008 and 1009, parts of the front pair are worked into twists. The method of doing this will be explained later. In the section (Fig. 1011) are shown the four uprights arranged in position; they form an oblong, 4 ft. by 18½ in. These may be fastened together by screwing upon them four tiers of rails at the front and ends, and by boarding up the back. The back boarding is of ½-in. wood, and it extends from the tops of the uprights to within 4 in. of their bottoms. The pieces are 3 ft. 11 in. long, the remaining ½ in. at

each end being made up, for the sake of appearance, with an upright strip. All the rails are of ¾-in. wood, 4 ft. 1½ in. long for the front and 19¾ in. long for the ends. The top, third, and lowest ranges of rails (A, C, and D, Fig. 1008, respectively) are 3 in. wide; the second (B, Fig. 1008) is 2 in. only. These rails are mitered together at the front corners. The rails A, B, and C are rounded off on their lower front edges, whilst C and D are rounded off on their upper front edges. Their bottoms are from the floor line as follows: rail D 4 in., C 3 ft., B 4 ft. 1 in., and A 5 ft. 9 in.; ½-in. stuff will serve for boarding up the two lower divisions of the ends. They are, as shown in Fig. 1008, quite plain. These boards are together 14½ in. wide, and their length is 3 ft. 9 in.; their upper ends are placed ¾ in. lower than the top of rail B (see G, Fig. 1012); they are screwed to the rails. The narrow end board of the upper division, which is of thicker stuff, will be dealt with presently.

Cabinet Top.—The top of the cabinet is of ¾-in. board, 4 ft. long and 19 in. wide. Its hinder edge comes flush with the back boarding. It is screwed down to the uprights and upper backboard; screws through rail A are also driven into its edges.

Lower Section.—The lower section of the cabinet is occupied by two large cupboards. The floor of these, H (Fig. 1012), is of ¾-in. wood, its upper surface coming flush with the top of rail D. It rests on four ledges, I, of which the two end ones are screwed to the uprights, and the middle ones (the four being placed at equal distances apart) are mortised into the front rail and backboard— the mortice in the front rail being so placed as to be hidden by the moulding which will be fixed there. As a top, these cupboards have the floor of the middle division—that devoted to drawers—for which ½-in. board is sufficiently strong K, (Fig. 1012). Its upper surface comes flush with the top of rail C. Its

of the partition, on both sides, to strengthen it and prevent warping. To fix it in place, screws are driven into it through the floors above and below, and through the backboard. In front of the partition stands the centre strip F (Fig. 1011), against which

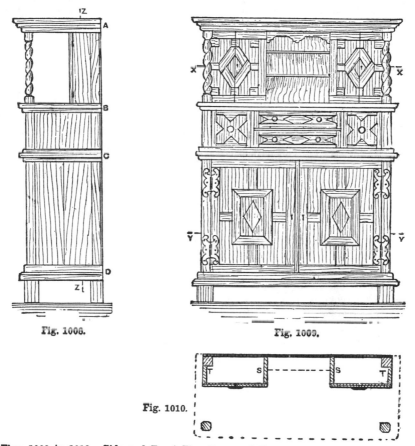

Fig. 1008.

Fig. 1009.

Fig. 1010.

Figs. 1008 to 1010.—Side and Front Elevations and Horizontal Section (on Line X X) of Appliqué Cabinet.

ends are supported by ledges L screwed to the uprights like those below, but its middle will rest on the partition which divides the cupboards.

Partitions, etc.—Half-inch wood will also serve for the partition, which is shown in section at E (Fig. 1011), the pieces being 13½ in. long and, together, 17½ in. wide. Strips of thin board M, say ⅓ in. by 2 in., should be screwed along the top and bottom

the two doors close. It is of 1-in. board, 2 in. wide and 34 in. long. An opening is cut for its lower end through the floor below, and it is screwed to the rails C and D. So much of it as is in sight has a ½-in. rebate cut into each of its front edges to receive the doors. The floor of the upper division N (Fig. 1012) is of ¾-in. wood ; its top comes flush with that of rail B. It rests on the end ledgers O O, and on the partitions P P. These partitions are also of ¾-in. board, 11¼ in. by 18½ in. ; they are fixed by screws driven into them through the floors above and below, through the backboard, and through the rail B. The floor on which the uppermost of

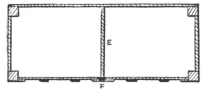

Fig. 1011.—Horizontal Section of Appliqué Cabinet (on Line Y Y, Fig. 1009).

the two shallow drawers slides, Q (Fig. 1012), is of ½-in. board, and has its ends let into V-shaped grooves in the upright partitions.

Upper Section.—The upper section of the cabinet is chiefly an open shelf, but at its back it has two shallow cupboards, and between them a recess with small shelves. The cupboards, which have an internal depth of 6½ in., have folding doors—an arrangement rendered necessary by the twisted pillars, which, if they were single doors, would interfere with their proper opening. Each pair of doors measures 16 in. across ; the recess between them has also a width of 16 in. The sides of the cupboards are of ¾-in. board, and 20¼ in. long. The outer ones, T (Fig. 1013), are 4½ in. wide only ; the inner ones, S S, are 6½ in. wide. Each cupboard has two shelves, as shown in the section (Fig. 1013), of ½-in. board, and flush with the sides at front. They fit into V-shaped grooves in the sides. Fig. 1014 shows the interior of side S, with the grooves. Fig. 1015 shows its exterior, with grooves for the shelves of the recess, which are only 3½ in. wide, and also a groove for the ornamental piece at the top of the recess. The cupboard sides are screwed to the floor and top, and to the rails A. The sides S S are also screwed to the backboard. The doors of these cupboards are 18 in. high ; there is, therefore, a space 2¼ in. wide by 16 in. long above each pair of doors, which will be filled with a strip of inch wood, screwed to the sides.

Twisted Pillars.—The twisted pillars at the front corners of this division will now

be considered. The twist has, of course, to be worked before the uprights are fixed in position. To cut a twist, the square piece is first reduced to an octagon by taking off the corners neatly. It is proposed to have a double twist ; that is to say, there will be two fillets with their intervening hollows running up the spiral. This kind of twist is said to have been introduced into English furniture in the reign of Charles II., the earlier twists being single. The double twist is quite as artistic in effect as the single, weakens the wood less, and is more easily worked. To set it out, take two strips of paper, each of which will represent the width of one of the fillets from the bottom of the hollow on one side to the bottom of the hollow on the other ; these are twisted spirally side by side round the wood. They will seem to fall into their places naturally. A slack twist—one, that is, that takes comparatively few turns round the pillar—always looks more artistic than one more tightly twisted. The slips of paper can be temporarily fixed with drawing pins, and when they are satisfactorily arranged, one of them must be taken off, split through the middle, and one half of it replaced on

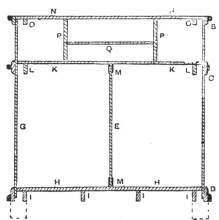

Fig. 1012.—Longitudinal Vertical Section of Appliqué Cabinet (on Line Z Z, Fig. 1008).

the wood and pasted there. The other strip will then be treated in the same manner. The paper will now represent the fillets, the bare spaces between them the hollows : these latter will have to be cut out. It will help the work if a cut is first made with the saw down the middle of each hollow, which can then be cleared out with gouges and mallet. This having been done regularly, the perpendicular edge left along the margin of

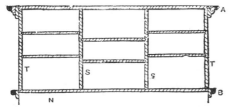

Fig. 1013.—Vertical Section of Upper Part of Cabinet (on Line Z Z, Fig. 1008).

the paper can be taken off with a chisel, and the fillet can be shaped. The use of a half-round file and glasspaper will finish the work. To make a twist in this way is a much easier matter than anyone who has not tried it would suppose.

Appliqué Mouldings.—The cabinet must now be fitted with the mouldings which lie upon the rails. Regarding cornice A, lying on these rails are strips of ¾-in. wood, long enough to mitre at the corners, and having hollow mouldings worked in their lower front edges. These are best seen in the section (Fig. 1013). If no plane is at hand, this moulding can, without much difficulty, be run out with a gouge. Again, lying on this strip is another strip 1 in. square, of which the lower front edge is simply rounded off. These are the longest strips used, that for the front being 4 ft. 5 in., and those for the ends 20½ in. Round the rails B runs a strip 1 in. square, the lower edge of which is rounded off, but not the upper. This lies, as will be seen, close upon the upper edge of the rail. The 1-in. moulding round the rails c differs from that above in having both its front edges rounded off, and in being screwed on the middle of the rail. The moulding round the bottom rails D is 1 in. thick, but 1½ in. wide ; its upper front edge is chamfered off, and it lies on the bottom of the rail. The bottom ends of the uprights which serve as feet are cased in ¾-in. board ; and this completes the carcase of the cabinet.

Doors.—The doors may now be considered. These are all made in the same way—that

is, by screwing two layers of thin board together so as to make them cross each other in grain, as far as is practicable. For the two large doors, take ½-in. board, the pieces being 29 in. long and, together, 21 in. wide. These run vertically, and form the inner layer ; and on them is fixed an outer layer of strips of the same thickness, the arrangement of which is clearly shown in Fig. 1008. It will be observed that the upright strip on the lock side of each door overlaps the inner layer by ½ in., to shut into the rebate in the central slip. For the sake of neatness, the edges of these ornamental pieces should be chamfered off ; the outside strips are shown as stop-chamfered. To give variety in the relief, the diamond pieces in the centre of the doors might be of ¾-in. board.

Drawer Fronts.—The fronts of the drawers in the middle section will be made in much the same way as the doors, but ¼-in. board for the ornamental pieces would perhaps look as well here. In making the small doors in the upper section, however, both layers should be of ½-in. wood. The small diamond in the centre of each pair is of ¼-in. stuff laid upon the larger diamond of ½-in. board.

Fixing Appliqué Pieces.—Purely ornamental pieces, in old appliqué, have been almost always glued on. But one rarely meets with an old example of this work from which more or less of the applied ornament has not come off, and, bearing in mind the untrustworthiness of most amateur gluing, the use of screws is advised. If the screwheads are thought unsightly, they can, in most instances, be driven from behind.

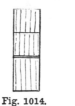

Fig. 1014.   Fig. 1015.

Figs. 1014 and 1015.—Interior and Exterior of Side of Cabinet's Upper Cupboard.

Yet it is preferable to see the mode of attachment frankly acknowledged ; round-headed screws, either brass or black, may thus be driven in from the front.

MISCELLANEOUS EXAMPLES AND DESIGNS

Examples Designed by Mr. W. S. Williamson

FIRST place in this, the concluding, chapter is given to some designs by Mr. W. S.

carved from original designs by him—illustrated in this section. Fig. 1016 (below) shows an oak settle designed in the Henry II. (France) style and excellently carved by Mrs. A. Chaffey. The dimensions are 3 ft. 6 in.

Fig. 1016.—Oak Settle.   Designed by W. S. Williamson.   Carved by Mrs. A. Chaffey.

Williamson, Society of Arts medallist, of Taunton, Somerset. This artist is a clever and versatile designer, as will be made apparent by the eighteen examples—all

by 3 ft. by 1 ft. 6 in.   Fig. 1017 illustrates a delicate and beautifully executed piece of relief carving, having openings of graceful outlines. There is evidence of mastery over the tool in the execution of the examples shown by Figs. 1018 and 1019 ; this is bold, striking work, well adapted to be used as ornament. An oak casket (the carving being the work of Miss Coleman) is shown by Fig. 1020. The dimensions are 12 in. by 8 in. by 6 in., and the design is in the French Gothic style. A solid oak chest, most appropriately and pleasingly carved,

Fig. 1017.
Panel Carved in Relief.
Designed by W. S. Williamson.

Fig. 1018.   Fig. 1019.
Figs. 1018 and 1019.—Figures. Designed
by W. S. Williamson.

is illustrated by Fig. 1021. It is 3 ft. 6 in. long, 1 ft. 8 in. wide, and 2 ft. 2 in. high. Other designs from the same source are shown later in this section.

Candlesticks

Three designs of turned and carved candlesticks are given by Figs. 1022 to

Fig. 1020.—Oak Casket. Designed by W. S. Williamson. Carved by Miss A. Coleman.

Fig. 1021.—Oak Chest. Designed by W. S. Williamson.

Fig. 1022   Fig. 1023.   Fig. 1024.

Figs. 1022 to 1024.—Turned and Carved Candlesticks.

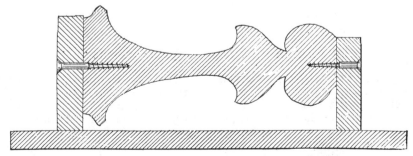

Fig. 1025.—Supporting Turned Candlestick for Carving.

1024. For these, oak, walnut, mahogany, or any other hardwood may be used; The sizes of the pieces are : Fig. 1022—$9\frac{1}{2}$ in. long by 4 in. square ; Fig. 1023—$9\frac{1}{2}$ in. long by 3 in. square ; Fig. 1024—$9\frac{1}{4}$ in. long ance is not necessary, as it is impossible to disguise the fact that it has been turned in the lathe. To fix the candlesticks in a suitable position for carving, make a stand out of three pieces of wood, as shown in section

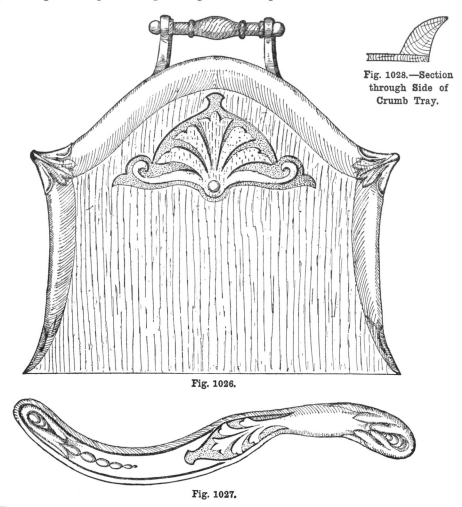

Fig. 1028.—Section through Side of Crumb Tray.

Fig. 1026.

Fig. 1027.

Figs. 1026 and 1027.—Crumb Tray and Brush Lightly Ornamented in Renaissance Style.

by 4 in. square. The material should first be roughly cut to shape, and then fixed in the lathe and turned to exact proportions. The section for turning should be slightly larger than the size after carving in the case of Figs. 1022 and 1023. This is to allow for plenty of cutting, to take away the machine-made appearance. For Fig. 1024 this allow-

at Fig. 1025 ; the distance between the two uprights should be such as to enable the candlestick to be held tightly between them. A screw through each end will hold the work secure, and will enable it to be turned round as required. The design may present some difficulty in drawing on the round wood ; but by dividing the circumference into four equal parts, the work will be facilitated. The tools must be particularly sharp for cutting across the end of the grain and into the corners. The candlesticks may be finished as follows; If in oak, they can be

polish. To harmonise with the fumed oak, the copper socket should be given an antique finish; with oiled American walnut or with mahogany, the copper may be bright-polished.

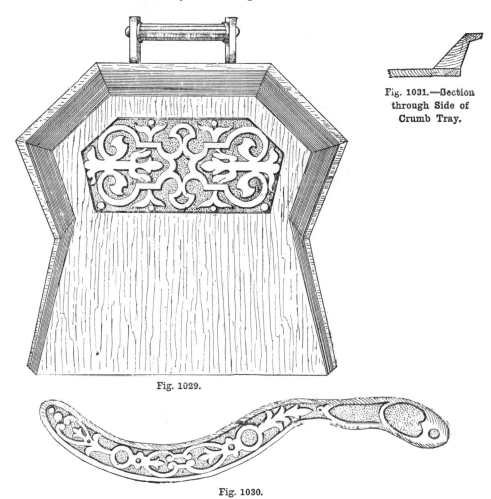

Fig. 1031.—Section through Side of Crumb Tray.

Fig. 1029.

Fig. 1030.

Figs. 1029 and 1030.—Crumb Tray and Brush Ornamented in Elizabethan Style.

fumed, oiled, and beeswaxed; fumed and beeswaxed; beeswaxed only; or simply oiled with raw linseed oil. If in American walnut, oiled with raw linseed oil, and (when dry) beeswaxed; or beeswaxed only. If in mahogany, they may be treated with bi-chromate of potash, and then either oiled or dull-polished with ordinary brown french

Crumb Trays and Brushes

Figs. 1026 to 1031 give two designs for a crumb tray and brush. Fig. 1026 shows a tray with a little ornament of the Renaissance style to relieve the plainness, Fig. 1028 being a section showing the moulded edge and flat portion. This tray should be made of hardwood such as oak, mahogany, walnut, beech, canary wood, or teak. The flat portion is about $\frac{1}{4}$ in. thick. The moulding can be cut out of wood, say $1\frac{1}{4}$ in. thick, worked to shape, and then fixed to the flat portion with fine brass screws. The leaf work at the corners can be carved in relief, if the moulding is left a little thicker at the corners and ends for this purpose ;

new back of the same wood as the crumb tray can be glued on and carved. The back should be elliptical in shape to give the best effect to the carving. A crumb tray in the Elizabethan style of ornament is shown by Fig. 1029, a section of the moulding and flat portion being given by Fig. 1031. This tray is constructed in the same manner as the one described above. The handle in

Fig. 1032.—Oval Frame.   Designed by W. S. Williamson.   Carved by Miss A. Ardagh.

or it can be incised. The ornament in the upper side of the flat portion is sunk about $\frac{1}{8}$ in., the ornament being left flat on the surface. The ground of the ornament can be left plain or matted as shown. The top handle is screwed at the back of the moulding, and should be brass with a wood spindle. A design for a brush suitable for this tray is shown by Fig. 1027. Crumb brushes of this kind can be purchased from any brush-maker ; then if the back is removed, a

this case can be entirely of metal. Dark oak or walnut would be the more suitable wood for this style of ornament. Fig. 1030 gives a design for the brush.

Frames Designed by Mr. W. S. Williamson

Four beautiful frames, suitable for mirrors or pictures, are illustrated by Figs. 1032 to 1035. The designs are due to Mr. Williamson, and the names of the carvers, where known, are given in the inscriptions to the figures.

Frames for Photographs and Picture Postcards

First Example.—The carved frames about to be referred to may be made in oak, wal-

formed by the addition of a $\frac{1}{2}$-in. slip, $\frac{3}{4}$ in. wide, mitered, glued, and bradded on the back of the carving. A cross section taken through the corner at Y Y (Fig. 1036) is given in Fig. 1039; while Fig. 1040 shows a fretted support forming the hinged strut for the back of the frame. The support is cut from

Fig. 1033.—Frame with **Oval Opening.** Designed by W. S. Williamson.

nut, or mahogany. A frame for an oval mount is shown in front and end elevations by Figs. 1036 and 1037. It measures $10\frac{1}{4}$ in. by $8\frac{5}{8}$ in. The front carved portion is cut from $\frac{1}{2}$-in. stuff, and is sunk as shown in the horizontal section (Fig. 1038). This also shows the rebate to receive the glass, the photograph, and the back, which is

$\frac{1}{4}$-in. stuff, and hung with a useful but simple hinge (Fig. 1041).

Second Example.—A frame of somewhat different character is shown in elevation in Fig. 1042. It is 9 in. by $7\frac{3}{4}$ in., and is made from $\frac{3}{4}$-in. stuff, which allows sufficient thickness for the rebate to be cut in the solid, as shown in the enlarged section

(Fig. 1043), in which is also given a section of the carving. A view of the back, showing the method of fixing with small clips or buttons secured with small brass tacks, is given in Fig. 1044.

in wood carving good practice in berry cutting. A section taken at x x (Fig. 1046) is given in Fig. 1047.

Fifth Example.—A stiff fret saw will be necessary to open up the flowing lines in

Fig. 1034.—Frame with Rectangular Opening. Designed by W. S. Williamson. Carved by Miss L. Underwood.

Third Example.—The long frame (Fig. 1045) is made from ¾-in. stuff, 2 ft. 8 in. long and 11 in. wide, and may be used as an overdoor, in which position it will form an effective decoration. The back may be secured the same as shown in Fig. 1044.

Fourth Example.—The double frame (Fig. 1046) is 1 ft. 2¼ in. by 9⅜ in. by ¾ in., and is simple in detail. This will afford beginners

the frame shown by Fig. 1048, as it should be made of ¾-in. stuff, and a fine saw is apt to run out of square in that thickness. A vertical section through the middle of Fig. 1048 is given at Fig. 1049. The outside measurements are 1 ft. 2 in. by 9⅜ in. Figs. 1046 and 1048 are rebated in the solid, as shown by dotted lines in Fig. 1048, and the backs are secured as shown in Fig. 1044.

Chippendale Overmantel

The overmantel shown by Fig. 1050 may be cut from 1-in. solid mahogany, which through the $\frac{1}{4}$-in. mahogany forming the panel, the latter being sunk in from the face and fixed by quadrant-shaped beads (*see* Figs. 1052 and 1056).

Fig. 1035.—Ornate Frame with Oval Opening.   Design Adapted by W. S. Williamson.
Carved by T. Darch.

forms the foundation of the carved work and scrolls (*see* Fig. 1051). The mirror is fixed in the rebate formed by the ogee mould-ing, and has also a deal backboard $\frac{3}{8}$ in. thick. The details given by Figs. 1051 to 1055, to a scale of 2 in. to the foot, are self-explanatory. The lozenge-shaped sinkings in the two upper side panels are pierced

Overmantel Designed by Mr. W. S. Williamson

An overmantel, designed by Mr. W. S. Williamson and ornamented with carving of the modern style, is shown by Fig. 1057. The actual carving was executed by the Rev. Mr. Kerthompson.

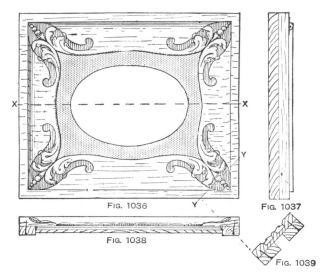

FIG. 1036

Fig. 1040.—Hinged Strut to Photograph Frame.

FIG. 1037

FIG. 1038

Y

FIG. 1039

Figs. 1036 to 1039.—Front and End Elevations, Horizontal Section (on Line X X) and Corner Section (on Line Y Y) of Photograph Frame.

Fig. 1041.— Hinge for Frame Strut.

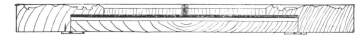

Fig. 1043.—Horizontal Section of Photograph Frame shown by Fig. 1042.

Fig. 1042.—Front Elevation of Another Photograph Frame.

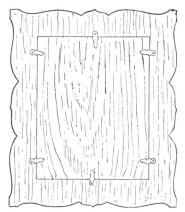

Fig. 1044.—Back Elevation of Photograph Frame.

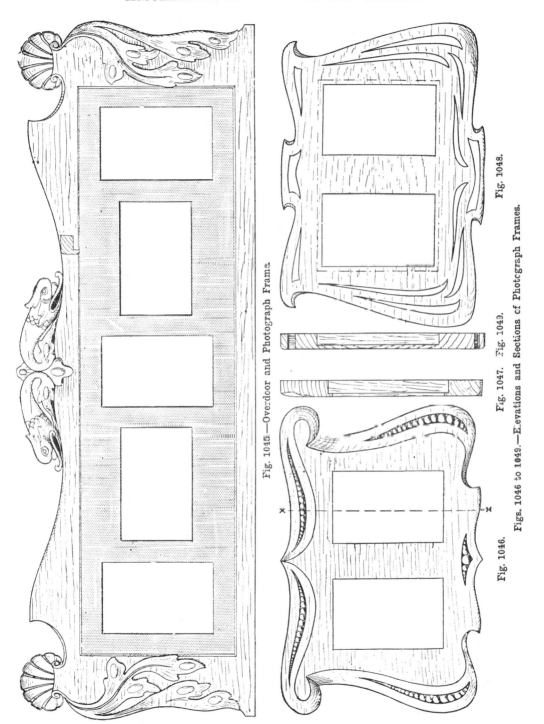

Fig. 1045—Overdoor and Photograph Frame.

Fig. 1048.

Fig. 1047.   Fig. 1049.

Figs. 1046 to 1049.—Elevations and Sections of Photograph Frames.

Fig. 1046.

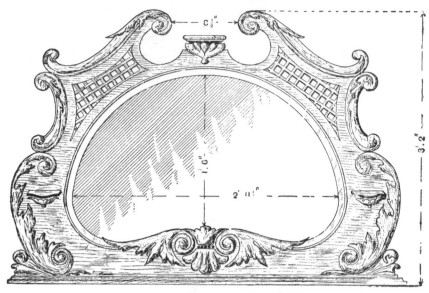

Fig. 1050.—Chippendale Overmantel.

Fig. 1052.—Cornice and Other
Ornamentation of Chippendale
Overmantel.

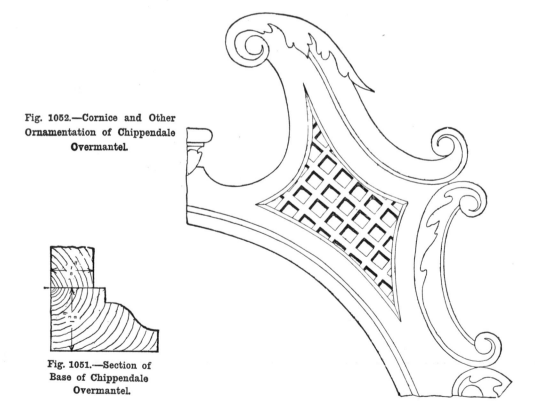

Fig. 1051.—Section of
Base of Chippendale
Overmantel.

Thermometer Panels

Figs. 1058 to 1060 represent thermometers mounted on an ordinary panel, and then framed with a deep moulding. The designs can be worked on $\frac{1}{2}$-in. oak or walnut, the panels being about 14 in. by 10 in. A plain seat is left in the middle of the panel for mounting the thermometer, which may be firmly affixed by means of two small screws driven in from the back, as shown by the holes in Figs. 1058 and 1059. The frame should be deeply moulded, so as to form a protection for the slightly projecting glass tube. The originals are bevelled at the joints in order that this protection may be increased. The design shown in Fig. 1063 is of a more advanced nature. The panel is about 11 in. by 22 in., and $\frac{3}{4}$ in. thick. The margin around the copy is about 1 in. wide, and the carving itself is fully $\frac{1}{4}$ in. in depth. The seat for the thermometer is routered out level with the other groundwork, as this accentuates the idea of the bird at the top being perched on the thermometer, itself. For those who prefer a carved frame

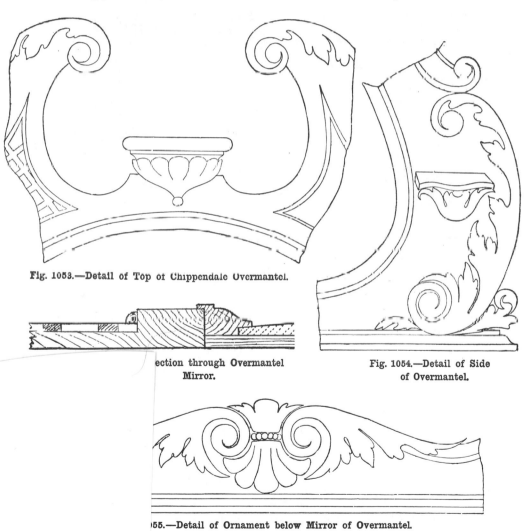

Fig. 1053.—Detail of Top of Chippendale Overmantel.

...ection through Overmantel Mirror.

Fig. 1054.—Detail of Side of Overmantel.

...55.—Detail of Ornament below Mirror of Overmantel.

the details of a sufficiently heavy moulding (Fig. 1061) and an effective repeating pattern (Fig. 1062) are given. Still another design is presented by Fig. 1064.

Grandfather-clock Smoker's Cabinet

In this cabinet (*see* Fig. 1065) is used a clock movement having a spring, but no pendulum. The dimensions depend upon the size of the clock-face. The all-over size of the article here illustrated is 37 in. in height, 10 in. in the widest part, and 8 in. at the greatest depth, the clock measuring

fully cut the corners clean, as they form part of the seats for the moulding eventually to be added. This back is again outlined in Fig. 1069, and is there indicated by the inner dotted lines. Regarding the sides themselves, start with the pieces second from the top, marked A in Fig. 1070. These will be 6½ in. by 15 in., and, besides exactly fitting the cut-out portion of the back, should be fitted exactly flush with it, as should all the other side pieces. There is nothing more to do to these side pieces beyond making the grooves to take the two shelves

Fig. 1057.—Modern Style Overmantel. Designed by W. S. Williamson.
Carved by Rev. Mr. Kerthompson.

4½ in. by 6 in. In Fig. 1066 the plain carcase is shown, with a pipe-rack and shelf in the upper space, while the lower compartment is occupied with two drawers, convenient for a smoker's belongings. Construct the dial-plate at the commencement to fit the clock face (*see* Fig. 1067), and then proportionately alter all the other parts of the construction; ½-in. stuff is used throughout, though the doors may be slightly thicker. Beginning with the back, a piece of ½-in. timber, 8 in. by 37 in., will be required. This should be sawn to the shape shown in Fig. 1068. The sides, which consist of four pieces each, are secured to this, and this single-piece back gives great stability. Care-

shown in Fig. 1066; but these could be made to rest on thin slips, either screwed or glued on the inside, if the operation of grooving is omitted. The side pieces coming next below B (Fig. 1070) are each 7 in. by 9½ in., and when in place should overlap the side pieces above by ½ in. Consequently, each can not only be secured to the back piece, but to the side pieces above them. The lowest side pieces C (Fig. 1070) overlap ½ in., and can each be fastened similarly to the foregoing. Before finally fastening, the cut-out portions at the base, shown in Fig. 1065, should be worked. The top side pieces D (Fig. 1070) are each 6½ in. by 11 in., and overlap ½ in. at the base; from each base,

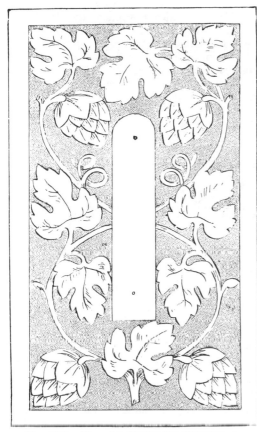

Fig. 1058.—Hop-vine Design for Thermometer Panel.

destined to hide its front edge. The board or seat for the clock-face should be 8 in. square, and its construction is illustrated in Fig. 1067. Cut out a circular space for the insertion of the clockworks about $4\frac{1}{4}$ in. in diameter, and let the lowest part of the circle be 1 in. from the bottom. Fit the clock into this, and make four screw-holes, one near each corner, to secure the dial-plate to the wood. Mark round the dial-face with a pencil, and remove the clock for safety until the whole article is finished off. Turn a pillar $1\frac{1}{4}$ in. by $5\frac{1}{4}$ in., and saw it in halves lengthwise. If not possible to do this, plant

for 8 in. upwards, $\frac{1}{2}$ in. of stuff is cut away at the front to allow the dial-board and front fittings presently to be placed in position. A careful study of Figs. 1069 and 1070 will speedily make this apparent. It will be wise to proceed next with the shelf-like divisions; the mouldings will hide all nails or screws used for fastening these shelves in place. Two pieces, each 6 in. square, will be required for the top and bottom of the division A (Fig. 1069). Let the upper one come flush with the bottom of the moulding, which will eventually cover it; also let the lower one come flush with the top of the moulding presently to overlay it. Another piece, about 7 in. square, will be necessary to floor the division B (Fig. 1069), and this should be kept flush with the top of the moulding

Fig. 1059.—Conventional Design for Thermometer Panel.

on reeded, moulded, or plain pieces in place of the half-pillars. Next take a piece of wood 5½ in. by 8 in., hollow an arc parallel to the circular top of the dial-plate, and carefully chamfer the circular edge. The ½-in. moulding eventually covers the base of this, and further up two pieces of 1-in.

Fig. 1061.—Section of Moulding for Thermometer Frame.

Fig. 1062.—Repeating Pattern for Thermometer Frame.

Fig. 1060.—Gothic Design for Thermometer Frame.

moulding will also rest upon it. Fit it to the allotted part, but before finally fixing be sure to insert a top piece to the clock, some 6 in. by 7 in., in order to keep all dust from the interior. The door A (Fig. 1069) is 7 in. by 12 in., and it can be beaded or moulded around the sides if desired. The

lower door B is 8 in. square, and the edges should be finished similarly to A. As these doors will not be framed, special care should be exercised in selecting the material for them. Get it as well seasoned as possible, for any subsequent warping will not only spoil the fitting, but the whole appearance of the front. The bottom front piece is 3 in. by 9 in., and after being fitted should have the lower part band-sawn, and finished to some such shape as that shown in Fig. 1065.

Completing the Cabinet.—Only the moulding remains to be fitted. About 12 ft. of 1-in. moulding, run in an ogee or similar pattern, as well as 3 ft. of ½-in. material, will be required. This should not yet be cut or fitted, as the various pieces of wood should be carved and fastened in their places before the moulding is applied. In Fig. 1065 various carving designs of an antique style are given for selection, or others may be adopted to suit individual fancy. When this is finished, the whole may be finally fixed, and it would be well to follow the sequence already suggested. When each piece is carefully fitted and firmly fixed, the mouldings

Fig. 1063.—Thermometer Panel of More Advanced Design.

Fig. 1064.—Thermometer Panel of Grotesque Design.

Fig. 1065.   Fig. 1066.

Figs. 1065 and 1066.—Grandfather-clock Smoker's Cabinet.

may be cut, mitered, and tacked or glued on. Before hanging the doors, carefully fit and secure the pipe-rack and shelves shown in Fig. 1066, and make and fit the drawers in the lower compartment. To get the top part of the upper drawer to fit nicely, some part,

Fig. 1067.—Seat for Clock Case.

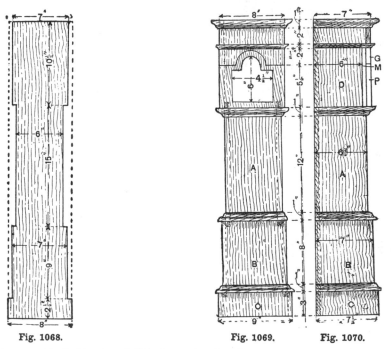

Fig. 1068.　　　　　　　　　Fig. 1069.　　　　　Fig. 1070.

Figs. 1068 to 1070.—Back, Front, and Side Pieces for Grandfather-clock Smoker's Cabinet.

say 1 in. or so, of the overlapping portions of the sideboards marked A in Fig. 1070 will have to be cut away. This is an important detail, and will demonstrate the wisdom of not finally fixing the carcase, etc., until every portion has first been fitted. The cabinet might stand on a side table, and be fastened to the wall by means of two picture fasteners and nails ; the top would then form a secure shelf for a vase or a piece of bric-à-brac.

the front. The two side columns or pillars are turned from oak, walnut, or any hardwood, leaving the square pieces at the top and bottom as shown. These pillars are shown enlarged at Figs. 1074 and 1075. The feet, as shown enlarged by Fig. 1076, may be cut out from wood $1\frac{1}{2}$ in. thick, carved on the front with the half circle and the leaf, and the roll foot with incised ornament on each side. These feet are dovetailed into the bottom square of the pillar or column.

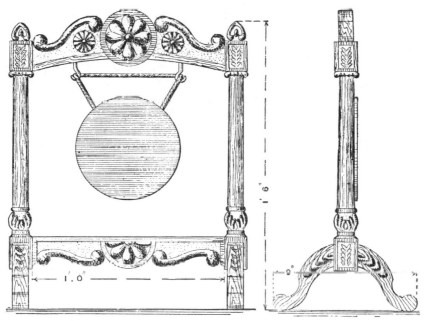

Fig. 1071.   Fig. 1072.

Figs. 1071 and 1072.—Gong Stand.

Gong Stand

Figs. 1071 and 1072 show a suitable design for a carved oak gong stand. The dimensions are : thickness of columns, $1\frac{3}{8}$ in. square, pediment 1 in. thick by 1 ft. long, claws $1\frac{1}{8}$ in. thick.

Fire Screen with Repoussé Metal Centre

Fig. 1073 shows a fire screen constructed of wood and ornamented with carving, and having a repoussé metal plate either of brass, copper, or nickel-silver screwed to

The upper and lower rails should be cut out of wood 1 in. thick, carved on the front, as shown in Fig. 1073, and dovetailed into the upper and lower squares of the pillars or columns. The position of the lower rail fitting into the square of the column is shown at A (Fig. 1076). A carved knob, as shown enlarged at Fig. 1074, is fixed to the upper square of the columns. The turned pillars or columns may be ornamentally carved as shown, or left quite plain. The repoussé centre should be a plate of copper or other suitable metal of, say, 17 B.W.G., cut to the shape shown, and with

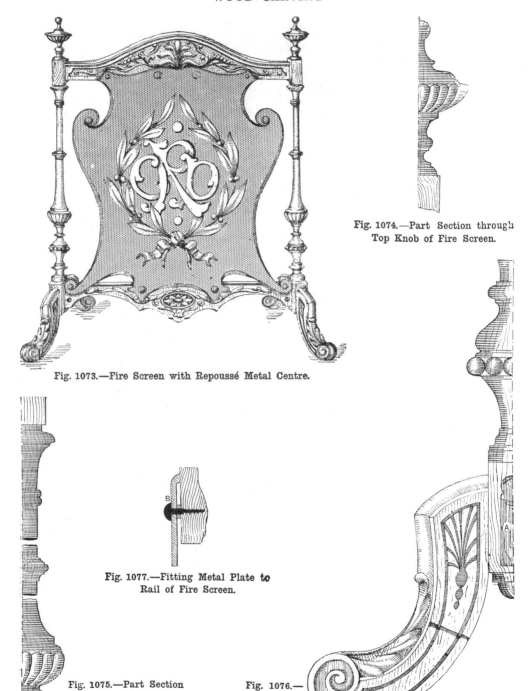

Fig. 1073.—Fire Screen with Repoussé Metal Centre.

Fig. 1074.—Part Section through Top Knob of Fire Screen.

Fig. 1077.—Fitting Metal Plate to Rail of Fire Screen.

Fig. 1075.—Part Section through Upper Part of Fire Screen Pillar.

Fig. 1076.— Fire Screen Foot.

the edges turned over. The repoussé pattern (which, of course, may be any ornament to taste) in the design shown is a monogram surrounded by a laurel wreath, and centre may be substituted for the metal centre if desired, and fluted silk stretched between the upper and lower rails would also give a very pleasing effect. The woodwork

Fig. 1078.—Fire Screen, Ornament based on the Aconitum. Designed by W. S. Williamson.
Carved by Miss L. Snelgrove.

should be hammered on the plate in the usual method on a pitch-block and fixed to the front of the screen with round-headed screws (*see* B, Fig. 1077). This copper plate may be either polished or bronzed brown or greenish or light fawn in colour, and will then match very well with either oak or walnut. A wood plate with a carved panel in the

may be left smooth with a dead finish, or it can be polished.

Fire Screens Designed by Mr. W. S. Williamson

Three fire screens, carved from the designs of Mr. W. S. Williamson, are illustrated by Figs. 1078 to 1080. That shown by Fig.

1078 is ornamented with a design based on the aconitum, and the carving was executed by Miss L. Snelgrove, the material being Quatorze style, the dimensions being 2 ft. 7 in. by 1 ft. 10 in. Fig. 1080 shows a screen most suitably constructed in wainscot oak.

Fig. 1079.—Fire Screen in Louis Quatorze Style. Design Adapted by W. S. Williamson. Carved by Miss L. Underwood.

walnut; the size is 31¼ in. by 23 in. The same material is used for the screen shown by Fig. 1079, and wainscot oak is also suitable; the carved ornament is in the Louis

Key-board

The key-board illustrated by Fig. 1081 is designed to save the inconvenience of losing or mislaying keys belonging to doors, cupboards, etc., in a house. Its size is about 18 in. by 11 in., so affording room for six ornamental brass-headed screw-hooks, as fine tool, the pattern left plain, and the groundwork lightly stamped. A naturalistic style is given in Fig. 1083, resembling

Fig. 1080.—Fire Screen in Wainscot Oak. Design Adapted by W. S. Williamson. Carved by Miss L. Wood.

shown in the sketch. Fig. 1082 shows a conventional pattern for fluted work, the seat for the screws being of a ribbon-like character. The work should be done with a very in character that shown in Fig. 1081. It should not be cut more than $\frac{1}{8}$ in. deep, and the modelling requires a light and careful touch. These patterns can be worked on

½-in. stuff, either in whitewood, oak, or walnut. When finished, in order to prevent a possible warping of the wood, three strips should be screwed to the back, as shown in Fig. 1084. The strip C should come immediately behind the seat for the ornamental screw-hooks. For deeper carving the material should be in ¾-in. stuff, and if the carving weakens the wood the strips can be affixed as already suggested.

to the back and front as indicated in Fig. 1087, the front is lightly tacked on, and finally glued and clamped together, using small triangular blocks C (Fig. 1087). E (Fig. 1085) is a hole for supporting the spill box on a nail.

Hanging Cupboard and Bookshelf

The hanging cupboard and bookshelf illustrated by Figs. 1088 and 1089 could be made

Fig. 1081.—Design for Key-board.

Spill Box

The spill box illustrated by Figs. 1085 and 1086 can be made out of any wood suitable for chip carving, ¼ in. thick. Fig. 1085 is a front view of the box, and Fig. 1086 an end view. The dimensions are : from top to bottom, 1 ft. ; width, 5 in. ; length of box part, 6 in. ; radius of circular part at the bottom, 1¾ in. The bottom of the box is 3½ in. from the bottom of the back. The curves may be fretted out. A and B (Fig. 1085) show the veining, which is cut lightly with a veining tool. The section of the top is square, and when the sides are screwed

of oak (and wax-polished), walnut, or mahogany. The following are the principal dimensions : Height from the bottom shelf to the top shelf over all, 2 ft. ; length over the ends, 2 ft. ; width from the back to the front, 1 ft. 2 in. ; height of the cupboard between the shelves, 1 ft. The ends should be ⅞ in. thick and cut to shape as shown in Fig. 1089 ; they project 1½ in. beyond the bottom shelf and 5 in. above the top shelf. The shelves should be ¾ in. thick, being dovetail-grooved into the ends. The grooves are stopped ½ in. from the front, and the shelves are notched to correspond. The back is ½ in. thick, and is rebated into the ends and top and bottom shelves, the back edge of the middle shelf being kept $\frac{1}{2}$ in. from the back edge of the ends when making up. The top of the back above the top shelf is $\frac{3}{4}$ in. thick, cut to shape as shown in Fig. 1088, and ornamented with a little carving; it is 11 in. high in the middle. The moulding across the top of the back is made up sepa-

rately and fixed on. The back is rebated into the ends, and fixed to the top shelf with screws from underneath. The framework of the doors is $1\frac{1}{2}$ in. wide by $1\frac{1}{8}$ in. thick, mortised and tenoned together in the usual way. The doors are hung with $1\frac{1}{2}$-in. brass butt hinges, and are fitted with a lock and key. The carved panels should be of wood

Fig. 1082.—Key-board: Conventional Design for Fluted Work

⅝ in. thick, the framework of the doors being boxed out to receive the panels, which are fixed in position by small fillet pieces. A suitable carving design for the panels is shown at Fig. 1090; the construction lines ruled across the outlined half of the design should be 1 in. apart in the full-size design, which it is desirable to prepare before carving.

Coin Casket

A carved casket for coins is shown by Fig. 1091. Inside the casket is a number of trays with circular sinkings to hold coins. The front of the casket is shown separately by Fig. 1092. The carved feet are secured as shown in Fig. 1093. Fig. 1094 shows the base strip, and Fig. 1095 the edge of the lid.

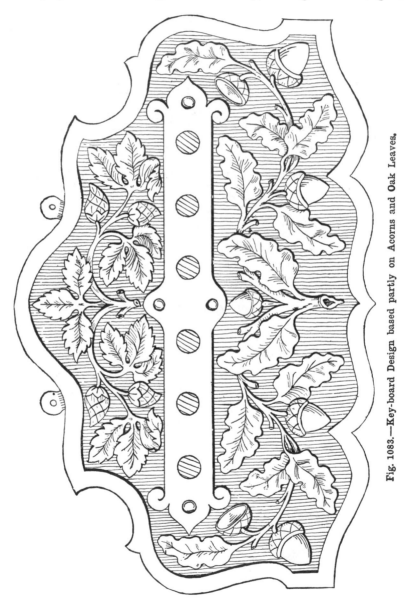

Fig. 1083.—Key-board Design based partly on Acorns and Oak Leaves.

Table-board

The table-board (Fig. 1096, p. 540) is made from a panel, with an ovolo run round edges, or **U**-shaped in section, and are cut with a **V**-tool or small gouge. Figs. 1103 and 1104 are half side elevations of Figs. 1101 and 1102 and are reproduced to the scale of 1 in. to

Fig. 1084.—Back of Key-board.

and the whole mounted on four small brass claw-legs. This figure gives a general idea of the article. It is 19 in. long by 7 in. wide, and is made of ½-in. stuff. Regard for the use of the article must rule in carving, consequently it should not be worked very deeply. An incised pattern, like that in Fig. 1099, looks very well, and it could be worked in yellow pine or in whitewood, and then stained and varnished. For hardwood—oak or walnut—the strapwork pattern given in Fig. 1100 is especially effective. It should not be cut more than ⅛ in. deep, and then depressed in places with a firmer chisel. If sufficient space is allowed for an ovolo to be run round the panel, the effect may be pleasantly heightened by carving a series of scollops round the edges, as illustrated in Figs. 1097 and 1098. Another easy method of finishing the panel is by mounting it in a beaded oak frame ; and besides the legs, handles to match may be affixed to each end.

Pedestal Flower-stands

The pedestal flower-stands shown by Figs. 1101 and 1102 (p. 543) are made of walnut or mahogany. The ornamental lines are **V**-

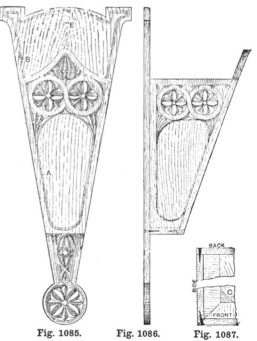

Fig. 1085.   Fig. 1086.   Fig. 1087.

Figs. 1085 and 1086.—Front and Side Elevations of Spill Box.

Fig. 1087.—Part Horizontal Section of Spill Box.

the foot. The chief dimensions are : height, 4 ft. 9 in. ; tops, 1 ft. 2 in. square ; width across top of legs 11½ in., and at the bottom 1 ft. 6 in. The lower part of Fig. 1101 is shown by Fig. 1102 is similar in construction. If a shaped top is preferred to a square one, see the alternative designs given in Figs. 1105 and 1106.

Fig. 1088.—Hanging Cupboard and Bookshelf.

Fig. 1090.—
Panel of Cupboard.

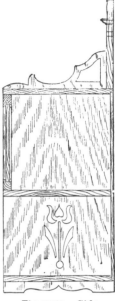

Fig. 1089.—Side Elevation of Cupboard

Fig. 1091.—Coin Casket.

enclosed, and forms a cupboard, one side being hinged and secured with a spring bullet catch and handle, or by a lock and the handle. The cross rails are connected to the legs by tenons and mortices. The stand

Lamp-stand

An ornamental lamp-stand that may be made from an old mahogany bedpost is illustrated by Fig. 1107. The twisted stem has a leaf husk at the centre. The portion of the foot, which is 3¾ in. square, may easily be adapted as shown. The lamp may be of polished brass or copper. As the mahogany is red in colour, a brass lamp may be better; to this may be screwed a wire frame on which the lace lamp shade may be placed. The pedestal should be hollowed to take the lampholder socket, which should be of circular tubing soldered to the bottom of the holder, and about 6 in. long. Fig. 1108 shows, enlarged, the mahogany brackets that are fixed underneath the lamp and holder to give effect to the upper portion of the pillar. The stand is formed of four carved legs, with mortice pieces at the upper ends to fit into the mortice holes in the lower part of the pillar (see A, Fig. 1109). The legs may be of mahogany, 2¾ in. square, with a carved leaf on the upper side of each

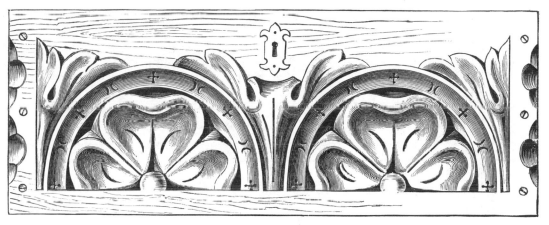

Fig. 1092.—Front of Coin Casket.

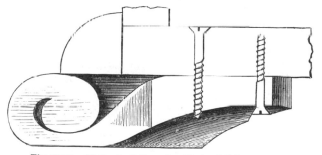

Fig. 1093.—Method of Securing Feet of Coin Casket.

Fig. 1094.—Base Strip of Coin Casket.

Fig. 1095.—Edge of Coin Casket Lid.

and with both sides carved with low relief scrollwork. The termination should be a square block, say 3 in. by 3 in., carved, as shown, on three sides with rosettes, its top having a carved knob, and the under portion having a reeded ball on which the leg rests. This must be flat at the bottom, so as to make a firm stand. Fig. 1110 shows, en-

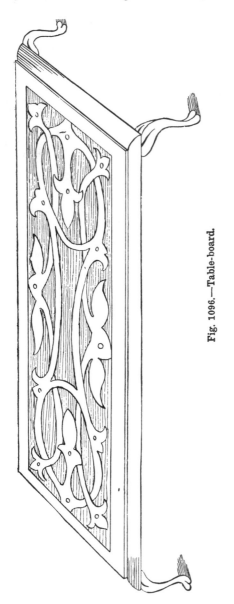

Fig. 1096.—Table-board.

larged, the brackets that, resting on the upper parts of the legs, make an artistic connection to the pillar. The new work should be stained to match the old pillar, and then polished.

Art Metal and Carved Oak Fonts

First Example.—An uncommon font is shown in elevation by Fig. 1111 and in section and part plan by Fig. 1112 (p. 545). From platform to top of basin it is 3 ft. 9 in high, and the greatest spread of the feet is 2 ft. $3\frac{1}{2}$ in., while the outside width of the basin is 2 ft. $0\frac{1}{2}$ in. The font is supported by a triangular stand ; the legs are prepared from 6-in. oak, and are dovetailed into the tapered hexagonal piece, which is sur-

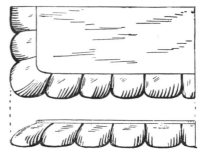

Figs. 1097 and 1098.—Edge and Corner of Table-board Panel.

mounted by a turned and carved finial. An elevation of the legs is shown in Fig. 1111. The basin and cover are circular, and would look exceedingly well with copper for the main parts and armour-bright steel mounts riveted on. The way in which the cover clasps the basin, while effectually securing it in position, presents a graceful appearance. The upper part of the cover is split, and the pieces are turned into scrolls, six of which clasp a ring, as is clearly shown in Fig. 1113. A section through B (Fig. 1111) and a part plan of the hexagonal platform are illustrated by Fig. 1112. The platform should be of oak ; $4\frac{1}{2}$-in. by 1-in. boards are suggested, to be cut on to the $5\frac{1}{2}$-in. by 2-in. rebated joists. The moulding is formed of a piece of 1-in. oak worked and cut round underneath the boards as shown at Fig. 1114. The joists are tenoned into the middle post,

Fig. 1099.—Incised Pattern for Table-board Panel.

Fig. 1100.—Strapwork Pattern for Table-board Panel.

which stands above the floor and is ornamented as indicated in Fig. 1115.

Second Example.—Figs. 1116 and 1117 represent another font of modern design.

through the middle. The sides of the basin turn out into scrolls at the bottom, and are screwed to a piece of metal that is fitted to the required size. Two tablets are fixed on

Fig. 1101.—
Pedestal Flower-stand.

Fig. 1102.—
Another Pedestal Flower-stand.

Fig. 1105.—
Shaped Top of
Stand.

Figs. 1103.   Fig. 1104.

Figs. 1103 and 1104.—Half Front Elevations
of Two Pedestal Flower-stands.

Fig. 1106.—
Alternate Shaped Top
of Stand.

The basin is octagonal, and the upper edge is turned over into scrolls, eight of which fall inside and the rest out, so as to receive the circular cover. For a plan of the scrolls and circle, showing the edge of the cover resting between, *see* Fig. 1118. The true shape of the cover and basin is given by Fig. 1119, which represents a section

the cover, on which suitable inscriptions may be worked in repoussé. Four carved columns, each 6 in. by 6 in., and arches prepared from ¾-in. stuff, support the basin. A section through these at c (Fig. 1116) is reproduced at Fig. 1117, together with a plan of the platforms and the middle post, which is both decorative and symbolical, and runs through both floors, receiving the joists of each. The platforms are ornamental as well as useful. The octagonal platform is 5 ft. from side to side, and $5\frac{1}{2}$ in. high, the other being $3\frac{1}{2}$ in. high. The height from the top of the octagonal floor to the

turned legs and rails, a drawer, and three top cupboards. The carving is bold, and is cleanly cut. The modern style of ornament is typified in Fig. 1122, which shows a table

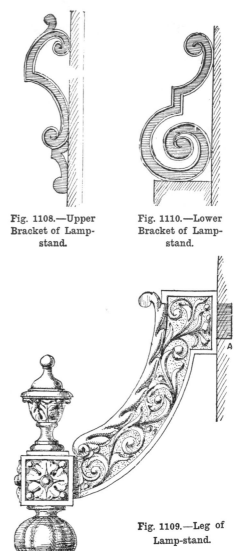

Fig. 1108.—Upper Bracket of Lamp-stand.

Fig. 1110.—Lower Bracket of Lamp-stand.

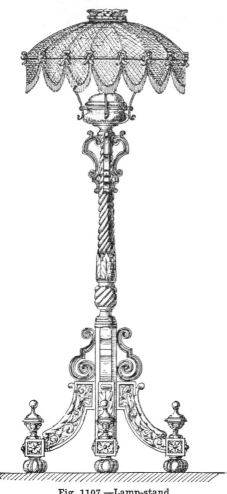

Fig. 1107.—Lamp-stand.

Fig. 1109.—Leg of Lamp-stand.

top of the basin is 3 ft. 9 in. Fig. 1120 shows the detail of the carved columns and capitals.

Tables, etc., Designed by Mr. W. S. Williamson and others.

A writing table, ornamented in the Italian Renaissance style, is illustrated by Fig. 1121. This was carved by its designer, and it has

with side, top cupboards, and two drawers. This example was carved by Miss M. Adlington. The table shown by Fig. 1123 is a pleasing piece of work. A reredos, the work of Mrs. M. S. Knight, is shown by Fig. 1124.

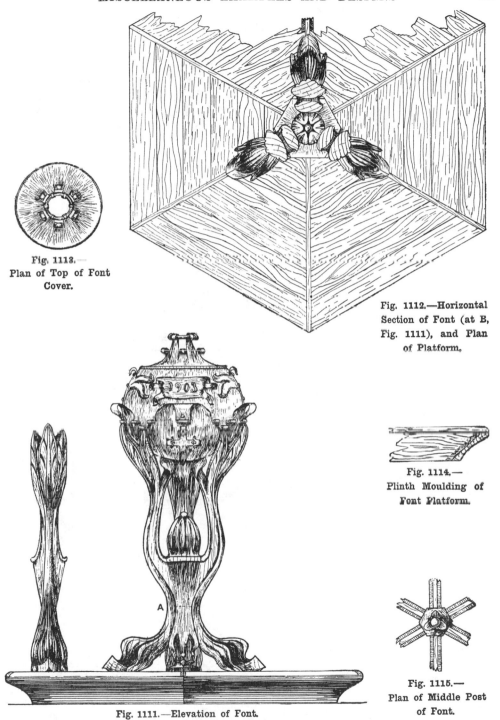

Fig. 1113.—
Plan of Top of Font
Cover.

Fig. 1112.—Horizontal
Section of Font (at B,
Fig. 1111), and Plan
of Platform.

Fig. 1114.—
Plinth Moulding of
Font Platform.

Fig. 1111.—Elevation of Font.

Fig. 1115.—
Plan of Middle Post
of Font.

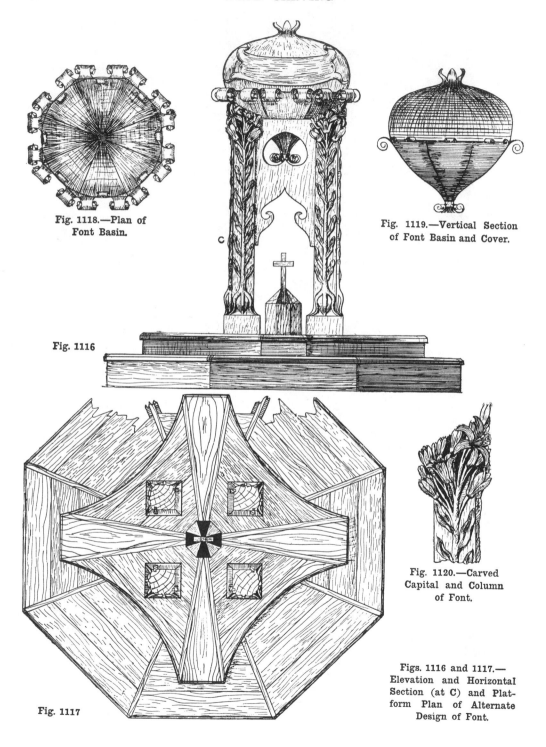

Fig. 1118.—Plan of
Font Basin.

Fig. 1119.—Vertical Section
of Font Basin and Cover.

Fig. 1116

Fig. 1120.—Carved
Capital and Column
of Font.

Fig. 1117

Figs. 1116 and 1117.—
Elevation and Horizontal
Section (at C) and Plat-
form Plan of Alternate
Design of Font.

Fig. 1122.—Writing Table, with Modern Ornament. Designed by W. S. Williamson. Carved by Miss M. Adlington.

Fig. 1121.—Writing Table, with Italian Renaissance Ornament. Designed and Carved by W. S. Williamson.

The hanging cabinet illustrated by Fig. 1125 was carved in oak by Miss A. Collins ; the dimensions are 2 ft. 6 in. by 2 ft. 9 in.

Standing Cabinet

A standing cabinet, constructed in solid oak, is shown by Fig. 1126 ; its height is

(*see* Fig. 1128). The long pieces must be mortised right through at 1 in. from the ends, the mortice holes being exactly central and square. These are for the tenons A (Fig. 1128) to fit into. The outside measurement of the doors, when put together, must be 32 in. by 16½ in. A rebate, ¼ in. wide and

Fig. 1123.—Square Table with Carved Sides.   Designed by W. S. Williamson.

about 6 ft. 6 in. Both designing and carving are the work of Miss O'Niell.

Chiffonnier

The carved oak chiffonnier (Fig. 1127) is made of ½-in. oak throughout, with the exception of the frames of the doors, consisting of 1-in. oak, and the back and shelves, which are of white pine. For the door frames, four pieces of oak, each 32 in. by 2½ in. by 1 in., and four pieces 16½ in. by 2½ in. by 1 in., will be required. These must all be planed true and square. The four 16½-in. pieces must have tenons cut at each end

⅝ in. deep, is taken off the inside of each door for the panel to drop into. The sides will be more easily carved before gluing together. The carved panels must have ¼ in. more of plain oak on the two edges, which will meet when the doors are closed. This is to leave room for a piece of oak beading, which makes a neater finish and which may be fitted on in the following way : cut a strip of oak 32 in. long to the section shown in Fig. 1129. Take off at the outside left-hand edge of the right-hand door a rebate ⅜ in. wide by ½ in. deep, and glue the strip firmly in its place, so that when the doors are on

Fig. 1124.—Reredos in Solid Oak.   Designed and Carved by Mrs. M. S. Knight.

Fig. 1125.—Hanging Cabinet.   Designed by W. S. Williamson.
Carved by Miss A. Collins.

the chiffonnier the part marked B (Fig. 1129) will overlap the edge of the left-hand door. The panels measure 27½ in. by 12 in. These must be carved, the back edges bevelled

Fig. 1126.—Standing Cabinet in Oak.
Designed and Carved by Miss O'Niell.

off, and then dropped into the rebate at the back and fastened securely in with panel pins. For the body of the chiffonnier, use two pieces of oak 37 in. long by 12½ in. wide and ½ in. thick when planed up. As this thickness would not be sufficient to carry

the doors, let the frame be further strengthened by gluing and screwing from the inside, with ¾-in. screws, a strip of oak 32 in. by 1 in. at each inside edge where the doors will be hinged on. The top should be made of ½-in. oak, to strengthen which, put on a false top of white pine first. The side elevation (Fig. 1130) shows how this is done : E is the pine top and D the oak ; the pine top comes right to the front and back, but the oak top must be ½ in. off the back (see H, Fig. 1130) to allow the overback to drop into position. The oak top projects 1½ in. in front. F is a piece of pine 33 in. long, planed up true to size and shape shown in Fig. 1131. Before putting this on, a strip of pine, 3 in. by 1¾ in., should be screwed on the back as at J, to make a stop for the doors to swing to. A piece of oak G, 34 in. by 1¼ in., should be glued over F, to which must be added the strip C, 35 in. by 1 in. by ½ in. ; this will give a heavier appearance to the chiffonnier. Pieces similar to G and C are carried across the tops of the ends, but F is left out. The piece C should be trued up, joined with hot glue, and smoothed down when set. Fasten the oak top to the pine with ¾-in. screws from the inside. The size of the oak top before C is put on is 34 in. by 14 in. The doors close flush on the bottom, or what is in reality a bottom shelf. To do this it must project 1 in. beyond the sides. A piece of oak 3¾ in. wide, carved with a simple design, is carried right across the front and ends at the bottom ; thus the bottom of the doors will be 3¾ in. from the floor. The end pieces are fastened by screws from the inside, and the front piece by gluing blocks of wood inside the bottom, and a strip of wood must be glued on the bottom shelf for the doors to close up to when shut. The back is made of pine, nailed on. The two pine shelves are made to rest on ledges. The doors can now be hinged on, a lock put on the right-hand door, and a small bolt at the top and bottom of the left-hand door. The overback should be the shape and size shown in Fig. 1132. This should not be carved within 1 in. of the bottom, and as oak can rarely be obtained 22 in. wide, it is best to carve as much as possible before joining up. It is attached to the chiffonnier back by a couple of stays, shown at M. The three brackets K are

Fig. 1128.—Plan of End-piece for Door
Framework.

Fig. 1130.—Side Elevation of
Chiffonnier Top

Fig. 1132.—Overback to Chiffonnier.

Fig. 1129.—
Section of
Beading.

Fig. 1131.—
Section of Door
Stop.

Fig. 1127.—Oak Chiffonnier.

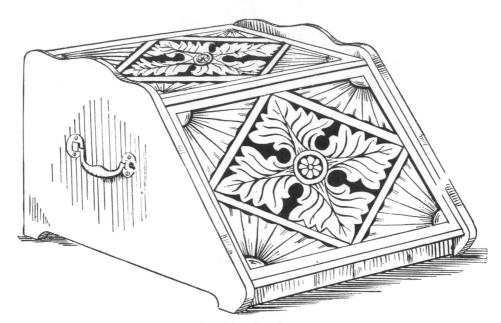

Fig. 1133.—Coal Box.

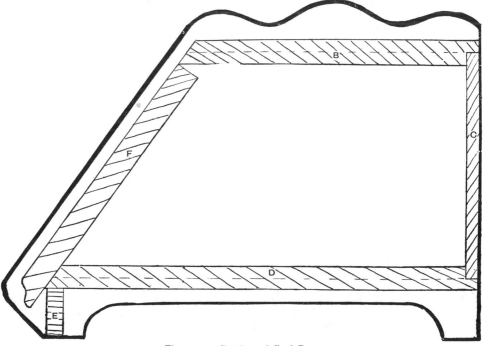

Fig. 1134.—Section of Coal Box.

attached by small screws from the back. The bracket supports are carved to match the back, but the little shelves are left plain.

Coal Box

Fig. 1133 shows a coal box which may be constructed in either oak or walnut, of stuff into a $\frac{1}{2}$-in. groove on the insides of the side pieces. The bottom piece D is about 12 in. by 18 in., and should be rebated in a groove similarly to the top, as great strength is here required. When fitted and glued, nails or screws should be added at will. The heads of the nails should be punched in, and then

Fig. 1135.—Alternative Design for Coal Box Front or Lid.

planed to not less than 1 in. in thickness. The sides (see Fig. 1134) should be band-sawn or otherwise shaped to the desired outline from a piece of stuff 20 in. by 14 in., tapering to 12 in. at the top. The hollow at the base is $1\frac{1}{2}$ in. deep, and allows for supports of the same length. The top piece is 11 in. by 12 in. The wider side allows for this top piece B (Fig. 1134) to be rebated and let filling applied to hide them. The screws should be countersunk and filled, or ornamental screws could be used with the heads exposed. This is a matter of taste. If the rebating and grooving (which is practically a haunched tenon) is too exacting a task, both top and bottom pieces could be finished in 11 in., jointed in the shooting-board, and simply fastened by screws or nails; but this plan would involve a certain amount of loss in strength and finish. Again, the back ends of both top and bottom pieces should be rebated endways to allow the back piece c (Fig. 1134) to be securely fastened in its place. Both back and bottom pieces could be of commoner wood, if desired, but this if desired, instead of moulded. The strip E is added to give a finish to the front view, and could be beaded or left plain. The sides are left plain, and handles can be fixed of any size or shape that fancy may dictate. The same may be said about the hinges and the knob for lifting the lid. Before beginning

Fig. 1136.—Alternative Design for Coal Box Top.

would necessitate staining to match the other parts as far as possible. The front end of the top piece is planed to an angle corresponding with the slope of the sides, but it is kept back about $\frac{1}{2}$ in. from the extreme front (*see* Fig. 1134). The lid F is about 11 in. by 12 in., the extra inch being for the ovolo or other moulding run along its bottom edge. It could be simply rounded or nosed, to carve any portion, it would be well to put the article lightly together and make any needed alterations. This would prove an awkward and possibly ruinous affair after the carving is finished. In Fig. 1133 is shown an antique pattern, which would look well on both lid and top. It is a surface pattern, with little grounding out, and is easy to execute. More modern and flowing in design is Fig. 1135, which shows a pattern which would look well on the lid, while Fig. 1136 provides another of similar character which would suitably adorn the top. They could be cut $\frac{1}{4}$ in. deep, and they afford scope for some artistic moulding of detail. When fixed together, a strong metal lining to the vase should be obtained.

Coal Cabinet with Cupboard

The coal cabinet and work cupboard illustrated by Fig. 1137 has been so designed

Fig. 1137.—Coal Cabinet with Cupboard.

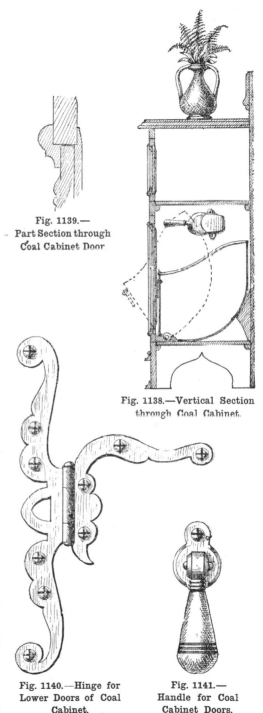

Fig. 1139.—
Part Section through
Coal Cabinet Door

Fig. 1138.—Vertical Section
through Coal Cabinet.

Fig. 1140.—Hinge for
Lower Doors of Coal
Cabinet.

Fig. 1141.—
Handle for Coal
Cabinet Doors.

that, whilst only taking up the space of an ordinary coal box, it shall be more in keeping with the other furniture of the room than is the usual coal receptacle. Fig. 1137 is a view of the complete article, which may be constructed of oak, walnut, or mahogany, as may be most in harmony with the rest of the furniture. The height to the top of the upper shelf is 3 ft., and the width from 22 in. to 24 in. These sizes may be varied to suit requirements. The upper flat top should have a moulded edge, on which vases of flowers or other ornaments may be placed. The back may be carved as shown, and the small panel decorated with a monogram or something similar. The cabinet is divided into two parts (*see* Fig. 1138), the upper part forming a small cupboard, and the lower a receptacle for coals. The doors should have

larged views of alternate designs for panels are given by Figs. 1142 and 1143. The groundwork of these panels may be left either smooth or matted. A good effect is obtained by having the panels of a lighter or darker wood than that employed in the construction of the rest of the cabinet.

Fig. 1142.

Fig. 1143.

Figs. 1142 and 1143.—Alternative Designs for Coal Cabinet Panels.

mouldings fitted round as shown in Fig. 1139, which is a sectional view; in this figure is also shown the method of fitting mouldings, doors, and panel. The upper doors may be fitted with panels of stained glass having circular bull's-eyes, as illustrated in Fig. 1137, and may be attached with ordinary brass butt hinges. The lower doors open to the coal cupboard, and are fitted with mouldings similar to those described above, and with carved wood panels. En-

The lower doors may be hung with polished brass hinges, as shown in Fig. 1137. These hinges, together with the handles, are represented by Figs. 1140 and 1141. They may be of polished brass or copper, as may be preferred. The coal receptacle may be made of galvanised wrought sheet iron; its shape is shown in section by Fig. 1138. This vase should have handles riveted on the front and sides to allow of its being lifted. A pin is riveted on each side at the front end, which

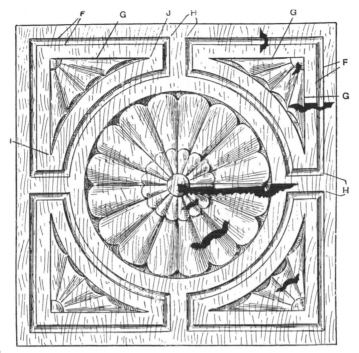

Fig. 1144.

Fig. 1145.

Figs. 1144 and 1145.—Door Panels for Cabinet Whatnot.   (See Fig. 1146, page 558.)

should drop into a wood block fixed to the bottom of the closet, on which the coal receptacle should work. This is shown in Fig. 1138 by the dotted lines. A wood block is placed at the back of the closet to lessen the jar of the fireplace. The carved panels in the doors (*see also* Fig. 1144) are effective without being very difficult of execution. The half of an alternative design for these panels is shown in Fig. 1145. The plinth forming

Fig. 1146.—Cabinet Whatnot.

on the back of the cabinet when the coal receptacle falls back. The shovel may be fixed on the one side as shown, and the coal tongs on the other side.

Cabinet Whatnot

The cabinet whatnot shown in Fig. 1146 is specially suitable for a recess at the side the base of the whatnot will prevent the articles in the lower portion from being too near the floor, where they would be liable to get dusty. Mahogany stained dark, walnut, and American ash stained green, finished with french polish, are suitable woods to use. The curtains may be made of any soft material, figured or plain.

INDEX

Illustrated subjects are denoted by an asterisk